DAYS
of the
DEAD

A YEAR OF TRUE GHOST STORIES

Sylvia Shults

Other Books by Sylvia Shults:

Fractured Spirits: Hauntings at the Peoria State Hospital

Fractured Souls: More Hauntings at the Peoria State Hospital

44 Years in Darkness: A True Story of Madness, Tragedy, and Shattered Love

Hunting Demons: A True Story of the Dark Side of the Supernatural

Spirits of Christmas: The Dark Side of the Holiday

Ghosts of the Illinois River

…and more!

© 2021 by Sylvia Shults

All rights reserved. No part of this book may be reproduced, stored in a retrieval system or transmitted in any form or by any means without the prior written permission of the publishers, except by a reviewer who may quote brief passages in a review to be printed in a newspaper, magazine or journal.

First Edition:
First printing

PUBLISHED BY HAUNTED ROAD MEDIA, LLC
www.hauntedroadmedia.com

United States of America

This book is dedicated to my father, David Zethmayr, the best storyteller I know. Thank you for raising me in a house full of books. And to "Uncle" Tom Sienkewicz, my college Classics professor, who let me write stories instead of papers and who pointed out, "You know, people make a living doing this." I'm beginning to believe you.

TABLE OF CONTENTS

Introduction	11
January	13
February	45
March	79
April	111
May	143
June	171
July	199
August	237
September	267
October	293
November	323
December	351
About The Author	381

"It is wonderful that five thousand years have now elapsed since the creation of the world, and still it is undecided whether or not there has ever been an instance of the spirit of any person appearing after death. All argument is against it, but all belief is for it."

   – Dr. Samuel Johnson

INTRODUCTION

Ghosts are with us, every single day.

Whether we are aware of it or not – whether we want to admit it or not – we walk hand-in-hand with the supernatural every day of our lives. From our first encounter with the monster under the bed, until we close our eyes for the last time and peek beyond the veil for ourselves, the spirit world is as close to us as our own shadow.

This thought might freak some people out. Others, like myself, find the idea comforting, even intriguing. Who hasn't daydreamed about meeting some famous figure from the past, or wished for just five more minutes with a lost loved one? Those of us who go out looking for ghosts, either on tours or on investigations, are just a little more vocal about our desire to run into any spirits that might be hanging around.

And people have been intensely curious about the paranormal for centuries. Way back in classical Greece, Odysseus conjured up the ghosts of the Trojan War. His séance involved a trench full of the blood of a sacrificed sheep. According to the rules of the séance, Odysseus had to stand guard over the blood with his sword drawn, and keep the thirsty ghosts away from the gore until he got to talk to Tiresias and ask him for details about the trip home to Ithaca. (And it *still* took Odysseus ten years to get home, even with guidance from a famous prophet.)

Contacting the dead got way less bloody (but no less weird) in the modern world. Surprisingly enough, as Gregory A. Coco writes in *A Strange and Blighted Land: Gettysburg – The Aftermath of a Battle*, lots of folks in the middle of the 19th century had no particular use for religion. However, with the Civil War raging (and the generally dismal proposition that people of that era were *way* too familiar with death as a fact of life), what they *were* keenly interested in was a way to contact the dead. Spiritualism, mediumship, and seances were all the rage in the 19th century, as people sought a connection with those they had lost.

The late Nineteenth Century saw the invention of the Ouija board, and it really took off around World War I. The Ouija board was just the latest incarnation in a long history of "talking boards". Cultures as widely spread as ancient Greece, Rome, India, and medieval Europe and China used automatic writing as a way to communicate with the spirit world. Other divination games, like Bloody Mary and Charlie Charlie, have joined Ouija boards to provide late-night entertainment at sleepovers for generations of excitable teenagers – and tweens, and adults.

There's a game that's popular in Japan, somewhat like Bloody Mary, but much more of a commitment. It's called 100 Candles. A group of people sit together in a dark room, a room lit only by – you guessed it – one hundred candles. Each person takes turns sharing a quick ghost story, then blows a candle out. When the final, hundredth candle is blown out, a hundred spirits surround you in the darkness. That's far more deliciously creepy than waiting for a precariously balanced pencil to move. (Plus, you get to hear a hundred ghost stories.)

Legend has it that the game was thought up by samurai warriors as a way to put their bravery to the test. During the Edo period (1603 – 1868) in Japan, Hyakumonogatari Kaidankai – "A Gathering of One Hundred Supernatural Tales" – was a popular parlor game. Kaiden, or collections of ghost stories, were already well known in Japan and China. In modern times, the game became the concept for a Japanese TV series. The show's characters use the game to retell classic Japanese ghost stories.

I'm proud to say that the book you are holding in your eager little paws brings you well over three times that many tales. Here you'll find a ghost story for every single day of the year. There's a story for your birthday. There's a story for your mom's birthday. Look up the day you got dumped by your high school crush – there's a story there too. (I hope that one is satisfyingly creepy.)

These spooky tales come from all across history and from all over the world. Sometimes I found more than one awesome story for a certain date. When that happened, I scooched one story to the next day or the day before. And sometimes, a haunting just takes place anytime during a certain month, or during a season. I used those stories to round out each month.

I wasn't at all surprised to discover that there are ghost stories for every single day of the year. What delighted me was getting the opportunity to discover the stories behind the hauntings. When we retell these stories, we find out who these spirits were, when they were alive. Telling their stories makes them human again. I hope you enjoy reading them as much as I enjoyed finding them for you.

And hey, maybe you don't believe in ghosts. That's okay – it's not my job to change your mind. As long as you enjoy the stories, that's fine with me. But do keep this in mind: Richard Estep, in his book *In Search of the Paranormal*, pointed out some food for thought.

"If *just one* of the ghost encounters you have ever read about (or personally experienced, perhaps) turns out to be real, then the scientific community has been ignoring or scoffing at one of the most important human experiences that we could possibly imagine."

So, settle down in your favorite reading spot, turn the page, and let's dive right in with January 1.

JANUARY

JANUARY 1
The Santika Nightclub Fire, Bangkok, Thailand (2009)

New Year's Eve in Bangkok, the hard-partying capital of Thailand. All of the city's nightclubs were open for business, but over a thousand guests and employees packed the Santika. It was a special night – the theme of the party was "Santika's Last Night" or "Bye Bye Santika", as the club was scheduled to move to a new location. The Thai band Burn (keep in mind, I am making none of this up) took the stage, lights flashing, music pounding, urging the dancers into a frenzy of celebration for the new year. True to their name, Burn's stage show featured the bright, colorful lights of sparklers and fireworks.

Minutes after the New Year's countdown, a fire broke out in the crowded nightclub. The tar paper and plastic sheeting used to keep the tropical rains out of the building caught fire and added to the blaze. The building's one fire extinguisher was pitifully inadequate against the inferno. Emergency teams raced to the scene, and paramedics tried desperately to reach people trapped on a staircase, but failed. The electrical system of the building shorted out in the intense heat. The exit signs dimmed, then went out, leaving the partiers trapped in the glowing hellscape, unable to find a way out.

No official cause was ever determined for the blaze that killed 66 people and injured 222, but it was generally accepted that the fireworks and sparklers of Burn's stage show were to blame. What had begun as a night of celebration turned to tragedy, as the revelers suffered burns, or smoke inhalation, or were crushed in the frantic stampede for the elusive exits.

Three days after the fire, some teenagers broke into the roped-off scene to take pictures with their cell phones. Thais believe that ghosts return to the scene of their deaths after three days, so these kids were there to ghost-hunt. No mention was made of them finding any ghosts on that visit, but they had the right idea.

The ravaged skeleton of the building has been torn down, but the ghost stories continue. Residents in the apartment complex across the street from the site report strange noises. At night, they'll hear the sounds of a huge party coming from the empty lot. The party noises are soon replaced with the sounds of people screaming.

Noel Boyd, the host of *Ghost Files Singapore*, visited the site of the Santika nightclub in 2015. He went to the site without his team, accompanied only by an employee of the hotel he was staying at in Bangkok. (He brought someone with him so he wouldn't be *completely* alone, which is always wise.) As he investigated the empty site, he became aware of negative energy surrounding him. Soon Noel felt very drained, and said that he saw black shadows rushing towards him.

Noel cut the investigation short – he was so powerfully affected by the site's energy, he just couldn't handle two hours there. He spoke with the ghosts, pointing out that he was visiting on "Buddha Day", when spirits are at their strongest. He promised to go to a temple the next day and pray for the souls of the 66 people who lost their lives in the fire. (To watch Noel Boyd's investigation, please look up "Santika nightclub ghost hunt" on YouTube.)

JANUARY 2
A Strange Story in the Paper, Nebraska (1888)

The *Chicago Tribune* for January 2, 1888, carried an article that told a very strange tale indeed. According to the article, a farmhand named William Aimison, who was working in Nebraska, had gotten married in Illinois about six years before. Three years into the marriage, his wife had died suddenly. Aimison attended the funeral, and watched as the coffin lid was closed and the coffin lowered into the grave. Shortly after his wife's death and burial, Aimison moved to Kansas, then ended up in Nebraska.

Shortly after reaching Kansas, Aimison got a letter in the mail ... from his dead wife. It was postmarked from his old home in Illinois, and signed "Lulie" (his wife's name). The handwriting was unmistakably hers – he compared it to letters Lulie had written to him before they'd gotten married. In the letter, his wife said that she was very lonely, and missed him terribly. She begged him to return home to her. That would have been creepy enough, but there was more.

One sentence of the letter went something like this: "You all thought I died, but I did not, and am much better than when I saw you last." Aimison could not explain this, to himself or to anyone else.

Aimison got more letters from his dead wife. They were lovely letters, full of endearments and sweet nothings, the kind of letter any loving wife would write to a husband who was away from home. (Aside, of course, from the fact that Lulie had been dead for a few years by then.) Just in case there was something *to* these letters, William wrote a letter to his wife, addressing it "Mrs. W. S Aimison", but it was returned.

The letters got weirder. One was postmarked Concordia, Kansas, where Aimison had spent some time before coming to Nebraska. In this particular letter, Lulie bemoaned the fact hat he'd left before she had reached him.

This was really starting to get disturbing. Aimison sent a few of the letters to his wife's parents, back in Illinois. His inlaws agreed that yes, it was their daughter's handwriting, but beyond that, they were just as stumped as he was.

The last letter from William's "wife" showed up about three weeks before the newspaper article appeared, from Table Rock, Nebraska. In the letter, Lulie wrote that she was at a hotel in Table Rock, sick and out of money. She begged William to come and help her.

These days, any one of us would suspect a scam. But those were different times. William took off for Table Rock as soon as he got the letter. When he arrived, he discovered that a woman had registered at the hotel under the name "Mrs. Lulu Aimison". She'd stayed in her room for a week, saying she was sick. Hotel employees described the woman, and their description was almost identical to that of his wife the last time he'd seen her alive. Of course, three years had passed ...

Here's where the story gets *really* weird. Aimison was thoroughly confused by the appearance and disappearance of this mystery woman, who claimed to be his wife, who looked just like her, and whose handwriting exactly matched hers. Aimison went back to Illinois and had his wife's body exhumed.

Lulie Aimison was there in the casket, right where she was supposed to be ... right where William had buried her three years before.

JANUARY 3
The Murder of J.P. Rademuller, Toronto, Canada (1816)

The lighthouse at Gibraltar Point is one of the oldest on the Great Lakes, and the first one built to serve Lake Ontario. It has been guiding sailors with the light atop its 82-foot-high tower since 1808. And like all the best lighthouses, it is haunted. Some visitors have reported phantom footsteps echoing through the stone lighthouse, and mysterious moving shadows that tease the eye and freeze the blood.

The first keeper of the lighthouse, J.P. Rademuller, served from 1808 to 1816. He was a recent immigrant from Germany, and he kept the lighthouse running with meticulous Teutonic efficiency. He took great pride in keeping the light's wicks trimmed properly and making sure the great lens was cleaned to a pristine polish. Rademuller was known for being fastidious and reliable.

He was also known for the quality of the beer he brewed, a talent he'd brought with him from Germany. It was common knowledge that he made the best pilsner on the lake, and his hospitality was legendary.

The soldiers at nearby Fort York knew of Rademuller's generosity, and they often stopped by the lighthouse for some good conversation and good beer. This congenial habit led to tragedy on January 2, 1816.

Three soldiers showed up at the keeper's house, already sloshed. Rademuller couldn't, in good conscience, serve them any more beer. He tried to get them to go back to the fort, or even sack out in the lighthouse until they sobered up. But the soldiers were drunk and belligerent, and demanded some suds.

One of the soldiers picked up a chunk of firewood and raised it, yelling at Rademuller to fill the mugs already, dammit! Again, Rademuller told them that no way was he giving them any more beer, they'd had quite enough.

The soldier brought the stick of firewood crashing down on Rademuller's skull, knocking him senseless. Then the men dragged the keeper up to the top of the lighthouse and pitched him over the side to his death.

Reality soon began to sober the men up, and thinking to hide the evidence of their crime, they cut Rademuller's corpse into pieces and buried him all over the grounds of the lighthouse. By the time they were done with this grisly task, they were completely sober. They freaked out, and ran.

Rademuller's disappearance was an unsolved mystery for a good while. A Mr. Halloway was appointed lighthouse keeper, and the light kept burning. Everyone in the area suspected that Rademuller had met with foul play, but no one had any idea what really happened.

Sometime after 1832, a keeper named James Durnam was digging near the lighthouse, and uncovered some human bones. He notified authorities, and they deduced that the remains were those of J.P. Rademuller. Durnam later claimed that Rademuller's spirit haunted the lighthouse, howling and groaning his way through dark and foggy nights, still searching for the soldiers who had murdered him over a mug of beer.

JANUARY 4
The Sinking of the Juanita*, Nova Scotia, Canada (1910)*

Mallory Arnott, a native of Nova Scotia, spent the summer of 2006 working on a lobster boat in Tor Bay. As a researcher studying the lobster population, her job was to count the crustaceans hauled up in the nets of the research boat. Mallory was no stranger to the area – her family still owned the cottage that was built by her great-great-grandfather in the 1800s.

The family connection was strong; Mallory's great-grandmother, Margaret, whose father Reuben Monroe had built the cottage, grew up there was well. Reuben was a seafaring man, the captain of the fishing boat *Juanita*. Margaret was born on August 27, 1886 – and Mallory was born on August 27, 1986, exactly a century later than her ancestor. Mallory was grateful for this link to her family's past.

One night, that past intruded on her present in a way she never could have suspected. Exhausted from a long day's work on the lobster boat, Mallory fell into bed. Her bedroom, in the cottage, may have been the very room used by her great-grandmother, Margaret. Mallory woke up every summer morning to peer out of the same windows through which Margaret had done, as she scanned the sea for her father's boat.

Sometime in the dark of the night, Mallory came bolt awake.

A stranger stood in the small doorway of Mallory's bedroom. Mallory later described the nighttime visitor.

"He was small, but he was gruff looking. He was wearing rain gear and a little hat. He was soaking wet, and he had pieces of seaweed on him as if he had come up from the ocean. He wore a dark beard, and had piercing eyes that stared right into me," Mallory said.

The dripping stranger came farther into the room, headed for the young woman. As she watched, frozen in terror, the figure suddenly vanished, and Mallory knew she'd seen a ghost.

The next morning, she shared the story of the terrifying apparition with her mother and sister. They had a simple theory for the spirit's identity. It had to be Reuben Monroe.

Reluctantly, Mallory agreed that their theory made perfect sense. Why shouldn't Reuben appear to her? After all, Mallory had been born exactly a century to the day after Margaret, Reuben's cherished daughter. The ghost had manifested as a dripping, drowned sailor festooned with seaweed and salt water – and Reuben had been lost at sea.

Intrigued by the ghostly visitation from her long departed relative, Mallory dug into the newspaper archives and did some research. What she found confirmed her belief that it had indeed been her great-great-grandfather standing in her bedroom doorway.

On Tuesday, January 4, 1910, fishermen from two Nova Scotia villages were out trawling for haddock when a snowstorm barreled through the area with no warning. Headlines in the *Halifax Herald* trumpeted the devastating news: "Forty Fishermen of Dover and Whitehead, Swept to Sea by Fierce Blizzard, Still Missing".

Miraculously, most of the men caught out in the storm survived, and limped their boats back to the safety of the shore. There was only one crew that did not make it home to Whitehead. The *Juanita* was lost to the storm. The crew consisted of 58-year-old Captain Reuben Monroe, his son, and his nephew. None of the men were ever seen again.

JANUARY 5
The Haunting of Kemper Hall, Kenosha, WI (1900)

Durkee Mansion was built in 1861, the palatial home of Senator Charles Durkee and his second wife, Caroline. They enjoyed the sumptuous mansion for several years until 1865, when the senator was appointed the territorial governor of Utah. Realizing that a cross-country move was inevitable, Senator Durkee gave his Wisconsin property to the Kenosha Female Seminary. By 1871, the mansion had been repurposed into a boarding school for girls, called St. Clair's Hall, run by the Episcopal community of the Sisters of Saint Mary. One of the buildings of the complex was named Kemper Hall in honor of Bishop Jackson Kemper, the first missionary for the Northwest Territory of the Episcopal Church.

Kemper Hall is haunted by the spirit of a young nun who had trouble adjusting to convent life. The nuns who lived in the former mansion dedicated their lives to the care of the needy, working closely with the poor of Chicago. Nuns in Kemper Hall, in particular, seemed to be prone to depression due to their work with orphans. The religious sisters were reluctant to speak out about mental health issues, but such things were a concern, even if they went unspoken. Sister Augusta discovered this – too late.

Kemper Hall hosted a retreat for the nuns in January 1900. On January 2, other nuns noticed that Sister Augusta hadn't shown up for the six o'clock service. Her sisters searched the grounds and buildings for some clue as to Sister Augusta's whereabouts. They even searched the nearby shore of Lake Michigan, fearing the worst, but the freshly fallen snow on the lakeshore revealed no footprints. She had taken only her veil and cloak, leaving behind everything else – including the cross that marked her status as a nun. The young sister was just … gone.

On January 5, a letter arrived at Kemper Hall. It was addressed to Sister Augusta, but the sister superior opened it, hoping to shed some light on the mystery. Reading the letter, the sisters realized that Sister Augusta had planned to leave convent life. The letter discussed Augusta's plans to move to St. Louis to live with a friend. But where was she now?

Three days later, two children strolling on the beach with their mother spotted something strange in the water, washed up on the rocky shoreline. The mother immediately notified the officials at Kemper Hall, and a party of nuns rushed down to the shore. Their worst fears were realized. The body of Sister Augusta, pummeled by the icy waves of Lake Michigan, was indeed lying limp on the rocky beach.

The nuns held a private ceremony for their lost sister. Afterward, her body was sent home to St. Louis, and Augusta was laid to rest in her family plot, next to her mother.

An inquest was held, and found that Sister Augusta had suffered from nerves and depression before her disappearance. Her work with the poor in Chicago had worn on her, and she had requested time off to go home to St. Louis for a rest. In a mournful twist, she had actually been granted a leave of absence. If she'd just waited a few more days for an answer, she would have been headed home. The coroner's jury ruled the young woman's death a suicide.

Sister Augusta wanted only to go home, but it seems that she has stayed on at Kemper Hall. In the 1930s, a young woman working in the bakery at Kemper Center was passing a staircase when she heard footsteps on the stairs. Reflexively glancing up, she saw a woman wearing a brown skirt and brown shoes standing motionless, one delicate hand on the stairway banister. The bakery employee froze at the sight of the intruder, then fled to the kitchen. She shared her story, and she and others searched for the unknown woman. They found no trace of her.

A tourist had an encounter with the ghostly nun much later. In an October 2003 newspaper interview, reporter Bill Robbins shared the story of a tourist who had been with a group at Kemper Hall. As the tour group moved past the main staircase, one man hung back. He gazed up at the staircase – and saw a nun, in habit and veil, leaning over the railing watching him.

The sight of the apparition unnerved him, but things were about to get much stranger for the hapless tourist. As he tried to collect his racing thoughts, he found his gaze drawn upwards again. This time, the phantom nun spoke to him in a soft voice. "*I've been waiting for you*," she murmured.

This was just too much, and the man backed away, intending to rejoin his tour group. But he couldn't resist one last look up the staircase.

This time, the nun was smiling at him, and gave him a little wave. His nerve broke, and he ran to catch up with the group.

JANUARY 6
The First Lady and the Spiritualists, Washington DC (1853)

The Spiritualism craze that swept the United States during the middle of the 19th century caught many people up in its promise of contact with deceased loved ones. And those high up in society weren't immune to this appealing prospect.

Franklin Pierce was nominated for president in 1852, and won the election. His quiet wife, Jane, was not thrilled by this. A private, intensely religious woman who suffered from tuberculosis, Jane fainted when Franklin was nominated. Political life held no appeal for her at all, but when Pierce was elected, the frail Jane dutifully accompanied him to the capital.

But tragedy far beyond the grueling social duties of a First Lady awaited the presidential couple. On January 6, 1853, the Pierces were traveling on a train not far from Boston when the car they were riding in uncoupled and jumped the track. The passenger car rolled down a rocky embankment, breaking apart as it smashed its way down the hill.

Franklin and Jane escaped with only minor injuries. But there was one fatality in the crash – their son Benjamin. The eleven-year-old was killed instantly and gruesomely. As the car rolled, Benjamin's head hit a large rock, cracking his skull and sheeting his face with blood and brains. The sight was horrifically traumatic for both parents, but Jane was nearly paralyzed with the shock of it.

And who can blame her? The Pierces had already lived through the loss of their firstborn son in infancy. A second son had died at the age of only four years.

Jane was still in deep mourning for her son when Franklin Pierce was sworn into office in March. Her grief affected all those who saw her suffering, including her husband. Franklin Pierce's presidency was subdued as a result of this gloom, and Pierce himself found it difficult to break free of the sadness that blanketed his life, and Jane's.

For her part, Jane became little more than a wraith herself. Already weakened by her illness, Jane retreated into a private, numb haze of desperate grief. She spent hours alone, writing letters to the lost Benjamin. White House servants spoke in hushed tones of hearing Jane playing with all three of her deceased sons. Was she just delusional? Or did she actually see the spirits of her young boys in the shadows of her gloomy evenings?

Soon, though, Jane was not content to lose herself in memories. She invited the famous Fox sisters to the White House for a séance in the hope of contacting her dead sons. Katie, Leah, and Maggie Fox were celebrities, so it made sense that these young women were called upon to perform the first séance ever held in the White House.

We have no idea what messages the Fox sisters produced from the Other Side. Whatever they said, though, gave Jane Pierce a great deal of consolation. The First Lady came away from the meeting convinced that her beloved lost Benjamin still lived on, in a different form.

JANUARY 7
The Haunting at Rosehill Cemetery, Chicago, IL (1885, recurring)

Rosehill Cemetery, in Chicago, Illinois, is one of the oldest cemeteries in the city. The land was purchased in 1859 from a man named Hiram Roe, who requested that the cemetery be named in his honor. So the burying ground was called Roe's Hill. It was a spelling error made by a city clerk that resulted in a change to Rosehill.

The cemetery, like many Chicago graveyards, has a hefty share of ghost stories. An employee of Rosehill saw a woman standing near the Peterson Avenue wall of the cemetery after closing time. He walked over to ask her to leave, but as he came closer, he realized that she was floating. Then she faded away and vanished into a mist as the man watched. The next day, a woman called the cemetery office with a strange story. She claimed that her deceased aunt had appeared to her in a dream to complain that her grave did not yet have a marker on it. The caller wanted to order a marker for the grave. Here's the interesting part: the unmarked grave was right where the employee had seen the phantom, just the night before. Once the headstone was installed, that particular ghost was never seen again.

But there are plenty more spirits roaming the grounds at Rosehill. One of the most famous stories is that of Charles Hopkinson. The real estate mogul was very wealthy when he died in 1885, and true to that era, he had grandiose plans for the monument that would mark his time on this earth. He drew up plans, included in his will, for a small cathedral (just a small one, mind you), that would serve as a tomb for himself and his family.

This did not sit well with the people who owned – and were planning eventually to use – the grave plots behind Hopkinson's tomb. They suspected that this grand edifice of his would block people's view of their own stones. The families took the Hopkinson family to court, where it was ruled that the other families should have known that something, sometime, would wind up blocking the views of their own tombs. (Besides, one could just, you know, approach the other graves from the opposite side of Hopkinson's tomb.) The cathedral was built, and Charles Hopkinson was laid to rest.

But apparently, he does not rest easily. Many witnesses have reported strange sounds coming from the tomb, including moaning and the rattling of chains. This eerie serenade can be heard at any time of the year, but it is most commonly heard on January 7, the anniversary of Hopkinson's death.

JANUARY 8
The Hanging of George Smiley, Holbrook, AZ (1900)

Frank J. Wattron had a dilemma.

Wattron was the sheriff of a town called Holbrook in Navajo County, Arizona, in the late 1890s. Wattron was pretty good at keeping order in the frontier town – as a matter of fact, he was setting things up for the execution of one George Smiley. Smiley was a railroad worker who had killed his boss. He was caught, tried, found guilty, and sentenced to hang.

And therein lay Wattron's dilemma. Smiley was to be the first person ever executed in Holbrook. So Wattron wasn't quite sure how to go about it. The mechanics were obvious, sure. But were there any social niceties to be observed? He was informed that yes, he needed to send out invitations to the hanging.

Wattron was a bit stumped as to how to word these invitations. How do you invite people to a public hanging? In the end, after much thought (and after discussing the matter jokingly with his men), Wattron decided to word the hanging invitation as though he were inviting people to a fancy society shindig.

"You are hereby cordially invited to attend the hanging of one George Smiley, Murderer. His soul will be swung into eternity on December 8, 1899, at 2 o'clock pm, sharp. Latest improved methods in the art of scientific strangulation will be employed and everything possible will be done to make the surroundings cheerful and the execution a success." The incongruously cheery invitations were professionally printed on gilt-edged paper.

This bombed, and rather spectacularly, too. President William McKinley, appalled by Wattron's complete lack of taste, complained to the governor of Arizona. The governor, equally mortified, postponed Smiley's execution so that Wattron could have another go at designing the tone-deaf invitation. This time, Wattron decided to tone it down, and modeled it after a sympathy card. This, at least, was a bit more appropriate.

"With feelings of profound sorrow and regret, I hereby invite you to attend and witness the private, decent and humane execution of a human being; name, George Smiley, crime, murder. The said George Smiley will be executed on January 8, 1900, at 2 o'clock pm. You are expected to deport yourself in a respectful manner, and any 'flippant' or 'unseemly' language or conduct on your part will not be allowed. Conduct, on anyone's part, bordering on ribaldry and tending to mar the solemnity of the occasion will not be tolerated."

Wattron got a bit of a jab in, though. At the bottom of the second invitation, he suggested that the governor should form a committee to maybe set up some guidelines on wording future execution invites, if he didn't like the way they were done in the first place.

George Smiley was hanged for his crime on January 8, 1900. Employees at the Navajo County Courthouse claim that Smiley is still there, haunting the place with the sound of slamming doors and other creepy noises.

JANUARY 9
The Murder of Margaret Burke, Christchurch, New Zealand (1871)

The lives of Irish immigrants in the 19th century were often difficult, full of toil, poor wages, and discrimination. Margaret Burke traveled to Christchurch, New Zealand, in search of a better life for herself. She found work as a domestic servant in several upper-class homes, but her good fortune was short-lived. On January 8, 1871, Margaret was viciously raped by Simon Cadeno, a Panamanian servant who worked for the wealthy William Robinson. The rape ended with Margaret's murder. In March 1871, Charles was charged with the crime, and the following month, he was found guilty. Cadeno was hanged at Lyttleton Jail.

Margaret was laid to rest in a pauper's grave on January 11. To make amends for their servant's appalling crime, the Robinson family paid for a granite headstone for Margaret's final resting place. The stone was erected in September 1871, and the Robinsons breathed easy, figuring they had paid their debt to poor Margaret.

But a month later, a reddish-brown stain began to spread over the pristine granite – a stain that, to those with vivid imaginations, looked an awful lot like spilled blood. The graveyard sexton scrubbed the discoloration with every cleaning agent he could think of, but the stain stubbornly stayed on the stone. The Robinson family replaced the marker with a fresh gravestone ... and soon that one was "bleeding" too. The rumor started, and quickly spread, that Margaret Burke was reaching out from beyond the grave, showing her anger at the rich people of Christchurch who had ignored her during her wretched life.

The "bleeding" headstone that marked Margaret Burke's lonely grave was a ghoulish tourist attraction for many years, but suffered frequent vandalism in modern times. The Department of Parks and Preserves finally removed the stone for safekeeping. History-minded citizens have asked repeatedly to have the granite marker restored, but the official line from the parks department is that the gravestone has mysteriously disappeared.

JANUARY 10
The Riverboat James T. Staples, *Alabama (1913)*

The stern-wheeler *James T. Staples* was once one of the finest vessels on the riverways of Alabama. It was designed, owned, and captained by Norman Staples, who named the ship after his father. The ship was built in 1908 at a cost of $40,000, and soon settled into a route on the Tombigbee River, running between Demopolis and Mobile.

The *James T. Staples* was an elegant riverboat, with clean lines and cargo space for 2,500 bales of cotton. But Norman Staples was beset by trouble in his operation. A large steamboat company wanted to take control of all the boats on the river, and they drove Staples to the brink of financial ruin. In December 1912, creditors seized Captain Staples' beloved ship, and turned it over to the competition. This broke Norman Staples, and on January 2, 1913, he held a shotgun against his chest and pulled the trigger.

A few days after Staples killed himself, his crew members began seeing a shadowy apparition hanging around the boilers in the ship's hold. The entire engine room crew quit, and the new owner of the ship had to hire an all-new crew to replace them – a crew that hadn't heard the ghost stories. A short while later, all of the rats onboard deserted the ship and swam to shore.

On January 10, 1913, the *James T. Staples* docked at Powe's Landing to take on a cargo of lumber. Exactly one week to the day that Captain Staples had killed himself – at nearly the exact minute – the boiler belowdecks exploded, scalding twenty-six men, including the new captain. The twenty-one crew members and passengers who made it off the ship alive were badly injured. The survivors were picked up by the steamer *John Quill*, and the stricken *James T. Staples* broke free from its moorings and drifted downstream for several miles. It finally sank at the grave of her former owner. Bladon Springs Cemetery is four miles inland from the spot in the river where the *James T. Staples* went to the bottom. The ship sank as close to Norman Staples as she could get.

There is a chilling coincidence to the sinking, too. Captain W. H. Gray, the acting captain of the ship and a longtime friend of Norman Staples, lived because of Norman's death. When Staples was forced from his ship, Gray took over as captain. On the day Staples was buried, Gary, grief-stricken over the loss of his friend, retired as captain, and accompanied Norman's family to the cemetery for the burial. One of the new owners, a Captain Bartee, stepped into the captain's role.

Bartee died in the explosion.

Captain Norman Staples still haunts Bladon Springs Cemetery. He hovers over the graves of his children Bertha, Mabel, and James, who all died in early childhood. (Another daughter, Jessie, lived into her early eighties and is buried at a different cemetery.) The apparition drifts protectively over the graves, seemingly content, most of the time, simply to watch over his babies. Sometimes, though, the spirit is seen with his head buried in his hands, suffering in the depths of despair or regret.

JANUARY 11
The Murder of the Teets Family, Barrington, IL (1979)

On January 11, 1979, Marlene Manke showed up for dinner at the home of her fiancé, Gary Teets. Teets lived with his parents in a secluded farmhouse in the woods near Shoe Factory Road in Barrington. Marlene knocked on the door, anticipating a pleasant evening with her fiancé and his family. But there was no answer.

Concerned, Marlene called Gary's brother, Earl Teets Jr. Earl caught Marlene's concern, and called the police. Two officers met him at the house, and they knocked again. The house was still silent, without even the barking of the family's four guard dogs to ease Earl's apprehension.

Sick with worry, Earl shouldered the door open with several lunging blows. The officers followed him into the house … and the three men walked into a scene of unspeakable carnage.

One of the family's guard dogs had been shot to death. The other three dogs had been locked up. The four brave animals weren't able to save their humans – Gary Teets and his parents were lying on the blood-soaked floor. They had also been shot to death.

At first, the police were confident about catching the murderer. Whoever had killed the Teets's knew the family kept guard dogs, and had taken precautions to avoid them or deal with them. The killer must have known the family well. They had probably been careless in their complacency, and left some sort of evidence.

Then, the snow started to fall. As the crime scene tape was being rolled out, the Blizzard of '79 began. In four days, the city of Chicago was brought to a standstill as 20 inches of snow blanketed the area. Snowplows were busy keeping paved roads clear for motorists; roads out in the country were a much lower priority, and the blizzard made them completely inaccessible.

The Teets case was to suffer another setback immediately after the snow stopped falling. Bodies had been discovered in the basement of John Wayne Gacy's home, and the scandalous Gacy murders pushed all other news to the side. Detectives were pulled off the Teets case and told to concentrate on the Gacy murders. Then, more bad luck for the investigators; an arsonist snuck into the woods and burned the Teets farmhouse to the ground. Any evidence that had been there was obliterated. The killer was never found.

The forested area where the Teets farmhouse once stood is now a part of a Cook County forest preserve, with a bike trail running through it. The hauntings here involve both the bike trail and the farmhouse site. In the woods adjoining the bike trail that leads to the farmhouse, people often report hearing the voices and laughter of children … sounds that seem to follow witnesses as they walk or bike along the trail.

People also report hearing voices at the foundations of the farmhouse and barn, but these are not the happy voices of laughing children. These are the voices of adults, raised in argument, or pleading for mercy from an unknown assailant. Witnesses often report feelings of overwhelming despair when standing in the foundation of the farmhouse.

JANUARY 12

The Grave of Mary Alice Quinn, Holy Sepulchre Cemetery, Chicago IL (1935)

Mary Alice Quinn was born December 28, 1920, to a family of devout Irish immigrants in Chicago. Even her name reflected her family's strong Catholic background; she was christened "Mary Alice" to honor the Blessed Virgin first, then her mother. Her parents, Daniel and Alice, were delighted with their first child. But their happiness was not to last. When Mary Alice was five months old, her parents noticed that her lips had a bluish tinge. They consulted specialists, who told them that Mary Alice's heart was enlarged to twice normal size. The child was not expected to see her second birthday.

But Mary Alice surprised the doctors by surviving. Her parents prayed constantly for her full recovery, and encouraged their daughter's spiritual growth too. By the time Mary Alice was three, she knew all her prayers by heart. She herself was discouraged by the fact that she and her parents had prayed very hard for her health, yet she wasn't any better. She told her mother, "God and all His angels and saints are very slow in making me well, but when I'm a big angel or saint I'm going to make everyone well."

The Blessed Mother appeared to her little namesake when Mary Alice was seven years old, and again when she was twelve. One morning when Mary Alice was in fifth grade, she received communion from Father Touhey, the pastor at St. Laurence Church, which the Quinns attended. During the sacrament, something happened that Fr. Touhey never did explain. All he would say was that Mary Alice would become a greater saint than Saint Therese, to whom the child had devoted her life.

Mary Alice Quinn succumbed to her heart ailment on November 5, 1935. She was not yet fifteen years old.

The miracles attributed to Mary Alice began even before the teenager was buried. Two nuns from St. Cyril's Elementary School "prayed for a favor and received it almost immediately", according to a letter written by Alice Quinn. Over the next few years, Mary Alice's spirit appeared to several people who were severely ill, including her own brother, Gorman Leonard Quinn. All of the people who received visits from Mary Alice were healed.

During the 1930s and 1940s, Alice Quinn, Mary Alice's mother, would give talks at area churches. She would provide the faithful with relics of her daughter – a scapular containing a photo of Mary Alice and a scrap of her clothing.

Even now, there are reports of desperately ill people being healed by Chicago's Miracle Child. Some of these dramatic healing episodes happen right at Mary Alice Quinn's gravesite, in Holy Sepulchre Cemetery in Worth, Illinois. Sufferers pray for a time at the grave, and are suddenly overwhelmed by the smell of roses. As soon as that sign from Mary Alice manifests, the patient's sickness goes into remission, or disappears entirely.

People have reported the scent of roses around Mary Alice's grave throughout the year, but it is most commonly experienced in January. Interestingly, only one row away from Mary Alice's grave is a nine-foot-tall sculpture of Saint Therese of Lisieux, known as the Little Flower. The saint holds a cross and a bouquet of roses. Curving above her head is the promise, carved in stone, "I will let fall a shower of roses."

JANUARY 13
Ghost Train, Pasadena, TX (1960)

It's never fun to get stopped by a train, especially a freight train, especially out in the middle of nowhere. Thomas Phillips was driving on Highway 36 through Texas when he had to stop for a freight train between Belleville and Sealy. The night was foggy, but Phillips could see the old-fashioned steam locomotive approaching through the mist, about 300 feet away on the right. Phillips sensibly stopped to let the train pass. But as he sat in his vehicle, watching as car after car flashed past, it began to dawn on him that there were no gates in front of where he'd stopped his car. No flashing red lights marked the time as the boxcars jogged past. No railroad crossing signs warned drivers of possible approaching trains. Even stranger, Phillips realized that the train passing in front of him seemed to be lit with a lambent glow, a glow that was not the reflection of his own headlights.

The last boxcar trundled past, and Phillips took his foot off the brake and pulled forward. Weirdest of all, his tires rolled over smooth pavement instead of bumping over train tracks. There was no railroad bed to break the line of the highway. There wasn't even a ripple in the pavement to show where train tracks had ever been.

JANUARY 14
Wreck of the Sagunto, *New Hampshire (1813, recurring)*

The east coast of the United States is an archaeologist's paradise. Shipwrecks leave their treasures to be washed up on rocky beaches, human habitation leaves its mark, and the romance of the sea casts its spell over the whole landscape.

One of the evocative parts of the New England coastline is the Isle of Shoals. This is a group of small islands about six miles off the coast, sitting on the borders of New Hampshire and Maine. The third largest of these islands goes by the delightfully odd name of Smuttynose. In addition to being the place where the pirate Blackbeard allegedly went on one of his honeymoons, Smuttynose Island has also been the site of a couple of tragedies.

One of these was the wreck, in January 1813, of the Spanish ship *Sagunto*. (At least, this may have been the name of the Spanish ship. It could have been the *Concepcion*. Or perhaps it was Portuguese. Sometimes the history of these shipwrecks can get a little woolly.) Whatever the ill-fated ship's name, wherever it's original port of call, it wrecked – hard – on the rocky shore of Smuttynose Island late at night on January 14, 1813. The ship was manned by a crew of fourteen sailors. When the *Sagunto* broke herself open on the rocks and surrendered herself and her cargo to the crashing waves, these men were tossed overboard at the mercy of the roiling water. They made their way to the beach through a blinding snowstorm, following the promise of safety – the yellow glowing light of a candle in the window of Sam Haley's cottage.

Haley, mindful of the ships that passed by the islands, kept a candle burning in his window for fifty years, until the White Island lighthouse was built. On that snowy night, the candle gave the sailors a direction to go, but sadly, not one of the men made it to the safety of Haley's cottage. Although a few made it all the way to the stone wall that encircled the cottage, they all froze to death during that long, cold, blustery night. Haley, warm and safe, knew nothing of the drama playing out just yards from his front door.

After the wreck, the men were buried right there on the beach where they had perished. Crates of cargo, raisins and almonds from Spain, washed up on the shore in the coming days. A watch, stopped at four o'clock, was found on the sand, fixing the time of the disaster.

In the spring, Sam Haley went exploring on the beach and found more treasure – a cache of silver ingots. Again, it's not really clear whether this silver was part of the *Sagunto's* (or *Concepcion's*) cargo, or if it was perhaps some buried treasure left behind by a pirate crew. Haley used four of the ingots to fund the construction of a breakwater to connect Smuttynose with Malaga Island. Other treasure hunters later found silver coins lodged in the rocks on the shore of the island.

Now, the ghostly apparition of the ship appears just off Smuttynose every January, around the anniversary of the wreck. The island is also haunted by both Blackbeard and one of his many wives. The pirate is either searching for his treasure or protecting it, and his wife is seen as a misty white figure or an apparition wearing a white dress. Blackbeard abandoned that particular wife on one of the Isles of Shoals, and sometimes the woman's ghost simply manifests as a whisper on the breeze, murmuring *"He will return."*

JANUARY 15
The Ted Bundy Murders, Tallahassee, FL (1978)

Even monsters can sometimes feel remorse.

On New Year's Eve 1977, the murderer Ted Bundy escaped from jail in Colorado. For the past two years, he'd been awaiting his trial for the murder of Caryn Campbell. During that time, he felt he'd made great strides in his personal growth. Bundy realized that he had a darkness within him, an evil force he later described as "the Entity". His breakout on December 31 was a chance not only at escape, but also at redemption. What better day to begin a new life than New Year's Eve?

Bundy ran from Colorado all the way to northern Florida. He ended up in Tallahassee and took a room at a boarding house called The Oak, named in a nod to the moss-draped oak tree that spread its branches in the front yard, a tree that was said to be a thousand years old.

Bundy was pleased with the way he'd landed on his feet. He planned to turn over a new leaf with the new year. He'd change his name, get a job, and just start over. He figured he'd finally come to grips with his personal demons, and had beaten the Entity.

He was wrong.

In the cold early morning hours of January 15, Bundy, restless in his room, decided to go for a walk. His stroll took him to the Chi Omega sorority house on the campus of Florida State University. Sometime between 3 am and 3:15 am, Bundy broke into the house and attacked four women, leaving two of them dead.

The attack left nearly every bone in Karen Chandler's face broken. Her roommate, Kathy Kleiner, was beaten so badly that her jaw was broken in three places, hanging off the side of her face, attached only by the hinge. She remembered lying on her bed trying to talk – trying to scream – but she just couldn't.

As badly as the two women suffered, they were not the only victims Bundy left behind at the sorority house. Lisa Levy and Margaret Bowman had been beaten and strangled to death. And Bundy's demon still wasn't sated. He left the Chi Omega house after the brutal attacks and went several blocks away, to Dunwoody Street. There, he crawled through a kitchen window into the home of Cheryl Thomas, a dance major at the university.

Cheryl shared the home with a roommate, Debbie Ciccarelli. Debbie lived in one side of the house, and Cheryl lived in the other side. The kitchen window Bundy came through was next to Cheryl's bedroom. Bundy attacked Cheryl, leaving her bloody and unconscious on the floor. She woke up in the hospital a few days later, with no idea what had happened to her.

Ted Bundy was caught after abducting and murdering 12-year-old Kimberly Leach in Lake City, Florida. He was executed by electric chair on January 24, 1989.

A few weeks after Bundy's execution, two women walking past The Oak noticed a man standing on the porch of the rooming house. One of the women casually remarked that the guy looked a lot like a young Ted Bundy. When the women looked again, the man had disappeared.

Had the ghost of Ted Bundy returned to the boarding house where he'd found a few days of contentment before his darkness had overtaken him again?

JANUARY 16
Barker Gang Shootout, Ocklawaha, FL (1935)

Lots of folks in the Midwest think it's a great idea to escape the cold snowy winter and hide out in Florida enjoying the sunshine for a few months.

In 1934, a couple of Chicago gangsters had the very same idea. The Karpis-Barker gang, twenty-five like-minded souls, had been on a rampage since 1932. Their agenda included three kidnappings, ten murders, and over $1 million in bank heists. They'd been busy, and they deserved a vacation.

They also needed to lay low for a while. The Barkers were members of one of the last remaining active gangs in the United States at the time, and J. Edgar Hoover had just vowed to destroy all organized crime. In fact, he'd just named the Karpis-Barker gang "Public Enemy Number One". Things in Chicago were getting pretty uncomfortable for the gang. So they turned their eyes to central Florida.

Carson Bradford owned a house on Lake Weir, in the town of Ocklawaha. He hadn't planned on renting it out, but a sweet old lady from Chicago, a Mrs. Blackburn, offered him loads of money. Bradford hesitated – he'd never rented that house – but Mrs. Blackburn was very persuasive. And so was the increasing number behind the dollar sign. Mrs. Blackburn and her sons just really wanted to get away from it all for the winter, and they were prepared to shell out big bucks to do it.

So, Bradford rented the Lake Weir house, and collected the cash.

The tenants enjoyed the lakefront house for about two months. Then, federal agents arrested Arthur "Doc" Barker in Chicago. In their investigation of Doc's apartment, they found a map of Florida, with a circle around the town of Ocklawaha.

Eight days later, FBI agents surrounded Bradford's house, and one of them knocked on the front door. Ma Barker answered the knock. Moments later, Fred Barker came out onto the porch and started raking the agents with machine gun fire. That opening barrage started the longest gunfight in FBI history: four hours of nearly continuous gunfire as the agents and the Barkers traded lead.

At noon, the agents sent Willie Woodberry, the Barker's colored cook, into the house to see what was going on. "It's me Ma, don't shoot," Woodberry yelled as he gingerly opened the front door.

The two gangsters lay dead in the house. Fred Barker had been gunned down on the stairs, shot in the back of the head. Ma Barker had caught a bullet in one of the bedrooms. Nearly 3,500 rounds had whistled through the air between 8 am and noon.

FBI agents found rifles, pistols, machine guns, and $14,293 in cash in the house. And Ma and Fred Barker, two of the most notorious names on the most wanted list, were dead.

The crime scene photo of Ma Barker shows her curled on the floor, cuddling a Thompson machine gun. But was Kate "Ma" Barker a criminal mastermind, or an old lady caught up in her sons' illegal activities? Willie Woodberry said of Ma, "She was the boss." And J. Edgar Hoover presented the image of Ma Barker as the cigar-smoking, machine-gun-toting brains of the Karpis-Barker gang.

Lee McGehee, the former police chief in Ocala, sees Ma Barker a bit differently. He thinks Hoover might have exaggerated Barker's ferocity. "I think they were afraid if she wasn't built up as a serious gangster the community wouldn't support him if she was killed."

One thing is for sure, though: as late as 2016, the spirit of Ma Barker was still at the house where she and Fred were killed. Elizabeth Cockrell and Carson Good, brother and sister, are Carson Bradford's great-grandkids. They spent time in the house as kids – sailing on the lake, digging on the beach for Mason jars full of gangsters' hidden money, swimming on hot summer days, and spending sleepless nights lying awake in the dark, listening to ghostly voices.

"I'm not a big believer of ghosts, but I heard a lot of sounds in that house," Carson says. "Voices. Furniture moving. People walking up and down the wooden stairs. I was told by my mother and grandmother and uncles that the first ten to twenty years after the shooting, people often heard loud talking, clearly voices, but couldn't discern exactly what was being said."

Carson's sister Elizabeth adds, "You'd often hear footsteps up and down the stairs in the middle of the night. And there would be sounds of people playing poker at the dining room table and the glasses chinking and people yelling at each other and laughing."

But those stories are tame compared to what Donald Weiss experienced at the Bradford house. The police patrolman from New York had retired to Ocala, Florida, and wanted to see the house where Ma Barker had met her end. As he crossed the yard, a voice snarled, "*Get outta here, lawman!*" And a shadowy figure appeared in a photograph he took of the front porch.

John Pendygraft, a photographer from the *Tampa Bay Times*, also captured a strange image in the picture he took of the front porch: the figure of a stout woman, her hair up in a bun, who looked like she was holding a machine gun. In that same visit to the house, in the fall of 2012, John had gone alone into the front bedroom, intending to take a few pictures through the window looking toward the lake, where the FBI agents had used the trees as cover as they approached the house. The front bedroom was where Ma Barker had died.

Suddenly he came barreling out of the house in a panic, nearly sliding down the stairs in his hurry to get away. He said he didn't know what happened, but a mattress fell through the bed frame without him touching it.

"I used to have an antique bed frame," John says. "I know modern mattresses are a bit smaller than old frames. They can easily fall through the middle if they get wiggled. I am more of a believer in good ghost stories than in actual ghosts ... but ... when that mattress dropped, I was outta there. All the way outta. Down the stairs, out the door and in the front yard outta there."

Carson Good sold the Lake Weir property in 2018. In late 2016, he donated the house to the county. The house was lifted, put on a barge, and floated across the lake, relocated to Carney Island. It is now a museum. Paranormal groups have investigated the house since the move, and it seems that the Barkers' energy is still there. The group Soul Sister Paranormal investigated the house on January 16, 2019, on the 84th anniversary of the shootout. In the upstairs bedroom, where Ma Barker died, a spirit box blurted out the word "Blackburn" – the alias used by Ma to rent the house.

So maybe when the house was moved, Ma and Freddie moved with it.

JANUARY 17
Mercy Brown, Exeter, RI (1892)

The Brown family was beset by troubles. George Brown had as much backbone as any Yankee farmer, but it was hard, so very hard to lose his family. One by one, they left him for the valley of death. His wife, Mary, passed away in 1883 from a mysterious illness. Six months later, his 20-year-old daughter, Mary Olive, was also taken from him.

The losses kept coming. Within the next several years, 19-year-old Mercy, another daughter, fell ill and died, and his son Edwin began to cough and waste away too. The doctor told George sympathetically that it was tuberculosis, or "consumption", that was ravaging his family. But George and his friends had a very different theory.

The men gathered at Chestnut Hill Cemetery on a chilly afternoon in March 1892. George exchanged worried glances with his friends, them jammed a shovel into the graveyard dirt. Over the next several hours, the men exhumed the bodies of George's wife and two daughters. The reason for this gruesome task, in their minds, was simple: there was a vampire on the prowl. One of the dead women had to be leaving her grave to suck the life from her living relatives. To save Edwin, the vampire must be found – and killed.

At last all three coffins had been dug up, the soil drying on the wood in the early spring breeze. The men opened Mary's coffin, then Mary Olive's. Both corpses, having been in the ground for nine years or so, were in an expected state of decomposition. The men opened Mercy's coffin … and recoiled in appalled horror.

Mercy had died January 17. She'd been in the grave for about two months, but her body appeared suspiciously well-preserved. Her fingernails and hair seemed to have grown during her time belowground. And when the men gingerly poked Mercy's corpse with a shovel, they found it was still full of fresh-looking blood. They had found their vampire.

George Brown cut out his daughter's heart and burned it on a nearby rock. Following the rules laid out by magical thinking, he mixed the ashes of the heart into Edwin's medicine and had the young man drink it. The folklore cure was, of course, useless. Edwin died less than two months later.

Nowadays, we can scoff at this tale of New England superstition. We know that hair and nails don't grow after death; it's simply an illusion caused by shrinkage of the surrounding tissue. And Mercy Brown had just spent the two coldest months of the year underground, sealed away in a casket. It's no surprise to us that her body was so well preserved. And we can easily recognize the wasting disease that carried off George Brown's family as tuberculosis.

It's disturbing, though, to realize that people as late as 1892 were still seriously putting so much stock in vampire lore. The 20th century was less than a decade away, and the fine folks of Exeter were exhuming dead bodies, looking for signs of vampirism. And up until 1900, there were enough rumors floating around that Rhode Island was, for a time, known as the "Vampire Capital of America".

JANUARY 18
The Bent House, Taos, NM (1847)

New Mexico in the 1840s was a place of unrest. It had become an American territory in 1834, during the Mexican War. Charles Bent, a mountain man who had made a name for himself as a trader and trapper, was appointed the first governor of New Mexico. Bent, his brother William, and Ceran St. Vrain had built Bent's Fort in Colorado, and had built the fort's reputation as a trading center for both natives and whites.

On January 18, 1847, an angry mob of Hispanic and Taos Indian rebels gathered in front of Governor Bent's house to protest the Mexican War. Bent went out to try to calm the crowd, but violence erupted. Bent was killed, along with several other men. The men were butchered – shot full of bullets and arrows, and scalped.

Bent's family managed to escape the carnage. They dug through the adobe wall of the parlor and crawled into a neighbor's house.

Having met such a grisly end, it's no wonder Governor Bent still haunts his former home. It's said that the men who attacked him are still hanging around the place too. An alarm went off on January 18, 2013, at the Moby Dickens Bookshop on Bent Street. The bookstore is located in what used to be the John Dunn house, right across the street from Governor Bent's home. A book had flung itself off of a top shelf and landed in the middle of the aisle, which is what tripped the alarm. No one was in the building at the time.

Was someone just trying to get attention on the anniversary of the massacre?

JANUARY 19
The Legend of Spanish Moss, Savannah, GA (1735, recurring)

Alice Riley and her husband Richard were servants in the home of William Wise, a wealthy Savannah businessman. Wise was a horrible boss, abusive and tyrannical to his hired help. Finally, the Rileys couldn't take any more of Wise's crap. Richard and Alice ran away from Wise's house on January 19, 1735.

There was a hitch in the Rileys' escape though. In their flight from Wise's home, they had left behind the corpse of their tormentor. William Wise had been strangled to death. Alice and Richard were the prime suspects in the murder. They were soon caught hiding on a nearby island, and brought back to Savannah.

The trial was quick, and justice swift. Richard was hanged in Wright Square in downtown Savannah. Alice's fate was delayed several months – she was pregnant at the time the couple was captured. As it was Alice, not her child, who had been sentenced to death, she was allowed to give birth before she was sent to the gallows. But in the end, that didn't save her. Proclaiming her innocence every step of the way did Alice no good either. She was hanged, and her body swung limply in Wright Square for three days before it was cut down and buried.

The spirit of Alice Riley now haunts Wright Square. In a nod to her final fate, she appears on January 19 and wanders the square for three days, searching for her lost child.

Was Alice Riley innocent, as she insisted before her sentence was carried out? Well, here's some food for thought: all the trees in Savannah are draped with silvery-gray Spanish moss, the hallmark of grand old trees throughout the South. All the trees … except the ones that grow in Wright Square.

According to folklore, Spanish moss will not grow where innocent blood has been spilled.

JANUARY 20
James Heyward, Charleston, SC (1805)

South Carolina can boast of being one of the original thirteen colonies. And the oldest city in this venerable state is Charleston. So of course, the town is simply stuffed with ghosts and haunted places.

One such place is the Hannah Heyward House. The house was built in 1789 by Hannah Schubrick Heyward. After her husband William died, Hannah was not only able to keep the luxurious home, but she also set herself up as a very successful rice planter. She lived a full, independent life – quite an achievement for a woman on her own during the late 18th-early 19th century.

But even with her fiery spirit, Hannah suffered tragedies … one of which has left its mark on the beautiful mansion. On January 14, 1805, her 19-year-old son, James Heyward, lost his life in a tragic hunting accident. The bullet tore through his jugular, and he died within moments.

James' ghost stuck around the place he'd died so suddenly. Hannah began to see his ghost in the house beginning later that year. James can still be seen in the mansion, wandering around the museum's collection as if admiring the art, needlework, photography, and antique furniture preserved there as a glimpse into Charleston's past. Visitors to the museum aren't frightened by James' quiet ghost; he's often seen in the library, reading or just gazing out of the window, still dressed in the green hunting jacket he was wearing when tragedy struck.

JANUARY 21
Take the Tree Down Already!, San Diego, CA (modern)

People who share their home with a ghost have to learn to be tolerant of their spectral roommate's likes and dislikes. Peggy Kellner discovered this in 1964, when she bought her historic (1906) home in San Diego, California.

Peggy believes her ghost is female, mostly because a friend of hers has seen the specter. Peggy was the wardrobe mistress of the Old Globe Theatre, and one day, Pat Collins, then the bookkeeper for the theater, was visiting. Peggy was in the kitchen brewing a pot of tea, while Pat was chatting with her through an open door. As Pat spoke, she idly ran her fingers across the strings of an old harp. Suddenly, a woman's voice said, *"Don't do that, just go sit down."*

Pat assumed it was Peggy speaking, so she didn't take the suggestion seriously. She kept plucking the strings of the harp. The woman's voice snapped again, more firmly this time, *"Don't do that! Just go sit down!"* Then, a woman in a long white gown appeared in the room.

That got Pat's attention, and she fled the house in such a hurry she left her purse behind.

The woman in the white dress may be Victoria Pedrorena Magee, who lived in California around the time it became a state. The daughter of a proud Spanish family, she brought her parents' wrath down on herself by eloping with a young American army doctor. Her parents hated all gringos, so they kidnapped Victoria, brought her back home by force, and had the marriage annulled.

Victoria was heartbroken, but determined more than ever to escape her restrictive family. A few years later, she married another army Yankee, a fellow named Lt. Henry Magee. This turned out to be a colossally bad decision. Magee quickly started to burn through his wife's fortune, spending it on booze and dancing girls.

Victoria had escaped her domineering family. She wasn't about to let her wastrel husband ruin her life. She petitioned the state, asking for permission to do business in her own name. She was one of the first women in California to be granted that right. She was able to salvage what was left of her inheritance. She taught school, and was able to save enough money to buy some land for herself.

Tragically, though, Victoria died at the age of forty-four, her health ruined by multiple pregnancies.

Victoria Magee never lived in Peggy Kellner's house, but her youngest daughter did, and gave birth to a son there. Maybe this is why the proud, spunky spirit is drawn to that house. Peggy realized right away that the ghost had her own ideas about how the house should be kept, and how things should be arranged.

One evening, Peggy got home after a long, tiring day. She lay down on the couch, intending just to relax for a bit. She was startled awake by a loud crash – a picture had fallen off the wall. But when Peggy jumped up to investigate, she found that the nail from which the picture had hung was still firmly fastened in the wall. Even stranger, the picture hadn't fallen face down on the floor. It was leaning neatly against the wall *facing inward*.

Peggy decided not to rehang the painting. Obviously, her ghostly roommate didn't care for it.

The spirit has made other silent comments on Peggy's relaxed approach to housekeeping. One Christmas season had been particularly hectic for Peggy. She spent December in a rush, that lasted well into January. On January 20, she still hadn't gotten around to taking down her Christmas tree.

On the morning of January 21, Peggy came into the living room and discovered that all the ornaments had been taken down, and packed neatly in their boxes beside the tree.

JANUARY 22
The Wreck of the Valencia, Pachena Bay, *British Columbia (1906)*

The waters around Vancouver Island are known as "the graveyard of the Pacific". The treacherous waters, breaking against the rocky coastline in a constant battering deluge, make maritime travel in the area a perilous proposition.

In January 1906, the small passenger steamer *Valencia* was one of the ships that braved this dangerous passage. She left San Francisco, bound for Seattle, carrying 60 crew members and around 94 passengers. The night of January 22 was stormy, the scudding clouds and pounding rain making it impossible to navigate safely by the stars. The *Valencia*, feeling her way along the coast nearly blind, struck a submerged reef at Pachena Bay just before midnight.

The ship was only about 55 yards from shore, so the captain ordered the crew to beach the ship. The waves heaved the *Valencia* off the reef, but immediately dashed her against the rocks again. The ship was pounded by the waves, making rescue impossible. Panicking, the crew launched the lifeboats without waiting for the captain to give the order. Three of the lifeboats flipped as they were lowered, three more reached the water only to capsize in the pounding waves, and the last one just disappeared into the storm.

Rescuers huddled on the shore could only watch helplessly as the tragedy unfolded. Survivors climbed into the rigging to avoid the pounding waves, and clung there for two days as the rain continued to lash the *Valencia*. Their struggle was in vain – the ship was eventually dragged under the waves, taking the exhausted victims with her.

Estimates of the death toll varied, but an investigation by the United States government fixed it at 136 souls lost. Only 37 men survived the wreck. Every woman and child who'd been aboard the *Valencia* perished.

The *City of Topeka* managed to pick up some of the survivors, and took them to Seattle. On the way, she passed another ship, and stopped for a bit to pass along the news of *Valencia*'s demise. The storm had died down by then, and the thick black smoke from *City of Topeka*'s smokestacks hung low over the water. Suddenly, a shape formed in the greasy dark cloud. It was the shadowy outline of *Valencia*.

The *Valencia* continued to make appearances to crews of ships sailing in the waters around Vancouver Island. It didn't appear drifting placidly along, either. Every sighting was a gruesome reenactment of *Valencia*'s death throes, with the ghosts of passengers and crew clinging to the sinking ship in the hope of rescue that would never come.

Ghosts populated the lost lifeboats of the *Valencia* too. Fishermen working along the coast still report seeing lifeboats bobbing in the waves, manned by skeletons. And remember the lifeboat that was swept away right after launch? Six months after the wreck, several Native Americans were exploring caves in Pachena Bay. They found a lifeboat floating in one of the caves. Peering into the abandoned boat, they were horrified to discover eight corpses slumped in the bottom of the boat. They'd been picked down to bare bones by seashore scavengers.

The cave was large, going back about 200 feet, but the entrance was blocked by a huge rock. The explorers puzzled over the mystery – how did the lifeboat get past the rock into the cave? As near as they could tell, a large wave at high tide had washed the lifeboat over the boulder and into the cave. Once there, though, the little boat and its passengers were trapped. Due to the treacherous waters at the mouth of the cave, the lifeboat was never recovered.

Even today, a century later, intrepid tourists who make their way along the West Coast Trail near Pachena Beach can still see pieces of *Valencia* rammed into the rocky sands of the beach. It remains the worst maritime disaster in the history of the Graveyard of the Pacific.

JANUARY 23
The Ghost of Takaluma, Kansas (1879)

A cowboy riding herd on his cattle near the Saline River in Kansas got the shock of his life on the night of January 23, 1879. He'd been out with the cattle all day, and night had caught him several miles away from his camp in Oak Canyon. His horse was tired from the day's work, but the cowboy wanted to get back to his base camp, so he urged the horse forward. When he got to the river crossing just below Phil Mock's claim, his horse balked and refused to move.

An unearthly yell startled the cowboy, and through the darkness he saw a tall Indian brave. The cowboy drew his revolver and fired at the man, but his bullet had no effect. The native laughed scornfully, and told the cowboy that he was the spirit of Takaluma, the chief of Inciennes. Then he said that he had a tale to tell, of a great wrong that needed to be put right.

The cowboy dismounted and built a small campfire, to encourage the storytelling. The native told the cowboy that a few months before, a local farmer had plowed a nearby field, disturbing the chief's father's burial site. The farmer had inadvertently scattered the bones, but had picked up the skull and taken it home. As a result, Takaluma had been tasked with wandering the area for an hour every night in an attempt to get his father's skull returned to its proper resting place.

Takaluma's ghost told the cowboy that he knew exactly who had stolen the skull, but that he didn't have the power to enter someone's home. He warned that unless the skull was returned to the burial site within two months, another more powerful spirit would be dispatched in search of the skull, and this spirit *would* be able to go wherever it wanted to. The chief asked the cowboy to pass along the message, and track down the skull. In this version of the tale, it peters out there, and the skull was never found.

But according to Mock family lore, the skull was never lost in the first place. There was a story handed down to the descendants of Phil Mock that went like this: a cowboy who was doing some work for the Mock family was on his way home when the spirit of an Indian chief appeared to him. The ghost told him to tell the family not to plow a certain pasture, as that was the burial place of his ancestors. The family had discussed plowing that particular pasture the next day. The cowboy passed the message along, and the Mocks put off their plowing for the day. When the cowboy walked home that night, the ghost appeared to him again, repeating its request not to plow the field. The cowboy duly reported this second plea to the family. The Mocks decided not to plow that pasture after all. The ghost never appeared again.

JANUARY 24
Confederate Troops, Petersburg, VA (1865, recurring)

Centre Hill Mansion is a beautiful historic home owned by the city of Petersburg, Virginia. Built in 1823 by Robert Bolling, it sits at the center of an eight-acre park, and visitors come to admire the gorgeous Victorian mansion. It keeps regular museum hours, except on January 24, when it stays open in the evening. It's the only day of the year the museum offers nighttime tours.

That's because it was around 7:30 on January 24 that 1870's resident Townshend Bolling heard boots stomping and sabers rattling up the staircase in the house. There was no one in sight. Bolling heard the ruckus the same day and time the next year. And the year after that.

Bolling started inviting friends over to the mansion every January 24 so they, too, could experience the eerie noises. The tradition continues today.

Uncharacteristically for paranormal phenomena, the noises are extremely predictable. At 7:30 in the evening every January 24, visitors to the mansion can hear horses stamping and blowing on the front lawn. Moments later, the front door opens, and soldiers are heard marching across the front hall. The phantom footsteps continue up the stairs to the second floor, headed for a room above the office. The footsteps are punctuated by the clattering of sabers slung at the ghosts' hips. About twenty minutes later, the cacophony starts up again as the soldiers come back down the stairs. They cross the hall and go out the front door with a resounding slam. Then all is quiet … until next January 24.

The mansion served as headquarters for both Union and Confederate armies during the Civil War. Paranormal investigators theorize that the ghostly brigade is made up of Confederate troops who were ordered to evacuate the city in 1865.

Interestingly, Townshend Bolling wasn't the first to experience the annual ritual. The sounds were first reported on January 24, 1866, by Union soldiers who were occupying the house at the time.

JANUARY 25
The Ghost Bear of Boon Hill, Staffordshire, England (1918)

One chilly day in January, 1918, two young miners in Staffordshire, England, were hurrying to their shift at the Halmer End mine. They were running late, so they decided to take a shortcut, which would lead them over Boon Hill.

At the top of the hill, the miners were startled by a huge bear who lumbered out of the trees, headed straight for them. Work was forgotten as the two men turned and ran for their lives.

As it turned out, they truly *were* running for their lives. Soon after they got home after their narrow escape, word reached the men that there had been a horrible accident at the mine. It was the largest loss of life ever recorded in Staffordshire. The men had escaped disaster thanks to their run-in with the bear.

Oddly enough, though, no one else had ever seen or heard of a bear roaming the area. Search parties were formed, and people fanned out over the whole countryside to look for the bear of Boon Hill. The bear was never found.

Legend and history may hold a clue to the mystery. At the end of the 12th century, Hugh de Audley, first Earl of Gloucester, was out hunting. Near midday, the earl and his hunting party found themselves at the summit of Boon Hill. A bear stood in a clearing, and Lord Hugh unslung his bow, ready to make the kill.

A squire noticed that a cub stood behind the bear, and realized that the bigger bear was the cub's mother. He begged Lord Hugh not to shoot. The earl nodded, and the hunting party moved off to seek their quarry elsewhere. The legend holds that the grateful mother bear vowed to protect mankind as a man had protected her.

To the locals in 1918, the conclusion was obvious. The two young miners who escaped death were descendants of the merciful earl, and the bear of Boon Hill saved their lives that fateful day.

JANUARY 26
The Flying Dutchman, *Cape Town, South Africa (1927)*

The Flying Dutchman is a multi-faceted tale of hubris and general doom and despair. The legend has several origins, and since this is folklore, we can consider none of them to be true – or all of them, why not? The German version says that a ship's captain named von Falkenburg was sailing in the North Sea when he gambled his soul to the Devil in a game of dice.

The story from Britain is a tale of misplaced pride rather than a warning against the evils of gambling. A captain (of a different ship, presumedly) shook his fist at the heavens and challenged God to sink his ship. An apparition appeared in the sky over the ship, and the captain, adding injury to insult, shot at it. The apparition, whoever it was, was deeply offended by the captain's poor behavior, and cursed the captain to sail the seas forever. The curse extended well past the captain; everyone who saw the doomed ship would fall prey to their own run of bad luck.

The most famous version comes from Holland (hence, The Flying Dutchman). A stubborn captain named van Stratten was determined to take his ship around the Cape of Good Hope, at that time (perhaps more honestly) called the Cape of Storms. His daring plan fizzled, his ship sank, and everyone aboard drowned – except for Captain van Stratten, who bargained with the Devil to save his own hide. Van Stratten found himself the captain of a ghost ship, doomed to sail until the end of time.

Ships that see the Dutchman and try to get close to her are thwarted, usually because the ship is seen in bad weather and poor visibility. If a ship does manage to draw near, the Dutchman suddenly vanishes.

But here's the funny thing about folklore: sometimes the tales come true. Just past midnight on January 26, 1927, sailors aboard the British ship *Carnervon*, rounding Cape Town, saw a strange light on the water, glowing dimly through a thick bank of fog. Fourth Officer N.K. Stone was called up on deck to investigate. He took the telescope and had a look.

Stone later recalled the sight in his journal entry for the day. "It was an old-fashioned sailing rig, like no other I'd seen before. It was green and bright and there was a luminous haze between the masts."

Five sailors, including Fourth Officer Stone, watched the ghost ship for several minutes. The phantom drifted closer – then, as the men watched frozen in terror, the ship simply disappeared. For the rest of his life, Stone was convinced he had seen the fabled Flying Dutchman.

The eerie ship seems to have drifted off all nautical charts, though. The last reported sighting was in September 1942, and oddly enough, it wasn't another ship that spotted the Dutchman. Four people sitting on their balcony in Cape Town saw the ghostly ship sail into Table Bay. As they watched, the apparition disappeared behind Robben Island, and it has never been seen again.

JANUARY 27
Redford Theatre, Detroit, MI (1928)

There wasn't a whole lot to do in Detroit around the turn of the last century. In 1910, a dozen or so young people decided to change that. They started off putting together stage shows, for their own amusement and that of the audiences that came to see them. After World War I, the shows became so popular that there was talk of building a theater that could seat over 2000 people.

It took several years, but once the project got rolling, the community really got on board with it. The designers loved the culture of the Far East, so the walls were decorated with colorful paintings in a Japanese motif. The auditorium was designed to make the audience feel like they were seated in the tranquil courtyard of a Japanese teahouse, with blue sky arching overhead and tree branches peeking over the tromp l'oeil roofs on the walls. Cloud machines on the roof of each organ chamber projected images of fluffy white clouds floating across the sky-blue ceiling. The proscenium arch was topped with a pagoda-style roof. On either side of the organ grilles were murals of Japanese figures in opulent Oriental costume.

Silent movies were still in vogue when the building was being designed, so a magnificent Barton pipe organ was installed to provide the soundtrack to the films. Writhing dragons, powerful symbols of good luck, guarded the organ console.

Ushers for the new theater were trained for four weeks. The highly efficient service system of the Kunsky Service was recognized as one of the finest in the country. Theatre staff were trained in military tactics and in theater etiquette, with the goal of providing sterling service to the patrons.

The building which housed the theater was also home to several stores. One of these stores was Bob-O-Link, which featured a sidewalk popcorn and candy cart. The nearby Smiley Drug Store began selling candy in a "theatre package". (Theaters originally didn't have food concession counters, so it was perfectly okay to bring your own snacks in with you.) The Haller Bakery got into the business too, offering to "check your parcels here while attending the new Kunsky-Redford Theatre".

The grand opening on January 27, 1928, was a week-long celebration in the community. The theater had held an essay contest for local school children, and the two winners, a boy and a girl, were given the honor of cutting the red, white, and blue ribbon that stretched across the foyer. Of course, every theater grand opening has to have a spotlight. The organizers mounted a six-foot tall tower on the tallest part of the building, and a revolving 7,000,000 candlepower aircraft beacon cast its beam of light in every direction.

With the December 7, 1941 bombing of Pearl Harbor came profound changes to the decoration of the Redford Theatre. The opulent Oriental murals were covered with drapes, or painted over altogether.

By the mid-1970s, the theater was no longer showing a profit. The company that owned the building, Community Theatres, sold the Redford to the Motor City Theatre Organ Society. The MCTOS was overjoyed at the chance to get the Redford, which still had its original pipe organ, one of only two left in Detroit.

The MCTOS restored the theater over the next couple of decades. The restoration of the Redford was really something special. The theater has been in constant operation since 1928, so it didn't suffer the deterioration experienced by some other venues. And the restorers at the Redford lucked out – for instance, they managed to track down chandeliers of Oriental design from the same era as the Redford's heyday. The Detroit Oriental Theatre had been demolished decades before, but the lobby was intact, hidden in the lower portion of an apartment building. The chandeliers were donated to the Redford, restored, and installed in the grand foyer in December 1981. In 1995, the panels on either side of the organ chamber openings were stripped of several layers of paint, revealing four Japanese figures that had been buried for the past fifty years. That same year, the blue sky ceiling was repainted by the same company that had painted it in 1927.

These days, the Redford Theatre is managed by the MCTOS and staffed by volunteers. A virtual tour on the website (www.redfordtheatre.com) shows the venue in all its majestic opulence.

And like all the best theaters, the Redford is haunted. Two benign spirits call the Redford home. One ghost, Sara, is a girl about twelve years old. People say they feel a presence near them when Sara is around, or that they even feel as if someone has brushed up against them.

The ladies' room is thought to be haunted by the spirit of Ethel O'Leary. This former theater volunteer lived to be 100 (see what volunteering can do for you?). Her choice of service was cleaning the bathrooms. Some of the female volunteers have tales of being the only one in the bathrooms, and getting a whiff of the bleach Ethel used in her job. Or they'll hear the shuffle of footsteps, the rustle of toilet paper, or the flush of a toilet.

Paranormal groups are cheerfully invited to experience the Redford Theatre. Motor City Ghost Hunters and Metro Paranormal Investigators have both hosted lock-ins, to let members of the public experience a ghost hunt.

Members of the Motor City Theatre Organ Society are there during these investigations, of course. They will happily fire up the old Barton organ and treat the investigators to the sounds of the theatre in the era of silent movies. And when the cheerful music plays, reminding us of the antics of Charlie Chaplin and Buster Keaton, the paranormal activity in the building really ramps up.

Apparently, the spirits of the Redford have fond memories of the organ music too.

January 28
Ghost of a Groom, Yorkshire, England (1954)

Ghosts don't always show themselves in the dead of night. Many spirits are simply going about their daily lives as they knew them, pottering around in broad daylight. At ten minutes to noon on January 28, 1954, 17-year-old Julie Groves was at work in an office in Bridlington, Yorkshire. Julie was a typist for a wholesale liquor firm. She was working alone in the office when she happened to glance out of the window.

From her office window, Julie could see the door of the warehouse across the yard. The door was padlocked … but as Julie watched, she could see a figure coming through the locked door.

"I saw a man come out of the warehouse, melting through the door," Julie said later. "He walked across the yard, then into the house opposite my window, walking half through the closed door and half through the brick wall … A minute or two later he came out by the same way, with a saddle under his arm, just walking through the wall. He then disappeared through the closed door of the warehouse. He was dressed in riding breeches, with leather leggings, and was wearing a light-colored jacket. He was slightly built, and somewhat hunchbacked."

Julie was understandably freaked out – seeing someone walk through a brick wall will have that effect. She told the area manager what she'd seen. The manager, Mr. J.H. Rodger, called the person who'd formerly occupied the premises. He repeated the secretary's description of the apparition, and was told that it fitted the description of one William Robson.

The warehouse had previously been stables. The building opposite the office had once been the coach house. Robson, who had worked at the stables as a groom, regularly had to go through the coach house to get to the tack room, where the saddles were kept. Robson was simply going about his duties, completely unaware that the stables had closed years ago, and that he himself had been dead for over ten years and was buried miles away.

JANUARY 29
Red Lion Square, London, England (1661)

The English Civil War was a time of strife and recrimination in the country. The English were divided into Royalists – those loyal to the Crown – and Parliamentarians, who had tried to overthrow the Stuarts and had beheaded Charles I. In 1660, Charles II returned from exile and began the Restoration of the Monarchy. But the three leading Parliamentarians – Oliver Cromwell, John Bradshaw, and Henry Ireton – had nothing to fear now that a Stuart was back on the throne of England.

Why? Because all three of them were dead, and buried quite prestigiously in Westminster Abbey.

But the king's justice demanded satisfaction. The court decided, hey, you can't just get away with committing regicide, for heaven's sake. You can't just behead the king of England and then cheat the executioner by *dying*. That's just not cricket, as the English would say. So on January 29, 1661, the three gentlemen were dug up and tried for the murder of King Charles I.

The three men – okay, the three corpses – were found guilty. The bodies of Cromwell and Ireton were kept overnight at the Red Lion Inn (where Red Lion Square is today). At dawn the next morning, they were chucked into a wagon and driven to Tyburn, where they were joined by Bradshaw's putrefied corpse. All three men – cadavers – were hanged by their necks until dead … well, they were already technically *really properly* dead, and beginning to go green … so they were hanged by their necks until late afternoon. Then the executioners (who really needed a reason to keep busy, as their job had already sort of been done for them) cut the bodies down and cut off their heads. The heads were stuck on spikes and displayed above Westminster Hall, while the bodies were flung into a deep pit dug underneath the gallows, and buried. (So much for burial in the hallowed sanctuary of Westminster Abbey.)

Oliver Cromwell, Henry Ireton, and John Bradshaw still haunt Red Lion Square. Their apparitions can be seen strolling diagonally across the square, deep in animated conversation, before gradually disappearing as they reach the edge of the square.

JANUARY 30
Imperial Castle, Vienna, Austria (1889)

Shakespeare's tale of Romeo and Juliet holds an eternal fascination. Doomed lovers, eager to sacrifice anything to be together … the tragedy tugs at our heartstrings with romantic notions of doomed love and the ultimate sacrifice.

The story of Crown Prince Rudolf of Austria and Baroness Marie Alexandrine von Vetsera was … not exactly that kind of story.

The baroness, known as Mary, was the youngest child of Baron Albin von Vetsera and his much younger wife Helene Baltazzi. The baron was 22 years older than his vivacious and socially ambitious wife. From the time little Mary was a toddler, she was being groomed for a socially prominent marriage. Unfortunately, the young girl had no illusions about this. She complained to her friend, Countess Marie Larisch, "Mamma has no love for me … Ever since I was a little girl,, she has treated me like something she means to dispose of to the best advantage."

The countess was sympathetic to her friend's frustration – maybe a bit too sympathetic. The countess's cousin was Crown Prince Rudolf, heir apparent to the Austrian throne. Mary Vetsera met Rudolf in Prater Park in Vienna, and was promptly smitten with him. She immediately agreed to become his mistress, and it was often Countess Marie who arranged their trysts.

But Crown Prince Rudolf was – and please forgive the word play – not such a prince of a guy. Sure, he was a well-educated man who spoke four or five languages, and he wrote several books. But he looked like Ron Howard with a good beard. Plus, he was thirty, and Mary was just seventeen. Plus, he was married, to Princess Stephanie of Belgium, and they had a little daughter. The marriage was not a love match. At the time of the marriage, Stephanie was a gawky schoolgirl of fifteen. She had little education, and a hot temper. Their marriage was solely a political one, but Rudolf soldiered through it. He treated Stephanie decently, regarding her with tolerance and a certain amount of affection. That didn't stop him having continuous affairs with many mistresses, though.

Mary, on the other hand, was a knockout. Louise of Coburg described her appearance at an ambassador's reception in January 1889: "I glanced at the seductress. Two brilliant eyes met mine. One word will describe her. Mary was an imperial sultana, one who feared no other favorite, so sure was she of the power of her full and triumphant beauty, her deep black eyes, her cameo-like profile, her throat of a goddess, and her arresting sensual grace."

Mary was regal and imperious, and knew exactly what she wanted: marriage to Rudolf. Her family and friends, though, knew that it was never going to happen. When her mother, Helene, discovered that Mary had sent Rudolf an engraved cigarette case, she flew into a rage, ranting: "She is compromising herself when she is scarcely seventeen years old and so is ruining her life but also that of her brothers and sisters and mother …"

Helene had good reason to be furious at Mary's bullheaded naivete. Everyone could see that Rudolf was never going to give up Princess Stephanie for Mary ... everyone, that is, but Mary. She honestly thought that by becoming Rudolf's lover, she was putting herself in a position to take over Stephanie's title.

But Mary was not Rudolf's only lover. He had several, including a pretty 24-year-old dancer named Mizzi Kaspar. He was serious about Mizzi – so serious that he proposed a suicide pact with her. Mizzi assumed he was joking, so she laughed him off.

So Rudolf turned to his second choice of suicide partner: Mary Vetsera.

Rudolf had a hunting lodge in Mayerling, about an hour outside Vienna. On the morning of January 30, 1889, in bed together in Rudolf's room, the lovers went through with their suicide pact. Rudolf shot Mary, then himself. Rudolf left a note demanding to be buried next to Mary, and Mary had sent a letter to her mother requesting to be buried next to Rudolf.

Mary's uncles were summoned to Mayerling to retrieve Mary's body as discreetly as possible. They managed this quite neatly: one story says they arrived that night and drove away in their carriage with Mary's corpse sitting up between them, propped up with a broomstick pushed up the back of her dress.

The lovers' last request, to be buried together, was of course thoroughly ignored. Crown Prince Rudolf was given a state funeral and buried in the Imperial crypt at the Capuchin Church. Mayerling, his hunting lodge and scene of his suicide, was converted to a penitential convent of Carmelite nuns, who were tasked with praying daily for the repose of Rudolf's soul.

Mary's body was taken to the Cistercian monastery and buried in the cemetery there. Her uncles had to persuade the abbot to give her a Christian burial because at first it was believed she had committed suicide too. (At the inquest, it was established that Rudolf had killed her, then himself.)

On May 16, 1889, Baroness Helene had her daughter's body exhumed, and had her re-buried a few yards away in a permanent grave. She also had Mary's wooden coffin replaced with a copper one.

Mary Vetsera seems to be the only one of the couple who has remained earthbound as a ghost. Her spirit is seen both at Mayerling and at the Imperial Palace, both places the lovers met for their trysts. At the hunting lodge, Mary's apparition drifts up the stairway, then glides down the hallway to Rudolf's room.

JANUARY 31
Haunting of Willington Mill, England (1830s)

The haunting at Willington Mill was one of the most complex cases of poltergeist activity ever recorded in England. The family involved, the Procters, suffered the attentions of a whole army of noisy ghosts for over eleven years.

The troubles began in the last several months of 1834. It was a nursemaid who first noticed the disturbances – heavy footsteps coming from an empty room on the second floor, right above the nursery. She stood it for as long as she could, but finally her nerves could take no more, and she quit.

The next nursemaid also heard the heavy phantom footsteps, and now other family members were beginning to hear strange noises too. The poltergeist made its racket in broad daylight as well as in the dark hours of the night. The ghost had a perverse sense of timing; if anyone tried to investigate, to wait up for the noises, or sleep in the empty room in the hope of catching some activity, all was quiet. As soon as the investigators left, though, the running footsteps would start right back up.

On January 31, the Procters were getting ready for bed when they heard a dozen loud thuds next to the bed. Strange sounds continued to manifest – someone winding a large clock, a baby sucking on a bottle, a heavy sack falling to the floor, a bullet whizzing past and striking wood. Voices moaned, cried, and yelped *"never mind"* and *"come and get"* over and over.

The poltergeist activity was not only audio phenomena. Furniture was tossed around, especially in the kitchen; the cook would often come down in the morning to find the kitchen chairs heaped in a tangled pile, the window shutters open, and utensils scattered all over the place.

Apparitions began to show up as well. One of the Procter children saw a man come into his bedroom, walk over to the window, fling it open, then pull it shut and walk out of the room. One of the weirdest manifestations was the monkey-like creature that tickled Edmund Procter's foot, pulled Joseph Jr's bootstrap, then ran out of the room into the next room and scurried under the bed, never to be seen again.

Joseph Jr. also had the deeply unnerving experience of seeing his own face peering at him from the shadows beside his bed. The poltergeist made itself into a double of the ten-year-old boy, even dressing itself in clothes identical to what the young Joseph was wearing at the time. The apparition walked back and forth between the window and the wardrobe before fading away.

By this time, the Procters decided that eleven years of putting up with the poltergeist's shenanigans on a daily basis was quite enough. Joseph Procter Sr. found another house, and after packing, he and his wife sent the servants and children on ahead while they spent one last night in the house.

Those dark hours were the most terrifying of all. The noises – thuds, moving furniture, bangs, footsteps – were continuous. After several hours, the Procters realized with horror that they had heard those sounds earlier that day; the noises were mimicking the hustle and bustle of moving day. The Procters wondered, terrified, if the ghost was indeed doing its own packing in order to move with the family to the new house.

To everyone's relief, the new house was blissfully ghost-free. The house at Willington Mill was soon divided into two apartments. The first two tenants were the foreman and chief clerk of a nearby flour mill. They heard some weird noises, but nothing too frightening. But in 1867, two new families moved in. These new tenants were so plagued by ghostly manifestations that one of the families moved out, refusing to return.

After that, the paranormal activity seems to have plummeted. The house sat empty for a while, and son Edmund and some friends spent a night there while it sat vacant. Nothing happened. The house was sold, and the new owners reported a few disturbances, but nothing major. Eventually, the house was further divided into several small apartments. Edmund Procter interviewed several tenants around 1889.

They had no tales whatsoever to tell.

FEBRUARY

DAYS *of the* DEAD

FEBRUARY 1
Not the Right Ghost, Colwall, England (1940)

A few months after the start of World War II, some young people in the English village of Colwall ran a small social club to cater to soldiers camped locally. The club was popular in the village, as the managers were issued extra rations for the club, to boost morale.

On the night of February 1, 1940, one of the volunteers, a schoolteacher named Olive Gosden, was running the club. When she arrived about half-past seven to open the club for the evening, she realized with dismay that in her busy school day, she had forgotten to pick up milk for the club's canteen. So, while other volunteers started making sandwiches, Olive grabbed an enamel jug and hopped onto her bicycle, intending to bike to the farm about a mile away.

Her moonlit route would take her down a lonely stretch of road known as "the haunted lane". Local legend held that one snowy night, a young woman had been thrown out of her home by her abusive husband. Carrying her infant in her arms, the young woman sought shelter in her father's house, but was turned away. She was found the next morning drowned in a small pond. Her ghost was supposed to be seen on moonlit nights coming up the lane.

Olive wasn't the nervous type, but the ghost story was in the back of her mind as she pedaled along the lane in the moonlight. She told herself firmly that her friends who lived on the farm took that road all the time, and had never had a problem. She reached the farm safely, got the jug filled with milk, and started back.

The ride back through the "haunted lane" ended in an uphill climb, and Olive had to get off her bike and push it for the last bit of the trek. She reached the top of the lane and congratulated herself. Here she was at the top, nearly back to the club, and the trip hadn't been so bad.

Then she yelped in astonishment. Crossing the road in front of her was a small procession of figures dressed in sweeping black robes. Olive got the impression that they were carrying a bier, on which rested the body of a young man. The man had been well-loved by all, and the other figures were bearing his body home as a sign of respect. Olive felt that the young man would be deeply missed, and that his friends and family would greatly mourn his death. She felt as if someone was standing next to her wordlessly telling her all these details – or that she already knew them. She got the feeling that the time period of the vision's setting was about 1400.

The procession seemed to go off the road onto a path that led down to some nearby farms. Once the ghostly parade had passed, Olive's reverie broke, and she hopped onto her bike and tore off down the road (which, from there, was mercifully downhill).

Then she got another shock. The apparition of a horseman in a cloak and plumed hat was thundering down the lane next to her, on her left side. Olive again had the feeling that this man was responsible for the death of the man on the bier, and was trying to escape. The phantom rode with her all the way to the railway bridge, just before the village green.

Olive made it back to the club, much shaken by the night's adventures. One of her friends commented that Olive had been very quick about running her errand. She laughed shakily. Of course, she hadn't dawdled going through the "haunted lane".

Sometime later, Olive told a friend about her experience that night. The friend told her that long ago, two young men who lived in the area had fought a duel, and one of them, the son of a family who lived in a house in the valley below the lane, had been killed. Was the ghostly procession headed to the house in the valley when they turned off the lane, to bring the young man's body home? Was the phantom rider the man's killer? Olive never found out if there was any connection between the old local legend and her strange experience that cold night in 1940.

FEBRUARY 2
Santa Fe State Penitentiary Riot, Santa Fe, NM (1980)

The night of February 2, 1980, began like any other evening in the Penitentiary of New Mexico. Prisoners stirred restlessly in their cells, some drinking homemade prison hooch to take the edge off their day. Mutterings of discontent rumbled through the hallways.

Conditions at "Old Main" were wretched, even by prison standards. The facility was desperately overcrowded: on the night of the riot, there were 1,156 inmates in an institution designed to house fewer than 963. The prison was overrun with mice and roaches, which got into the food.

Even worse was the "snitch game", which pitted inmate against inmate as guards searched for incriminating evidence. Cell Block 4 housed many of these snitches.

Elsewhere in the prison, many of the most violent criminals were being held with very little security. E-2 dormitory was designed for low-level criminals, but because of construction at the prison, some of the most violent prisoners were being housed there.

The rumblings began late that night. An inmate in Cell Block 2 heard men nearby planning to jump the guards if they didn't lock the door to the dorm during the 1 am head count. The guards didn't lock the door, so the prisoners rushed them. Twelve guards were taken hostage. The prisoners fanned out, breaking into the infirmary and stealing box after box of drugs. High on paint thinner, raisin jack and stolen drugs, they went on a rampage, headed for Cell Block 4.

The construction workers had left their equipment behind, ready for the next day's work. Inmates grabbed acetylene torches, yelling "Kill the snitches", and started cutting through the cell bars to get at the prisoners in protective custody. Some of the attackers, impatient with the slow going, just threw flammable liquids into the cells and ignited them. When the cells were opened, victims were stabbed, tortured, burned, bludgeoned, hanged, and hacked apart. The hatchet marks from one brutal beheading can still be seen on the concrete floor in Cell Block 4.

Inmates rampaged through the prison for 36 hours. A former inmate described the scene as a "zombie apocalypse". "The hallways of the prison were filled with acrid black smoke from the fires. You had all these high, angry, and armed inmates stumbling around. It was unreal." By the time the whirlwind of violence was spent, 33 inmates were dead, and hundreds more suffered injuries or drug overdoses. It is still considered the most violent prison riot in American history.

For this reason, the New Mexico State Penitentiary is one of the most haunted places in the world. The hauntings began to be reported just a year after the riot, in 1981. That was the first sighting of a shadow figure, a figure that's been seen by members of the New Mexico National Guard as well as by guards at the prison. Unexplained noises break the silence of the halls, from clanging cell doors to more insistent metallic sounds, as though an inmate has grabbed the bars of his cell and is shaking them in rage and frustration.

FEBRUARY 3
Conley's Money, Dubuque, IA (1891)

In 1891, a farmer named Conley traveled to Dubuque for medical treatment. Sadly, the treatment didn't work. On February 3, Conley's body was found in an outhouse near the boarding house where he was staying. The body was taken to Hoffman Funeral Home for preparation.

Matthias Hoffman, the coroner, examined the body. He found $9.75 in Conley's pockets, but nothing else of value. The farmer's clothes were not much more than tattered rags, hardly a respectable suit in which to be buried. So Hoffman dressed the body in a white shirt, black suit, and new satin slippers.

Hoffman sent a telegram to Conley's son Pat, who arrived in Dubuque with a wagon and a friend to claim his father's body. When Pat arrived home, Conley's daughter Elizabeth fainted, even though the coffin was still in the wagon and closed. Several hours later, she came to, with a strange story to tell.

When Elizabeth had been in her swoon, she'd had a spectral visit from her father. "He had on a white shirt and black clothes and slippers. When I came to, I told Pat that I had seen father. I asked Pat if he had brought back father's old clothes and he said no. He asked why I wanted them. I told him that father said he had sewed a roll of bills inside of his gray shirt, in a pocket made of a piece of my old red dress. When I awoke, I told Pat we must go and get his clothes."

Pat Conley sent a telegram to Matthias Hoffman, who retrieved the clothes from the rubbish pile in the morgue, wadding them up in a bundle. Pat went back to Dubuque, and he and Hoffman opened the bundle together. Inside the tattered gray shirt, they found a hidden pocket made of red cloth. Inside the pocket was a roll of bills totaling $35.

FEBRUARY 4
The Murder of the Donnelly Family, Ontario, Canada (1880)

In the 1840s, many immigrants from Ireland showed up on the shores of the New World, seeking a better life for themselves and their families. The Donnellys were just more faces in the crowd of humanity that sought to improve their lot in life. James Donnelly, his wife Johannah, and their son James Jr. emigrated from Ireland, to London, Ontario, sometime in 1845 or 1846. James found work, and soon another son was born. William was born with a deformed foot, and would be known all his life by the nickname "Clubfoot Will".

City life held no appeal for James, who wanted to farm the land on which he lived, making a good honest living for his family. The Canada Land Company was offering land to Irish settlers, leasing it with an option to buy. But the Donnellys were poor folks, and James knew he could never afford to buy land.

So he squatted on 100 acres instead. He wasn't alone; it was common practice for poor people to do this, especially on the frontier. James settled on land belonging to an absentee landlord, John Grace. He threw a shanty together and began to clear the land. Over the years, five more boys would be born to the couple: John, Patrick, Michael, Robert, and Thomas. All went fairly well until 1855, when the absentee landlord sold 50 acres to Michael Maher.

James was furious at the impending loss of "his" land. He dared anyone to take the southern fifty acres from him. Surprisingly, no one challenged him.

No one, that is, except Patrick Farrell.

Farrell had rented the land from Michael Maher, the new absentee owner. He and Donnelly went to court over the dispute. The court ruled a tradeoff: James was allowed to keep the northern fifty acres of the property. But he had to give up the southern half to Farrell.

On June 25, 1857, William Maloney hosted a logging bee. Bees were very common in pioneer days as a way for neighbors to help each other. These were also opportunities for socializing and, of course, drinking.

James Donnelly and Patrick Farrell were both invited to this logging bee, and they both showed up. It's not really clear how the fight started. Words were exchanged, which led to violence. Farrell grabbed up a tool called a handspike. Donnelly grabbed one too, to defend himself. Moments later, Patrick Farrell was lying on the ground, with a handspike jammed into his left temple. He died two days later.

James Donnelly was now a murderer. A warrant was issued for his arrest, but when constables showed up at the farm, James was nowhere to be found. He stayed hidden for the next eleven months. But before the next winter, James turned himself in. He was found guilty and sentenced to death by hanging. The execution was set for September 17, 1858.

Johannah was devastated by the news. She started a petition for a lighter sentence. In July 1858, her persistence paid off. James's sentence was reduced to seven years in prison. He was released in 1865.

In May 1873, William Donnelly started up a stagecoach business. "Clubfoot Will" was generally agreed to be the smartest of the Donnelly brothers, and the Donnelly stagecoach line was a roaring success. But there were other stagecoach businesses, and they deeply resented the Donnellys.

The Stagecoach Feud, between the Donnellys and the Flanagan & Crawly Stage, erupted in violence. Coaches were smashed, stables were torched, and horses were beaten and even killed. The Donnellys began to get a bad reputation. They were accused of everything from trespassing to attempted murder.

Unfortunately, feuds like this were a way of life in Biddulph. Biddulph was settled mainly by Irish immigrants, who brought the feud between Catholics and Protestants with them to the New World.

In June 1879, Father John Connolly organized a group he called the Peace Society. In August, a splinter group of the Peace Society, also organized by Fr. Connolly, started meeting in Biddulph. They called themselves the Vigilance Committee.

The spark that touched off the final confrontation came on January 15, 1880. Patrick "Grouchy" Ryder's barn burned down. Everyone – spurred on by the Peace Society – blamed the Donnellys.

On February 3, life at the Donnelly farm went on as usual, with James Jr., John, and Tom leaving around 4 pm to pick up a neighbor boy, Johnny O'Connor. Johnny often helped the Donnellys with farm chores.

When they got back to the house, John and Tom put the horse away, then John left to visit Will. Then everyone settled down for the night. The Donnelly house was small, so Johnny bunked with James in the front bedroom. Johannah slept in her own room with Bridget, her niece, who was visiting from Ireland. Tom had his own bed in a room off the kitchen.

About one in the morning on February 4, members of the Vigilance Committee gathered at the Cedar Swamp Schoolhouse. The group included Grouchy Ryder, whose barn had been torched, and James Carroll, one of the constables Johannah Donnelly was known to swear at. In all, 34 men showed up at the Donnelly home that night, thirsting for blood.

At a signal from Carroll, the men outside stormed the house. They were all armed with sticks, clubs, and various farm tools, and they began beating the three adults.

James Donnelly was the first to fall; the men beat him in the head, pulping his skull. Johannah was also bludgeoned to death. One of the men bashed Tom's head with a shovel. The men found Bridget Donnelly upstairs, and killed her too.

They went to the front bedroom, poured coal oil all over the bed under which Johnny lay quivering with terror, and lit the bed on fire.

Then the men went hunting for more Donnellys.

Will Donnelly lived with his wife Nora in Whalen's Corners, not far from the Donnelly homestead. On the night of February 3, he and Nora had two visitors, brother John, and Martin Hogan, a friend. Nora went to bed around 9 pm, and the men stayed up talking, finally turning in around 12:30.

Will had been asleep for about two hours when he was woken up by someone yelling "Fire!", trying to get Will to come out. But it was John who opened the door – and was gunned down. After milling around for a while longer, the mob drifted away. Will, Nora, and Martin huddled on the floor next to John's body until dawn.

No one was ever punished for the massacre. But the Donnelly property still bears the psychic imprint of the ghastly crime. The paranormal activity on the land is extreme. Horses seem to be especially sensitive to the psychic residue. Horses ridden near the property late at night on February 3 will refuse to go any further, or go berserk as if possessed. If they are forced to go any further after balking, the horses soon die mysteriously. This has happened to at least three mounts.

The weirdness doesn't stop with the doomed horses. Blue balls of lightning have been seen rolling down the road next to the Donnelly land on the anniversary of the killings. Photographs of the Donnelly tombstones on the property show strange figures and light anomalies.

Robert and Linda Salts moved into the Donnelly house in 1988, and have experienced paranormal activity from the very first day. The original house no longer stands, of course. In 1881, a year after the massacre, the surviving family members, sons Will, James Jr., Patrick, and Robert, restored the middle part of the house. The rest of the house was built around this.

The Salts family hear footsteps going up the stairs late at night, and shadowy figures move through the house constantly. The ghosts of James and Johannah are dressed austerely in somber black, while the spirits of the Donnelly sons appear in white clothes. Will's ghost can sometimes be seen in the yard behind the house, as that was a favorite place of his.

Even the barn, built in 1877, is haunted. Tourists visiting the barn have experienced a heavy feeling pressing down on their chests. Visitors have also reported phantom footsteps, and, more chillingly, the sound of screams.

FEBRUARY 5
The Wreck of the *Montreal* (1877)

What makes a haunting?

Some say it is tragic, unexpected death, life snuffed out in an instant. Others point to hand-wringing, gut-wrenching guilt. A spirit may revisit the scene of an accident to bemoan the possibility that they could have prevented it, if only ... Still others believe that ghosts can have feelings of abandonment, just as survivors do after tragedy strikes.

On February 5, 1877, the *Montreal Express* was on its regular route, running between Boston and Montreal. The train was about ninety minutes behind schedule, but the passengers were in a festive mood. Many of them were on their way to Montreal for the winter carnival.

One of the passengers had just come from a successful speaking engagement. Henry Tewksbury, a well-regarded lecturer, has spent the evening in Windsor, Vermont, talking to an enraptured crowd about the Battle of Gettysburg. A friend of his, Smith Sturtevant, was in the audience. Sturtevant had fought in the Civil War as a teenager. After the talk, the friends took a train north to White River Junction. Tewksbury planned to get a hotel room for the night. Sturtevant had another train to catch; he worked on the *Montreal Express* as a conductor.

The two friends parted ways in White River. Tewksbury stopped at the Junction House, but it was booked solid. So he walked back to the train station to catch the *Montreal Express*. His home in Randolph was just thirty minutes down the line.

Tewksbury joined the rest of the 77 passengers, finding a seat near the front of the train. Sturtevant, collecting tickets as he walked down the aisle, teased his friend about the change of plans.

About ten minutes later, as the train sped toward a bridge near West Hartford, Tewksbury felt a jolt as the car swayed back and forth. A strange rumbling told him that the train's wheels were not running smoothly on the rails, but bumping over the railroad ties. The train was derailing.

Tewksbury and Sturtevant both lunged for the bell-cords to pull to sound an alarm. Brakeman George Parker grabbed a lantern and jumped from the train. He landed in the deep snow and rolled down the embankment, sliding to a stop on the thick ice of the White River. Parker then raced to a nearby farm, borrowed a team of horses, and headed to White River Junction, just four miles back down the tracks, for help.

The rear sleeper car jumped the tracks first, pulling three other cars with it as it plunged off the bridge and down to the river, forty feet below. A connection finally snapped under the weight of tons of metal. Only the locomotive and the mail car directly behind it were spared.

The ice on the river was thick, but still it shattered under the weight of the train cars that had plummeted from the bridge. Some passengers were killed in the initial impact. Others succumbed to fire that raced through the cars – oil lamps and coal stoves toppled in the crash, setting upholstery and window curtains alight. Still more drowned as the train cars settled further into the frigid water.

Tewksbury was pinned in his seat, watching in horror as the flames licked their way closer to him. The veteran of Gettysburg clenched his eyes shut and pulled his hat down over his face "to hide the dreadful view of approaching death."

Two crew members reached him just in time, and tried to pull him from his mangled seat. The men braved the fire, pulling at Tewksbury in a frantic bid to save a life. The heat of the flames drove them back.

"I begged them to try once more – to pull my leg off if they had to, but not let me burn. They pulled – and oh, with what a joyous feeling did I feel my feet gradually slipping from my shoes. I cried out that I was moving – to pull, pull, pull! I felt one of my legs break, but I was released."

Tewksbury's friend, conductor Smith Sturtevant, was not so lucky. His fellow crew members saw him crawling through the car, the back of his clothes on fire. They shoveled snow on him through a broken window, but by the time they could pull him out, he was badly burned. He died several hours later.

Sturtevant, Tewksbury, and other injured passengers were carried to the farmhouse of Oscar Paine. The farmhouse was used as a makeshift hospital – and a temporary morgue. The Paine House still stands, and it is a hotbed of paranormal energy. The kitchen ceiling still bears the bloodstains of the injured and dying. Crash victims were brought to an upstairs bedroom, and their blood soaked through the floorboards. The house still echoes with mysterious voices, moans, and sobbing.

Sturtevant, the conductor, still patrols that stretch of track at night. He yanked the alarm cord to warn the engineer to stop, but he couldn't prevent the derailment. Perhaps, as a conductor, he still feels responsible for the loss of life.

And what about survivor's guilt? One of the passengers was a thirteen-year-old boy named Joe McCabe. Young Joe survived the wreck … but he watched his father burn to death. Joe's spirit, too, seems to be trapped by the tragedy. His ghostly figure can be seen hovering over the river's surface, aching with the loss of his father.

FEBRUARY 6
Expiration Date, Portsmouth, VA (1784)

The Battle of Yorktown, which ended the siege on October 19, 1781, effectively marked the end of the Revolutionary War. The new young country went wild with the news. Church bells pealed in celebration – the bell at Trinity Church in Portsmouth, Virginia, actually cracked, so vigorously was the bell-ringer celebrating American victory.

The second rector of the church, Reverend John Braidfoot, came home soon after that. He'd been in charge of the parish since 1773, but had left for a while to serve with George Washington as an infantry chaplain. Now he was back, and ready to serve his flock once more.

After the Revolution, though, many Anglican churches were closed. Reverend Braidfoot didn't let this stop him. He simply kept in touch with his congregation by riding around the parish to visit them. Reverend Braidfoot spent a lot of time on the road, but he didn't mind the travel, as long as he could still minister to his people.

As he drove home one evening, Reverend Braidfoot's horse suddenly stopped in the middle of the road, and refused to go any farther. The reverend looked to see what had made the horse balk – and saw an apparition standing in the road. Reverend Braidfoot was stunned to see the ghost, but not alarmed. He waited quietly to see what the apparition would do next.

The phantom spoke to Mr. Braidfoot, telling him that he would die, at home, on February 6. Then it faded away.

That was an unsettling announcement. Mr. Braidfoot clucked to his horse and went home.

When he got there, he told his wife the unfortunate news.

Mrs. Braidfoot didn't want her husband dwelling on this news from the Other Side. She planned a large dinner party for the fateful day. The reverend was preoccupied, of course – the phantom had appeared to him several more times on his travels, and had repeated the same dire prophecy – but he appreciated his wife's efforts. The party went off without a hitch, and Reverend and Mrs. Braidfoot welcomed their guests.

Halfway through the dinner, the reverend excused himself and went up to his room. When he didn't reappear, Mrs. Braidfoot became concerned.

Reverend John Braidfoot was found dead in his room. There were no signs of violence, and he had been in perfect health.

FEBRUARY 7
The Haunted Pillar, Augusta, GA (1878)

The Farmer's Market in Augusta, just blocks from the riverboat landing on the Savannah River, was once the bustling hub of commerce for the city. Built around 1830, it was a gathering place for merchants of all kinds. The marketplace was marked by a brick and concrete pillar ten feet tall.

In 1878, a traveling fire-and-brimstone preacher rode into town, on fire to preach his jeremiads to the sinners in the marketplace. Local merchants, once they heard the tone of his evangelizing, felt that the preacher's haranguing would drive away their customers. They complained to the city officials, who tried to shut the preacher down.

The preacher was furious at being thwarted in his divine mission. He stood in the middle of the crowded marketplace and declared that a great wind would come and smite the wicked, ungrateful citizens of Augusta. The only thing that would remain, he said, would be one pillar, left as a reminder of the divine destruction. And whoever would dare to move the pillar, destroy it, or even touch it, would be struck down, as punishment for disrespecting a messenger of God.

At a few minutes after 1 am on February 7, 1878, a freak winter tornado tore through downtown Augusta and destroyed the Farmer's Market. One lone pillar was left standing.

That's the version of the story put out by the Augusta Chamber of Commerce. Another origin story for the pillar is much darker. The Farmer's Market was a place that saw the buying and selling of not only produce, cotton, and livestock, but human beings as well. One day, during a slave auction, a slave who was chained to the pillar pronounced a curse on the pillar, a symbol of bondage.

We'll never know which of these stories is true, or if the real story is something else entirely, lost to history. All we know is that *someone* cursed the old pillar at the corner of Broad Street and Fifth. And they did a very thorough job.

Some while ago, city officials decided to tear the pillar down, saying that it was obstructing pedestrian traffic. They hired a contractor to demolish the pillar – and the contractor died unexpectedly. So did the next contractor, and the next, and the next. These deaths were all attributed to natural causes ... but there were an awful lot of them. It seemed that whoever was put in charge of the pillar's removal just dropped dead. The city eventually gave up on the project.

But they hadn't forgotten about the old-fashioned pillar just sticking out of the sidewalk. Several years later, the city decided to widen Broad Street, and wanted to just move the pillar – to preserve it, they said. The city hired two men to move the pillar out of harm's way. As the men prepared to shift the pillar, a bolt of lightning came out of a clear blue sky and struck them dead.

Just a few years ago, a driver lost control of his car and ended up hitting the pillar. It was a minor fender-bender, no harm done … except that when police arrived, they discovered the man dead behind the wheel.

FEBRUARY 8
Murder in Golden Gate Park, San Francisco, CA (1981)

Golden Gate Park, in San Francisco, is not the kind of place you'd want to go camping. But Leroy Carter, Jr., had no choice. The 29-year-old African American had survived the Vietnam War, but things hadn't gone his way when he returned to civilian life. He had ended up homeless, a petty criminal, just another casualty of the war. On February 8, 1891, Carter unrolled his sleeping bag next to Alvord Lake, crawled into it … and never came out.

When police arrived at the scene the next morning, they discovered a headless corpse rolled up in a sleeping bag. Fingerprints told investigators Leroy Carter Jr.'s identity, but they couldn't tell the police why Carter's head was missing. Or why there was a headless chicken about fifty yards away. Or why Carter had two kernels of corn and a chicken wing jammed into the stump of his neck where his head had been the day before.

The police department assigned Officer Sandi Gallant to the case. Gallant had worked on the recent Jonestown Massacre, and had become the SFPD's resident expert on cults, Satanic murders, and religious ritualistic killings. With help from Charles Wetli, the coroner in Dade County, Florida, Gallant came up with a theory.

Both Gallant and Wetli were convinced that the murder had something to do with the dark rituals of Palo Mayombe, an offshoot of Santeria that focused on black magic. According to Gallant's research, Carter's head had been taken for use in a ritual that called for human body parts – the brain, and maybe the ears and nose too. The potion would be finished in 42 days, and to complete the ritual, the head would have to be returned to the scene of the murder.

It was a solid theory, but no one was convinced … not even Gallant. On March 22, the 42nd day after the murder, none of the police were at the park. Gallant had second-guessed herself, and she and her partner decided not to set up a stakeout. The killer completed the ritual, placing Carter's head in the weeds near Alvord Lake.

The head revealed no new clues, and the case went cold. Leroy Carter Jr. was buried in Arlington National Cemetery in Virginia. His murder remains unsolved.

FEBRUARY 9
The Legend of Black Annie, Mount Vernon, IL (1888)

Southern Illinois, or "Little Egypt", is a haven of weirdness. Mount Vernon suffered the attentions of a specter known as Black Annie. In the mid-19th century, the citizens of the town were plagued by a "witch" who threatened their cattle. They ran the old woman out of town, and thought that was the end of the matter.

But on February 9, 1888, a tornado ripped through the town, killing 37 people, injuring as many as 800, and demolishing homes and businesses in a swath of destruction half a mile wide. Several witnessed claimed to see a woman dressed in black wandering the wreckage of the town, cackling and screaming. The legend of Black Annie was born.

In 1918, an old woman dressed in black wandered around Mount Vernon harassing people. In Lebanon, Illinois, in 1921, Black Annie was seen peeping in windows at night, hidden in the shadows by her black clothing. In the 1930s, she made other appearances in the area. She showed up in Carlisle, Illinois in the early 1930s, following people on the street and just generally being a creeper. And in 1936, Black Annie was blamed for throwing sleeping powder through windows in a bizarre series of attacks. She seems to have disappeared from the historical record since then, but not from local folklore. Parents still sometimes threaten misbehaving children with a visit from Black Annie.

FEBRUARY 10
A Haunting in Massachusetts, Salem, MA (1980)

Witches aren't the only supernatural inhabitants of Salem. The town also has its fair share of plain old haunted houses.

One of these is a house on Allen Street. On February 10, 1980, the house caught fire. Two young girls were on the third floor. Neighbors did their best to try and reach them, but by the time they propped a ladder against the house, the blaze was raging out of control. The girls both died.

New owners decided to renovate, rebuilding after the tragedy. The renovations went slowly, though – workers kept getting spooked and quitting. The girl who lived next door kept seeing the ghosts of the two dead children through the windows. She saw the spirits so frequently that she kept her shades down all the time.

In 2001, the house was sold, and a new family moved into the home. The spirits of the two little girls seemed to enjoy this, as the family had a girl of their own. Lucy and Carter moved into the house with their daughter Sarah. Lucy began to see bright white orbs, about the size of a silver dollar. The orbs would dart around the room, or simply hover, as if watching the family. The orbs showed up most often in the upstairs bedroom.

The orbs seem to be especially attracted to Sarah, following her around the house. Lucy says, "You can't take a picture of my daughter in that house without orbs." Sarah's boyfriend has seen the spirits of the young girls as apparitions, rather than orbs. The phantoms were climbing the back stairs, on their way to the third floor.

The young ghosts still think of themselves as little girls, and they enjoy a good prank.

Lucy's brother was staying at the house, and used the shower in the upstairs bathroom. He came thundering down the stairs moments later, dripping and furious. Someone had turned the lights off when he was in the shower. He yelled for whoever had done it to turn them back on. The lights came back on – then went off, and he hollered again. This happened several times, and each time, he heard two girls giggling in the hallway. Thinking the culprits had to be his niece Sarah and a friend of hers, he stalked out looking for someone to blame.

But Sarah and her friend weren't there. They had left the house as soon as he had gone upstairs for his shower.

FEBRUARY 11
Diana of the Dunes, Gary, IN (1925)

When I was a kid, every summer our church would host a trip to the Indiana Dunes. I can still remember the flat, pleasantly musty smell of our old canvas tent, the sight of the scrubby dunes, and the slightly spooky feeling of the waters of Lake Michigan pulling the sand away from under my toddler toes. And one of the reasons I have those memories is because of a woman named Alice Mabel Gray.

Alice was born in Chicago in 1881. She was whip-smart, and lucky enough to be able to indulge her passion for learning. She was educated at the University of Chicago, starting there at the age of sixteen. By the time she graduated in 1903, she had a bachelor's degree with honors in Latin, Greek, mathematics, and astronomy.

This fierce intelligence led Alice to make a decision that was revolutionary for a woman in the early 20th century. She refused to join the rat race. She had a special loathing of working for a paycheck, calling it "slavery".

By 1915, she was fed up with the effort it took to support herself in Chicago. She felt that her career had stalled, because women weren't offered the same opportunities for advancement as men. She was vastly overqualified for the jobs she *could* find. She moved out to the Indiana Dunes – basically, she decided to become a beach bum. As a grad student, she had come to the Dunes often, and had fallen in love with the wild beauty of the lakefront. In October 1915, she moved into an abandoned shack, intending to write and live a simple life, Thoreau-style. She supported herself by editing manuscripts for the University of Chicago, which were mailed to her.

She wasn't a total hermit, though. The Miller branch of the Gary Public Library was within walking distance of her shack, and Alice regularly hiked into town to stock up on books. She also made trips to Chicago to visit the museums.

In the early 20th century, the Indiana lake shore was seen as wasteland, and land developers were eager to turn the Dunes into industrial parks. Gary, Indiana, known for its factories, was built along seven miles of Lake Michigan's shoreline. By 1909, conservationists realized that the entire dune area was in danger of being lost.

Alice threw herself into conservation efforts. By the time she'd survived her first winter living alone, newspaper reporters were seeking her out for interviews. Legend says that local fishermen had seen Alice skinny dipping in the lake, and had told reporters about this nutty lady who ran around the dunes naked. Reporters soon came up with a catchy nickname for the woman of mystery – Diana of the Dunes, comparing the free-spirited Alice to the Greek goddess of the hunt.

Alice really would have been happy just hanging out in her driftwood shack, reading library books, writing, and venturing out once in a while to get provisions or to visit a museum. But the ecology of the dunes was being threatened. Alice parlayed her newfound notoriety as Diana of the Dunes into a passionate voice for conservation of the lakefront's natural resources. One of her most stirring speeches was at an event held at the Art Institute of Chicago on April 6, 1917.

"So, the glacier which came down from the north to give Illinois its chief treasure – its deep, rich soil – tarried at Chicago on the way back to give birth to the lake ... To the east, in Indiana, it left a somewhat narrower strip of fine level sand ... To see the Dunes destroyed would be for Chicago the sacrilegious sin which is not forgiven."

Alice spent five years living alone on the dunes. Around 1920 or 1921, she raised eyebrows again by starting a relationship with a man named Paul Wilson. Wilson was a fisherman who also made driftwood furniture. Alice and Wilson moved into another shack on the beach, in the western part of Ogden Dunes, a place they christened "Wren's Nest".

Alice's relationship with Wilson was ... complicated. Wilson was a tall, powerfully built man with a violent temper. The couple had two daughters, but the relationship was volatile. In 1922, a body was discovered in the dunes near Wren's Nest, and Wilson was accused of murder. He was later cleared, but the murder was never solved.

Deputy Sheriff Eugene Frank also accused Alice and Wilson of stealing fish and breaking into local cottages. When Frank came to Wren's Nest with these accusations, a fight broke out. Wilson was shot in the foot, and Alice suffered a skull fracture. When the couple returned to Wren's Nest after treatment, they found that their home had been ransacked.

Their troubles continued. In spite of Alice's efforts, development continued to encroach on the dunes. In 1923, the Dunes Highway was completed, linking Gary and Michigan City, Indiana. The highway made it easy for Chicagoans to visit the Dunes, which was good, but it passed within a mile of Wren's Nest, which sucked for Alice. Reporters had even better access to Diana of the Dunes, and any hope of privacy Alice had cherished was pretty much gone.

In early 1925, Alice became seriously ill with kidney failure. Sadly, this was probably due to kidney damage caused by Wilson beating her. Just after her second child was born, in mid-February 1925, Alice died in her little shack on the beach. Her daughters were taken into protective custody, and Wilson just disappeared.

But Alice has most certainly not disappeared into the sands of history. There are reports that Diana of the Dunes still wanders the shore of Lake Michigan, enjoying the lake spray on her bare skin.

Whether or not the ghost stories are true, Alice Mabel Gray's legacy does live on. Her tenacity in fighting for the conservation of Lake Michigan's wild lakefront led to the creation of a nature preserve, now called Indiana Dunes State Park. This is, in turn, surrounded by Indiana Dunes National Park, with beaches, hiking trails, camping, picnic shelters, bird observation towers, and the Ancient Pines Nature Area, a prehistoric forest revealed by wind erosion of some of the dunes.

And Indiana has this beautiful natural treasure because a young, free-spirited intellectual decided to shuck city life and go skinny-dipping.

FEBRUARY 12
The Execution of Lady Jane Grey, London, England (1554, recurring)

Lady Jane Grey has to be one of the most tragic figures in English history. (With the nickname "the Nine-Day Queen", you know right from the jump that Jane's story doesn't end with a happily-ever-after.)

Lady Jane had a very tenuous claim to the English throne; her mother was Henry VIII's niece. Jane herself was the great-granddaughter of Henry VII and the cousin of King Edward VI. Jane and Edward were about the same age, and they had almost been married in 1549, but those plans didn't work out. In May 1553, fifteen-year-old Jane was married to Lord Guildford Dudley.

Soon after this, King Edward fell deathly ill with tuberculosis. John Dudley, Guildford's father and the duke of Northumberland, convinced the dying king to name Jane queen of England. Edward's half-sister Mary had been in the line of succession to the throne, but she was Catholic. Jane was Protestant – and John Dudley's daughter-in-law. Edward died on July 6, 1553, and four days later, Lady Jane Grey was proclaimed Queen of England.

She and Guildford went to the Tower of London to prepare for her coronation, but those plans fell through rather spectacularly. The Royal Council supported Lady Jane's ascendance, but the populace believed that Mary was the rightful heir to the throne, and supported her. Lady Jane had been queen for just nine days when the Council changed their minds and declared Mary queen instead.

On July 20, Jane's stay in the Tower of London became involuntary. Instead of making preparations for her coronation, she was now under arrest for high treason. On November 13, she and Guildford were both found guilty and sentenced to death, but Mary didn't order the sentence carried out. She felt that the teenagers were too young to be sentenced to death; besides, they were just mostly innocent pawns in this political game. John Dudley had already been executed on August 23, so Mary was inclined to be merciful.

But in early 1554, Jane's father, Henry Grey, helped lead a revolt against Mary. The queen decided she'd had enough of her political opponents, and signed death warrants for Jane and Guildford on February 7. On the morning of February 12, 1554, Jane watched through a window as Guildford was led to Tower Hill to be executed. Two hours later, Jane herself was beheaded.

Lady Jane Grey still wanders the halls of the Tower of London. Her most famous appearance was on February 12, 1957, when a couple of guards said they saw a white figure walking above the battlements at the top of the Tower. Lady Jane usually makes her rounds on the anniversary of her beheading. She appears as a shimmering white figure that forms from the mists on the Thames. She glides from the river to the green lawns of the Tower grounds, then slowly fades away.

FEBRUARY 13
The *Lady Lovibond*, England (1748)

True love, bitter jealousy, and superstition. Swirl them all together and you get the tale of the *Lady Lovibond* ... a tale that has resulted in a ghost ship that returns to the waters off of Kent, England every fifty years.

On February 13, 1748, the *Lady Lovibond* set sail from London. The three-masted schooner was on her way to Portugal. The captain, Simon Reed, thumbed his nose at one of the oldest and most enduring maritime superstitions: he brought a woman on board his boat. Reed had just gotten married, and he brought his bride, Annetta, with him for the voyage.

There was one man aboard who didn't join in the celebrations belowdecks. John Rivers, the first mate, had stood as best man for the happy couple ... but he was secretly in love with the beautiful Annetta. The sounds of his crewmates toasting the captain and his new wife were more than Rivers could stand.

The Goodwin Sands is one of the most dangerous passages of the English Channel, a nine-mile stretch of shifting sands and treacherous eddies. Over a thousand ships have been wrecked here since 1298. It's just a very bad place for ships.

As the *Lady Lovibond* made her way through the channel, Rivers overpowered the helmsman and steered the ship onto the Goodwin Sands. The ship was destroyed, and everyone aboard was lost.

Fifty years later, on February 13, 1798, the crew on at least two ships sighted the *Lady Lovibond*. The apparition was so real that the master of the *Edenbridge* thought his ship had nearly collided with it.

In 1848, the ship appeared again, and again, its appearance was so lifelike that fishermen in the area thought a boat had actually grounded itself on a sandbar. They came out in lifeboats hoping to rescue survivors ... but there were none. Nor did they find any trace of a wrecked ship. She appeared again in 1898. She looked so real and solid in her distress on the sands that several other ships in the area sent out small boats to aid her. But as soon as they got close, the wrecked ship disappeared without a trace.

The sighting of the *Lady Lovibond* in 1948 was well-documented. Captain Bull Prestwick wrote about his encounter with the phantom ship: "It came straight out of the fog like a moldy shadow, its rotted old timbers creaking and groaning, its ripped and mangled sails flapping and cracking in the cold night wind like the laughter of Satan himself ... She looked real enough, but there was a curious green glow about her that gave us all a bad fright." Prestwick and his crew watched the ghost ship sail towards them for about five minutes before it was swallowed up by the fog.

The *Lady Lovibond* appeared reliably every fifty years ... but it failed to show up in 1998, disappointing the crowds that had gathered on shore to catch a peek at the legendary ship. Maybe it will appear again in 2048.

We'll just have to wait and see, won't we?

FEBRUARY 14

The Haunted Chocolate Shop, Chester, England (present day)

Chester is considered one of the most haunted towns in Britain. One of the places contributing to this creepy reputation is, oddly enough, a chocolate shop.

Thornton's has been making quality chocolate since 1911. It's like the UK's equivalent of

Fannie May Candy. One of their shops is located in Chester on Eastgate Street. It's haunted by a ghost named Sarah.

Legend says that Sarah was a pretty young woman who lived on Eastgate Street in the late 18th or early 19th century. She fell in love with a man named Wilhelm, and they planned to get married. But the groom-to-be got cold feet, and didn't show up on the day of the wedding. Sarah, humiliated, went home and hanged herself.

Now, she seems to delight in harassing men who come into the shop. An electrician who went into the basement to read the meter came up before the job was done, saying he felt like he was being watched by something unpleasant. An American tourist who dismissed the ghost stories was immediately pushed down the stairs.

Sarah has also exhibited poltergeist activity. Her restless spirit takes out her revenge on boxes of chocolate, the quintessential symbol of romantic love. In 1991, she took offense at a Valentine's Day display in the shop. The heart-shaped boxes of chocolates were often found scattered all over the floor … but the regular boxes of candy, boxes that were stacked in front of the display, were left undisturbed.

Sarah's dislike of men proved helpful once. Late one night, a burglar broke into the shop and stole the day's cash from the safe – but he felt so spooked that he fled, leaving behind all his tools, and a beautiful set of fingerprints.

FEBRUARY 15
The Murder of Mary Schlais, Elk Creek, WI (1974)

Bridges seem to be fertile spots for ghost stories. One such place is the bridge at Elk Creek, in Dun County, Wisconsin. Unfortunately, this bridge is haunted by a tragedy.

In February 1974, a young woman named May K. Schlais was hitchhiking from Minneapolis to Chicago. The pretty 25-year-old left her home around 10:30 am on February 15. Later that same afternoon, the sheriff's department in Dunn County got a call from a resident. He'd been on his way home when he'd seen a man standing near the trunk of a small gold-colored car parked at the side of the road near Elk Lake Dam. The man had been kicking snow and leaves over something large on the ground, and the caller found that suspicious.

The sheriff sent investigators out, and sadly, the caller was right to be concerned. The police found the body of Mary Schlais. She had been stabbed over a dozen times.

The caller wasn't able to give a good description of the man, nor had he seen the license plate of the car. The case went cold, and has never been solved.

Paranormal activity is rampant and varied at the site. Photographs taken at the bridge show strange white mists, or full-body apparitions. Witnesses have seen a young woman standing near the dam on the shore of Elk Lake. One of these witnesses was a boy fishing on Elk Lake with his dad. The two had been out since dawn, and around noon they dropped anchor near the dam, hoping that the dark waters would yield good fishing. The boy saw a floating woman out of the corner of his eye. He turned his head to get a better look, and saw the phantom, glowing and nearly transparent. She gazed at him with a blank, chilling stare, then vanished.

Several witnesses, including paranormal researcher and author Chad Lewis, have heard disembodied screams at the dam. Other researchers have experienced their equipment mysteriously failing to work at the dam. This experience of mechanical failure isn't limited to paranormal investigators. The dam is in need of repair, but contractors who are hired to work on the dam often find that their machines won't start.

Virginia Hendricks had a much more pleasant encounter with the spirit. Virginia lived close to Elk Lake Dam, and in the fall of 1994, she began to have regular visits from a mysterious young woman who called herself "Mary". Virginia described the woman as being in her early 20s, quite pretty, with shoulder-length blonde hair. The young lady, who invariably dressed in a pink angora sweater and white capri pants, would walk up to Virginia's house through the garden and tap on the window. Virginia tried to be a good hostess, often offering her visitor a snack, but she found it odd that the girl always showed up at the exact same time.

The other odd thing about Mary's visits was that Virginia was the only person who could see her.

FEBRUARY 16
The Teddi Dance, Rochester, NY (present day)

Elizabeth "Teddi" Mervis was diagnosed with a brain tumor in 1979 when she was twelve years old. Suddenly thrust into an adult world of doctor visits, lab tests, and days and nights of pain and heartbreak, Teddi faced it all with grace under pressure. But like so many other children with terminal illnesses, Teddi was missing out on her childhood.

Her father, Gary, founded a camp and called it Camp Good Days and Special Times. Here, Teddi and other kids could enjoy the pleasures of summer – fishing, hiking, canoeing, swimming, and telling stories around the campfire. Teddy enjoyed the serenity and happiness of the camp until her death in February 1982.

Teddi's legacy lives on, and Camp Good Days still helps terminally ill children enjoy their childhood. About a thousand children attend the camp every summer. Such philanthropy needs money. Soon after Teddi's passing, Dr. Lou Buttino, a professor at St. John Fisher College and a friend of the Mervis family, was telling his class about Teddi's valiant struggle and the devastation he felt at her loss. The class came up with an idea: why not hold a 24-hour dance marathon to raise money for the camp which had brought such joy to Teddi's life?

And so the Teddi Dance for Love was born. The first year, a few dozen dancers took part, and raised $7,500. St. John Fisher College has hosted the dance marathon every February since then. About 500 dancers show up, and they raise an average of $50,000 a year. The Teddi Dance raises funds for the Teddi Project, which makes it possible to fulfill wishes for terminally ill children.

The 24-hour marathon is a physical and emotional challenge. Knowing that your dancing makes it possible for a sick child to visit Disneyland allows you to push past the all-night ordeal. That kind of repetitive physical exertion can lead to some wild experiences, too. Dancing has been used for centuries to induce a trance state, and when you're dancing for twenty-four hours straight ... yeah, it can get intense.

Many dancers, still on their feet in the wee hours of the morning, report hearing a young girl's voice softly crooning their name in an encouraging, hope-filled tone. The weary dancer will turn to look, but the child is nowhere to be found – nowhere but in a fresh burst of energy to keep on dancing.

At the end of each year's event, as the footsore dancers shuffle into the final dance of the marathon, hundreds of balloons are dropped from the ceiling in celebration. Some years – and the Teddi Dance for Love website will back this up – some years, a single pink balloon will be seen floating somewhere off by itself, as if wanting to be noticed.

The organizers never order any pink balloons. Teddi Dance lore says that this is Teddi's spirit, still alive, still joining in the dance.

For more information on the Teddi Dance for Love, please visit www.teddi.sjfc.edu.

FEBRUARY 17
A Midnight Visitor, Dixville Notch, NH (1995)

If you're looking for a place to get away from it all, the Balsams in Dixville Notch is an amazing opportunity. The resort hotel sits on 15,000 acres of New Hampshire wilderness. Stately Victorian-era buildings welcome visitors with gracious hospitality. The Balsams, in all its incarnations, can boast of being one of the oldest resorts in the United States; even before the first hotel was built, the Huntsman's Lodge had been entertaining guests since the late Colonial period.

The Dix House hotel was founded in 1866 to give rest to weary travelers making their way through the White Mountains. By the time the Dix House was joined by the Hale House in 1895, the resort had already gotten a reputation for first-class service. In those days of railroad barons and fin-de-siecle wealth, the rich families of business and industry moguls would enjoy the resort for months at a time. The Hampshire House was built in 1916, bringing the resplendent resort to 400 rooms. Guests still visit the opulent Balsams for four-season excitement, including golf, hiking trails, an extraordinary wine cellar, a performing arts center with festivals, and some of the finest snowmobiling in New England, on the US/Canadian snowmobile "superhighway".

Apparently, it's home to several ghosts as well.

The Balsams gets a renovation of some sort or another every ten years or so, and that keeps the paranormal activity stirred up. One of the hotel owners, Steve Barba, has worked at the hotel since 1959, and has been documenting the ghostly occurrences at the resort from the beginning of his time there.

The occurrences are many and varied. Toilets flush on their own. There is a one-armed man who mysteriously disappears. There are three old ladies, merrily laughing together at some ancient private joke, who also disappear. There is the Vanishing Beauty who hangs out in the hallways of the Dix House, and has been heard laughing in delight in the John Dix parlor. On one occasion, a man heard her peal of giggles and tried to find her. As he passed a mirror, he glanced over to it, and saw a beautiful woman in the reflection smiling at him. When he turned to see the real girl, there was no one there.

In February 1996, a sergeant in the Massachusetts state police and his wife were spending the night in Room 120. At 12:30 in the morning, the wife woke up and realized there was a naked man standing at the foot of the bed. He was dripping wet, as though he'd just gotten out of the shower and hadn't yet reached for a towel. The wife was a bit concerned. Why was her husband taking a shower after midnight?

"Honey, are you alright?" she called.

A sleepy mumble came as answer – from next to her in bed. Her husband had been sound asleep. So, who was the naked, dripping man?

Some research turned up a possible answer. In the early 1930s, the era of the Big Bands, bandleaders often stayed in Room 120. One of them had mysteriously drowned in the lake on the grounds in front of the hotel.

Maybe it wasn't shower water glistening on the man's body, but water from Lake Glorietta.

FEBRUARY 18
Bettie Brown's Birthday, Galveston, TX (recurring)

Ashton Villa is a breathtaking Italianate mansion in Galveston, Texas. James Moreau Brown was a wealthy, powerful businessman who made his fortune in hardware. In typical Texas fashion, he decided to show off his riches by building a huge, ostentatious home for himself and his family. Built in 1859, Ashton Villa served as headquarters for the general of whichever army, Union or Confederate, happened to be in charge of Galveston during the Civil War. It was also used as a hospital for Confederate soldiers.

After the war, the immense palace was home to the free-spirited Bettie Ashton Brown, who inherited it on her father's death. Born in 1855, Bettie never married, but spent her life in pursuit of pleasure. Bettie paid no attention whatever to social conventions of the time. She smoked in public, she traveled alone to foreign places like Morocco and Egypt, and collected gorgeous clothes and exotic souvenirs. She was blonde, beautiful, voluptuous, and beloved in Texas society, if a bit shocking. Bettie could always be counted on to bring the entertainment to the parties she hosted at Ashton Villa. Once, her guests were amused, but not particularly surprised, to see Bettie sweep into the Gold Room with several kittens catching a luxurious ride on the train of her dress.

Ashton Villa was the setting for many of these parties and gala dinners. But the Brown family had its share of troubles too. Mathilda "Tillie" Brown, Bettie's sister, married Thomas Sweeney in 1884. Seven years later, their marriage was in shambles. Thomas was an abusive husband, bad enough that when he came home from work ready to use his fists on his wife, his children would run and hide from his wrath. When the situation escalated into divorce, Bettie, to help her sister's case in court, went around to the mansion's staff and neighbors in search of witnesses. She found no shortage of compassionate voices willing to testify to Thomas's domestic abuse. The divorce was granted.

The sisters still make their presence known at Ashton Villa. One of Bettie's many souvenirs from her extensive travels, a chest of drawers that she brought back from the Middle East, spontaneously locks and unlocks, even though the key has been missing for years. Confederate troops wander the mansion's halls and the grounds, perhaps remembering the care they received here when the house was used as a hospital. In the Gold Room, furniture moves without human help, and clocks stop for no reason.

One question that intrigues researchers is this – which Brown sister actually haunts Ashton Villa? The answer would seem to be … they both do. The Gold Room, scene of so many soirees and piano recitals during Bettie's life, still echoes with piano music, even late at night. Once, a caretaker was awakened by the sound of the instrument, and when he went to the Gold Room to investigate, he saw a young woman sitting at the piano, playing a delicate tune. As he watched, both the music and the apparition faded.

But Bettie never learned to play the piano. It was Tillie who played both piano and violin, and she was quite accomplished on both instruments. And Ashton Villa held a special place in Tillie's heart. She'd grown up there, and she loved the mansion. She didn't travel the world, like Bettie did. Ashton Villa was her happy place. And it was the place she went to escape an abusive marriage, a safe haven for herself and her children. It is probably Tillie who still enjoys giving piano recitals in the Gold Room.

The beautiful apparition seen on the staircase landing in 1991, dressed in a turquoise gown and carrying an ornate Victorian fan, her light blonde hair swept up in a Gibson-girl updo, is obviously Bettie. And the ghostly activity at the mansion always gets more intense around February 18, which was Bettie's birthday. It's likely that both sisters are still there, sharing the prestigious house that is their family's legacy.

FEBRUARY 19

City Hall Haunting, Sao Paulo, Brazil (1974)

Sao Paulo is a city of 20 million people, so city administration is, understandably, a complicated business. But people who work in the 12-story city hall building have something else to contend with: their workplace is haunted. *Really* haunted. Witnesses have reported dozens of paranormal events – people appearing then disappearing, phantom footsteps, unexplained lights that wander the hallways, and perhaps the most irritating, phones that ring, but with no one on the other end.

One night, a council member and his staff were in the building very late, having worked past midnight. They had wrapped up their business and decided it was time to head for home ... but the door wouldn't open -- the door that only locked from the inside. To make the situation even more disturbing, the councilman and his staff began to hear voices outside the door. Then they heard furniture being moved around. Now thoroughly freaked out, they called security. A security guard showed up only moments later, and easily opened the door. The guard assured the councilman that no one else was in the building.

It's well-known that Sao Paulo City Hall is haunted. What isn't clear is why. There are a couple of theories, though. The one that seems to hold the most water is this: in February 1974, there was a fire in a newly-built skyscraper near City Hall. Dozens of people were trapped in the high-rise by the flames, and many victims jumped to their deaths rather than face being burned alive. City Hall was turned into a makeshift morgue. It's possible that there are souls wandering the building and that they are very confused as to how they ended up trapped in their city's municipal offices.

Of course, maybe they just assume they're in hell ...

FEBRUARY 20
The Revenge of "Old Mary", Boyle, Ireland (1919, recurring)

The town of Boyle, in Ireland, has its fair share of pubs and alehouses. And the people there are not shy about frequenting those watering holes – except on February 20. That's one day during the year that Boyle turns "dry". Pubs are closed, their shutters fastened tight. No one throws a party on February 20, and even if they did, no one would come.

The reason Boyle turns into a town of teetotalers for the day goes back to before the turn of the last century. In the late 19th century, the Widow Kelly, also known as "Old Mary", was the local temperance leader. She was absolute death on drinking, hated liquor of any kind, and she made regular visits to the pubs of Boyle. Armed with her shillelagh, she would burst in and bust up the place.

Of course, this destruction of property led to Old Mary's arrest. The magistrate sentenced her to one month in prison, which she accepted gladly, calling it her "martyrdom". And the moment she was released, she was right back at it, bringing her shillelagh to bars, clubs, parties, anywhere good Irish whiskey could be found. Many celebrations were spoiled by this tireless, self-styled "reformer".

But age, stiff fines, and longer prison sentences took their toll on the crotchety old woman. "Old Mary" Kelly died in prison in 1919. With her dying breath, she vowed to "come back and check up on Boyle every single winter".

She seems to have kept her promise. According to the *American Weekly* dated February 20, 1944, one local resident, Martha Ann Wylder, said she had seen "Old Mary" on at least twenty-two different occasions. Mrs. Wylder had known Mary Kelly, and recognized her old acquaintance. "She always comes in from the south, brandishing a big, ugly shillelagh, and makes straight for places that sell liquor."

Two Boyle bartenders, Frank Kennedy and Hobson Moore Jr., had their own experiences with the cranky ghost. In the 1944 article, Kennedy said that Old Mary "came into my place late in the evening last year [1943], or at least I saw a shillelagh sailing through the door ... I lost two of my last bottles of imported bourbon." (Remember, this was during wartime. The loss of imported bourbon would have been a serious blow at any time, but during World War II, it was even more of a hardship.)

Moore reported that on the same night that Kennedy lost the bourbon – and at nearly the exact same time – "I felt a cold breeze, and all of a sudden a good half-dozen quarts of Irish whiskey toppled to the floor."

"Old Mary" had struck again.

FEBRUARY 21
The Battle of Olustee, Olustee, FL (1864)

The fighting in the Civil War raged all the way down to Florida. The largest battle in Florida was fought at Olustee on February 20, 1864. Union general Truman Seymour planned to march his 5,000 troops – mostly colored soldiers – west to cut transportation lines that were running supplies from central Florida to Confederate troops in northern Georgia. Seymour's advance was blocked by 5,200 Confederates under General Joseph Finegan. The battle was short but bloody, a Confederate victory that left 203 Yanks and 93 Rebs dead in the woods.

In 1912, the site was marked with a historical monument. And the Battle of Olustee has been remembered in other ways. Every February, thousands of spectators come to watch reenactors bring the past to life through battles, living history displays, sutlers' tents, and a Civil War ball.

The reenactors, it seems, are not alone.

During the annual event, people take lots of pictures, both of the battlefield and of the gracious dancers at the ball. Many of those pictures display orbs and ribbons of light snaking across the photo. Witnesses have seen phantoms hovering in the pine forest that surrounds the battlefield.

If you've never been to a reenactment of a Civil War battle, the reenactors do try to make the experience as authentic as possible for the spectators. That includes soldiers playing dead on the field. While lying in the grass during one mock battle, one reenactor said he had "an eerie feeling." He kept hearing a voice saying, "*Have you seen the elephant?*" – a Civil War-era euphemism for being in combat.

Ray Barlow had a stunning experience in 2002. He was helping his friend, who had a sutler's booth, set up for the weekend. After they finished setting up the booth, Ray decided to take a walk along a trail in the surrounding woods.

"I get a good ways down the trail and see this guy decked out in Confederate garb, I mean, he really looked the part, and on top of that he was barefooted. He was sitting next to a pine tree and had a small campfire going. So, he says, 'Howdy,' and I answered back but noticed he looked pretty skinny, like really ragged … Anyway, he asked if I had a 'chaw', so I pulled a square of chewing tobacco out of my shirt pocket. A lot of reenactors chew and spit – it adds realism to the whole business of reenacting. I handed it to him and he unwrapped the cellophane, cut off a plug with his knife, and put it in his mouth. Then he held the cellophane up and looked through it at the sun. He studied it for a bit and then asked me, 'What's this made of?'

"I said, 'It's cellophane.' I figured he was making fun of me, having something that didn't fit the period theme. He didn't say much, but asked if he could have a piece of that cellophane. I obliged his request, put the tobacco back in my pocket, and went on down the trail."

Half an hour later, Ray walked past the spot again on his way back. There was no sign of the other man – and no sign of his campfire. Ray kept an eye out for the reenactor, but he didn't see him for the rest of the weekend. When he got home, Ray hopped onto his computer and did some research. He discovered that cellophane wasn't invented until 1908. So was this a time slip? Or did Ray share some tobacco with a ghost? You decide.

FEBRUARY 22
Time Slip, Ebenezer, NY (1966)

When the Becker family built a new home in rural New York, they knew that the land they had bought had originally been part of the Seneca Indian reservation. What they didn't know was that the past would come back …

On the night of February 22, 1966, Carolyn Becker took her dog for a walk along the creek. She and the dog were enjoying a lazy evening ramble when Carolyn heard the howl of a strange dog. Her own dog heard it too. The hackles on his neck stood up as he froze to listen.

On the bank of the creek, Carolyn saw a tall pole decorated with colorful strips of cloth ... a pole that, moments before, hadn't been there. And at the base of the pole, a Native American man dressed in buckskin was kneeling. Carolyn gasped in horror – the man was strangling a beautiful white dog.

As Carolyn watched, the man wrapped the limp body of the dog in brightly colored strips of cloth, and strings of wampum around the dog's neck. Then her other senses began to come alive, feeding her more information about the scene unfolding in front of her. She saw the dim glow of campfires and heard the steady beat of drums in the nearby encampment. The smell of tobacco smoke stung her nose. As the man finished his grisly task, the scene slowly faded, leaving Carolyn and her dog standing next to the creek bank.

Carolyn knew that the eerie scene must have been connected to the Seneca tribe that had once roamed those woods. She did some research, and discovered that the Senecas' new year ceremony involved the sacrifice of a pure white dog, who would bear the burden of the tribe's sins for the year. She also learned that the last time the ceremony had been performed was in 1841.

FEBRUARY 23
Death of John Quincy Adams, Washington DC (1848)

John Quincy Adams belonged to the generation after the Revolution. He was the oldest son of John Adams – the second president – and Abigail Adams. John Quincy Adams also served as president from 1825 to 1829. After losing to Andrew Jackson in the 1828 election, Adams did not retire from public service. He was elected to the House of Representatives, where he served from 1831 to his death in 1848.

As a matter of fact, being an orator on the floor of the House is what led to his demise. Adams was particularly opposed to the Mexican-American War and the annexation of Texas – he felt it was just another excuse to extend the reach of slavery. On February 21, 1848, the House was discussing ways to honor army officers who had served in the war. Adams had been an outspoken critic of the war, believing it to be unjust. As his colleagues rose one by one to vote "aye" in favor of the resolution, Adams stood up and yelled, "NO!" His exertion brought on a stroke, and the 81-year-old Adams collapsed. He was taken to the Speaker's Room in the Capitol Building. Two days later, on February 23, he died, with his wife Louisa at his side.

Adams still returns to his old seat on the House floor, the location of which is now marked with a plaque. Visitors and security guards have reported hearing Adams still shouting his famous "No!"

FEBRUARY 24
Alpha Theta Frat House, Hanover, NH (1934)

Dartmouth College is an Ivy League school founded in 1769. It's one of nine colleges chartered before the American Revolution.

With such a distinguished pedigree, you know there are bound to be a few ghosts floating around the venerable old campus. And Dartmouth, like many other colleges, has quite the roster of ghostly inhabitants.

The ghosts at Alpha Theta fraternity house, unfortunately, all crossed over the veil on the same night. The tragedy dates back to 1934, when the building housed a chapter of Theta Chi fraternity. On Saturday night, February 24, nine young men at the house died in their sleep from carbon monoxide poisoning. The coal furnace had been improperly banked, and everyone in the building died. The other eight fraternity brothers only survived because they happened to be away for the weekend.

The tragedy was a serious blow, not only to the college, but also to Theta Chi. The shadow of death meant that the fraternity had serious difficulty finding pledges. The Dartmouth chapter was in danger of folding entirely. In 1940, the building was demolished, and a new fraternity house was built on the same site. Theta Chi moved elsewhere, and the new building was taken over by Alpha Theta.

The ghosts, though, seem to have stayed. Some of the stones from the original house were incorporated into the laundry room, which is located in the basement near the back stairs. Current members of Alpha Theta have witnessed supernatural activity. They feel uneasy when they have to go down to the basement. But that's not all: laundry has been known to move around by itself, and sometimes, food randomly shows up, which no one can account for. The creepiest aspect of the haunting is that some of the fraternity siblings have reported seeing phantom men in 1930s dress … and some of these faces can also be found in old college photos, in the 1934 yearbook's In Memoriam section.

FEBRUARY 25
The Murder of Carrington Harvey Witherspoon, Miami, FL (1962)

Students of the paranormal have discovered that one of the best ways to create a haunting is to experience sudden death, and leave behind unresolved issues. That's exactly what happened to Carrington Harvey Witherspoon.

The Witherspoons lived in a pretty terra cotta house in Miami, Florida. The setting may have been paradise, but life in the Witherspoon home was violent and terrifying. Carrington Witherspoon was an abusive husband and father, terrorizing his family on a regular basis. The house would tremble with the tumult of his abuse as he smashed furniture over his wife and children. He even, in his uncontrollable rage, fired a shotgun at his family.

On February 25, 1962, the Witherspoon home once again shuddered with breaking furniture and shouting. Carrington, overcome with fury yet again, was beating his teenage son with a chair. And yet again, a shot rang out … but this time, it was Mrs. Witherspoon who stood over the bleeding body of her husband. She had decided to end Carrington's abuse for good.

Mrs. Witherspoon went to trial, but she was acquitted of the homicide. There were plenty of witnesses who testified to Carrington's violent temper and physical abuse.

Unfortunately for the people who later moved into the Witherspoon house, Carrington's torment carried over into his afterlife. The crashing of furniture being thrown around rang out from the living room at night. The activity even continued during the day – furniture in the sun room would move as if pushed by unseen hands. People in the house often suffered with feelings of deep discomfort, and were sometimes overcome by a horrible stench that pervaded the house.

In May 1967, the harried owners of the house brought in psychic medium Harry Levy to make contact with Witherspoon's antagonistic spirit. Levy discovered that the man's appalling temper had not been tamed by his violent death. Carrington Harvey Witherspoon, after being shot by his wife, had vowed with his dying breath to return from the grave to get even with her.

FEBRUARY 26
The Milford Mine Disaster, Crow Wing County, MN (1924)

The Milford Mine was an integral part of Minnesota's steel production. The mine produced manganese ore, which was shipped to Duluth, then on to steel factories in cities like Cleveland and Detroit.

The mine opened in 1917, and by 1924, it had reached a depth of 200 feet and was producing 70,000 tons of ore. Mining was dangerous, nasty work, and the Milford Mine was known as a "wet" mine. There were parts of it where the miners had to wear rain hats and slickers to work.

This was because the eastern end of the mine was very close to Lake Foley – many of the miners knew that, in fact, parts of the mine shaft were under the lake. Some miners quit rather than risk their lives. Others stayed, but only because they hoped that the ground would freeze and become a little more stable. But water and mud that deep underground just won't freeze over the course of a winter.

On February 4, 1924, the miners were hard at work underground. It was about 3:30 in the afternoon, the shift was nearly over, and every man was looking forward to getting back above ground.

Suddenly there was a quick rush of warm wind. The gust was so strong that it blew out the carbide gas lamps on the miners' hats – or blew the hats off altogether. There was a liquid roaring sound. Then everything happened with incredible speed.

Frank Hrvatin Jr., fourteen years old, worked with his father at the mine. Both father and son had only planned to work there for a short while, as they were well aware of the dangers of the lake. So, when Frank Jr. heard the sound of rushing water, he knew immediately what had happened. He was at the second level, at 175 feet, working with Harry Hosford when the gust of wind hit him in the face. He glanced down to the lowest level of the mine, 200 feet below the surface, and saw a brown river of rushing water.

Frank Jr. ran for his life. "The lake is coming in!" he screamed as he scrambled along the shaft. He and the other miners fled for the only exit – a ladder that led 200 feet up to the surface, quite a climb on a normal day. Matt Kangas, an older miner, was above Frank on the ladder, and he was struggling. Frank bulled his head and shoulders under Kangas' legs, shoving him upward in desperation as the water below them surged higher. Even with Frank's panicked assistance, the seven men on the ladder barely outclimbed the flood. When Frank reached down to pull his partner, Harry Hosford, off of the ladder, Hosford was waist-deep in water.

He was the last miner to make it out. Within fifteen minutes, the mine was filled with mud and lake water. People standing on the shore of Lake Foley could see the ice crack as the water level in the lake dropped.

In the confusion and panic, a sound blared stridently, filling the air with noise. It was the warning whistle. Clinton Harris had been manning the electric hoist when the flood roared through. Harris, being right next to the lift, could easily have escaped. Instead, he stayed at his post to sound the alarm, hoping to alert miners on the upper levels to the danger. Harris may have become entangled in the pull cord that sounded the warning whistle. Or, knowing that his choice to stay was a guaranteed death sentence, Harris quickly tied the cord around his waist so that when he perished, the alarm would continue to sound.

The alarm blared for nearly five hours after the mine flooded. An engineer finally managed to disconnect it. Then all was deadly quiet.

Forty-one miners died that day, including Frank's father, Frank Hrvatin Sr. Thirty-one of them were married. Eighty-eight children were left orphans by the worst mining disaster in Minnesota's history.

The tragedy struck so suddenly that everyone knew the seven men standing muddy and gasping at the top of the ladder were the only survivors. There would be no rescue attempt, not from a mine filled with mud and lake water. It would be a recovery operation, not a rescue.

It took months to pump all the filthy water out of the mine. The shafts were also alive with fish and turtles, many of which were handed out to the miners' families for food. By late March, enough mud had been pumped out of the mine that recovery teams could go down to search for bodies. One account tells of the horrifying conditions in the mine.

"The air underground had the smell of death, not only from the bodies to be found, but also of the rotting fish and frogs." As the human bodies decomposed, they added a singular stench to the air. The searchers used hoses to wash away the grime from each body they found. Usually, the first thing to be revealed with the flush of clear water was "the grotesque white face" of the corpse, "swelled to look like a rag doll, peering out of the black muck."

The last body was recovered on November 9. The mine resumed operation soon after that. Legend has it that the first men down the ladder when the mine reopened got a nasty shock.

The translucent figure of Clinton Harris was at the bottom of the shaft, his hands wrapped around the ladder, gazing wistfully upward toward the light of day. Some of the men even swore they heard the phantom shriek of Harris's alarm whistle.

The Milford Mine closed for good in 1932, when the Great Depression curtailed the demand for steel. The site is now a memorial park honoring the forty-one men who lost their lives in an instant. Walking trails crisscross the land, picnic shelters provide an area for relaxation, and forty-one trees have been planted as living memorials.

FEBRUARY 27
The Fire at Old Kenyon, Gambier, OH (1949)

Kenyon College, in Ohio, has a long, proud history. The first permanent structure to grace the campus was Old Kenyon, built between 1827 and 1829. By 1949, the dormitory housed almost a quarter of the student population. It was an iconic fixture on the campus grounds.

There was a persistent legend about fireplaces at Old Kenyon. Everyone knew they were there, but no one knew where they were. There were four chimneys that rose from the center of the building. But only one was ever used: a fairly new fireplace had been chiseled into the flue in the first-floor parlor of Middle Kenyon.

On Saturday February 26, some students enjoyed a small fire in that fireplace. By 9 pm, it had burned down to embers. Someone tossed a bit of scrap paper onto the glowing coals. A quick flame flared up, then guttered out as the paper burned to gray ash.

At about 10 pm, the students in the dorm started to head off to bed. More students straggled in later from a dance. There had been a raucous party that night, called the Sophomore Shipwreck. Partygoers had been instructed to dress as if they were stranded on a tropical island. The students at all-male Kenyon College even had dates for the evening, many of them from nearby Denison University, which was coed. (One of the Kenyon students, a veteran of World War II and a pilot, had taken to the skies and dropped leaflets over the Denison campus, suggesting that the young women there visit Kenyon for this party and see what the nightlife at an all-male college was like. This did not thrill the male students at Denison.)

By 2:30 am, the men of Old Kenyon and their dates had settled in for the night. By 4 am, the girls had left, and the last partygoers were fast asleep.

But tragedy never sleeps. A few pops from the embers of the dying fire, and sparks escaped through a crack in the flue. They kindled in an enclosed space between the walls, then exploded into a raging inferno.

William Wenner ('52), whose dorm room was in Middle Kenyon, was probably the first to see the fire. He was passing the first-floor parlor on his way to his room when he glanced in and saw fire running up the drapes next to the window on the far right of the room. He ran to get the fire extinguisher at the bottom of the steps, but by the time he came back up, he was blasted back from the parlor doorway by a wall of smoke and heat.

Fire crews from neighboring towns rushed to the campus, but the fire consumed the building so quickly that their efforts were pitiful. The dorm was gutted down to the walls by the inferno. Seven students were trapped in the building in their third-floor rooms, and two students who lived on the second floor died of skull fractures suffered when they leaped from the third floor. (The fire escapes were simply steel rungs embedded in the rear wall between windows. To reach a rung, students had to stand on a window ledge and lunge sideways, hoping to snag a rung. It's not clear whether those two students actually jumped to escape the searing heat, or if they were trying to grab hold of a rung and missed.)

As dawn broke and the fire slowly died down, a roll call determined that six students were missing. When the parents of the missing boys arrived, they clung to the hope that maybe their sons had escaped the fire and were hiding in the woods next to the building. Volunteers combed the woods for survivors. They found none.

The bodies of the six missing students were soon found in the smoking wreckage of the dorm and returned to their grieving parents. All, that is, except for Stephen Shepard. His parents refused to believe that the charred bones were all that were left of their boy, so they declined to accept them. The shards of Stephen's bones now rest in a small grave in a cemetery near the campus quad.

Old Kenyon was rebuilt over the next summer. Students, alumni, and members of the community all wanted to see the grand old building rise again, so funds were collected and construction began. Photographs were taken of the ruins, and the dorm was rebuilt as accurately as possible. The walls were torn down, a new basement was excavated, and a steel and concrete structure put up. Then, the old stones were meticulously attached to the walls, forming a veneer that reproduced the look of the original building. Amazingly, the "new" Old Kenyon opened to students on September 11, 1950, ready for the beginning of the academic year.

With the tragic deaths of nine young men, ghost stories abound at Old Kenyon.

Thomas Marvin Hill ('52) had an experience with the ghosts of Old Kenyon that he says happened within a few nights of the fire. He'd spent the evening at his fraternity house, and he walked home alone in the dark.

He had to pass the college chapel, which was on his right as he walked down Middle Path. As he came closer, he saw a line of men coming from the far corner of the chapel. The men were silent and expressionless. Hill realized with a start that the men crossing the path in front of him were ghosts – the spirits of the students who had so recently died in the fire.

"I was on the edge of panic. A voice told me as I passed the chapel: 'Do not run, keep silent. Stay calm.' I continued on, shaking with fear. Ahead of me, perhaps 150 yards away, was a street light …" Hill reported that the voice assured him he would be fine once he passed under the light.

"As I passed beneath the light, my panic abruptly disappeared. I felt the burden of my fears lifting. Within seconds, all was well."

On the anniversary of the fire, a student came into his room and found a 1949 yearbook open to a memorial page listing the nine fire victims. Another student, who lived in a room where one of the students was trapped, heard someone pounding on his door yelling "Get out!" When he ran to the door and yanked it open, no one was there. One of the most unnerving encounters happened to yet another student. He was shaken awake by a rough, invisible hand. A voice shouted, "Ed, wake up, fire!" Edward Brout had once lived in that room. He also died there – he was one of the students trapped in the building.

The most common haunting phenomenon at Old Kenyon is the sight of one or more of the victims walking down the corridor. However, witnesses report that the specters don't so much walk as glide – because they appear only from the knees up. Still other witnesses tell of seeing disembodied legs poking through the ceiling. (This is because the new foundation is about ten inches higher than it was in the old building. The ghosts are simply walking on the original floor.)

The hauntings don't only happen during the school year. One sultry night in July, two safety officers, Dan Turner and Renee Joris, were sent to Old Kenyon because someone had seen a light on in one of the West Wing windows. No students were in residence at the time, so the security guards went to check it out.

The guards went into the sweltering building. The temperature had been in the 90s that day, and the air on the fourth floor was stifling. They turned the light off and went to check the rest of the building. As they pushed open the door that leads from the West Wing to the middle section of Old Kenyon, they suddenly saw each other's breath. The temperature had plummeted when they opened the door.

The two guards hurried out of the building and huddled, wordless, by the door. Four cigarettes later, their walkie-talkies crackled to life.

"That light is on again, the one in the West Wing …"

Turner looked at his partner, "I don't care," he said.

"I don't either," Joris muttered. Neither of them went back into the building that night.

FEBRUARY 28
Strange Goings-on at Gonzaga University, Spokane, WA (1970s)

Gonzaga University, in Spokane, Washington, is known for its stellar educational programs and its competitive sports teams. Its history, though, hasn't always been so worthy of a full-color brochure printed on slick paper.

The school was founded in 1887 by Joseph Cataldo, a Jesuit missionary. He had come to the Pacific Northwest in 1865 to minister to the Upper Spokane Indians. In 1880 he built a schoolhouse to serve Native children, but he and his fellow Catholics were concerned about the influence of Protestant schools on the Native people.

 The city of Spokane offered to help pay to build a new college, as long as it was a whites-only school. Father Cataldo wanted to educate the Native population, so this was exactly the opposite of what he'd envisioned for a college. He wrote to Rome for help, but the Church leaders there warned that the Methodists and other Protestants were continuing to build schools too. They worried that city funding would go to the Protestants if the Catholic school wasn't built soon enough. So, Fr. Cataldo had to swallow his dreams of educating the natives. Later faculty members also tried to enroll Native American boys, but were turned down. Non-Catholic boys were also refused admittance in the college's early years.

But we're here to visit Monoghan Hall, the music building on campus. This Victorian mansion was built in 1898 by James Monoghan, a millionaire and supporter of Gonzaga University. The university acquired the three-story mansion in 1942 as a home for the music department.

The hauntings took place over several months during the 1974-1975 academic year. One Friday evening in November, a housekeeper stopped by the building to pick up something she'd forgotten earlier that day. The front door of the hall was unlocked, and the housekeeper could hear organ music playing, coming from one of the practice rooms upstairs. No students were allowed in the building so late, so the housekeeper went up to roust the errant student.

The door to the room was locked, and no light shone from under the door. The housekeeper unlocked the door, turned on the light, and went in. The organ's keys were still moving as if unseen fingers were dancing in a melody. The music was still playing … but the room was empty and the windows were locked.

In January 1975, Father Walter F. Leedale, a Jesuit priest and associate professor of music, heard flute music outside his Monoghan Hall studio. He went out to see who was playing, but saw no one. In mid-February, Fr. Leedale was noodling around on the piano in his studio. He was playing an 8-note snippet of music, the only bit he could recall from the phantom flute music he'd heard a few weeks earlier. The housekeeper overheard Fr. Leedale's piano puttering, and burst into the studio. She thought she was going to catch the culprit who'd snuck into the building. When she found only Fr. Leedale, she told him his melody was the same she'd heard being played on the organ that night in November.

Father Leedale was already familiar with the building's haunted reputation. He'd been approached in September 1974 by several music students who'd had odd experiences in the building. They'd heard strange footsteps, and had seen pianos playing by themselves. At first, Leedale didn't believe them. He figured the experiences were just down to the overactive imaginations of impressionable college students. To humor his students, Leedale spent the night sleeping on a couch in his office. He was kept awake all night by inexplicable noises, and the morning sun found him much less skeptical.

As the weeks went by, Leedale's experiences mounted. He was finally convinced that something paranormal was going on when a locked door handle turned and opened on its own. There was "an absolutely locked door just opening in front of me as I went to put my key in the lock. The handle turned, and it opened. I went in, and the room was empty."

The activity really ramped up in February. There had been several thefts of musical instruments, so Monaghan Hall was patrolled by several security guards, and a live-in student caretaker provided another set of eyes. One day, Leedale and the student caretaker were checking the building when they heard a growling coming from behind a locked door. Leedale suggested that it was just a draft rattling the door, and the two men moved on. Leedale came back later, alone, and unlocked the door. The room was empty except for an old bass viol missing its strings. And there was no draft.

Later in the month, Leedale, the caretaker, and two security guards were standing outside the building with Daniel Brenner, the chair of the music department. The group was about to do a walkthrough of the hall when one of the guards thought he saw something in a third-floor window. Both guards then saw something in a second-floor window. The whole group raced inside to investigate. They found no one inside, and nothing unusual on the first or second floor. But on the third floor, the group was accosted by a powerful invisible force. Leedale and one of the guards felt their skin tingling and prickling with some unknowable force. The other guard felt cold hands around his throat, strangling him, and the student was nearly brought to his knees, overwhelmed by some "oppressive presence."

None of the men saw a thing.

By February 24, Fr. Leedale decided that enough was enough. For four days, he went through Monaghan Hall intoning the cleansing prayers of the exorcism ritual a total of six times. Although it was not a formal rite of exorcism, the prayers got something riled up. The candles lit for the experiment repeatedly blew out. Daniel Brenner assisted with the cleansing, and he said later that as Leedale spoke, the 8-inch, half-pound crucifix around the Jesuit's neck began to swing – and it kept on swinging. "It simply wouldn't stay the right way. I was assisting Father Leedale with prayers, holding the holy water so that he could hold the prayer book and keep the cross still at the same time."

Father Leedale spent four days going through the building floor by floor, reciting the prayers over and over. On February 28, the live-in caretaker met Leedale and Brenner as they arrived at the hall for the fourth day of prayers. The student had smelled smoke in the building, and was trying to find the source of the smell. No fire was found, but the second floor reeked of sulfur – a classic sign of demonic activity. Fr. Leedale said that on February 28, he felt the ominous presence disappear, and he declared that the haunting was over.

(Some people aren't convinced that the presence has been fully laid to rest. In 1979, security guards in the attic saw a large blackboard on wheels roll silently towards them across the wooden floor until it bumped into one of the guards, pinning him. The other guards moved the blackboard, freeing their coworker, but it wasn't easy. This was the same area where Leedale, Brenner, and the others experienced the terrifying ominous presence in February 1975.)

So, who is responsible for the oppressive experiences in Monaghan Hall? Ghost lore points to John Robert Monaghan, James Monaghan's son. (You'll recall that James built Monaghan Hall in 1898.) John was a member of the first graduating class of Gonzaga College (as it was then known), graduating in 1887. He attended the US Naval Academy at Annapolis, graduating in 1895. In 1899, John was serving on the cruiser *USS Philadelphia* when it was sent to Samoa to put down a war between two tribes. British and American forces landed, but were ambushed. Lt. Phillip Lansdale was shot in the leg. Ensign Monaghan tried and failed to rescue him; he stayed with his comrade until the tribesmen overran their position. Both Lansdale and Monaghan were beheaded by the natives.

John Monaghan's body was returned to his family for a hero's funeral. His body lay in state in the family home, surrounded by flowers, as was customary in those days. But there is a curious detail to be seen in the photos of John Monaghan's viewing. There are several crucifixes in the photograph.

And they are upside down.

Even creepier, another photograph was found stuffed into a hole in the dirt wall in the basement of Monaghan Hall in the 1970s. This picture showed a coffin, covered with flowers, sitting under a tent at a gravesite. On top of the coffin, propped up among the blooms, was a photograph of a young man, identified as John Monaghan. Two crosses, one black and one white, hung from the tent -- both upside down. The housekeeper for the building reported that someone, long ago, had tried to burn the photograph, but it refused to catch fire. So it was buried in the basement instead.

If a picture is worth a thousand words, what story would that photograph tell?

FEBRUARY 29
Death in Deerfield, Deerfield, MA (1704)

The tiny British settlement of Deerfield, Massachusetts, was in a precarious position in 1704. Queen Anne's War was raging around it, as the British and French fought for control of the New World. The settlers prudently stayed within the tall wooden palisade.

They weren't expecting to be attacked in the middle of winter, but on February 29, at about 4 am, a band of 50 French soldiers and 200 Abenaki and Caughnawaga Indians raided Deerfield. The war party slaughtered nearly fifty townspeople, and rounded up over a hundred for a 300-mile forced march into Canada. The trek, through heavy snow, took its toll: twenty of the captives died along the way.

John Williams, the town's minister, was taken prisoner along with his wife and five of his children. Two more children, six-year-old John Jr. and six-week-old Jerusha, were immediately killed, as was Parthena, the family's black slave. Mrs. Eunice Williams was one of those lost on the trek, but Reverend Williams survived. Nearly three years later, he and about sixty others made their way back to Deerfield. Williams returned home with four of his children.

Some of the captives chose to stay in Canada, and joined either French or Native American society. Eunice Williams, John's daughter (named for her mother), stayed and joined the Mohawk tribe. She converted to Catholicism, and even took a native name, A'ongote, meaning "She (was) taken and placed (as a member of their tribe)." In early 1713, she married into the tribe. She made four trips back to New England to visit her relatives over the years, but she always returned to her tribe. She ended up being the last surviving member of those taken in the raid.

Queen Anne's War ended in 1713, and life on the frontier returned to normal. But the ghosts remained. Eunice Williams (John's wife) is said to haunt a covered bridge that still stands today. Eunice was one of the first to be killed along the grueling trek to Canada. As the party crossed the Green River, Eunice, still convalescing from childbirth, lost her footing and collapsed from exhaustion. A warrior struck her down with his tomahawk.

People give varying reasons for Eunice's continued presence at the bridge that bears her name. Some say she's tied there by her violent demise in the icy water, hacked to death just hours after seeing her newborn and second youngest child killed. Others say she mourns the fate of her namesake, the daughter who abandoned her family and the religion her family valued so much.

MARCH

DAYS *of the* DEAD

MARCH 1
The Stevens Pass Avalanche, Wellington, WA (1910)

Snow in the mountains of the Pacific Northwest can be treacherous. The engineers on the train traveling from Spokane to Seattle in late February, 1910, knew the dangers of late-winter snowfalls. But passengers were expecting a comfortable trip through the mountains.

The Great Northern tracks were steadily being obliterated by falling snow. Snowplows were running day and night to keep the trains on schedule, even with a snow delay on February 23. But the soft white flakes were relentless. One of the snowplow operators later said that the snow was eight to ten feet deep on the level, with drifts 15 to 20 feet high. The storm was dropping a foot of snow an hour.

Just west of Stevens Pass, near the town of Wellington, two trains finally ground to a halt. One, the Spokane Express, carried passengers. The other was a mail train. The snowplows just couldn't keep up. Laborers were sent out with shovels, but at 15 cents an hour, they soon gave it up as a bad job. The trains were stuck.

One day became three, then five, then six. Passengers waited with increasing impatience. Even then, it was a matter of inconvenience, not danger. The men who worked on those trains had never known that stretch of track to suffer an avalanche. That didn't mean things weren't dire, though. The coal in the bunkers was being used to heat the trains to keep the passengers marginally comfortable, not to fuel the trains. And the coal was running low.

Some passengers lost patience with the wait and decided to take their chances outside. They tackled the deep drifts in their street clothes, wading through piles of snow and sliding hundreds of feet down the mountainside on their rumps. All of the passengers who made this risky decision actually made it out okay, but for the children on the train, and their parents, it just wasn't feasible.

The weather changed on February 26, but not in a good way. A "pineapple express" roared through, warming things up and changing the snow to rain. Then on February 28, an electrical storm pounded the mountain with thunder and lightning.

Just after midnight on March 1, the passengers were asleep on the train, along with many of the train's crew. Others were sleeping in shacks in the nearby town of Wellington. At 12:05, the storm was at its fiercest. A streak of lightning jagged across the sky, and a loud clap of thunder followed it. Then another, longer roar drowned out the noise of the storm.

Countless tons of fresh, wet snow broke loose from the mountainside and cascaded down on the town of Wellington and on the trains. The train cars were thrown from the tracks and rolled over 150 feet down into the Tye River Valley, ending up buried under forty feet of snow. Thirty-five passengers were killed, and 61 train employees lost their lives. The last body was recovered in July, later that year. The death toll of 96 makes the Stevens Pass disaster the worst avalanche in United States history.

Over a century later, the area is still haunted. Iron Goat Trail follows a 7.5 mile stretch of the Great Northern Railway line. Hikers can visit a snow shed, built in 1911 to prevent further avalanche deaths, and see an interpretive sign within the shed that describes the tragedy. Many investigators like to record at the historical plaque in the hopes of catching ghost voices. People report feeling a heaviness in the snow shed, and seeing strange shadows. Witnesses also hear disembodied voices, and snippets of old-fashioned music.

The 1998 International Ghost Hunters Society Western Ghost Conference was held in Washington, and investigators visited the town of Wellington, near the avalanche site. (The depot there closed in 1929, and the town was abandoned.) As the investigators were leaving, six of them heard the phantom shriek of an old-fashioned steam whistle … a sound that hadn't been heard in that area for decades.

MARCH 2
The Martha Washington Hotel, New York City, NY (1903)

When the Martha Washington Hotel opened on March 2, 1903, it filled a distinctive niche in the residential hotel market. Women at the start of the 20th century were beginning to demand more freedoms, including leaving home to pursue professional careers, to travel, or just to go on a shopping excursion to the city. The 450 rooms at the Martha Washington were advertised proudly as being exclusively for women. This was such an appealing idea that on opening day, the hotel was fully booked, with 200 names already on a waiting list.

The hotel continued to be popular with women's groups, and became the center for the nation's suffrage movement. In 1907, the entire second floor was devoted to offices in which women worked tirelessly to get the right to vote.

But our story takes place ten stories higher. A woman who had rented the room noticed the day she moved in that the room was redolent with a foul but unidentifiable odor. She took the room anyway, but her first night there was not a restful one. She was kept awake by footsteps that went back and forth between the chair and the door, and the sound of a newspaper rustling, as if someone was turning the pages.

After a few weeks, the woman had a theory as to who was haunting the room. She figured that the spirit of an older woman was still in the room, and was irritated to have an uninvited guest in "her" room. The ghost made her feelings very clear one night – the woman woke to see two withered hands holding a pillow over her head as if planning to suffocate her. The guest left the room in a hurry.

Later, she learned that two other hotel guests had been found dead of unknown causes in that room. One had been found dead in a chair and the other had died in the bathtub.

MARCH 3
Federici's Curtain Call, Melbourne, Australia (1888)

The Princess Theatre in Melbourne is a Victorian confection of the arts, glowing with stained glass and intricate stonework. Completed in 1886, it's still a vibrant part of Melbourne's theater life. It got a complete refurbishing inside and out in 2018; it was the site of a production of *Harry Potter and the Cursed Child* – only the third location after London and New York.

And, of course, the Princess has a resident ghost. On the evening of March 3, 1888, the theatre was showing a production of the opera *Faust*. The opera was supposed to end with a dramatic flourish – the sight of Mephistopheles sinking through a trapdoor on his way to the fiery pit of Hell, taking the soul of Dr. Faustus with him.

The trapdoor worked great. The baritone playing Mephistopheles, an actor named Frederick Baker with a rich, deep voice who went by the stage name "Frederick Federici", sank dramatically from view on his way to the basement, and the audience thrilled to this stunning bit of stagecraft. Unfortunately, Federici was in the throes of a swift and violent heart attack. By the time the platform reached the basement, the actor was dead. He was only 38 years old.

The show must go on, and the opera was staged again, with an understudy taking Federici's place. The actor's spirit was none too pleased with this recasting. His ghost had insisted, the night he died, on making a final appearance. Federici died almost immediately, and never made it back onstage to take his leading-man bows. But the other actors said that yes, Federici had been onstage with them for that final curtain call. Some of them didn't realize he'd just passed.

For the rest of the opera's run, the understudy who took Federici's place in the role of Mephistopheles said that whenever he stepped forward to take a bow, invisible hands would shove him backwards. Federici must have gotten over his pique, though, because he has stayed at the theater ever since his demise.

In the early 1900s, a fireman on duty at the theater saw Federici's ghost standing center stage. The imposing apparition was a tall, well-built man dressed in evening clothes, complete with a cloak and top hat. In 1917, another fireman and the wardrobe mistress saw Federici sitting in the second row. The sightings have continued through the years, and it is considered good luck for the production if the ghost is seen on opening night.

I wonder how he liked the Harry Potter play?

MARCH 4
The Shooting of Fatty Walsh, Coral Gables, FL (1929)

The Biltmore Hotel, built in 1926, was the place to see and be seen in the Roaring Twenties in Coral Gables. Boasting what was then the largest pool in the world, the Biltmore hosted aquatic galas including synchronized swimming and alligator wrestling. Johnny Weissmuller, who won gold at the summer Olympics in 1924 and 1928, was a swimming instructor at the hotel. He would later go on to fame in Hollywood playing Tarzan.

Other famous guests enjoyed the lavish hospitality of the Biltmore in the pre-war years. Fred Astaire, Ginger Rogers, Bing Crosby, and Judy Garland all stayed there, as did the Duke and Duchess of Windsor. Franklin D. Roosevelt used the hotel as a temporary White House office.

Some of the entertainment was not quite as wholesome. Al Capone had a favorite room at the Biltmore, and the booze flowed freely in spite of Prohibition. Local gambler Eddie Wilson rented the entire thirteenth floor of the hotel and ran a gambling hall and speakeasy.

Just before dawn on March 4, 1929, a ten-hour poker marathon was drawing to a close. Only two players were left at the table: Eddie, and mobster Thomas "Fatty" Walsh. Eddie raised, and Fatty folded. Fatty, a sore loser, demanded to see Eddie's hand. But Eddie shoved his cards into the middle of the deck.

Fatty was furious. He exploded up from his chair, knocking it over, and lunged at Eddie across the table. Eddie drew a pistol and shot Fatty. The gangster crashed to the floor, his poker-playing days over forever.

When World War II broke out, the Biltmore was commandeered by the government. In 1942 the hotel was repurposed into a hospital to care for wounded soldiers.

Nurses who served at the hospital noticed that the private elevator that went to the thirteenth floor always reeked of cigar smoke. Even stranger, the click of poker chips and the shuffle of cards could be heard behind doors on that floor – but when the nurses would open the door, the room would be empty. The sounds were so pervasive that an army nurse later said, "Everyone who worked there visited the thirteenth floor just to hear what was going on. They said it was Fatty Walsh still shuffling and dealing cards … years after he was shot dead."

And Fatty still plays his eternal poker game at the Biltmore, which was restored in 1987 to the tune of $55 million. The quiet sounds of poker chips being stacked and cards being slapped down on the table still echo on the thirteenth floor. And the elevator still carries a whiff of Fatty's cigar smoke.

MARCH 5
The Boston Massacre, Boston, MA (1770)

Tensions were running high in Boston in the spring of 1770. Over 2000 British soldiers had been occupying the city since 1768, and their presence had been tolerated … for a while. Colonists were finding tax burdens increasingly repressive, and there were mutterings about taxation without representation. Patriots began to vandalize stores selling British goods.

On February 22, patriots attacked a store belonging to a known loyalist. Ebenezer Richardson, a customs officer, lived near the store. He tried to break up the crowd by firing a gun through his window. The shot killed eleven-year-old Christopher Seider. This inflamed the patriots.

On the evening of March 5, Private Hugh White was on guard alone in front of the Custom House on King Street, where the take from the taxes was stored. (Basically, his job was to guard the King's money.) A restless group of angry colonists began to gather in front of the building. Soon, about fifty people were milling around, insulting Private White and threatening violence.

At some point, White had had quite enough, and he lashed out and struck a colonist with his bayonet. The colonists started to throw snowballs and chunks of ice at White. White yelled for help, bringing Captain Thomas Preston with six more soldiers. Even with this additional show of force, the angry mob refused to break up. The snowball throwing escalated, and now some of them were packed with rocks. The soldiers retaliated with blows from clubs.

No one's really sure what happened next, but someone yelled the word "fire". A British soldier took this literally, and shot into the press of people. More shots followed – then a shocked silence fell. Several colonists lay on the frozen cobblestones. Crispus Attucks, a black sailor, was dead, shot twice through the chest. Samuel Gray fell with a hole the size of a fist in his head. Five others were shot. Four of the men died.

You can visit the Granary Burying Ground today, where victims of the Boston Massacre are buried. People have reported feeling chilled when looking at the headstones of the five victims. Fun fact: there are 2300 gravestones in the cemetery … but it's estimated that over

5000 people are buried there. This discrepancy may be why the cemetery is home to so many paranormal phenomena, including faces showing up in photographs, floating lights, and shadowy figures wandering among the stones.

MARCH 6
The End of the Alamo, San Antonio, TX (1836)

Patchy moonlight lit up the desert as over one thousand men crept close to the small adobe mission. It was about 5:30 in the morning but the men, women, and children inside the mission were wide awake, waiting for the attack that was sure to come.

In 1835, General Antonio Lopez de Santa Anna was president of Mexico. American citizens who had settled in the Mexican province of Texas chafed under Santa Anna's dictatorial regime. An uprising in Texas pushed the Mexican military south across the Rio Grande. Soon the revolutionaries weren't content with simply freeing themselves from Santa Anna's rule. They wanted Texas to be an independent state.

Santa Anna was having none of this. He led his forces back across the Rio Grande, and ordered his soldiers to kill any insurgents they found. Santa Anna marched his troops towards the Alamo, a Spanish mission, now abandoned, that had been built in 1764 to bring Christianity to the natives. The general knew that a group of several hundred rebels were holed up there.

Santa Anna was ruthless – he drove his troops onward without mercy. Midwinter in Texas is still winter, and men and horses died by the hundreds as the Mexican army struggled to reach San Antonio. On February 23, Mexican troops surrounded the Alamo, pounding it with cannon shot to break down the adobe walls. Thirteen days of siege followed, while the defenders waited for reinforcements. Santa Anna positioned his troops outside the Alamo and ordered nearly continuous cannon and rifle fire, figuring that the constant barrage would wear the defenders down. It did – but the deafening attack also gave the defenders a bit of cover. Several messengers slipped through, and on March 2, a small group of reinforcements arrived from Gonzales, the only town to send help. The Alamo was defended by nearly two hundred men, including heavyweights of American frontier history Jim Bowie and Davy Crockett.

At 4 am on March 6, 1836, Santa Anna ordered his men to begin the final attack on the Alamo. Just as the dawn was breaking, the Mexican bugle players blared out a mournful tune called El Deguillo, or No Quarter. (Mexican-born Tejanos fighting in the Texan army recognized the song and interpreted it for the other defenders.)

The defenders filled cannons with any metal they could find – chains, door hinges, nails, horseshoes – and fired into the crowd of attackers. Nine-pound cannonballs tore through the Mexican lines. Some of the Mexican fighters turned away from the carnage, seeking retreat, but officers forced them back into battle at sword point.

The barrage of artillery fire from the Alamo was enough to repulse Santa Anna's first charge, and then the second. But troops in the third attack managed to scale the walls, at enormous cost. (Out of 800 men in one battalion, only 130 were left alive.) Fighting was room-to-room and hand-to-hand with pistols, clubs, knives, knees, and fists.

After ninety minutes, it was all over. All of the Texan men were dead (a few women and slaves were spared). But they sold their lives dearly – 1500 Mexicans were killed, and over 500 were wounded.

This butchery left its mark on the small mission. The first ghost sighting at the Alamo was reported just a few days after the massacre. A contingent of Mexican troops was sent to the Alamo with orders to finish destroying it. But the spirits of the place weren't finished defending it. The men saw six huge spirits, flaming phantoms they called "diablos" (demons), guarding the blood-soaked mission. The soldiers fled in terror.

By the end of 1846, the Alamo was again in the hands of the United States. The army reclaimed the ruins and rebuilt the mission. But they couldn't rid the Alamo of the spirits that still patrolled the crumbling walls.

The Alamo now sits in the middle of downtown San Antonio. Near the end of the 19th century, the city used the Alamo as its police headquarters and jail. The ghosts were furious at having to share their eternal home with common criminals. The spirits of the proud defenders made their displeasure abundantly clear; guards and prisoners alike were attacked with punches, gouges, kicks, screams, cold blasts, moans, and rattling cell bars. Soon, authorities had to move to a different facility.

Even now, the spirits of the Alamo make their presence known. Guests at nearby hotels tell of hearing the explosion of cannon fire and the screams of the wounded and dying. Witnesses have seen the defenders of the Alamo still patrolling the walls dressed in the bloody tatters of the clothes they died in. Other ghosts haunt the Alamo as well. A young blonde boy wanders the grounds every February, looking for his father. A woman draws water from a well near the church. A large Indian creeps up on people and glares at them. Staff and visitors smell the stink of gunpowder and burning wood, and experience cold spots and feelings of dread.

And always, always, the battle of the Alamo is not forgotten.

MARCH 7
The Lighthouse at St. Simon's Island, GA (1880)

Lighthouses seem to attract ghosts – or to put it more accurately, they seem to attract the kind of people who end up as ghosts.

Take St. Simon Island Lighthouse, for example. The original lighthouse there was destroyed during the Civil War, blown up by the Confederate Army to frustrate Union gunboats as they searched for a way into St. Simon's sound. After the war, in 1872, the lighthouse was rebuilt, with living quarters for two families. And here's where things got problematic.

The keeper's house was a two-story building, with the two floors connected by a central stairwell. The keeper in 1880 was a man named Frederick Osborne. He and his family lived on the ground floor, and his assistant, John Stevens, lived with his family on the second floor.

When two families share the same house, even if they're on separate floors, there's bound to be some friction at times. Unfortunately, tempers flared between Osborne and Stephens. Stephens barked that Osborne had said something "inappropriate" to Stephens's wife. On Sunday morning, March 7, the men went outside to discuss the matter. The discussion ended with Stephens firing a double-barreled shotgun at Osborne. A few pellets of the shot hit

Osborne, and he fell, writhing, to the ground. He clung to life for several days, but lost his battle at 3:30 Wednesday March 10.

Soon after that, the rumors began to fly that the lighthouse was haunted. Frederick Osborne was still watching over his lighthouse, and he was, it seemed, willing to help the living keepers as well. In 1908, the wife of a later keeper was tending the lighthouse while her husband was away. The mechanism developed some problems, and the wife was getting frustrated. She spoke out loud to Osborne, asking for his help from beyond the grave. She heard a rattling sound, and saw the spirit of the former lighthouse keeper bending over the lampworks. She fainted – and when she came around, she heard the reassuring "click-click" of the light functioning just as it should.

The ghost seems to have a playful side as well as a helpful nature. Carl Svendsen, the keeper from 1907 to 1935, complained that the ghost would constantly harass his dog Jinx.

Even now, the spirit of Frederick Osborne has been seen going up and down the old spiral staircase late at night as he continues to tend the lighthouse that was in his care. The brick cottage at the base of the lighthouse has been turned into a museum.

MARCH 8
Three-Fingered Riley, Lake Superior, MI (1920)

It's said that Lake Superior never gives up her dead. It's true that many ships have been lost on the lake, with many sailors never seeing the light of day again, their bodies fated to spend eternity in the murky depths.

The steamer *John Owen* was one of those unfortunate vessels. She had a crew of 22; 21 men and one woman. (The woman was the wife of Magnus Peterson – the two were stewards on board the ship.) The steamer was making a run from Duluth to Sault Ste-Marie with a hold full of barley when she was lost in a violent storm on November 13, 1919. The wreck happened, as far as anyone could tell, somewhere northwest of Whitefish Point, along Lake Superior's Shipwreck Coast. Everyone on board was killed, and the wreckage was never found.

The United States Coast Guard manned stations all along the shores of the Great Lakes, and the four stations in the forty miles of wilderness west of Whitefish Point were particularly desolate. Still, men patrolled the lonely stretches of woodland, even in the dead of the long winter's nights.

The following March, a Coast Guardsman was out with a team of sled dogs making a mail run when he found a body in the ice just off the shore at Crisp's Point. The corpse was chopped from its frozen tomb and taken by sled to a nearby station. The body was in excellent condition, but missing two fingers, possibly lost when the corpse was chopped free from the ice.

The body was identified as William J. Riley, an engineer on the *John Owen*. The guardsmen stored the body, still frozen, as long as they could while waiting for further instructions. But eventually, Riley had to be buried in the station cemetery – without his two missing fingers, which never did turn up.

Since then, the guardsmen who have the lonely job of patrolling the forests on the shore of Lake Superior along Shipwreck Coast have had company. "Three-Fingered Riley" still wanders the shore, looking for his missing fingers. Sometimes he'll walk right behind a patrolling guardsman, close enough for the living to hear his ghostly footsteps.

MARCH 9
John Glenn's Close Encounter (1962)

In the field of paranormal research, perhaps no evidence is more polarizing than orbs. Some researchers see orbs as vehicles for spirit energy, as a way for the soul to travel after its material life has ended. Others dismiss orbs as dust on a camera lens, or a bug that swooped down too close and too quickly for focus.

When astronaut John Glenn returned from his five-hour trip around the Earth, he shared the experience with Life magazine for their March 9, 1962 issue. He told the interviewer that the strangest sight of his three orbits around the planet came when he was crossing the Pacific, headed towards the United States. He glanced down to check the instrument panel, and when he looked up again, his entire field of vision was covered in orbs. He actually double-checked his instruments to make sure he hadn't tumbled to face outwards into deep space.

"There, spread out as far as I could see, were literally thousands of tiny luminous objects that glowed in the black sky like fireflies," Glenn said. "I was riding slowly through them, and the sensation was like walking backwards through a pasture where someone had waved a wand and made all the fireflies stop right where they were and glow steadily. They were greenish yellow in color, and they appeared to be about six to ten feet apart."

Glenn never did find out what those orbs were – all he could say was that he was certain that they hadn't been caused by anything coming out of his space capsule. "As far as I know, the true identity of these particles is still a mystery," he said.

MARCH 10
The Death of Zelda Fitzgerald, Asheville, NC (1948)

F. Scott Fitzgerald and his wife Zelda are icons of the Jazz Age. The glamorous couple personified the excess of the Roaring Twenties, only to see it all fall apart.

The Fitzgeralds married in 1920, just weeks after the publication of *This Side of Paradise*, Scott's debut novel. The book was a hit, and the couple traveled, partied, and basked in Scott's newfound fame. But the good life was not to last. The Fitzgeralds' marriage eventually crumbled under the strains of their excessive, unsustainable lifestyle. Mental instability took its toll as well.

The couple's daughter, Frances, was born in 1921, but her arrival didn't really cramp Scott and Zelda's style. They hired a nanny, then later shipped Frances off to boarding school.

In 1924, they moved to France, as friends told them the living there was cheap, and money was getting tight. Scott began work on *The Great Gatsby*, while Zelda painted.

Zelda flirted with painting for a while, as well as writing stories. Then she turned to ballet, practicing up to eight hours a day. But her daughter later revealed Zelda's creative flaws, saying, "It was my mother's misfortune to be born with the ability to write, to dance and to paint and then never acquired the discipline to make her talent work for, rather than against her."

Zelda suffered her first mental breakdown in 1930 in Paris. This led to years of struggle with mental illness. She was diagnosed with schizophrenia, and began to cycle through stays in institutions.

Scott and Zelda were two very creative people who loved each other, but ultimately, the pressure of trying to live together destroyed their relationship. They were both flawed artists, driven to create, but helpless to help each other fight their demons. Scott once admitted, "Perhaps 50 percent of our friends and relatives would tell you in all honest conviction that my drinking drove Zelda insane – the other half would assure you that her insanity drove me to drink."

Health problems plagued the Fitzgeralds as well, as their hard-partying ways in the 1920s caught up to them in the 1930s. Scott died of a massive heart attack in 1940. He was only 44 years old.

Zelda outlived her husband, but not by much – she didn't last a decade without him. Beginning in 1936, she was in and out of Highland Hospital, a lunatic asylum in Asheville, North Carolina. In early March 1948, doctors assured her she was well enough to leave. Zelda decided to stay for a few more weeks to make sure she was well enough to live on her own.

Late at night on March 10, Zelda and several other women were on the top floor of the Central Building at the hospital. Zelda had been getting electroshock therapy for years, and on that night, she was waiting for her next treatment. Electroshock therapy at Highland was given at night so the sudden surge in electricity usage wouldn't blow fuses on top of normal daytime use.

A fire started in the hospital's kitchen and spread up through the dumbwaiter shaft. By the time firemen arrived, shortly after 1 am, the four-story building was engulfed in flames. Zelda and eight other women died in the fire, their screams echoing in the blazing night. Zelda and four others had been heavily sedated. In addition, the windows of the rooms were locked and barred, and someone had cut the phone lines. A crowd of a thousand people could only look on helplessly, listening to the shrieks of the trapped women as they burned alive.

Willie Mae Hall, an aide at the hospital, later turned herself in to police and asked to be charged with arson, saying she "may have" set the fire. (She was also the one who had cut the phone lines.) Hall had been a patient at Highland, and had been released as cured, then hired. She wasn't charged, but she was committed to a different mental hospital.

Zelda Fitzgerald's spirit still haunts the grounds of the hospital where her troubled life ended. When Zelda appears, she sometimes holds a paintbrush, and many times her ghost wears red slippers – when her body was found, that was how searchers identified her charred corpse, by the fact that she was wearing red ballerina shoes.

Psychic Angelique Clark, from Arizona, joined Ghost Hunters of Asheville on their Haunted Montford tour. She and another investigator heard someone invisible whistling a peppy tune right beside them. Later, Clark captured a ghost photograph that appeared to be a running figure ablaze.

MARCH 11
Spirits of the Tsunami, Japan (2011)

For six minutes in the afternoon of March 11, 2011, a 9.1 magnitude earthquake rocked the sea floor in the Pacific Ocean near Japan. That quake shoved the mainland of Japan more than seven feet to the east, and sent waves crashing through the Pacific. Waves over six feet high dashed the coast of Chile, 11,000 miles away. But the waves that pummeled Japan caused the most damage, leveling houses, sweeping thousands to their deaths, and causing a meltdown at the Fukushima Daiichi nuclear power plant.

In mere minutes, nearly twenty thousand people were killed. Another 2,500 were missing, their bodies lost forever. Stunned survivors wandered through a wasteland of debris – smashed cars, dead animals, dead people, trees ripped from the ground, cars and boats tossed to the tops of buildings, themselves destroyed by the implacable power of nature.

In the days and weeks following the tsunami, survivors picked their way through the destruction and began to rebuild their lives. The dead were often right there alongside them, trying to wrap their minds around their sudden demise. Witnesses saw lines of ghosts queued up outside abandoned shops, waiting for the fractured building to open. Others spoke of seeing apparitions of ghostly figures running inland in terror, as if trying to outrun the wave, before vanishing in mid-stride. Still other witnesses saw people they knew, people that had perished in the disaster, who came to them asking for help before disappearing.

Taxi drivers reported picking up phantom fares – spirits just trying to get home. One driver spoke of picking up a young woman a couple of months after the disaster. She wanted to go to the Minamihama District, which had been razed to rubble by the tsunami. The driver told the woman that there was nothing left there to drive to, and she gave him a mournful stare. She calmly asked, "Have I died?" – then disappeared.

One elderly woman who had died in the tsunami developed the unsettling habit of dropping by a refugee camp for a refreshing cup of tea. Apparently, the senior citizen left behind big splotches of seawater wherever she went. The folks who encountered her felt so bad, they just couldn't bring themselves to tell her she was, in fact, dead.

MARCH 12
The Phantom Truck, Florida (1985)

Truck driver Harriette Spanabel of Brooksville, Florida, wrote in to *Fate* magazine in 1986 to tell about her experience with a phantom truck. Spanabel hauled produce from Florida up the East Coast. She claimed that a phantom truck would sometimes follow her on her runs. It usually appeared at night, and only showed up when she was returning from a trip.

In March 1985, Harriette and a friend, Kelly Rose, were coming back from Miami when they both saw the truck. The phantom truck joined them around 11:30 pm on the night of March 12. It followed them for about two miles on US 98, headed north. Harriette turned onto State Route 471, and the truck followed the friends for a while.

The truck appeared again when the friends were driving on a narrow two-lane road that ran through a state forest. It stayed behind them for thirty miles, then suddenly vanished. Kelly had been watching the phantom truck, and yelped when it disappeared. Harriette stopped her truck, and the friends got out to look.

On that stretch of road, there were no side roads, and very narrow shoulders, right up against the treeline. There was no place for a truck to pull off without either tipping over or landing in the forest. The other vehicle was just gone.

MARCH 13
Rex of Sunnybank, Pompton Lakes, NJ (1916)

Albert Payson Terhune was an extremely prolific author who wrote many books about what he knew best – dogs. He lived on a country estate called Sunnybank, where he raised thoroughbred collies. The dogs were prominent characters in many of his books, notably *Lad of Sunnybank*, *Buff: A Collie*, *Wolf*, and *Lochinvar Luck*.

The dogs in Terhune's novels were the epitome of canine heroism. They were loyal, trusting, devoted, obedient, perfect guard dogs, and they worshiped their master. In real life, though, Terhune's dogs were sometimes not so noble. One day in March, 1916, two of Terhune's dogs, Rex and the famous Lad, got into a scrap. Lad was one of Terhune's purebred collies, and Rex was a large mixed-breed dog. Rex had a nasty scar across his forehead, which made him look more vicious than he was. But on this day, he had an issue with Lad. The scrap turned into a fight, and the fight turned into an all-out running battle. The fight started in the woods on the estate and moved to the front lawn.

Both dogs were tearing savagely at each other, and the air was filled with apocalyptic barks and snarls. Rex had Lad pinned and was about to tear out his throat. Terhune acted without hesitation to save one of his dogs. He pulled out a hunting knife and stabbed Rex, killing him instantly.

Rex had been devoted to Terhune, lying at his feet for hours while the author wrote. Many months after Rex's death, Terhune had a visit from a friend of his, Henry Healy. Healy knew how much Terhune had loved his big dog, but apparently no one had told him that Rex had been killed. At the end of the evening's visit, as Healy was leaving, he sighed wistfully and told Terhune, "Bert, I wish there was someone or something on earth that adored me as much as Rex worships you. I watched him all evening. He lay there at your feet the whole time, looking up at you as a devotee might look up to his god."

That's when Terhune, shocked, told Healy that Rex had been dead for a year and a half.

MARCH 14
A Premonition of Death, Ireland (1873)

A writer from Ireland in the 19th century had a strange tale to relate, one that held a particular fascination for him: it happened to a member of his family.

One morning at the breakfast table, his great-aunt announced that she'd had a peculiar dream. His father, who had an interest in the strange, got out his notebook and wrote down the details as the old woman talked.

She'd dreamed that she was in a cemetery, which she'd recognized as Glasnevin. As she looked around at the gravestones, one of them caught her eye – because it had her name on it. The stone read: Clare S. D___, Died 14th of March 1873, Dearly Loved and Ever Mourned, RIP. What made this even odder was that the date on the headstone was exactly a year away from the day she'd had the dream.

The old lady wasn't superstitious, and soon the dream faded, as dreams tend to do. Months passed. One morning, she wasn't in her usual place at the breakfast table. She was very religious, and the family assumed she'd gone out to church. But when she failed to come back later that morning, the writer's father sent someone to the great-aunt's room to see if she was indeed there. She was found kneeling at her bedside, quite dead. The date was March 14, 1873, the date she'd seen on her own headstone in a dream, exactly a year before.

MARCH 15
Massacre of the Cathars, Languedoc, France (1244)

In the early Middle Ages, Christianity was beginning to take hold as a major world religion, but Christians still didn't have a lock on it. For one thing, even more than a thousand years after Jesus lived, people were still arguing about Christianity's exact tenets and meaning. There were dozens of fragmented sects, each with their own interpretation of Christ's teachings.

One of these groups was a gentle, unassuming group of folks who called themselves Cathars, or "the Pure Ones". In the 13th century, they were persecuted because they believed that the soul's redemption could be attained by following the example of Christ's life on earth. This infuriated the Catholics, who taught that salvation came through involvement in the Church. In 1209, Pope Innocent III declared a crusade to eliminate the Cathar "heresy".

As you can imagine, it was impossible to tell the Cathars from the Catholics just by looking. So, the pope's representative decided to err on the side of caution, and ordered *everyone* slaughtered. In one single day of this, over twenty thousand men, women and children were killed.

By 1243, the last of the Cathars were holed up in the last safe place they could find – Montsegur Castle in Languedoc, France. For ten months, they endured an onslaught of ten thousand crusaders. Finally, the crusaders got sick of messing around. On March 1, 1244, the Cathars were given two weeks to renounce their faith or be burned alive.

On the morning of March 15, the crusaders lit a huge bonfire outside the castle gates, and prepared to storm the castle, fully intending to make good on their threat. But just before the attack, the gates of the castle opened. The last Cathars, 216 of them, walked slowly down the hill in silence. One by one, they stepped into the bonfire voluntarily, giving up their lives rather than their beliefs.

The place where the Cathars martyred themselves is now called The Field of the Burned. Visitors to Montsegur Castle can sense the emotional energy there, even after centuries.

Witnesses have even seen the misty forms of the Cathars walking down the hill to their deaths.

MARCH 16
The Starved Rock Murders, Utica, IL (1960)

Starved Rock State Park is a place of incredible beauty. Hiking trails wind through the green depths of primeval woods, opening up into richly carved canyons that echo with the eternal dripping music of the water that formed them.

But this peaceful paradise was tainted by violence in 1960. On March 14, three women from Chicago – Frances Murphy, Mildred Lindquist, and Lillian Oetting – came to the park for a three-day getaway. They checked in at the Starved Rock Lodge, had lunch, then decided to hike to St. Louis Canyon.

That evening, Lillian Oetting's husband George tried to call her, just to check in and find out how the vacation was going. George tried calling Lillian at the lodge several times over the next two days, getting more and more worried when his calls went unanswered. On Wednesday, he called the lodge office and asked staff to check the women's rooms. That's when staff found out that the women's bags hadn't yet been unpacked, nor had their beds been slept in. The women had arrived in Frances Murphy's car, and a check of the parking lot revealed that the car had been in the same spot since their arrival on Monday. On Monday evening, a blizzard had dumped six inches of snow in the area.

George Oetting was now frantic with worry. He contacted authorities, and soon police were searching the park for the women. Later that day, their bodies were discovered in St. Louis Canyon. The women had been bludgeoned to death – a tree limb, its end covered with blood, lay nearby. The three women were laid out side-by-side, on their backs. They had been sexually assaulted. Two of the women were tied together with common white twine.

Investigators floundered for several months. With no suspects, the investigation went slowly. Then in September, they caught a break. They traced the twine to the kitchen at the lodge. Detectives questioned Chester Otto Weger, a former dishwasher at the lodge. After he failed a lie detector test, he became the prime suspect in the murders. Eventually, he confessed. Weger was convicted and sentenced to life in prison.

Ghosthunter Dan Norvell did an investigation deep inside the cave where the women's bodies were found. A spirit box session captured a voice saying *"Fourteen"* – a number with significance, as March 14 was the day the women went missing. While deep within the cave, Dan heard a woman's voice whisper *"help me"* from behind him.

Starved Rock Lodge has had many reports of paranormal activity, such as lights turning on and off, black apparitions, cold spots, and doors opening and closing by themselves. People hiking the trails have also reported seeing strange lights on the paths at dusk.

Of course, the three vacationing women who were killed in 1960 are not the only people to lose their lives at the park. Half a dozen people have fallen to their deaths from the sandstone cliffs over the years. And in the 1760s, a scuffle between the Illiniwek and Ottawa tribes ended up in a siege which gave Starved Rock its name. Chief Pontiac of the Ottawa was stabbed by the Illiniwek chief Kinebo at a tribal council meeting. Chief Kinebo and his warriors fled to a tall cliff in the area, pursued by the furious Ottawa tribe. Chief Pontiac's outraged warriors besieged the Illiniwek, who eventually died of starvation, thus christening Starved Rock.

MARCH 17
Crisis Apparition (1917)

Crisis apparitions, where a spirit appears to loved ones at the moment of death, seem to happen often in wartime. Such is the case of Captain Eldred Bowyer-Boyer. The 22-year-old pilot was shot down in a dogfight over France on March 19, 1917. Eldred's spirit was sensed by three people in three different places that day.

Mrs. Spearman, the captain's sister-in-law, was at the Grand Hotel in Calcutta, India. She was sitting with her newborn baby when she turned to see Eldred, who looked delighted to see her. She put the baby down, intending to give Eldred a hug in greeting, but when she stood back up, he had vanished. This startled her terribly, and she wrote to Eldred's mother about the incident.

At about the same time, Cecily Chater, Eldred's sister, was at home. She was still in bed, and her young daughter, Eldred's niece, came in to see her. The not-quite three-year-old chirped, "Uncle Alley Boy is downstairs!" This was the family's pet name for him. Cecily told her daughter that her beloved uncle was actually in France, but the girl insisted she'd seen him. This prompted Cicely to write to her mother later, with the observation of how cute it was that Betty remembered her uncle and spoke of him. A few days later, Cecily heard that her brother had been killed – on the day Betty had seen him downstairs.

The third incident was not a sighting of Eldred's ghost, but rather a feeling of impending doom. The captain's mother got yet another letter, this one out of the blue from an elderly friend, a Mrs. Watson. She wrote, "Something tells me you are having great anxiety about Eldred. Will you let me know?" The letter was dated March 19, 1917. A few days later, the report came of the captain's death. His mother had three somber letters to write back, replying to her trio of correspondents.

MARCH 18
The Hanging of Albert Howard, Gonzales, TX (1921)

Time waits for no man, not even for convicted criminals.

Albert Howard was convicted of an exceptionally brutal rape in January 1921. He was sentenced to hang on March 18, 1921 – the last man hanged in the county, but that bit of trivia was cold comfort for the man who would actually lose his life.

From his cell in the Gonzales County Jail, Howard could see the north face of the clock on the county courthouse, right next door. The courthouse was a regal stone building with a three-story tower. That tower housed a clock with four faces, each facing a cardinal direction. Howard could see only one of those faces, but he developed an obsession with the clock. He knew it was ticking away the minutes and hours he had left to live, and that weighed on him.

The fateful day arrived, heralded by the finite ticks of the grand Seth Thomas clock. Albert Howard, still brooding, was led out of his cell and up to the gallows. Before he mounted the gallows steps, he snarled a curse on the clock that had measured out the last hours of his life, saying that after he was hanged, it would never keep time accurately again, and never count down the minutes of anyone else's life.

As Howard was the last man hanged in Gonzales County, that part of his curse did come true. But so did the other part. Ever since the day he died, the clock has shown a different time on all four of its faces.

In the 1990s, a Gonzales resident spent $11,000 on repairing and restoring the clock. It didn't help. Author Ed Syers visited Gonzales and saw the courthouse. He left town at 5 pm, but made a circuit of the courthouse before he left. No two of the clock's faces showed the same time. The north face, the one Albert Howard could see from his cell, read 7:15.

The staff at the Gonzales County Jail Museum will admit to hearing strange echoes in the building. Doors slam, lights turn on and off with no human hand on the light switch.

But it is the tower clock that stands as the most visible reminder of Albert Howard's curse.

MARCH 19
The Millstadt Axe Murders, Millstadt, IL (1874)

A quiet house – too quiet – still and silent in the morning air. Break-of-day chores left undone. A concerned neighbor peering in through a front window. An entire family brutally murdered, hacked with an axe as they slept.

This scenario is a perfect description of the infamous Villisca Axe Murders. Unfortunately, this scene took place hundreds of miles from Villisca, and decades before that tragedy.

On the morning of March 19, 1874, Benjamin Schneider noticed that his neighbors, the Steltzenreides, were not up and about their first chores of the day. The horses and cows penned in the front lot had not yet been watered or fed. Schneider lived near the Steltzenreides on Saxton Road, outside Millstadt in southwestern Illinois. Schneider had come to collect some seed potatoes, but as he approached the house, he could tell something was horribly wrong.

Schneider knocked on the front door, but there was no answer. He peered through the window into the darkness of the house, but no movement within caught his eye. Schneider took his courage in both hands, turned the doorknob, and pushed the door open.

Frederich Steltzenreide, aged 35, was lying in a pool of blood just inside the door. His throat was slashed, and he'd been savagely beaten, badly enough that three of his fingers had been sliced off. Frederich's wife, Anna, 28, was found dead in her bed, also with her throat cut. With her were her children, Carl, 3 years old, and 8-month-old Anna. Anna was lying across her mother's chest, her tiny arms wrapped around her mother's neck. All three of them had also been bludgeoned to death. Carl's face was a pulpy, sodden mass of flesh, unrecognizable as human.

In the hallway lay the body of Carl Steltzenreide, the family patriarch, aged 70. He had been hacked with an axe so many times that he was nearly decapitated. His body was found sprawled on the floor in the hallway between his bedroom and the room in which the others were found. Investigators later theorized that Carl had heard an intruder come into the house, and that he had been attacked and killed as he tried to defend his family.

The only living creature in the house was the family's dog, a German shepherd named Monk. Monk was found keeping silent watch over the bodies of Anna and her children. Monk was very protective of the family, and known to be savage toward strangers. The dog's presence turned out to be a clue – the murderer had to have been someone Monk knew and trusted.

There were a couple of suspects in the vicious murders. Footprints led away from the house, along with a deep gouge in the ground, a furrow that looked like someone had been wearily dragging an axe behind him. The bloody footprints led straight to the front door of Frederick Boeltz, the younger Steltzenreide's brother-in-law.

Boeltz was married to Anna Steltzenreide's sister. He had borrowed $200 from the family, and had never repaid the debt. This led to bad blood between Boeltz and his in-laws. Boeltz was arrested and tried for the murders. Astoundingly, the jury found him not guilty.

The house in which the Steltzenreides were slaughtered no longer stands, but another house has been built on the site. And the land remembers. In 1986, Randy Eckert, a Millstadt local who grew up hearing about the murders, bought the farm and lived in the house for a couple of years.

A couple of years was enough for him.

Every year around the anniversary of the killings, Eckert and his wife would notice strange activity in the house – doors opening and closing, mysterious footsteps.

One year, the activity was very specific. Eckert and his wife were woken from sleep by the shivering and whining of their small dog. The wife said, "Do you hear something?" Eckert said he did. Suddenly the silence of the night was pierced by the ghostly howl of a dog – a dog that had lived a hundred years ago.

Then things got even stranger.

"We heard someone pounding on the door," Eckert says. "The door to the house has glass windows and it's a very small house. One step out of the bedroom and you can see the door, and that door was bounding. Somebody was beating on that door." Eckert walked to the door, keeping an eye on the window the whole time, and not seeing anyone outside. The sound faded the closer he got to the door, and by the time he reached the door, the pounding had stopped.

MARCH 20
Chief Buffalo Child Long Lance, Los Angeles, CA (1932)

Sylvester Long was a talented writer and noted activist on behalf of Native Americans. Ridiculously handsome, with high cheekbones, straight jet-black hair, and a physique that lent itself to the picture of a bare-chested brave in buckskins, Long was the very epitome of Native American cultural pride. He wrote popular articles in national magazines like *Good Housekeeping* and *Cosmopolitan*. He wrote a wildly successful autobiography in 1927, touted as a boy's adventure book, which quickly became an international bestseller. He was asked to star in a silent film in 1929, called *The Silent Enemy: An Epic of the American Indian* (the "silent enemy" being hunger). The movie, released in 1930, was the most realistic depiction of Indian tribal life up to that point. Sylvester Long was the consummate representative of Native American culture.

There was only one problem, an elephant in the room, but one that only Long knew about. He was not a full-blood Blackfoot Indian, as he claimed in his autobiography. Nor was he half-Cherokee, as he claimed earlier in his life.

Sylvester Long was, in fact, the son of former slaves who could claim just a tiny portion of Indian ancestry. Long's father, Joseph, was a school janitor in Winston-Salem, North Carolina who claimed to be half-white and half Cherokee, but he'd been born a slave. Long's mother, Sallie, was apparently seven-eighths white and one-eighth Croatan or Tuscarora.

Because racial law of the time deemed the Long family to be "colored", Sylvester wasn't allowed to attend the white West End School, where his father swept floors and emptied garbage cans. Instead, he had to attend the Depot Street Graded School for Negroes.

Sylvester was obsessed with Indians from a very early age. Genetics was kind to him: he had straight black hair, eyes with a bit of exotic tilt to them, and high cheekbones. In 1904, 13-year-old Sylvester ran away to join a Wild West show, and he seldom looked back. Passing as an Indian, he picked up some Cherokee from another performer. Using this knowledge and his looks, he talked himself into acceptance at the famous Carlisle Indian School in Pennsylvania.

He graduated in 1912 and Indianized his name to Sylvester Long Lance. He continued on to higher education, including a scholarship to St. John's Military School. Whenever anyone asked, he claimed to be Cherokee. He later refined this to "a Cherokee from Oklahoma", further distancing himself from his mixed-race origins.

Long Lance moved to Canada in 1916 – the United States hadn't yet entered World War I, and he wanted to fight. He enlisted in the Canadian army and was badly wounded in France in 1917. He came back to Canada in 1919, and picked up a job as a reporter. Later he began writing articles on the Indians of western Canada – articles that appeared in major American magazines.

This work on behalf of his adopted culture didn't go unnoticed, and in 1922, Long Lance was adopted into the Blood tribe, part of the Blackfoot Confederacy. He chameleoned again, now using his adoptive name, Buffalo Child, and presenting himself as Blackfoot.

In 1927, Long Lance moved to New York. In addition to writing articles that portrayed the rich culture of Native Americans, he wrote an "autobiography" commissioned by Cosmopolitan Book Company. (To be fair, he intended the book to be historical fiction, but his publisher promoted it as an autobiography.)

He'd reached the top. Little Sylvester Long, son of former slaves, who couldn't even go to a white school, had morphed into Chief Buffalo Child Long Lance, son of a Blackfoot chief. Critics called the book "authentic" and an "unusually faithful account." If this praise caused Long Lance any sleepless nights, he wasn't about to mention it.

The success of his book led to a movie deal. *The Silent Enemy* was another triumph for Long Lance. When it was released in 1930, *Variety* gushed, "Chief Long Lance is an ideal picture Indian, because he is a full-blooded one ... an author of note in Indian lore."

And in January 1931 it all fell apart.

A Native American consultant on the film, Chauncey Yellow Robe, had heard rumors whispered that Long Lance wasn't actually Indian – that, in fact, he was colored. He confided his suspicions to the studio's lawyers, and Long Lance was asked to prove his Indian ancestry ... which he couldn't do. To be fair, he did have some faint echoes of Indian heritage way back in his family tree. He just wasn't the full-blooded Indian he claimed to be ... or even the half-blood he'd posed as earlier. His genetics gifted him with an Indian physique, but genetics also dictated that he was black, and therefore considered inferior.

Long Lance was suddenly snubbed by New York society. He moved out to California to act as a bodyguard for socialite Anita Baldwin. Hounded by the idea that he'd been outed as black, Long Lance knew he couldn't return to the stifling racism of Winston-Salem where he'd begun. On March 20, 1932, he shot himself in the Queen Anne Cottage at Baldwin's estate.

The estate is now the Los Angeles Arboretum, and the cottage where Long Lance took his own life still stands. As a matter of fact, it's the house depicted in the opening scene of *Fantasy Island*. The tower perched on top of the cottage is where Tattoo rang the signal bell and shouted his famous weekly line, "De plane, boss! De plane!" And suave, elegant Mr. Roarke came out of the front door to say to each week's guests, "Welcome … to Fantasy Island."

True to his calling as an actor, a career tragically cut short by a .32 round, Chief Buffalo Child Long Lance has appeared as an extra in a crowd scene on *Fantasy Island*. Members of the crew not only saw him when the show was in production, they occasionally spoke with him. Someone finally figured it out – Long Lance was still sneaking in where he really didn't belong – and they got a photograph of the 1930s actor and showed it around on the set. Many of the crew recognized him as "the guy who kinda hung around". Producer Aaron Spelling didn't mind the uninvited extra. After all, this was one actor who wasn't going to demand a paycheck!

MARCH 21
The Headless Motorcyclist, Elmore, OH (1918 – recurring)

One aspect of casual paranormal investigation is the hobby of legend tripping. It involves a specific place (a lonely stretch of road, a bridge), a long-ago tragedy (a murder, a murder-suicide, a ghastly car accident), and a certain amount of magical thinking (if you turn your car off and put it in neutral, the ghosts of dead kids will push your car across the railroad tracks to safety).

The small town of Elmore, Ohio, is the site of one of these adventure stories. The "legend" part of the story says that a local boy had gone off to fight in World War I, leaving his girlfriend behind. He pined for the young lady constantly as he huddled in foxholes and dodged enemy fire. When the war ended, he came home and hopped on his motorcycle, intending to go straight to his ladylove's home to visit her and profess his undying adoration. But when he got there, he found his girl in the arms of another man – her fiancé.

The man stormed out of the house in a rage and threw a leg over the bike. He gave the throttle a savage twist and roared away from his faithless girlfriend's house. Just a few hundred yards away was the bridge over Muddy Creek. The rider lost control of his bike at the bridge, and crashed into a farmer's barbed wire fence. They found the rider and his motorcycle in pieces. The bike had been wrecked, and the headlight had been knocked off. The rider was decapitated.

And now, if you go to that bridge on the anniversary of the motorcyclist's death, on March 21, and blink your lights three times and honk your horn three times – the magical summoning power of three – you'll see the headlight of the phantom motorcycle leave the driveway of the abandoned farmhouse, speed around the curve, and disappear halfway across the bridge.

On March 21, 1968, Richard Gill and a friend went out to investigate the haunted bridge. They set up two cameras, a video recorder and a still camera, and a tape recorder. They got everything set up, then did the "summoning" ritual.

A light formed, raced down the farmhouse driveway, and came right towards the two men, vanishing halfway across the bridge. Just as advertised!

The men were jazzed at their success, so they decided to experiment. They tied a string across the bridge, then summoned the light again. It repeated its performance … and the string was left intact.

They decided to take the experiment a little further. This time, Gill would summon the light from his car, as advised … and his friend would stand in the middle of the bridge to intercept the light.

This experiment nearly ended in disaster. The light appeared as summoned, and barreled right for the investigator standing on the bridge. Gill waited for a few minutes, but his friend didn't come back to the car. Gill went looking – and found his friend at the side of the road with the crap kicked out of him. The friend had zero clue how he'd ended up in the ditch – he had no recollection of the event at all.

The friends decided to do one more experiment. (These were some dedicated investigators.) They positioned the car facing the bridge, pointing away from the farmhouse. They blinked the lights three times, honked three times, then started across the bridge. The light came out of the farmhouse driveway on cue, then it overtook them, passed through the car, and disappeared in its accustomed spot on the bridge.

These were all thoughtful, sound experiments. So, you might ask, what did the cameras and recorder pick up? Well, the results were disappointing. The movie film was simply blank. The still camera recorded some kind of unidentifiable light. And the sound recorder picked up some high-pitched noises, also unidentifiable.

MARCH 22
The Haunted Doll, Hokkaido, Japan (1918 – recurring)

The Japanese believe that dolls have "souls" – not too hard to imagine, in my opinion. When an old, well-loved doll gets too tattered and frayed to be played with any more, a Japanese family will bring it to a temple to be exorcized or burned.

There is one doll, though, that has a place of honor in Mannenji Temple on Hokkaido Island. It is said to be haunted by the spirit of a toddler.

The doll was purchased in 1918 by a young man named Eikichi Suzuki. The teenager was visiting the shops at Tanuki-koji, and the doll reminded him of his two-year-old sister Okiku. He bought it for her, and brought it home as a gift for the toddler.

Okiku adored the doll and played with it every day. Unfortunately, Okiku's life was cut short; she died shortly after that of a vicious cold. The girl's grieving family put the doll in a place of honor on the household altar, a reminder of the sweet child they had lost, and a focal point for their prayers for her soul.

Some time later, Okiku's parents noticed that the doll's hair was growing. In 1938, the family donated the doll to the Shinto priests at the Mannenji Temple. By that time, the doll's hair had grown down to its knees.

The doll has been safeguarded in the temple ever since, and its hair has miraculously continued to grow. Every Spring Equinox, the priests give the doll a haircut. Even so, the doll's hair grows several inches a year.

MARCH 23
Mr. Brossart's Rocking Chair, Muscatine, IA (1950)

In 1942, Floyd Holladay and his wife bought a rocking chair. There was nothing special about it; it was simply a pleasant, utilitarian piece of furniture, a platform rocker with red upholstery.

In 1950, the Holladays moved into a house they rented from relatives, Floyd Brossart and his wife. On March 17, Mr. Brossart died. Six days later, the rocking chair began to rock. And it rocked steadily for weeks.

The Holladays moved the chair to every room in the house, and the chair continued its placid rhythm. It had been Brossart's favorite chair when visiting, and it seemed the gentleman was still enjoying it.

The television show "We The People" did a story on the haunted rocking chair. By the time the episode aired on May 12, 1950, the chair had been rocking for fifty days straight. The television audience saw what a flood of visitors to the Holladays' home had already witnessed: a comfy-looking red rocking chair, rocking slowly at times, then more energetically.

Tragedy struck as the chair made its way back to Iowa. The chair was crated after its television appearance and taken to the airport for shipment. Vandals at the air freight depot in New York broke into the crate, and ripped the upholstery and tore up the fabric and bracing on the back.

Mrs. Holladay tried to straighten the back bracing, and tacked the upholstery back down. The chair still rocked, but only for five or ten minutes at a time. And it never rocked with the same enthusiasm as before. (This is why we can't have nice things.)

MARCH 24
The Ghost of Judy, Norfolk, England (1883)

In March 1883, Mary Bagot and her daughter went on vacation to Minton, France. They had left their dog, a black and tan terrier, at home in Norfolk. Judy was being cared for by the family's gardener.

Mary and her daughter were sitting at dinner in the hotel's dining room when Mary saw her dog run across the room. She unthinkingly exclaimed, "Why, there's Judy!" The incident was weird enough that her daughter mentioned it in her journal entry for the day.

A few days later, Mary got a letter from home. In it was the sad news that Judy had suddenly taken ill and died. Mary was convinced that the little dog had died on the day she'd been seen in the hotel dining room.

MARCH 25
The Triangle Shirtwaist Factory Fire, New York City, NY (1911)

In the early 1890s, immigrants flocked to America in search of a better life for themselves and their families. When they got here, though, they discovered that the streets of New York City were not, in fact, paved with gold.

Many of them found work in the factories that were springing up in American cities. Factory owners jumped on this source of cheap labor. Many immigrants worked in factories like the Triangle Waist Company in lower Manhattan, which made women's blouses. Working conditions were abysmal, with workers – mostly immigrant women in their teens and twenties – putting in twelve-and-a-half hour days for $6 a week. Even worse, they had to supply their own thread, needles, irons, and sometimes, their own sewing machines.

The conditions at the Triangle factory were excruciating. The women couldn't even use the building's bathroom, and doors were locked so they couldn't slow down production by going outside for a break. Most egregiously, even though the Triangle factory had water buckets for extinguishing fires, they were empty.

Deplorable working conditions at the Triangle and other garment factories led tens of thousands of workers to strike in 1909, seeking a 20% raise, safer working conditions, and a 52-hour work week. Most factory owners settled, but the Triangle's owners, Isaac Harris and Max Blanck, were real jerks about the whole situation. They were very hostile to the unions, and when the strike ended in February 1910, the workers at the Triangle factory went back to the same old jobs with the same wretched conditions.

On the afternoon of Saturday March 25, 500 people were working on the top three floors of the 10-story Asch Building. Shortly before the 4 pm closing whistle blew, someone tossed a cigarette butt into a bin of scrap fabric on the eighth floor. Within fifteen minutes, the top floors of the building were ablaze, turned into what one firefighter called "a mass of traveling fire".

Women, girls, and a few men panicked and ran for the exits. Firefighters later found a pile of bodies six feet high jammed up against the door to the back stairway. The single fire escape collapsed under the weight of people trying to get to safety.

The ladders of the fire trucks only reached to the sixth floor. People, seeing that the ladders were several floors down, chose to jump two and three at a time to avoid burning to death. One woman reached the elevator only to find an open, empty shaft. Desperate to escape the flames, she wrapped a muff around her hands and leapt into the shaft, grabbing the cable and sliding to the bottom. She was pretty banged up from her daring escape, but she survived.

Others weren't so lucky. Seventeen men and 129 women perished in the fire. Most of them were Italian and Jewish immigrants. The oldest was 43. The youngest, eleven. Some 350,000 people filled the streets for the funeral procession.

Harris and Blanck were tried for manslaughter, but incredibly, they were found not guilty. They did pay out $75 in compensation to the families of each victim – but they raked in $400 per death from the insurance.

The upper floors of the building were destroyed by the fire, but were rebuilt, and became a library and classrooms for New York University. The Asch Building is now known as the Brown Building, and the echoes of the horrific tragedy still reverberate within its walls.

Many students and staff working on the upper floors of the building have felt an irrational sense of panic, of wanting to get out of the building no matter what. Some people do buckle under the feeling and leave.

Another phenomenon manifests as disembodied screams. These usually ring in the halls in late afternoon, at the end of the work day. Some witnesses smell the reek of smoke and burning flesh.

Perhaps the most unnerving aspect of this haunting is the mirror on the ninth floor. There is a tall rectangular mirror just outside the elevator. Sometimes, a person will look in the mirror and not recognize their reflection. It's all there – height, clothes, way of standing – but the head and face move slightly, as if seen through a flickering flame.

MARCH 26
The Devil's Coins, Romania (1925)

Eleonore Zugun was feeling great. The ten-year-old Romanian girl was on her way to visit her grandmother in Buhai, a few miles away from home. Eleonore skipped along, humming a little tune under her breath. She clutched her coat tightly as the February cold gnawed at her.

Suddenly she stopped. Something had winked at her from the side of the road. She bent down for a closer look. There in the dust were several shiny coins. Eleonore picked them up and rubbed them on her skirt. She'd not seen much money in her life – it was 1923, and nobody in her village had much – but it looked like … well, a lot. Maybe not a lot, but enough to buy something …

Eleonore stopped at the store before she went to her grandmother's house. She pushed the coins across the counter at the shopkeeper, and shyly pointed at jar after jar of candy until the shopkeeper stopped putting sweets in the bag. Eleonore grasped the bag and trotted out of the store, a grin spreading across her thick, plain features.

Eleonore hid behind a tree, stuffing sweets into her mouth. They were so good! She didn't want to share. She finished the last piece of candy, then went on her way to her grandmother's house.

She'd forgotten, though, that her rotten little cousin was going to be at Grandmother's too. Her cousin raced up to her, then stopped short. "You've had chocolate! I can smell it on your breath!" her cousin shrilled accusingly. And just her luck, Grandmother heard the whole thing.

The ancient woman hobbled out to see what all the fuss was about. Grandmother was over a hundred years old, and people said she was a witch. Eleonore was a little scared of her. Grandmother pointed a gnarled finger at her, and she quailed. "Where did you get candy, child?"

"I … there were some coins … I picked them up," Eleonore stammered.

Grandmother flinched, then spit between her fingers. "Dracu – the devil – left them there to tempt you! Now you'll never be free of him!" She spun on her heel and hobbled out of the room.

So began the most-studied poltergeist case of the 20th century. After Eleonore's confrontation with her grandmother, poltergeist activity started to plague the house. Stones crashed against windows, and the sound of shattering glass filled the house. Eleonore's superstitious grandmother was convinced that Eleonore was possessed by the devil, and ordered her back to her home in Tulpa.

Three days later, the activity began again. Furniture crashed around rooms. A jug full of water rose slowly into the air and floated several feet without spilling a drop. Eleonore's family panicked and sent her to the monastery at Gorovei. They were convinced that the telekinesis was a sign of demonic possession.

But the violent activity followed Eleonore there. The monks performed an exorcism on her, but it didn't change a thing. She was forced to leave the monastery, and her parents had her committed to a lunatic asylum.

Fortunately, newspaper accounts of her bizarre experiences made their way to the outside world. The Austrian psychical researcher Fritz Grunweld heard of Eleonore's case, and sprung her from the asylum. He got her sent back to the monastery where she could be observed.

In September 1925, Austrian countess Zoe Wassilko-Serecki came to see Eleonore at the monastery. Countess Wassilko was fascinated by the paranormal, and also had an interest in psychoanalysis. She was also part Romanian, so she could speak to Eleonore in her own language. While at the monastery, the countess saw poltergeist activity for herself. She took copious notes, eventually writing a book about Eleonore's case. By January 1926, she had convinced Eleonore's family to let the girl come to Vienna with her.

The poltergeist activity continued, and many psychical researchers were able to watch Eleonore and interact with her. Eleonore was the focus of many physical attacks, apparently by the malevolent "Dracu". She was slapped, thrown out of bed, scratched, and bitten. She had her hair yanked viciously, and a couple of times she found her shoes filled with water. Starting in March 1926, Eleonore began to complain that it felt like her hands and fingers were being pricked with needles – and sometimes actual needles were found embedded in her flesh.

Despite being totally illiterate, Eleonore occasionally was seized by a compulsion to do automatic writing. What flowed from her pen was coherent Romanian. One letter revealed the location of a lost set of keys, which the countess's secretary had misplaced.

On April 30, 1926, famed ghost hunter Harry Price arrived in Vienna to visit Eleonore and the countess. He came away convinced that the telekinetic phenomena happening around the 13-year-old could not be explained by normal means. Price invited the countess to bring Eleonore to London to his National Laboratory of Psychical Research.

One of the most perplexing of these telekinetic phenomena was witnessed in the lab. A small metallic letter C disappeared from a locked cupboard, where letters for a notice board were stored. Eleven days later, the letter turned up. It was found clipped around the metal rim of a pocket knife case belonging to Professor Tillyard, clamping it shut. Tillyard had used the knife several times that day, and the letter hadn't been there the previous times.

The countess observed that the phenomena surrounding Eleonore had two stages. The first stage was the astounding amount of telekinesis going on around the young girl. About six months later, the marks – scratches, bites, welts like stigmata – started showing up on Eleonore's skin. The bite marks didn't correspond with Eleonore's teeth. They were consequently blamed on "Dracu".

After Eleonore and the countess left London for Berlin, the telekinetic phenomena began to fade. The biting and scratching, though, continued … and now the bites were smeared with what appeared to be saliva. This slime was tested and found to be teeming with microorganisms … germs that were different than those cultured from Eleonore's mouth.

Dr. Hans Rosenbusch invited Eleonore and the countess to his home for a sitting. Shortly afterward, he claimed that he saw the countess scratch Eleonore's neck while pretending to brush her hair, and declared Eleonore to be a fake. Harry Price stepped up in Eleonore's defense, saying that the tests he'd done with her had all been rigidly controlled. What's more, the countess hadn't been there for any of the tests, and still, unexplained phenomena had occurred. Countess Wassilko sued the doctor for libel.

All this controversy became irrelevant in 1928, when Eleonore had her first period. All paranormal activity stopped entirely. Eleonore Zugun moved back to Romania, became a hairdresser, got married, and lived out the rest of her days.

MARCH 27
Hell's Mouth, North Adams, MA (1865)

The middle of the 19th century was a time of expansion and innovation in the United States. Railroads crisscrossed the country, transporting freight, livestock and people all over in a fraction of the time those trips had taken previously. The "iron horse" was dominating the country.

In North Adams, Massachusetts, construction began on the Hoosac Tunnel in the early 1850s. This was a marvel of engineering. The tunnel had to cut through nearly five miles of the rocky Berkshire mountainside, forging a path through the earth itself. The tunnel was 24 feet wide and 20 feet tall, plenty of room for the trains that would soon run through on their way to the west. The excavators started at each end of the 2,000-foot-high mountain – and amazingly enough, using nothing but plumb bobs, wire, and pencils, they met in the middle, less than one inch off of perfectly square. When the tunnel was finished, it became the most popular route in New England, with forty trains a day passing through the mountain.

The tunnel is elevated in the middle, and slopes slightly down from there to each end. This allows water to drain out, but it also blocks a clear view through the tunnel. Anyone standing at either end cannot see the proverbial light at the end of the tunnel – it just looks black and forbidding.

Construction was plagued with issues from the beginning. The new excavating machine the diggers were using immediately got stuck in the rock. The crew had to choose a different spot to start digging. The project ended up taking 24 years to complete, at a cost of over $21 million (about $300 million today). During construction, workers walked off the job on a regular basis, saying the project was cursed. Approximately 195 workers were killed during the construction of the tunnel. It's no wonder the Hoosac Tunnel is considered one of the most haunted spots in New England.

The tunnel's most tragic accident happened on October 17, 1867. Crews were busy digging the central shaft, a thousand-foot-high vertical space that would mark the halfway point of the tunnel. It was designed with a giant bucket sort of arrangement. The idea was that when the shaft was completed, workers could be lowered down to the tunnel from the middle, instead of having to hike in two and a half miles from either end.

The lamps used were fueled with volatile naphtha, and fumes from one of the lamps exploded. The hoist house at the top of the shaft caught fire and burned. The shack was also used to store the explosives used in blasting, and the oil for the lamps. The wooden floor of the shack soon collapsed. Three hundred newly sharpened drill bits being stored in the shack rained down on the men below in a deadly hailstorm of metal. The winch mechanism plummeted down the shaft next, followed by flaming chunks of the hoist house. The air pumps failed, leaving the thirteen men in the shaft without oxygen, and the shaft, sixty feet deep, began to fill with water.

In the days that followed, a worker was lowered into the shaft several times to look for survivors. (Before going down for the first time, he prudently made out his will.) He had to be pulled up quickly the first time, as he had passed out from lack of oxygen.

A year passed before workers could pump the water out of the shaft. During the winter of that year, people who lived near the tunnel reported seeing shadowy, indistinct shapes near the central shaft. Workers said they saw apparitions of their colleagues carrying axes and shovels, shades that would appear for a moment, then vanish. They never left any footprints in the snow.

When the shaft was cleared, and the oxygen pumps restored, workers ventured down and made a grisly discovery. Some of the thirteen men in the shaft had been killed by falling debris … but some had survived. The survivors had managed to construct a crude raft, hoping to ride the rising water to safety. But they had died, either of asphyxiation or starvation.

Once the bodies of the men were recovered and buried, their ghosts were not seen again, although people did hear the occasional anguished groan from the shaft.

In October 1874, just seven years after the central shaft disaster, Frank Webster vanished into the tunnel. Days later, searchers found him … but he was not the same. He claimed ghostly voices had lured him into the tunnel. Once inside, shadowy apparitions had taken his hunting rifle and beat him with it. When found, he had cuts and contusions … and no rifle.

One hundred years later, in 1973, Bernard Hastaba decided to walk all the way through the tunnel (a colossally foolish idea, by the way – trains still run through it). He went into the tunnel on the North Adams side.

He never came out.

And he couldn't be found inside, either. He'd just walked into the tunnel and vanished.

One of the weirdest stories to come out of the tunnel was the March 1865 disaster. Since the tunnel took 24 years to complete, technological advances during construction made the job easier at times … and other times, it went horribly wrong.

On March 20, 1865, a team was working on the tunnel under the direction of an explosives expert, Ringo Kelley. Instead of old-fashioned black powder, Kelley was using a new explosive: nitroglycerin. The workers were supposed to place the charge, then take shelter in a safety bunker. No one knows why, but Kelley touched off the blast prematurely, killing his two companions, Ned Brinkman and Billy Nash. The explosion brought tons of rock crashing down, crushing the two men to paste.

Soon after the explosion, Ringo Kelley vanished. (There were some people who thought that he deliberately set off the explosion before his coworkers had time to take cover, so he might have been trying to save his bacon.) Exactly a year later, though, Kelley reappeared … he was found strangled to death, in nearly the same place where Ned and Billy had been killed. Had the spirits of Ringo's coworkers gotten revenge for their untimely deaths?

MARCH 28
The Bethnal Green Disaster, London, England (1943)

Londoners during the Blitz really learned the meaning of "Keep Calm and Carry On". The Luftwaffe carried out nighttime bombing raids on London and other British cities from September 1940 to May 1941. The raids caused enormous destruction of property, and casualties were severe. Some 43,000 British civilians were killed, and another 139,000 were wounded. London was pounded for 76 nights in a row – enough to wear down anyone's nerves.

But the British people were unbowed. During the second month of the Blitz, Princess Elizabeth addressed the nation. The clear, piping voice of the fourteen-year-old princess came over the airwaves, reassuring her people that she shared their pain. "We are trying, too, to bear our share of the danger and sadness of war," she said. "We know – every one of us – that in the end all will be well."

Londoners, especially, tried to make the best of the situation. The government allowed people to use the Underground system as air raid shelters, a decision that saved thousands of lives. People put children to bed in hammocks suspended between the tracks. They passed around cups of tea, and sang songs to keep their spirits up.

But one night in March 1943, tragedy struck the Bethnal Green tube station. The horrors of the Blitz had begun to fade – Britain's Darkest Hour was a couple of years past. But the skies still held the possibility of danger. Earlier, Allied planes had bombed Berlin, and they'd done a thorough job. Londoners were understandably nervous. German bombers had been concentrating on Russia, but that could change.

Around 8:30 on the night of March 3, an air raid siren wailed a warning. Hundreds of people headed for the Bethnal Green station, not yet operational. Anti-aircraft artillery in nearby Victoria Park began launching rockets, but here's the thing: a shell headed up sounds an awful lot like a shell headed down. About 1500 people had made it to safety underground, but there were about 300 people crowded on the sidewalk when a cry went up: "It's a bomb!"

Rain had made the nineteen steps to the bottom slick, and the only light came from a dim 25-watt bulb. To their credit, people tried not to panic, tried to make their way down the treacherous steps in an orderly fashion.

But three steps from the bottom, a woman carrying her young child lost her footing and fell.

An elderly man stumbled and fell on top of the two. No one could see much of anything, so those in the back of the crush didn't see any reason not to keep pressing forward. Within fifteen seconds, the crowd of people had surged forward into a death trap, suffocating 173 people in the narrow stairwell. The victims were overwhelmingly women and children. Some of the bodies were so badly mangled they had to be identified by their clothing. All of them were a sickly shade of purple from the asphyxiation.

The government suppressed the story. There had been no air raid, and no bombs had been dropped. But 173 people – 62 of them children – had been killed in a panicked stampede. Authorities felt that the truth would be a blow to morale, so they leaned on newspapers to report that the casualties were the result of a direct hit by the Luftwaffe.

Fifty years later, a memorial plaque was installed at the Bethnal Green station. In December 2017, the Stairway to Heaven memorial was unveiled. It's a full-sized replica of the fatal staircase, with the names of the victims carved into the teak wood of each step.

But the victims of the tragedy don't seem to be satisfied with a memorial, beautiful though it is. Workers at the station have reported hearing children sobbing, women screaming, and sounds of mass panic. The sounds start quietly at first, then rise to a crescendo of terror. Quite the unsettling experience late at night in an empty station.

MARCH 29
Voorhies Castle, IL (1923, recurring)

Nels Larson emigrated from Sweden to America in 1867. He came, like so many others, to seek his fortune. Unlike many of his fellow immigrants, he actually found it. He settled in Piatt County, on the Illinois prairie. He went to work for a landowner named William Voorhies. Voorhies owned vast tracts of land in the area, but found the management of all that property overwhelming. Larson saved every penny he made, and soon began renting land from his boss. Renting became buying, as Larson grabbed up more and more land. In 1872, he sent word to his fiancée, Johannah Nilson, still in Sweden, that she should join him in America. She did, and when she arrived later that year, they got married.

Larson's success continued, and soon he was renting property to other farmers. In fact, he eventually had the entire town of Voorhies under his thumb, renting businesses to the townspeople.

Nels Larson never gave up the greedy, grasping habits that helped him claw his way to the top. He was generally disliked by ... well, pretty much everyone – his tenants, his employees, even his family.

If this bothered Larson any, he didn't show it. By 1900, Larson was comfortably ensconced in his little empire on the prairie. He built himself a huge manor house, designed to look a grand home in the Old World style, a reminder of the Sweden he'd left behind.

The castle was a strange hodgepodge of architectural styles. The house was lavish, built of only the finest materials. Larson was extremely exacting – many times, he would send entire loads of lumber back to the warehouse because he'd discovered one or two boards with knots in them.

One of the oddest parts of the estate was the clock tower barn, built in 1910. Larson was fascinated – some said obsessed – with clocks. Voorhies Castle was filled with timepieces, from small clocks in the bedroom to the large grandfather clock in the reception hall. Nelson indulged his obsession with the construction of a clock tower. He ordered a Seth Thomas clock, then had the barn built to house the magnificent piece. The barn took five years to build, even longer than the house. The tower itself was 68 feet tall, and had to be reinforced to support the mechanism of the clock, which weighed two tons.

Legend says that when Nels Larson died on March 29, 1923, the clock struck thirteen times to mark his passing. The clock continued this strange chiming each year for the next fifty years. The tower was destroyed by a tornado in the summer of 1976 ... but stories say that the phantom clock continues to chime thirteen times every March 29, in honor of the anniversary of its owner's death.

MARCH 30
The Biltmore Hotel Fire, Boston, MA (1963)

In the early morning hours of March 29, 1963, the party was still going strong at the Sherry Biltmore Hotel in Boston. Cast and crew members of *The Sound of Music* were having a bittersweet celebration: one of the cast members was leaving the touring production. Suites 601 through 611 rang with laughter and music as the actors and crew shared drinks and memories.

In addition to the partying adults, an eight-year-old boy was still awake at that late hour. His mother played one of the nuns in the musical. Bored with the party, he had wandered away to Room 655, which was unoccupied. He brought a book of matches with him.

The boy sat down cross-legged on the floor and took out the matches. He pulled one from the book and snapped it alight. The match made a satisfying fizz sound, and the boy smiled. He dropped it and lit another. Pop … fizz … what a fun sound!

But the boy's innocent amusement would have fatal consequences. One of those matches, lit in fun, started a fire that engulfed the sixth floor of the hotel. An actress stepped out of the room to get away from the cigarette smoke, and found that the hallway was filled with smoke of a different, deadlier kind. One of the partygoers clawed a fire alarm to blaring life, but oddly, the alarm wasn't set up to alert the fire department. A police officer happened to be passing by the hotel on his rounds, and became concerned when he noticed lots of people climbing out of the windows. Seconds later, he saw the flames. He called it in, and soon help was on the way. Ten ladder trucks raced to the scene, and were able to rescue about 75 people from the blaze. Forty of those rescued were members of the cast and crew of the musical. They climbed out through a small window and stood on a terrifyingly narrow ledge awaiting rescue.

Even with the heroic actions of the firefighters, 27 people were injured and four people died in the inferno. Those deaths left their mark.

Berklee College of Music bought the hotel in 1972 and repurposed it into a dorm. Students that live there are quite familiar with their ghostly roommates. Even after the college renovated the building in 1999, people continued to experience the supernatural. One student, who reported their experience anonymously, told of something that happened when they lived there in 1985.

"My roommate and I [were] sitting doing homework and the TV [went] flying across the room … Oftentimes at night and sometimes in the afternoon, there would be knocking on the door … frantic knocking. We'd open it while the knocking was happening, and there wouldn't be anyone there."

Another spirit that haunts the dorm seems to be obsessed with water, perhaps a reaction to having perished in a fire. Faucets will turn on by themselves, filling the sink, then flooding the room and the hallway beyond. The spirit's fascination even extends to the toilet, which flushes by itself.

MARCH 31
The Old Barfoot House, Troy, AL (1932-1937)

There's nothing creepy about the Old Barfoot House in Troy, Alabama. Well … nowadays, there's nothing creepy. But the family that lived here in the 1930s were terrorized by a horrifying poltergeist that eventually scared them so badly that they left.

And they never came back.

Imagine this: you're sitting with your partner in the living room. The night is pressing up against the windows, but inside, all is cozy. The kids are in bed, and it's just you two having a snuggle at the end of the day.

Suddenly, there's a man standing there, right in your house, right there in front of you. He's wearing black pants and a white shirt that practically glows. His hair is black too, and his eyes … his eyes stare at you with hatred burning in their unfathomable depths. He glares at you for several long moments … and that's when you notice all the blood. Blood is dripping from his shoulders, running down his waist to his legs, pooling in unspeakable puddles on the floor.

The man gives you one last withering look, then turns and walks away, leaving puddles of blood as he goes. He leaves the living room and goes through the dining room as you stare at your partner, still stunned at the appalling apparition. Then it hits you – the man is heading for the back bedroom – ohmigod the kids are sleeping in there! You both shoot off the couch and chase after the man, following the bloody footprints. The trail of shocking gore leads all the way to the children's room … but when you throw the door open, no one is in there, except for the kids, sound asleep.

The family escaped some supernatural tragedy that night, but the apparition kept haunting them. The family stuck it out for five years, but five years of waking up to see a bloody spirit standing at the foot of the bed staring at them with pure malevolence was enough. The family moved – and the spirit was never seen again.

The history of the house might provide a clue to the restless spirit's identity. In the late 1800s, Troy was ravaged by a violent crime spree. An axe murderer was on the rampage – twenty-one men, women, and children were hacked to death, their bodies spread all over town.

When panic sets in, a community can lose sight of justice. The townspeople looked around for someone to blame. Suspicion fell on a drifter named Tom Johnson. Lynch law prevailed. A gallows was set up in the front yard of the Barfoot House, and Johnson was hanged on March 31, 1899. Coincidentally or not, the hanging also marked the end of the mysterious killing spree.

So was Johnson guilty? Maybe, maybe not. But thirty-odd years later, a bloody apparition stalked the Barfoot House. Was it the ghost of an evil murderer looking for more victims? Or was it the tortured spirit of an innocent man seeking revenge for an unjust death? We'll never know.

APRIL

APRIL 1
The Phantom Hitchhiker, Cape Province, South Africa (1978)

The well-worn story of the phantom hitchhiker tends to drift, sometimes, from paranormal business into the realm of urban legend. An experience from South Africa, though, has details that push it firmly back into the category of "ghost story".

One evening in April 1978, Corporal Dawie van Jaarsveld was riding his motorcycle along a road in Cape Province, South Africa. He saw a young woman standing at the side of the road, and stopped. He was headed for his girlfriend's house, and would be passing the town of Uniondale, so he asked the girl if she wanted a ride into town. She mumbled something in reply, which he took to be "yes" – he was wearing a helmet, so his hearing was muffled. He had also been listening to his radio through an earpiece. He gave the girl his spare earpiece so she, too, could enjoy the radio, and his spare helmet. She buckled the helmet on, threw a leg over the seat behind him, and settled herself for the ride.

They had gone about ten miles when Dawie felt the back wheel of the motorcycle skid. He slowed, then stopped; he wanted to check to make sure the back tire wasn't going flat. He heeled the bike over on the kickstand and looked behind him to tell the girl to dismount first.

That's when he realized she'd disappeared.

His heart slammed for a few moments. She hadn't fallen off, had she? The answer, clearly, was no. The spare helmet she'd been wearing was strapped to the passenger seat. Dawie undid his helmet strap and clawed his helmet off. That's when he got another nasty jolt.

He was still wearing his own radio earpiece. The earpiece he'd lent the girl, to listen to music? It was in his other ear.

Almost exactly two years later, on April 4, 1980, Andre Coetzee was riding his motorcycle along the same stretch of road. As he passed the place where Dawie had picked up his phantom passenger, he felt someone put their arms around his waist from behind. Andre panicked and cranked the throttle, trying to outrun the eerie feeling. Something popped the back of his helmet, three quick sharp raps. Andre pushed the bike up over 100 mph before he felt the unseen presence depart.

The young lady didn't only target motorcyclists. Several car drivers during that time reported picking up a young woman on that same stretch of road, and always in early April. Their stories agreed in the details of her appearance – she was even dressed the same in every account. Every story ended the same, too: the hitchhiker vanished sometime during the ride.

The story got around, and eventually, a pilot came forward with a tragic tale. His fiancée, Maria Roux, had been killed in a car accident on April 12, 1968 … at the exact location where the phantom hitchhiker would habitually be picked up. The hitchhiker's description matched Maria's, even down to the clothes she was wearing when she'd been killed.

APRIL 2
The Singing Nurse, Selma, AL (1865)

The three-story building that now houses the Vaughan-Smitherman Museum was built in 1847. The stately red-brick building is fronted by four elegant marble Ionic columns that reach from ground level three stories up to the pediment that graces the building's brow. Located just two blocks from the Alabama River in Selma, the building was constructed in 1847 as the Central Masonic Institute, a school for orphans and for the children of Masons who'd fallen on hard times. It has also served as a courthouse, a military school, and from 1911 to 1960, as Vaughan Memorial Hospital. Nowadays, it's a museum that displays Victorian antiques, exhibits of medical equipment, and Civil War memorabilia.

It is from the Civil War that the gentle haunting at the museum comes. During the war, Selma was one of the South's major manufacturing centers, churning out munitions, including Southern warships. Selma was home to a shipyard, a naval foundry, an army arsenal, and gunpowder works. The North had the South beat hollow when it came to industry and manufacturing, so Selma was crucial to the South's war effort.

The Battle of Selma was fought on April 2, 1865, just one week before Lee's surrender at Appomattox. Led by Major General James H. Wilson, 13,500 Federal troops invaded southern Alabama as part of the Union campaign through the South known as Wilson's Raid. Wilson's troops met Southerners – only 2,000 of them, mostly boys and old men – under Lieutenant General Nathan Bedford Forrest. Forrest's troops got trounced at Ebenezer Church, and he retreated to Selma. Union troops followed, and overran the flimsy defenses. The Union forces destroyed the arsenal and navy factories at Selma, dealing a devastating blow to the Confederacy.

After the battle, wounded soldiers were cared for at the Masonic building. One of their caretakers was a kind, beautiful young nurse, who went about her gruesome duties with a cheerful heart. She even celebrated a rainy day – as refreshing spring rains fell in Selma, the young nurse sang in a clear, lilting voice.

Her grateful moments of joy still linger in the halls of the Vaughan-Smitherman Museum. The nurse's pretty singing can still be heard along the corridors of the museum's third floor, and in the gardens on the grounds, whenever it rains.

APRIL 3
Disaster at Split Rock, Syracuse, NY (1918)

In April 1980, Tim Zorn was taking a bicycle trip through New York State. Just west of Syracuse, he stopped for the night next to a quiet road in farm country. He unrolled his sleeping bag in the shelter of a roadside embankment, had a light supper, then turned in for the night.

His sleep was less than restful. The sleeping bag gave him some protection from the chilly spring night, but still, he shivered. Tim woke, feeling that something about the night just wasn't right. He left the small comfort of his sleeping bag and crawled to the top of the embankment.

Peering over, he saw a rock quarry that he hadn't noticed in the fading light of the night before. Balls of fluorescent green light were darting around on a hillside in the quarry. Tim watched the glowing lights for ten or fifteen minutes. The lights seemed to move with purpose, as if they were alive. Soon, the night chill overcame his fascination, and he made his way back to his sleeping bag.

The next morning's ride took him into Syracuse, and he stopped at a diner for some food. Over breakfast, he shared his strange experience with the guy at the counter. The man shook his head, and told Tim that he'd run into the ghosts of the Rock.

The ghost lights of the quarry date back to World War I. Semet-Solvay, a chemical manufacturing company, used the rock quarry for its ore mining and processing business. And it was a vital part of the company's business. The minerals mined at the quarry were used to make picric acid, a yellow crystalline substance used in making tri-nitrotoluene (TNT). In early 1917, the company had gotten a huge order for TNT from Russia. The factory ramped up production to three shifts a day, working around the clock.

At around 9:30 pm on April 2, 1918, a gear in a grinding machine overheated and caused a fire. The flames spread rapidly. A ton of toluel detonated, and the explosion rained down rock, steel shards, and acid on almost 800 workers. The accident left 50 workers dead and 100 injured. A mass grave in Morningside Cemetery holds fifteen unidentified corpses and many random body parts. Sadly, the families of the workers lost in the explosion had little time for grieving. With the urgency of the war effort, the factory swung back into production the very next day.

Tim Zorn was not the only person to experience paranormal events in Split Rock in the 1980s. For some reason, six decades after the tragedy, activity in the quarry suddenly ramped up. A Syracuse psychic and some of her friends, also psychic, shared their experiences with a reporter from the Syracuse *Post-Standard* in the summer of 1980. The psychic said she'd had a conversation with a deaf man who complained of "hearing screaming" when driving past the site. The other psychics visited the quarry and saw greenish-yellow figures standing along the rock ledges. Just about every witness, from Tim Zorn to several different groups of investigators, reported seeing greenish-yellow, glowing apparitions.

There's a really interesting reason for this. Picric acid, the toxic yellow crystal produced at the chemical company, turns clothing yellow and green. Perhaps the phantoms or ghost lights are taking their color from the stuff that killed them.

APRIL 4
The Sullivan Brothers (1942)

American patriotism ran high in the early days of World War II. After Pearl Harbor, young men enlisted to fight in the war, just as their fathers had done a generation before.

The five Sullivan brothers – Albert, Francis ("Frank"), George, Joseph ("Joe"), and Madison ("Matt") – enlisted in the Navy on January 3, 1942. George and Frank had served in the Navy before, but the others had not. They had a sister, Genevieve, who served in the WAVES. Her boyfriend, Bill Ball, was killed on the *USS Arizona* when Pearl Harbor was bombed. The Sullivans joined the Navy to avenge Ball's death.

Their only request was that they be allowed to serve together, assigned to the same ship. After all, they said, nothing bad could happen to them as long as they stayed together. The Sullivan brothers were an unbeatable team. The Navy had a policy of separating siblings, but this wasn't strictly enforced.

So in February 1942, all five Sullivan brothers were assigned to the *USS Juneau*. The ship saw months of action in the Guadalcanal Campaign, beginning in August 1942. Early in the morning of Friday November 13, the *Juneau* was hit by a Japanese torpedo. It limped away from the battle, and huddled with other damaged warships. Later that day, as the surviving ships prepared to leave the Solomon Islands for the Allied base at Espiritu Santo, the *Juneau* was struck by another torpedo. The ship didn't survive the second hit – the torpedo probably hit the thinly armored ship near the ammunition stores. The *Juneau* exploded and quickly sank.

Later reports said that Joe, Frank, and Matt Sullivan died instantly. Around 100 of the *Juneau's* crew survived the initial explosion and the sinking and were stranded in the shark-infested waters. Al drowned the day after the ship sank. George also managed to drag himself to a life raft, and survived five days. George's death was particularly difficult: he spent those five days swimming from raft to raft in search of his brothers. He eventually succumbed to delirium, either from hypernatremia (an over-concentration of salt in the bloodstream) or simply from exhaustion and grief at the loss of his brothers. He slipped over the side of his life raft and gave himself to the waves. He was never seen again.

The brothers' parents, Tom and Alleta Sullivan, threw themselves into the war effort as a way of dealing with their profound grief. They gave speeches at war plants and shipyards, encouraging production, and promoted the sale of war bonds.

On February 6, 1943, a destroyer was officially named *USS The Sullivans* in honor of the lost brothers. Alleta Sullivan sponsored its construction, and on April 4, she helped launch the ship that memorialized her sons. The ship served for more than 20 years. She saw heavy combat in the Marshall Islands and the Philippines, as well as in the Korean War, but miraculously, no crew member of *The Sullivans* was ever killed in action while serving on the ship. The ship's motto? "We stick together."

The ship was decommissioned in 1965, and is now in drydock in Buffalo, New York. In 1986, it was designated a national historic landmark. The ship now functions as a museum.

Reports of paranormal activity aboard the decommissioned ship are many and varied. There are lots of electronic malfunctions – cameras punk out, batteries go dead in seconds. Rolls of film or memory cards spontaneously erase themselves. There are knocks, bangs, and disembodied voices. Orbs of light wander around belowdecks.

One tour guide on the ship had a terrifying experience. He was making his rounds when a floating torso with a horribly burned face launched itself through the darkness at him, vanishing just before it would have collided with him.

The most well-known part of this haunting is the claim that if you stand in the room designated "the Sullivan Brothers Memorial" and take a photograph, the portraits of four of the brothers will appear normal, but George's portrait will appear as a smear of white light. As tempting as it is to call this effect paranormal, it does have a logical explanation. The portraits of the five brothers are displayed on a wall, and they are framed and covered in glass. Since there are five pictures, a person taking a photograph naturally tends to center themselves on the middle picture – the one of George. The picture is taken, the flash goes off, and the glare bounces off the glass protecting George's portrait. The glass is a nonglare type, which produces a blurred, diffuse reflection of the camera's flash. Debunked, but still part of the Sullivan brothers' ghost lore.

APRIL 5
The Woman in Black, Central City, Colorado (1887, recurring)

The Masonic Cemetery in Central City, Colorado, is haunted by the ghost of a woman in black. She glides up to the grave of John Edward Cameron, puts a nosegay of blue columbine flowers on the grave, then silently departs. She visits twice a year, on April 5 and November 1.

Cameron, only 28 years old, died on November 1, 1887. A beautiful woman, garbed in a black satin dress, attended the funeral. For years, she came to the cemetery every April 5 and on the anniversary of Cameron's death, November 1. She always left flowers on the grave. No one knew who she was, or what her relationship was with Cameron, or the significance of the second date, April 5. Rumors spread that the mysterious woman was actually a ghost, the spirit of a former lover who killed herself after Cameron married another woman.

By 1899, everyone in the area was consumed with curiosity. They'd convinced themselves that the woman in black was a phantom, but they wanted to settle the matter once and for all. On November 1, over a dozen people gathered at John Cameron's grave to see if they could catch the ghost.

The lady appeared as sundown was fading into dusk. Clad in her customary black satin gown, she was one with the shadows. When she stooped to placed a bunch of flowers on the grave, two men lunged for her. She escaped their grasp and hurried away, vanishing over the crest of a nearby hill.

APRIL 6
The Battle of Shiloh, Shiloh, TN (1862)

On April 6, 1862, 42,000 Union troops, Grant's Army of the Tennessee, were encamped on the Tennessee River. At dawn that morning, 45,000 Confederate soldiers under the command of General Albert Sidney Johnston struck the Union forces in a surprise attack. The Union troops had been at this location for about a month. Since Grant was planning an offensive strike, he didn't order the troops to throw up any defenses around the camp. The Confederates pounded the Federal troops, driving them back towards Pittsburg Landing.

Many of the soldiers on either side had little combat experience, and the violence was wanton and horrific. At one point, the Union troops formed a line in a wooded thicket and tried desperately to hold it. So many bullets were whizzing through the air that the Confederates decided it sounded like a massive swarm of angry hornets. That area has forever after been known as the "Hornet's Nest". The Union troops struggled here for nearly six hours before falling back. But those hours were well if bloodily spent. Help was on the way.

That afternoon, Union reinforcements began to arrive; 20,000 more troops under General Buell. Heartened by the support, Grant's men shored up the sagging Union line. General Johnston was struck by a bullet as he rode forward to lead the Confederates in another attack. The bullet hit his leg, severing an artery, and he quickly bled out. General P.G.T. Beauregard took command of the Southern troops. At nightfall, with the Union line driven back two miles, he called a halt to the Confederate advance.

The next day, Grant counterattacked. With the addition of Buell's 20,000 troops, the

Union forces now outnumbered the Confederates. The battle raged on again, this time in reverse, as the weary Confederates retreated over the same ground they'd taken the day before. As they went, they inflicted heavy casualties on the Union lines. Shiloh was a Union victory – and the first major victory for Grant – but it came at a terrible price. The battle was the first real test of just how far each side was willing to go. By the end of the battle, there were over 23,000 casualties, with 3,400 men dead (1,700 on each side). It was the bloodiest battle of the war ... so far.

One of the legends of Shiloh says that when the Union encampment was first attacked, at dawn on a Sunday morning, Union commanders at first decided to retreat. In all the confusion, a drummer boy got mixed up, and beat out the rhythm for "attack" instead of "retreat". In the frantic rush to battle, the young boy was caught up in the crush of men, and was killed. His spirit is now seen throughout the park, but especially at the Hornet's Nest.

Another spirit haunts the area of the battlefield known as "Bloody Pond". A field hospital was hastily set up to treat the battle casualties. So much blood was spilled here, they say, that it stained the water in the brackish pond a permanent reddish-brown color. (This is the product of legend and imagination. The stagnant, coffee-colored water in Bloody Pond is the result of overgrowth of vegetation.) The ghost here is that of a young woman, possibly a local nurse brought in to treat the wounded. She usually appears as a white mist, but several people have seen her manifest as a pretty young woman standing by the pond. She seems real enough to speak to – that is, until she dissolves.

APRIL 7

The Psychic Knows, Rome, Italy (1960)

Iolanda Addolori was a lovely woman. Her thick, honey-blonde hair, good figure, and golden-brown eyes brought stares and whistles as she walked down the streets in Rome. The 27-year-old bore it good-naturedly – after all, she was Italian herself, and she knew her people appreciated life's beauty.

Iolanda had come to Rome from Venice with the blessing of her father, Ferruccio, to study costume design. It was her father, too, who had guided her development as a medium. Ferruccio had seem Iolanda's natural psychic abilities and encouraged them, teaching her to read tarot cards as well as he himself did. Ferruccio was renowned in the family for his psychic talents, amplified and refined by the cards. Encouraged by her father's guidance, and by the good fortune he'd foretold for her, she made the move to Rome to study.

On the night of April 7, 1960, at 7 pm, she picked up the ringing telephone to hear terrible news from Venice. Ferruccio, the beloved Papa of the family, had suffered a heart attack, and was fading quickly. Iolanda raced to the train station, but no trains were leaving Rome at that hour.

Iolanda was the youngest child, and very close to her Papa. Distraught, she turned to her cards for comfort. But every spread she laid out on the table was heavy with death. Iolanda staggered to bed with an aching heart and finally fell into a troubled sleep.

At 2 am, she heard her father's voice calling to her, drawing her gently from dreams. But the beloved voice held no joy for her. She snatched up the phone and dialed her family in

Venice. She already knew the answer to her unspoken question. Ferruccio had died at the exact moment she'd heard him calling to her.

Iolanda inherited her father's deck of cards as well as his talent for reading them. The cards had predicted that she would one day be famous, and that her marriage would be reported by the newspapers. A year later, in 1961, Iolanda Addolori met the actor Anthony Quinn, already famous for his roles in such films as *Ulysses*, *The Hunchback of Notre Dame*, and *The Guns of Navarone*. They were married in 1966.

APRIL 8
The Ghost of George Sitts, Sioux Falls, SD (1947)

Donna O'Dea is a psychic medium who lives in Sioux Falls, South Dakota. She has been getting messages from the Other Side since she was six years old. Now, as an adult, she helps people by providing messages from those who have passed on. Sometimes, she helps by "translating" spirit activity. If a client has a ghost in their home, Donna finds out why it's there and what it wants. Sometimes, she convinces it to leave.

In 2007, Donna got such a request from the owner of a hair salon in downtown Sioux Falls. The shop was in an old brick building in the historic section of town. The owner was not happy that hair dryers were turning on and off by themselves. The owner suspected there was a ghost involved.

Donna visited the salon after closing time one night. In her mind's eye, she saw a young man sitting in the chair reserved for pedicures. He lounged in the chair with a belligerent sneer. Donna discerned that his name was George.

The ghost spoke up. "They thought they killed me, but I escaped the penitentiary." Donna realized that the man had been executed in the electric chair. Furthermore, he had no idea he was dead. In his arrogance, he thought he'd cheated death and was on the run. He was "hiding out", going from building to building. His ghostly antics had attracted attention.

Donna sent George's spirit into the Light, freeing him from his earthbound existence (and freeing the salon owner from George's restless ghost).

As it happens, only one man in South Dakota had ever died in the electric chair. George Sitts had been convicted in 1945 in Minnesota for the murder of a liquor store clerk during a botched robbery. He spent three weeks sawing through the bars of his cell in the Minneapolis city jail. The day before he was to be transferred to a state prison, Sitts and three other men escaped. In South Dakota, he shot and killed Special Agent Tom Matthews and Sheriff Dave Malcolm on January 24, 1946. He fled to Wyoming, but was arrested February 5 and returned to South Dakota.

The state had instituted the electric chair as a method of execution in 1939, and Sitts was the fourth person sentenced to die by electrocution. The first three sentences were commuted to life in prison.

Sitts was not so lucky. At 12:15 am on April 8, 1947, he used his last words to joke with the witnesses to his execution, saying, "This is the first time authorities helped me to escape prison."

APRIL 9
A Tragic Wedding, Grand Tower, IL (1839, 1859)

This story begins with a wedding – a happy occasion, but this one ended in tragedy. The wedding took place on April 9, 1839 at Grand Tower in southern Illinois. The wedding party, seeking a dramatic vista for the ceremony, crossed the river to hike to the top of Tower Rock. Tower Rock is an island in the middle of the Mississippi River, a rocky landmark just across from Grand Tower.

The island made the Native Americans of the area nervous, because they thought it was haunted by a manitou, or demon, that ate travelers. The explorer Jacques Marquette discovered the secret of the "manitou"; it was a small cove in the side of Tower Rock which caught the whole current of the mighty Mississippi, creating a ferociously noisy whirlpool.

The wedding party, on their way back from Tower Rock, had the misfortune to be sucked into this whirlpool. Their little boat never stood a chance against the river's strength. The only survivor was a slave.

On the day of the wedding, the bridegroom's niece was born. For her 20th birthday, she and her family decided to hold her party at the top of Tower Rock.

As the party was in full swing, the guests were horrified to discover that they had company. The bride, groom, priest, and other members of the ill-fated wedding party rose from the murky depths of the Mississippi River. The priest silently handed the birthday girl a parchment scroll. Then, still without a sound, the ghostly party crashers sank back beneath the water.

With shaking hands, the niece unrolled the parchment. It predicted a great war in which families would be torn apart. Two years later, in April 1861, the Civil War began. One of the niece's brothers enlisted in the Union army, and another joined the Confederate cause. During a battle in Missouri, the Union brother killed the Confederate brother.

The scroll's dire prophecy had come true.

APRIL 10
The Death of Major-General Wallace, Savannah, TN (1862)

Ann Wallace was proud of her husband, and she had every reason to be. William had been a lawyer before this horrible War Between the States began, and he'd even had a hand in Illinois politics. Now, William had offered to help his friend and colleague, Abraham Lincoln. Lincoln had given William command of the Eleventh Illinois Infantry. He'd risen through the ranks, and now he was Major-General William Wallace, commanding one of the six divisions in General Grant's Army of the Tennessee. In his most recent letter to her, William had mentioned that his division was camped near Pittsburg, Tennessee, at a place called Shiloh.

Yes, Ann was proud of her William – but she was also worried sick. Everyone kept saying that the war would be over in just a few weeks, but it had dragged on for nearly a year. Maybe it was that grim anniversary headed their way, but Ann had been feeling sick with dread for weeks. March wore on, and the Illinois snows began to melt. The earth was waking to spring, but Ann could not shake her mounting feeling of approaching catastrophe.

She had to see William, she just had to. But well-bred ladies just did not go haring off into a war zone.

Late one night, though, the urgency overcame her. Even though it was midnight, Ann threw some clothes and a bit of food into a carpetbag, and set off alone for Tennessee.

The Illinois River took her as far as Cairo, in southern Illinois. There, she ran into a snag. Try as she might, she couldn't find a captain willing to let her aboard. It was only a short jaunt – the Illinois had taken her this far. She just had to go up the Ohio several miles to Paducah, and find a boat heading down the Tennessee River, which ran right past Pittsburg. From there it would be child's play to get to Grant's encampment at Shiloh. But no captain was willing to risk the safety of a lady in those dangerous times.

Ann refused to give in to despair. She would get to William, no matter the danger. Then luck smiled on her. In Cairo, she ran across a delegation from Ottawa – her very own home. Even more fortuitous, the men were carrying a new flag for the Eleventh Illinois – William's regiment – to replace the unit's old, battle-damaged standard.

It took some fast talking, but Ann convinced the men to allow her to continue on with their errand. Finally, it was agreed. She would be the one to bring the new flag to the regiment, a color guard of one. Ann had gotten her dearest wish … but it would come at a terrible price.

Ann arrived at Pittsburg late at night on April 6, 1862, and landed in the middle of hell. The Battle of Shiloh had raged all that day, and the Union forces were in a panicked retreat. Half of Grant's army was either dead, injured, or captured. Ann's resolve held strong. She had come this far. She was so close to William she could almost feel his presence. She'd come hundreds of miles to find him. What was the length of a battlefield compared to that?

That night, Ann's luck continued to hold. General Buell's reinforcements arrived to shore up Grant's sagging troops. As they were being ferried across the river, Ann joined them, still carrying the new regimental flag for the Eleventh Illinois. The soldiers would carry on in the morning, and so would she.

Chaos reigned on the far shore. The Union troops were in a rout in the darkness, struggling against the instinct to bolt. Soldiers crowded the dock and riverbank, preferring a cold dunking to hot Confederate lead. Buell's troops had to fix bayonets and force their way off the ferry. Behind them huddled Ann, still clutching the flag … and hope.

Ann finally found the Eleventh Illinois. Familiar faces broke the news: William Wallace was missing in action, presumed dead. His position had been overrun by Confederate forces. Now he was lying somewhere out there on the battlefield in the driving rain.

There was no time to search for one missing man. The battle began again the next morning, and this day belonged to the Union. The North took back all the ground they'd lost the day before. When they came to the sunken road of death nicknamed the Hornet's Nest, a feeble cry of triumph struggled up from the wet ground. General Wallace was alive. Soaked to the skin, badly wounded, barely conscious, but alive. Soldiers found him wet, shivering, wrapped in a blanket. A compassionate Rebel soldier had covered the wounded general. The enemy had shown kindness.

Field medics hustled Wallace off of the battlefield and bundled him aboard the steamer that had brought Ann to him. The couple was reunited, but William's situation was precarious. His head wound was serious, and he'd spent the night outside in the cold April rain. The steamer took them to Savannah, Tennessee, where Grant had his headquarters. William was ensconced in an upstairs bedroom at Cherry Mansion, with Ann finally at his side.

Even that powerful medicine couldn't save William. He rallied at first, and everyone thought that Ann's loving presence was helping his recovery. But soon he began to fade, "like a fire going out" as Ann described it. He died on April 10, 1862.

Ann accompanied William's body back to Ottawa, and he was given a hero's funeral. But it seems that a part of him has remained at Cherry Mansion. Witnesses have seen a man staring out from an upstairs bedroom window. He wears the dark blue uniform of the Union army, and a broad-brimmed officer's hat. Maybe William Wallace is reliving his final days, spent at the mansion … and remembering that his beloved wife moved heaven and earth to get to him.

APRIL 11
Assassination of General Canby, CA (1873)

The 1870s were the height of the Indian Wars in the American West. One of those was the Modoc War, which, if you look at the percentages, was one of the costliest wars in our history. American troops in the area numbered around 600, and there were only 60 Modoc warriors. But the war ended with 53 United States soldiers, 17 civilians, and 15 Modoc braves dead (only five of these died in battle; the rest were executed).

The Modocs lived in the wooded mountains of northern California and southern Oregon. The conflict here was much the same as in other Indian wars: the Modoc tribe had land, and the government wanted to take it from them. Whites were settling along the Lost River and on the shores of Tule Lake, in Modoc territory.

White settlers demanded that the Modoc be removed to the Klamath reservation. What most whites didn't know (and if they did, they likely wouldn't have cared) was that the Modoc and the Klamath were historic enemies. The Modoc arrived at the reservation, saw the Klamath already there, said oh hell no, and went right back to their land at Tule Lake.

The Modoc wanted their own reservation on Lost River, but the government decided there wasn't enough land for both a reservation and a white settlement, and of course the whites took precedence. Oregon Indian Superintendent Alfred Meacham convinced the Modoc, led by the young leader Kientpoos, to move back to the Klamath reservation. They went back to the reservation, confronted the Klamath again, said oh hell no again, and returned to Lost River. (Actually, both tribes said hell no. When the Modoc got to the reservation, the Klamath harassed them unmercifully. They didn't want them there any more than the Modoc wanted to be there.) The governor of Oregon decided that the Modoc were renegades, and the army was called in to force them to return to the reservation.

In November 1872, troops confronted the Modoc. Shots were fired, and the village was burned. The Modoc disappeared into the nearby lava field, hiding quite effectively from the army. All winter, troops tried to winkle the natives out of their natural hiding places in the lava beds, and all winter, the small band of natives held off a force twenty times their number.

The army troops were led by General E.R.S. Canby, who had been ordered by General Sherman to resolve the conflict peacefully if at all possible. Canby tried. Kientpoos asked several times if the Modoc could just have a reservation of their own, one they wouldn't have to share with the hated Klamath. Canby passed the requests along to Washington, but the government said that there was no money for the formation of another reservation.

Kientpoos had, as his advisors, the leaders of several other bands of Modoc. "Hooker Jim" had retaliated against the settlers for the army's unprovoked November attack. He killed fourteen settlers, but only the men – he left women and children alone, following Modoc war customs. This led to Hooker Jim being indicted for murder.

Unfortunately, Kientpoos took in Hooker Jim and his war party at his Lava Bed camp. On his advice, and that of the shaman Curly-headed Doctor, Kientpoos decided to take the reservation request in a much different direction.

Desperate for a conclusion to the war, Kientpoos met with General Canby and others on April 11, 1873 for yet another peace conference. Kientpoos asked once again for a Modoc reservation. Once again, Canby said it was impossible.

So Kientpoos drew a pistol from his shirt and shot Canby dead.

This squashed any hopes for peace. The army cut the Modoc off from their water supply, but the Modoc snuck off and escaped to the south. On April 26, a patrol of 69 soldiers was ambushed by the Modoc. In 45 minutes, two-thirds of the patrol was killed or wounded. The Modoc retreated further south.

Then things got bad for the Modoc. A surprise attack on troops camped at Dry Lake ended in defeat. The Modoc began to splinter into small, demoralized groups. Kientpoos and his followers went one way, Hooker Jim and his band went another. Troops looking for Kientpoos found Hooker Jim instead, who surrendered, then offered to betray Kientpoos to the army. Kientpoos surrendered on June 1, 1873. The Modoc War was over.

Lava Beds National Park is on the California-Oregon border just south of Tule Lake. The remains of army camps can still be seen, and the primeval lava formations that gave shelter to Kientpoos and his people. Apparitions walk the trails along with the tourists. One woman, after a visit in 1992, told of walking near the rocks on a trail, and seeing what looked like a child or a small woman wrapped in a gray blanket, who disappeared into thin air.

Other hikers have heard the soft chants of native song echoing in the air, or have seen the phantom of an army soldier in a hat, long coat, and light blue shirt: a uniform worn in the Modoc War.

APRIL 12
Fort Sumter Falls, Charleston, SC (1861)

Construction began on Fort Sumter in 1827, but it was still unfinished at the end of 1860. (The fort is massive. Sitting on a sandbar at the entrance to Charleston Harbor, it boasts walls five feet thick and fifty feet high. This was a fort worthy of the name, and it did not go up overnight.)

Major Robert Anderson commanded the army forces in South Carolina. He and his troops were stationed at nearby Fort Moultrie. Anderson, though, felt that Fort Moultrie was too big to be defended with the resources he had; he was in command of 127 troops, and a garrison of at least 300 was needed for Fort Moultrie. So on December 25, 1860, Anderson gave himself and his troops a Christmas present. He loaded his men, and everything else they could fit, onto two schooners and headed for Fort Sumter.

The Confederacy was … displeased by this action. On December 30, the *Charleston Courier* printed an article pointing out that Anderson had basically just started a civil war. On December 31, the *New York Times* reprinted the article.

Nobody was happy with Major Anderson, but people were still trying to be polite about things. These were Southern gentlemen dealing with a situation in a Southern harbor, and they were determined to be genteel. On April 11, 1861, Confederate Brigadier General P.G.T. Beauregard sent a politely worded letter to Anderson.

"I am ordered by the government of the Confederate States to demand the evacuation of Fort Sumter. My aides, Colonel Chestnut and Captain Lee, are authorized to make such demand of you. All proper facilities will be afforded for the removal of yourself and command, together with company arms and property, and all private property, to any post in the United States which you may select. The flag which you have upheld so long and with so much fortitude, under the most trying circumstances, may be saluted by you on taking it down. Colonel Chestnut and Captain Lee will, for a reasonable time, await your answer. I am, very respectfully, your obedient servant, P.G.T. Beauregard, Brigadier-General Commanding." (TL, DR: Get out of our fort.)

Beauregard didn't have to wait long for the answer. The same day, Anderson wrote back, in language that was just as fulsomely polite, but just as firm.

"General: I have the honor to acknowledge the receipt of your communication demanding the evacuation of this fort, and to say, in reply thereto, that it is a demand with which I regret that my sense of honor, and of my obligations to my government, prevent my compliance. Thanking you for the fair, manly and courteous terms proposed, and for the high compliment paid me, I am, General, very respectfully, your obedient servant, Robert Anderson, Major, First Artillery, Commanding." (TL, DR: Go kick rocks.)

At 4:30 in the morning on April 12, 1861, General Beauregard gave the order to start shelling Fort Sumter. The Confederates pounded the paste out of the fort. Fort Sumter, and the men inside, suffered through 34 hours of near-constant bombardment. Amazingly, the only casualty was a Confederate horse.

After a day and a half of this barrage, Beauregard again asked if Anderson might not consider giving up. This time, Anderson said yes, provided that Beauregard's offer of honorable surrender was still valid. Beauregard, being a Southern gentleman and an officer, said that of course it was.

During the bombardment, the United States flag was torn to tatters by the whistling shells. Sergeant Peter Hart braved the hurricane of lead to climb the flagpole and run up a smaller flag, called the Storm flag. It was this flag that was to be lowered, and honored with a 100-gun salute, on April 14, 1861.

Private Daniel Hough, born in Tipperary, Ireland and an emigrant to the United States sometime in the 1840s, was assigned to gun #47 in the 100-cannon array. No one's really sure what happened, but a hot ember was in the wrong place at the wrong time. When Private Hough tamped down the gun, it exploded, killing him instantly, and making him the first man killed in the Civil War. Anderson's salute was abbreviated to 50 guns, and Hough was buried on the parade ground.

The hauntings at Fort Sumter take several forms. Some people smell gunpowder. Some see puffs of smoke appear, as if a phantom cannon has just fired. But it is the Storm flag that gives us the most enduring phenomenon.

Anderson was allowed to take the Storm flag with him to New York when he surrendered. Soon after the surrender, the flag went on tour, to muster support for the Union cause. On that tour, people viewing the flag noticed that just to the right of the middle star, an image had formed … an image that looked uncannily like a bearded man, seen almost in profile, wearing a dark blue US army cap and uniform. Soldiers of the First US Artillery Regiment who had served with Daniel Hough swore it was the face of their late comrade.

APRIL 13
Clara's Dress, Loudonville, NY (1865)

Clara Harris smiled at her fiancé, Henry Rathbone. It was such a pleasure to be out with him, enjoying the humor of a play. The war was over at last, thank God. The nation could finally begin to heal, and she and Henry were about to start their life together.

A soft click – Clara barely heard it below the audience's laughter and the president's chuckle to her left. Mrs. Lincoln was smiling; it looked good on her. And it was so very good to see the president's face relaxed into a grin as well.

A bang! and Lincoln's great head fell forward, as if he'd nodded off during the funniest part of the play. A scream from Mary Lincoln. Henry was up and struggling with someone. He grunted in pain. The dark blue of his sleeve turned a darker shade; blood showed through a gash in the fabric.

Then Mary Lincoln's screams resolved into words. "My husband's blood!" she shrieked, pointing at Clara. Clara looked down at herself and nearly swooned.

Her white satin dress was spattered with shocking red splats of blood.

Everyone in the president's box at Ford's Theatre the night of April 14, 1865 suffered grievous psychological wounds. Mary Lincoln died in 1882, mourning the loss of her beloved husband and three of her sons, all who'd gone before her. Her eyesight failed near the end; her corneas were ulcerated with all the tears she'd shed. Major Henry Rathbone wallowed for the rest of his life in the guilt that plagued him. His inability to save his President was a wound far deeper than the slice on the arm he'd gotten from the assassin as Booth made his escape.

Clara never got over the shock of seeing Abraham Lincoln's lifeblood soaking her dress. In early summer 1865, she and Henry retired to a summer house her family owned in Loudonville, just north of Albany, New York. Clara hung the bloodstained dress in her bedroom closet.

Then she shut the closet door, and had it sealed and covered with wallpaper. She couldn't bear to get rid of the dress. But she could make sure she would never have to see it again.

Time marched on. The year rolled around, and soon it was Good Friday again. Clara went to bed early on the night of April 13, 1866. All she wanted to do was sleep, to escape into dreams and avoid the memories.

A sound drew her from sleep around midnight. In the moonlight, she saw her rocking chair moving with a rhythmic creak. Then she heard a man's low chuckle. It was lunacy, but she could have sworn the laugh sounded familiar. Where had she heard that voice before?

Then Clara saw a figure seated in the rocking chair, and let out a low moan. It was him, Lincoln, the president, his ghost right there in her room! He was smiling, as she had last seen him in life. He looked as though he was once again watching that play, enjoying the antics of "Our American Cousin". Clara gasped, and Lincoln's head turned.

He looked straight at the closet door behind the wallpaper.

The clock chimed midnight, and Lincoln vanished. The rocking chair slowed, then stopped, and Clara burst into tears.

When she told her family about the apparition, everyone brushed it off as a nightmare … until other people who stayed in that bedroom at Loudon Cottage told of similar visitations. One man saw the bloodstained dress hanging in the closet, as if the wall had temporarily turned transparent.

Despite their shared tragedy, Clara Harris and Henry Rathbone got married. They moved to Germany, but Henry was never able to escape the demons of his guilt. In 1883, Henry murdered Clara and attempted suicide. He spent the rest of his life in an asylum.

Eventually, the Harris family sold Loudon Cottage. One later owner, Daisy Ransome, ran it as a boardinghouse. One of the rooms she rented was Clara's old bedroom. One Good Friday evening, Daisy's tenant had an experience in his room that shook him to his core. He, too, saw the sad-looking man sitting in the rocking chair. The man was joined by a young lady who wore a white satin gown. The lady sobbed uncontrollably as she leaned against the rocking chair. A shot rang out, and suddenly the lady's white dress was splashed with red. The boarder, terrified, fled the house and never returned.

We don't know what happened to Clara's dress. Some believe Henry Rathbone Jr., Clara's son, took the dress out of the closet and destroyed it before he put the cottage up for sale. It's also possible that Daisy Ransome did some exploration of the haunted room, uncovered the closet, and got rid of the dress just to stop the haunting (and keep her boarders).

But the haunting didn't stop. Early in the 1900s, the governor of Massachusetts visited his cousin, Hobart Thompson, who owned Loudon Cottage at the time. He, too, saw Lincoln rocking placidly by moonlight. But as he reached for the light switch, he knocked over a pile of books, and the ghost vanished.

Loudon Cottage was moved in 1927, about 500 feet away from its original location. Subsequent owners have not reported any paranormal activity since the move.

APRIL 14
Grandfather's Clock, Clarksburg, WV (1865)

The Robey household was tense and on edge that Friday night. Everyone had been irritable, and no one knew why. Spring fever, maybe. It was the middle of April, and the children were fretful and naughty from being cooped up all winter.

Grandfather Robey went to bed early. He was simply exhausted. Grandmother settled down in her rocking chair with some mending in her lap.

Grandfather tossed and turned, sleeping fitfully and whimpering once in a while. Suddenly, he sat bolt upright, then threw the covers off and leapt from the bed.

"My god, Abraham Lincoln's just been shot!" he yelled.

Grandmother tried to soothe him. "I'm sure it was just a nightmare. Go back to sleep."

But Grandfather swore he'd seen it happen. He crossed the room to the clock that sat on the fireplace mantel. Grabbing a pencil, he marked the position of the clock's hands, and in tiny print, he wrote down the date on the clock face: April 14.

News traveled slowly in those days, but about two weeks later, a stagecoach stopped in Clarksburg. Soon, everyone in town heard the shattering news: Abraham Lincoln had been shot. And it had happened on the exact day and hour that Grandfather Robey had marked on the clock's face.

APRIL 15
Pictures in the Cemetery, Dahlonega, GA (1953)

Madeline Anthony leaned on her rake and armed a thin film of sweat from her temple. Cemetery cleanup was hard work, but satisfying. Her church committee had asked for volunteers to clean up Mount Hope Cemetery, and Madeline was happy to help.

The cemetery looked tidy with the winter's debris cleared away. They'd done a good day's work. Madeline wandered the cemetery for a while, snapping pictures. She figured the committee might like some photos of the neatened grounds. The cemetery was a historic treasure, too. Many early settlers were buried there, people who'd come to the area to make their fortune in the Georgia gold rush that began in 1829. Madeline finished the roll, and wrote the date on it – April 15, 1953. Then she dropped it off to be developed.

When she picked up the photos, she flipped through them, like she usually did. One of them caught her eye. She took it out of the pile and held it up for a closer look.

There was a girl in a long, old-fashioned dress standing beside a tree. There was a grizzled grandfather. There was a handsome young man with a beard. There – she squinted – there was a baby wearing a sweet little ruffled cap. The picture was filled with faces from the past.

Madeline marched back into the studio and thrust the picture at the developer, demanding to know why he'd tampered with it. She was an avid photographer, she'd trusted him with her film for years, so why this? Why now?

The technician took a long, professional look at the photograph. He shook his head and handed the picture back. He explained that to create a photo like that, he'd have to find all those old pictures. He'd have to enlarge or reduce them so they'd all be the same scale. He'd have to arrange them on something, blur the edges, photograph that, then print her negative and his fake on the same sheet. Short answer? It would be a monumental pain to do, and for what purpose?

Convinced he was telling the truth, Madeline asked how, in his professional opinion, he thought all those faces could have gotten onto the photograph. He told her in all seriousness that it was impossible ... unless she'd taken a picture of a gathering of ghosts.

APRIL 16
The Battle of Culloden Moor, Inverness, Scotland (1746, recurring)

The last battle to be fought on British soil was the Battle of Culloden Moor, a bloody clash that was critical to Scottish history. Prince Charles Edward Stuart, known as Bonnie Prince Charlie, was trying to claim the throne of England for his father, James Francis Edward Stuart. (The prince's grandfather was James II of England.) The elder Stuart was snottily known in England by the reigning Hanoverians as "the Old Pretender". Prince Charlie was called "the Young Pretender", because if his bid to put his father on England's throne succeeded, he'd be next in line to rule.

The Hanoverian British government was having none of this, and sent the Duke of Cumberland to squash the rebellion. The Highlander army was in no shape to fight a battle; they'd just marched several days back from England. In just twenty minutes, most of the Scots were mowed down by English artillery fire. Over 1,500 of the Highlander army died in the battle (versus around fifty of the government troops). Cumberland ordered his men to range over the battlefield after the fighting was over, and butcher any Scotsman they found, even the wounded. The Scottish dead were buried in a mass grave on the battlefield, with stones marking the resting place of each clan.

In the aftermath of the battle, the Scottish Highland way of life was blown apart. The clan chiefs who supported Bonnie Prince Charlie were stripped of their lands, and traditional Scots cultural trappings, like bagpipes and kilts, were banned. Hundreds of Scots were exiled to the colonies, destined to live as slaves. Bonnie Prince Charlie himself dodged government troops for five months throughout the Scottish Highlands. He eventually escaped to Italy, and never saw Scotland again.

The blood-soaked land has not forgotten the slaughter of its sons. On the anniversary of the battle, the sounds of steel-on-steel ring out again, and soldiers are seen wandering the battlefield. One of the spirits seen most often is that of a tall man dressed in tartan. He wanders the grounds looking dejected. When approached, he mumbles "Defeated," then wanders off.

A tourist in 1936 got a nasty shock when she lifted a tartan cloth that was covering one of the grave mounds. The ghost of a gruesomely murdered Highlander was lying on the ground underneath the cloth.

One day, a National Trust of Scotland park employee was manning the desk at the visitors' center when two ladies came in looking for some information. They wanted to know the route taken by the Scottish army on their night march before the battle.

The Duke of Cumberland, who was leading the government troops, was celebrating his 25th birthday. The Scots had the bright idea of sneaking up on Cumberland's troops in the dark. They'd surprise the troops, who were likely to be ill-prepared for a night attack, especially after an evening of toasting Cumberland's health with the two gallons of brandy per regiment they'd been issued. It was a good plan … but it didn't work.

Two divisions of Highlanders set out at about 8 pm. They soon got separated, blundering around in unfamiliar woodlands under a driving rain. At about 2 am, the commander of one division gave the plan up as a bad job, and headed back to Culloden. The other division kept going, and were almost at the Duke's camp when they got the message calling them back.

The two ladies knew the story, but they wanted to know exactly where all the Highlanders had passed by. The park employee got out a map and showed them the routes taken by each division.

One of the ladies tapped the map excitedly. "That's my house!" she squeaked. Looking at the map, she could see that one group of soldiers had passed right through what was now her garden. This explained why, about five times in the past ten years, she'd been awakened in the wee hours of the morning by the sound of a large number of armed men going past her house. When she'd hurry to the window to look, there was never anything to see. She'd only heard the sounds of an army on the move.

APRIL 17
Launch of the Mississippi Queen, *Memphis, TN (1873)*

On April 17, 1873, the riverboat *Mississippi Queen* left Memphis, headed for New Orleans. She was last seen around midnight that night, about twelve hours after she'd set off.

After that, no one ever heard from or saw the riverboat again.

How does something the size of a riverboat, made of steel and wood, carrying freight and bearing dozens of unsuspecting passengers, simply vanish, taking everyone on board with it? There were river pirates on the Mississippi, of course. But no wreckage was ever found, nor any trace of the dozens of crew and passengers on board. There are lakes deeper than the Mississippi River, and the Mississippi is certainly not the Bermuda Triangle.

The riverboat, and her passengers and crew, were just … gone.

APRIL 18
The Hand of Death, Chicago, IL (1924)

The firemen who worked at the Chicago Fire Department's Engine Company 107 had always taken it in turns to do the daily chores that kept the firehouse in good working order. Some of them weren't glamorous; there were only so many times you could wash the firetrucks and check over the gear to make sure everything was ready for the next call. That was how, on April 18, 1924, Frank Leavy happened to be washing the building's first-floor windows.

The normally cheerful Frank seemed to be in a funk. He slowly rubbed at the window with a rag, ignoring the afternoon sun pouring in. His fellow firemen couldn't help but pick up on his sullen mood. The whole company was on edge.

It didn't help that the telegraph system was bringing them the news that a four-alarm fire was burning at the Union Stockyards. Engine Co. 107 was too far away to be expected to respond, but all the men were nonetheless thrown a bit off-balance by not being able to fight that fire.

Edward McKevitt happened to be standing next to Frank Leavy when Frank paused in his work, rested his left palm on the glass, and sighed, "This is my last day on the fire department."

What a gloomy thing to say! Edward thought. He started to ask what Frank had meant by that odd pronouncement, but just then, the alarm bell blared. A call came in – Curran Hall, southwest of Chicago's Loop, was on fire, and the stations in that area were already at the Stockyards fire. Edward and Frank, along with their colleagues, scrambled into helmets, coats, and boots and piled into the truck.

The fire was roaring on the second floor. The fire crew wrangled a hose up to the fire escape, crawling in to aim the water at the base of the flames. There was no breathing apparatus available to firefighters in the 1920s, so the men had to take breaks periodically, following the hose back to the window for a few precious sips of fresh air.

They'd been fighting the flames for about half an hour when tragedy struck. One of the building's outer walls collapsed, knocking out the electricity and trapping eight firefighters inside. Frank Leavy was one of the men killed. His eerie prophecy had come true.

Edward McKevitt survived. The next day, he was telling the other firemen about Frank's weird premonition. They happened to be standing next to the window Frank had been washing not 24 hours before. As he spoke, Edward gazed at the window.

He blinked. There on the glass was a stain that looked kind of like a handprint. He pointed it out to the others, wondering out loud if it was Frank's handprint. The stain creeped them out, especially the fact that it had showed up the very next day after Frank had leaned against that same window and made the eerie prediction about his own death. Frank's friends scrubbed at it, using every cleaning agent they cold think of, but the handprint seemed to be etched into the glass.

A city official got a copy of Frank Leavy's thumbprint, and came to the station hoping to debunk the handprint. His plan was to compare the window to Frank's print, proving that the weird stain on the glass was definitely not the handprint of a dead man.

His plan backfired. When the two prints were compared, the thumbprint part of the stain on the glass was an exact match to Leavy's thumbprint. The official had just proven, without a doubt, that the spooky stain was the handprint of Frank Leavy.

The stain remained on the glass for two decades, stubbornly resisting periodic cleaning, scraping with razor blades, and all explanation, and providing a unique attraction for visitors to the firehouse. But one spring morning, an enthusiastic but careless paperboy chucked the daily paper at the firehouse – and hit the window. The glass shattered, and the handprint was destroyed. The mystery would never be solved.

And for a last little bit of spooky, the date on the paper that was thrown through the window was April 18, 1944 – exactly twenty years to the day that Frank Leavy died.

APRIL 19
The Ghost of George Fikes, Oswego, NY (1877)

The April 18, 1877, issue of the *Oswego Palladium* ran a delightful article on a local ghost that had begun to make regular visits to the home of a prominent citizen of Oswego, New York.

The story began on July 3, 1876, when this "prominent citizen" (who was never named in the article, for reasons of privacy) took his daughter to see the fireworks. The young lady enjoyed the light show, but she was also quite interested in the young men in the audience. One the way home, the girl asked her father, with studied carelessness, "Pa, who was that young soldier who stood next to you?"

The father was not at all happy with his daughter's question. He was about to brush her off when she pinched his arm and whispered excitedly, "There he is now!"

The father turned his head to see a young man in an old-fashioned uniform hurrying away from them. Not trying to hide his irritation, he told his daughter that the man was just some dork who'd gotten ahold of an old British uniform and was getting his jollies by running around in it. The guy was probably just a tramp, anyway. The young man was promptly forgotten by the father, if not by the daughter.

On the next Friday evening, father and daughter were sitting in the dining room of their house, when they both heard music – someone was playing the piano in their parlor. The father grabbed up a poker and went to investigate, with his daughter close behind him.

To their astonishment (and the daughter's delight), it was the soldier from the fireworks show. He stood up from the piano, bowed politely, and introduced himself as George Fikes. He told them he'd been a private in the British army, and had died at nearby Fort Ontario in 1782.

This made sense, historically. Fort Ontario had been destroyed by the Americans in 1778, but had been rebuilt by the English in 1782, and a garrison had been stationed there. The fort was surrendered to the Americans in 1796.

Private Fikes proved to be a pleasant guest, and when he left, both father and daughter invited him to call again. He took them up on the offer, and began to visit every Friday evening. They kept their ghostly visitor a secret for months, but finally spilled the beans.

The *Oswego Palladium* sent a reporter to the house to interview the family and their ghost. With a little research, the reporter was able to find a gravestone near the fort with the name "George Fikes". On meeting the ghost, the reporter was convinced that the ghost was indeed the spirit of George Fikes, a private in George III's army. He always wore the British uniform. Every Friday night, at the same time every week, he would just appear in the parlor, not bothering to come in through the door or even float spectrally in through the window. He would make pleasant conversation, play the piano for a bit, then vanish, never overstaying his welcome.

The reporter was convinced of George's ghostliness by the fact that the ghost would materialize without the help of a medium. One moment he wasn't there, the next moment, poof, there he was. His departures were just as sudden. The reporter found George to be "a polite, affable and accomplished gentleman, as the British private notoriously is."

The author of the newspaper article, though, was annoyed that the reporter who interviewed George didn't ask him any questions about Heaven or the afterlife, or about the business of dying. He just asked him a few questions about life in Oswego a hundred years before. The author felt that the other reporter had thrown away a golden opportunity.

"Perhaps in time the reporter, by mere accident, will ask an intelligent question; but unless he does, Mr. Fikes' return to earth will be of no benefit to anyone except the daughter of the leading citizen," the article snarked. The author did admit, though, that Oswego had produced the best ghost ever.

APRIL 20
The Ludlow Massacre, Ludlow, CO (1914)

The Triangle Shirtwaist Fire is perhaps the best-known of the tragedies that arose from struggling workers in the first decades of the 20th century, but there were others too. One of the most egregious of these would become known as the Ludlow Massacre.

The coalfields of Colorado, many owned by John D. Rockefeller's Colorado Fuel and Iron Company, were wretched places to earn a living. Employees were forced to live in company towns with exorbitant rent, and were paid in company scrip, only good at the stores in town, which had ridiculously inflated prices.

Even worse, wages were determined by the amount of coal produced. "Dead work", like building maintenance, shoring up tunnels, and laying track to transport the coal, was often unpaid, so workers were forced to cut corners on safety just to keep food on the table. The death rate in Colorado's mines rose to nearly double the national average.

To add to the misery, many mine workers were immigrants, mostly from Serbia, Greece, and Italy. They didn't share a common language, and the company's management took advantage of this by assigning workers to teams of mixed nationalities so they couldn't communicate with each other.

On September 13, 1913, encouraged by the United Mine Workers of America union, around 10,000 miners got fed up enough to strike. When they walked off the job, the company evicted them from their homes in the town. The UMWA setup tent colonies to house the striking mine workers. The largest of these settlements, at Ludlow, housed about 1,200 strikers and their families.

CF&I hired the Baldwin-Felts Detective Agency, a gang of thugs really, to intimidate the strikers. They patrolled the perimeter of the camp in an armored car, which had a machine gun mounted on it. Periodically, they would strafe the camp. Strikers dug pits under the tents, so their families would have somewhere to hide.

The National Guard was called in, but they sided with the company. In April 1914, it was decided that it was too expensive to keep the National Guard at Ludlow, so their numbers were reduced. This just inflamed the violence. On Sunday, April 19, the National Guard encircled the camp and set up a machine gun on a bluff overlooking the strikers.

No one can agree on what touched things off the next day. We do know that three strike leaders came out under a flag of truce, and were executed in cold blood. One of them, a Greek-American named Louis Tikas, was shot three times in the back. The National Guard opened fire, raking the camp with thousands of rounds from the machine gun. The strikers shot back, losing ten more of their men, but soon they were running low on ammunition. They retreated into the countryside around the camp.

That evening, thinking that the camp had been abandoned, guardsmen came through the camp, soaking tents in kerosene and setting them on fire. They figured that if the strikers had no homes to return to, they would give up and knuckle under.

The next day, a telephone linesman was wandering through the smoking ruins of the Ludlow camp. In one of the tents, he lifted up an iron cot frame ... and made a gruesome discovery. The cot had been hiding the pit that had been dug underneath. And huddled in that pit were the charred, twisted remains of two women and eleven children. They had hidden in the pit, seeking safety. Instead, they died, suffocating on fumes and burning alive.

The massacre at Ludlow resulted in child labor laws being enacted, and the creation of the eight-hour workday. The UMWA put up a monument to the lost workers and the innocents who perished, and the town of Ludlow, now abandoned, is under the care of the union. The cellar where the women and children died is still there.

The site is extremely haunted, typical for places where sudden and unjust deaths have occurred. Many ghost photographs have been taken here, showing misty forms of people going about the lives they led while in the camp – a man and woman crossing the street, miners walking around, two small children staring shyly at the camera.

DAYS *of the* DEAD

APRIL 21
The Death of Otto Klein, New York City, NY (1915)

Michelle (not her real name) raked the leaves carefully from around the gravestone. She enjoyed her job as a groundskeeper at Naperville Cemetery, even though it creeped some of her friends out. Michelle always told them, truthfully, that she'd never had a run-in with a ghost at work.

She took pride in her job, that's all. Some of these graves obviously hadn't had visitors in a very long time. Her job was to keep the place tidy, even if there was no longer any family to visit.

Take this grave. Somebody named Otto Klein was buried here. He had passed in 1915; it was now the early 1990s, so he'd been gone almost eighty years. Someone had loved him once, Michelle was sure. His gravestone was cheerfully decorated with carvings of flowers, a horseshoe, a lariat, and a cowboy hat. Guy must have loved horses.

A stubborn leaf right next to the base of the stone was resisting the tines of her rake. Michelle knelt down to grab it, and rested her hand on Otto's gravestone for support.

Instantly her mind took her … somewhere else. She smelled sawdust and the earthy, honest smell of horse. She heard the roar of an enthusiastic crowd, and a bright, tinny tune coming from all around her. She sensed that she was in some sort of arena. One thought stampeded around her head, despite the cheerful atmosphere: "Why me? Why now?" Michelle heard the plea in her mind. She knew it was Otto asking the plaintive question, but it felt like her own mind was wailing.

Michelle yanked her hand away and stared at the gravestone. She was herself again … but who was this Otto Klein?

She did some research. Otto Klein was a trick rider with the Barnum and Bailey Circus. He had a repertoire of many death-defying feats. At 28 years old, he had already made a name for himself as one of the top trick riders in the country, performing with his mare, Kitty.

One of Otto's and Kitty's tricks involved Otto leaping off of the horse, touching down, then leaping back over Kitty as she galloped around the arena at top speed. Otto and Kitty trusted each other implicitly, and the bond between man and horse was so strong that Otto routinely leapt back and forth over Kitty's back for two laps of the ring before landing in the saddle and coming to a stop.

The circus gave a performance at Madison Square Garden on April 21, 1915, and Otto and Kitty were in top form, Otto vaulting gracefully from side to side as Kitty thundered around the track. But near the end of the second lap, Otto lost his grip on the pommel of the saddle. His momentum sent him face-first into a wooden box, and he was knocked unconscious. Otto was carried from the arena and taken to the hospital. He died there a few hours later, the second Barnum and Bailey performer to die in as many years. Both deaths were at Madison Square Garden.

The other performers were stunned at the loss of one of their own. But, following the old motto, "the show must go on", the next performance, later that same day, went on as planned. Arthur Maywood performed in Otto's place, doing Otto's routine – including the daredevil stunt that had killed his friend just hours before.

Michelle also found out why Otto's consciousness had cried out "Why me? Why now?" in her mind. At the time of his death, Otto had just gotten married. While Otto went on the road with the circus, his young wife was here, in Naperville, Illinois, hundreds of miles away.

The next time Michelle went to clean that part of the cemetery, she brought a bunch of flowers to put on Otto's grave. She wanted him to know that he was not forgotten.

APRIL 22
Larry the Poltergeist, London, England (1958-1962)

Beginning in 1958, Graham Stringer and his family played host to a springtime poltergeist. Not wanting to alarm their 4-year-old son, who asked about the column of vibrating light that hung around the house sometimes, the Stringers decided to name the ghost Larry, and treat it like a person rather than an unexplained entity.

Larry laid low for most of the year, but during the Easter season, it caused mysterious fires in the London home. It first visited the Stringer home on Good Friday 1958. It manifested as a column of milky, fluorescent, vibrating light about as tall as a man. Shortly after seeing the entity, the Stringers smelled smoke coming from the baby's room. They discovered that something had burned a hole through the middle of a pile of the baby's clothes, just as neatly as if a blowtorch had done it.

In 1959, Larry was up to its tricks again. It yanked a pair of shoes out of Graham's hands. Then in 1960, it burned up another pile of clothes.

In 1961, the Stringers decided to end Lent with an exorcism of their home. A Catholic priest performed the rite just before Larry was scheduled to make its appearance. Easter Sunday that year was spent in peace. But Larry had just been taking a vacation. It was back in the spring of 1962, with more activity than ever. The living room furniture burst into flames. Their son's bed burned down to the springs. The Stringers called in a spirit medium.

The medium had a stunning message for the Stringers. During her visit on April 21, 1962, she told them that "Larry" was actually the spirit of Mrs. Stringer's baby brother Charles. Charles had died from burns twenty years earlier at the age of eighteen months. The medium promised: now that Charles had communicated the truth about the "poltergeist", he would leave his sister's family in peace.

Larry – or Charles – did find rest. After that, the Easter poltergeist never returned to the Stringer house.

APRIL 23
The Ghost That Wasn't, London, England (1240)

You know that scene in *Monty Python and the Holy Grail*, where the lord of Swamp Castle boasts that he had to build the castle four times? "The third one burned down, fell over, and THEN sank into the swamp, but the fourth one STAYED UP!" Well, that actually happened to a gate at the Tower of London.

In 1240, King Henry III ordered the construction of a gate to fortify the defenses on the side of the Tower that faced the Thames River. Since the land there on the riverbank was swampy and gross, setting the foundations was problematic. Builders constructed the gate – which collapsed into the river. They built another one – which also slid into the Thames.

The king noticed that both of the collapses happened on April 23, St. George's Day. He asked the contractors if they had any explanation for this. The builders didn't want to admit incompetence, so this being the Middle Ages, they cooked up a religious explanation. They said that both times, when they'd had the gate nearly built, the ghost of Thomas Becket had appeared and smashed the tower with his crozier, or bishop's staff of office.

Henry's own grandfather, Henry II, had been the king who was responsible for Becket's death. Henry II and Becket had once been the greatest of friends, until Henry named Becket Archbishop of Canterbury. Becket began to enforce the laws of the Church rather than those of the king, and by the time he was done, Henry loathed him. Deep in his cups with his barons one night, Henry had snarled, "Will no one rid me of this meddlesome priest?" The barons took him seriously, rode for Canterbury, and stabbed Becket while he was saying Mass.

Henry III was well aware that Becket's murder was the result of his grandfather's rash words. He ordered that in addition to rebuilding the tower once again, the contractors should also put up a chapel in honor of St. Thomas Becket.

His plan worked, and the tower has survived for nearly 800 years, held up by swampland and superstition.

APRIL 24
Madame LaLaurie's House of Horrors, New Orleans, LA (1834)

New Orleans has always been a place of free-spirited living, a place where people are encouraged to enjoy the good things life has to offer. But, as a bastion of the Deep South, it was also home to several huge slave markets. For the people who were bought and sold there, the good times did *not* roll.

One citizen of the town visited the slave markets quite often to choose merchandise, but for her own twisted reasons. Madame Delphine LaLaurie did not go to the slave auctions to find cute kids to dress up as pageboys. She didn't go to find talented cooks or seamstresses, or strong men to work her fields. Delphine LaLaurie was a predator. She bought slaves with the express knowledge that sooner or later they would probably be murdered at her hands.

Delphine abused her slaves. Everyone knew it – at least everyone gossiped about it. Some owners were like that, especially the ones who were rich enough not to count the cost of the human lives they purchased. But Delphine was different. Her cruelty was extravagant.

It was said that Delphine had killed one of her slaves, an eight-year-old girl named Lia. Some said that Lia had been brushing Delphine's hair, and the brush had caught on a stubborn tangle. Delphine jumped up from her chair in a rage, caught up a whip, and chased the girl up to the roof, lashing her unmercifully all the way. Lia, trying to escape the bite of the whip, fell shrieking to her death from the roof. Her body was hastily disposed of, but a neighbor had seen the rooftop scene. The LaLauries were investigated by the police. In the end, they were fined, and nine of their slaves were sold. Unfortunately for the slaves, the buyers at the auction were friends and relatives of the LaLauries. They were all bought and returned to bondage in the home of their abuser.

Of course, just to make historians' jobs harder, there is no legal record of nine slaves being forfeited by the LaLauries. But in 1828, Delphine sold six of her slaves to a family friend, Louis Brugniere. He turned around and sold four of them (Celestine, Ben, Juliette, and Edouard) to Andre Dussemir, another family friend. In 1830, Dussemir sold all four of them back to Delphine. Three of them – Celestine, Edouard, and Juliette – are recorded as dying in Delphine's possession sometime between 1831 and 1834.

The situation at 1140 Rue Royale was finally brought to light on April 10, 1834. Firefighters were called to the LaLaurie mansion because, most accounts say, the kitchen slave deliberately started a fire. She was in her seventies, and she spent her existence imprisoned in the kitchen, her world restricted by a 20-foot chain. When firefighters responded, what this slave told them brought the police running too.

As Delphine tried to shoo firefighters and looky-loos away from the blaze, the slave told firemen and police that she would rather burn to death than be a slave at the LaLaurie mansion for one more day. She was getting old, she said, and would be taken up to the attic soon, and people who went to the attic never came back. Then she single-handedly blew the lid off of years of abuse.

She told the firefighters that there were more slaves chained upstairs.

Rescuers hurried to the mansion's garret. Breaking through the locked door to the attic apartment, they revealed the depths of Delphine's depravity.

Some newspapers, with typical 19th-century reticence, drew a curtain over the whole scene, preferring to allow their readers to use their imaginations. Other papers, with typical 19th-century sensationalism, dwelled on the gory details to fascinate their readers. All we know now is that the scene up in that attic would have made Quentin Tarantino stumble to his knees and puke.

All seven of the slaves in the attic were naked and chained to the wall. They hadn't eaten in days. Some of the women had their stomachs sliced open, and their intestines pulled out and wrapped around their waists. One had her mouth stuffed with animal excrement, then sewn shut. Another had her limbs broken and re-set at odd angles.

The men had suffered even more horribly. They were found with fingernails pulled out, eyes gouged out, or with gaping, festering wounds where chunks of flesh had been sliced away.

Some accounts were even more graphic. One man was said to have had his severed hand sewn to his stomach. Another, found hanging lifeless from his shackles, had a hole drilled into the top of his skull, with a stick protruding from the hole. It had evidently been used to stir his brains.

Please note: these explicit details were reported in a book written over 110 years after the discovery, by Jeanne De Lavigne. In her 1946 book *Ghost Stories of Old New Orleans*, the author claimed that the first responders to the 1834 fire had found the slaves in this condition, but newspapers of the day, like the *New Orleans Bee*, did not report these details. We simply know that the seven slaves were chained, starving, and had been horribly abused, with limbs stretched and ripped from their bodies. All had been whipped savagely, and some had iron collars around their heads preventing them from lying down to sleep. And one man, according to the *Courier*, did have a hole in his head.

The law was immediately brought in, and demanded to know the details behind the abuse. Delphine's husband tartly replied that "some people should best stop meddling in the affairs of others." This insolence infuriated the people of New Orleans, and mob justice was invoked. The angry mob destroyed the LaLaurie mansion, finishing what the small fire had started.

The mansion stood in ruins for several years, until a new owner bought it in 1837 and refurbished it. Over the years, it has been a boarding house, a school building, a bar, a furniture store, and a luxury hotel. Paranormal phenomena reported over the years include sightings of the ghost of Dr. Leonard LaLaurie, a girl's scream echoing in the courtyard, and the phantom of a mutilated black man in chains.

How much of this is historical, and how much is hearsay? It's difficult to tell, especially after nearly two centuries have gone by. There really is no evidence that Delphine was abusive towards her slaves until she got married for the third time. Delphine's second husband died in 1818, and she remained unmarried for ten years. In 1825, she met Dr. Leonard Louis LaLaurie, who'd just arrived from France. He was 25, she was pushing 40. He specialized in treating spinal conditions, and Delphine's daughter Pauline suffered from a spinal deformity. She hired him to treat Pauline.

What began as a professional relationship turned personal, and in 1828, Delphine gave birth to Leonard's son. Leonard's brother talked him into doing the honorable thing, and the couple married later that year.

It was not a happy marriage, and in 1832, Delphine requested a separation. It doesn't seem to have been permanent, though, as Leonard was back at the house at the time of the fire in 1834.

Here's the interesting thing: there are no records of Delphine being investigated for cruelty to her slaves before her third marriage in 1828. And of the twenty slaves who died while owned by Delphine, twelve of them died between 1831 and 1833. So maybe it was Dr. LaLaurie's influence that made Delphine go bad. We'll never know for sure.

APRIL 25
The Mystery on Annan Road, Scotland (1962)

For sheer paranormal weirdness, it's hard to beat the experience shared by Dereck and Norman Ferguson. The brothers, aged 22 and 14, had been on a short vacation in Scotland in April 1962. They were returning to their home in Annan, and were nearly there when they stopped for gas just before midnight. They filled the car, then got in and headed for home, about fifteen miles away. Dereck was driving.

The moon was shining, and the road was lit by their car's headlights. They were alone on the road ... or so they thought.

Suddenly, what looked like a large white bird flew directly at the windshield. Dereck swerved to avoid the thing, but it disappeared before it hit the car.

Then, the brothers saw an old woman running down the middle of the road, waving her arms and screaming. Dereck jerked the wheel, and again, the strange old woman vanished.

Then came an entire menagerie of phantasmic figures, all looming out of the darkness and hurtling themselves at the car. Giant cats, birds, savage-looking dogs, shapes that were vaguely human ... and they all vanished just before the moment of impact.

And the weirdness wasn't only outside the car. Inside the car, the temperature began to drop. Dereck's hands felt very heavy on the wheel, and it felt as if some other force was trying to gain control of the car. He wrenched the steering wheel, trying to avoid hitting the phantasms outside, but he was having more and more trouble controlling the car. Both brothers were drenched in sweat, so Dereck rolled his window down a little.

That was a mistake. It was bone-chillingly cold outside the car, and as soon as Dereck cracked the window, the brothers could hear the screaming, cackling, and high-pitched laughter that filled the air.

Finally, Dereck stopped the car. Immediately a powerful force began to buffet the car, rocking it on its springs. Instinctively, Dereck opened the door and jumped out, while Norman huddled in the passenger seat. As soon as Dereck was outside the car, the shaking stopped, the noise dimmed, and all was quiet and serene.

Dereck got back into the car, and all hell broke loose again. The car started rocking and shaking again, and it felt like invisible fists were pounding on the windows. Horrible laughter filled the air.

Dereck decided to drive, slowly and carefully and without stopping, to Annan. He started driving again, trying desperately to ignore the ghostly figures that surrounded the car on all sides.

Finally, ahead of them, Dereck and Norman saw the red tail lights of a large truck. Both brothers felt themselves relax – at last, there was a sense of normalcy returning to their trip. But relief soon morphed into fear when Dereck realized he was coming up on the truck too fast. He wrenched the steering wheel from side to side, but the car didn't respond. He stamped on the brakes … nothing. Just when the car was about to slam into the back of the truck – the truck vanished. It was yet another phantom.

The brothers finally reached home. It felt like an eternity, but their bizarre trip had only lasted half an hour. Dereck was sure that if they had stopped for any length of time, they would not have survived the strange experience.

APRIL 26
The Death of Kate Penfound, Cornwall, England (mid-17th century, recurring)

They say that the difference between Britain and America is that the Brits think a hundred miles is a long way, and Americans think a hundred years is a long time.

The oldest part of Penfound Manor in Cornwall was built in Saxon times, before the Norman Conquest in 1066. Later additions kept the grand old home livable. With nearly a thousand years of continuous occupation, Penfound Manor is the oldest inhabited estate in the country.

The manor takes its name from the Penfound family, who from about the 15th to the 17th centuries were the leading family in Cornwall. The tragic tale of Kate Penfound, which has given us this ghost story, occurred in the mid-17th century.

Trebarfoot Manor, three miles from Penfound, was home to the Trebarfoot family, a family equally as honorable as the Penfounds. As a matter of fact, Kate Penfound and John Trebarfoot fell in love, and wanted to marry. But the marriage had not been arranged by Nicholas Penfound, Kate's father, and so was forbidden. So, Kate and John, exchanging letters in the hollow trunk of a tree, made plans to elope.

On the night of April 26, Kate waited until the whole household had gone to bed. Then she climbed out of her bedroom window via a ladder that John had brought for her. Kate made it safely down to the courtyard, and was soon in John's waiting arms.

But Nicholas Penfound had stayed up late that night. He heard Kate coming down the ladder and rushed out, sword drawn. In the confusion of the swordfight, Kate threw herself between John and Nicholas. All three of them were killed.

They say that the tragic scene is re-enacted at midnight every April 26. But Kate doesn't seem to be bound just to exist as a residual haunting. She has been seen wandering through the manor, which is open to the public. She always disappears at the head of the main staircase. And as tragic as her end was, her spirit is not malicious or unhappy. She leaves a feeling of great joy and tranquility whenever she appears.

APRIL 27
Lincoln's Funeral Train (1865)

When Abraham Lincoln was assassinated on April 14, 1865, the entire nation – South as well as North – reeled in shock. The South had lost the man who could have directed Reconstruction "with malice towards none". The North had lost their hero, the president who had led them to victory and had restored the Union. The Great Emancipator was gone.

When the first sharp shock had worn off, the thoughts of the nation turned to a state funeral. Not just any funeral would do – Lincoln was the first president to be assassinated, and he had to be honored in grand style.

The North wanted to mourn its fallen leader as publicly as possible. It was decided that a train should follow, in reverse, the route Lincoln had taken to get to Washington from Springfield, Illinois (adding a stop in Chicago). The route traced a path of 654 miles through seven states, rolling through 444 towns, and stopping in eleven cities for funeral processions and lying-in-state. The train never went over 20 miles an hour, so the doleful trip could be seen by anyone near the tracks.

On April 22 and 23, Lincoln lay in state in Philadelphia's Independence Hall, where the Declaration of Independence was signed. On April 25, future president Theodore Roosevelt was one of the citizens who filed past Lincoln's coffin in New York City. On April 27, 100,000 people paid their respects to the fallen leader, including former president Millard Fillmore and future president Grover Cleveland.

The funeral car was the Presidential train car, built for Lincoln during his time in office. It was the pinnacle of 1860s travel – ornate, gorgeous, ostentatious luxury on wheels as befitted the Chief Executive. It was basically the Air Force One of the 19th-century. But true to his modest personality, Lincoln shunned it. He never used the Presidential train car in life … only in death.

The train carried not only Lincoln's coffin, but also the small casket of his son Willie, who died at the age of eleven in 1862 of typhoid fever during Lincoln's second year in office. Father and son were to be buried together at Oak Ridge Cemetery in Springfield.

When the train had passed by each town, and the men had replaced their hats on their heads and the ladies had put away their hankies, everyone turned away from the train tracks thinking that they'd had a once-in-a-lifetime experience. They had … but it would be seen again. And again.

Lincoln's funeral train still makes its solemn, silent way along the tracks, following the route it took in April 1865. Sightings generally occur in April, as if to note the somber anniversary. The train itself makes no noise – it's as if the tracks are muffled in black carpet – but some people say that a band of skeletal musicians dressed in tattered military uniforms now accompanies the funeral car, playing mournful tunes as they sit on a flat car. It's said that when the spectral train rolls through a station, all the clocks in the area stop, as if in deference to the passing president. After the train passes, the clocks start up again.

The emotions of grief and loss and desolation experienced by people along the train's route certainly formed a matrix for a recurring haunting. But there is one other factor to consider in this story: the funeral car itself, the one that bore Lincoln's body home, is also a ghost. Decades after the train had completed its solemn duty, a private collector bought the Presidential car, intending to restore it. It was stored in a trainyard outside Minneapolis, Minnesota. In 1911, a prairie fire devastated the area, including that trainyard. The historic car was destroyed in the conflagration.

APRIL 28
A Deadly Explosion, Maryville, MO (1951)

The website of Northwest Missouri State University (nwmissouri.edu) mentions Roberta, the school's most famous ghost. On April 28, 1951, a gasoline storage tanker was parked on a railway siding of the Wabash Railroad tracks directly behind the Women's Residence Hall, the only female dorm on campus. The car exploded, sending steel beams and debris into the building and setting the structure on fire. Thirty female students were hurt, four of them quite badly. One of those critically injured was a girl named Roberta Steel. She died a year and a half later of complications from her injuries. The dorm was rebuilt, and named Roberta Hall in her memory.

Roberta's ghost is a playful prankster. She loves to throw hairbrushes at the girls in her dorm. She'll turn lights off if she thinks they're staying up too late, and she'll turn the volume down on loud music. She's quite the musician herself; she often plays the piano in the empty basement.

Roberta has also been known to lock or unlock doors and windows, and she seems to have a thing for keys, because they often go missing. When Roberta appears, it's usually in the form of a dark, indistinct shadow. On one occasion, though, the ghost materialized and tried to climb into a bed already occupied by a sleeping student.

APRIL 29
Higher "Dead-ucation", Bowling Green, KY (1979)

Colleges and universities do tend to attract spirits. Something about all that youthful energy, kids getting out on their own as young adults, students pulling all-nighters in search of good grades, it all coalesces into a swirl of emotions. Here's another ghost story from ivy halls.

Western Kentucky University sits on a 200-acre campus in the hills of Kentucky. Its website, too, has a page devoted to the tales that have been reported in nearly a dozen buildings on campus. (Visit wku.edu, and click on the History tab. There's a page there labeled "Ghost Stories".) The campus has even been featured on SyFy's *Ghost Hunters*.

Potter Hall was built in 1921 as a women's dorm. During the 1980s and 1990s, the building was abuzz with paranormal activity. Lights would turn on and off, desk drawers would rattle, disembodied footsteps would wander the halls, furniture would move, and cold winds would blow through the dorm rooms. In addition to this garden-variety activity, students would also hear coins dropping into the vending machine, and some even heard their names being whispered.

With all this activity in a college dorm, it was inevitable that someone would bring in a Ouija board. The spirit that came through sassily named itself "Casperella", although it also responded to the name Allison. Through the board, it told the sitters that it liked to play pranks on people, and that it loved to move things that weren't supposed to move on their own. This spirit really knew how to get people's attention!

It's generally accepted that "Casperella" is the spirit of Theresa Watkins, who lived in Room 7 on the basement level. In April 1979, she hanged herself with a belt from the heating pipes in the room.

Potter Hall is now an administration building, housing the Office of Admissions. With no students to pester, the ghost of Theresa Watkins has been lying low since the changes. But sometimes, staff members working on the ground floor of the three-story building will come into their offices in the morning and find random pennies lying around. They've nicknamed this generous spook "Penny", but it might very well be Casperella.

APRIL 30
A President's Sorrow, Richmond, VA (1864)

Abraham Lincoln. Jefferson Davis. Both men served as presidents of their chosen countries. Both men guided their countries through the turbulent days of the Civil War, and watched in agony as their soldiers fought and died for the cause they believed in.

The men were linked in another tragic way: both Lincoln and Davis suffered the loss of a child during their time in office.

In February 1862, Willie Lincoln died at the White House from typhoid fever. Abraham grieved the loss of the 11-year-old boy, and Mary Lincoln was inconsolable. A doting father himself, Jefferson Davis sent his sincere condolences to Washington. The differences of war took a back seat to very personal pain.

Jefferson and Varina Davis were parents to Margaret, Jefferson Jr., and Joseph. At the start of the war, the Confederate government rented a home in Richmond, Virginia to serve as the Executive Mansion. Two more children would be born there, William and Varina (nicknamed Winnie). The children brought joy to Jefferson's life, and a respite from the cares of the presidency. Davis adored all his children, but he made no secret that Joe was his favorite. He often said that Joe was his greatest joy in life.

On April 30, 1864, both Jefferson and Varina Davis had gone out for the day. Early that evening, Joe, who had just turned five, was playing on the railing of the balcony. He lost his grip and fell, landing on the pavement fifteen feet below the portico.

Jeff Jr., only seven years old himself, came out and frantically asked passersby for help, but nothing could be done. The fall had cracked Joe's skull, and a Confederate officer who stopped to help said he thought the boy had internal injuries as well. Joe died just as his parents came home. Jefferson Davis refused visitors immediately after Joe's death. Shortly after the funeral, he had the balcony removed from the house and destroyed. Some say that Davis never really recovered from the loss. Abraham Lincoln sent Davis a heart-felt letter of sympathy, just as Davis had done for him when he'd lost Willie.

Joe was buried in Hollywood Cemetery in Richmond. Less than a year later, on April 2, 1865, Union forces captured Richmond. The Davis family escaped, but Jefferson Davis was later arrested in May. While the family had been on the run, Lincoln had been assassinated, and most people figured that Jeff Davis was somehow involved.

In all the hubbub of the fall of Richmond, and Davis's escape and later arrest, the little ghost of Joe Davis was left behind. Dozens of witnesses claimed to see the phantom of a young boy who looked a lot like Joe wandering around near the executive mansion. The boy would ignore the people around him. He would simply mumble, "He's gone! He's gone!" before disappearing.

Jefferson Davis died in 1889. His body lay in two different cemeteries before Confederate veterans convinced his widow Varina to bury him in Richmond Cemetery in 1893. When Davis reached his final resting place, Joe was exhumed and buried next to his father.

Interestingly, it was at that time that the apparition of the little boy who haunted the street near the executive mansion, the one who wandered aimlessly, whimpering "He's gone!", suddenly stopped its melancholy appearances. It was never seen again.

MAY

MAY 1
Cursed, Or Not?, Chicago, IL (1914, recurring)

The discovery of the tomb of King Tutankhamen in 1922 energized the dusty world of archaeology, and the rest of the world too. The glorious art of ancient Egypt – everywhere, the glint of gold – captured everyone's imagination. Plus, the tomb had a curse attached! Can't get much cooler than that, can you?

Darius Miller is buried in Rosehill Cemetery, on the north side of Chicago. He rests in a gorgeous Egyptian-revival tomb. Legend has it that Miller, a curator of Egyptology at the Field Museum, was part of the expedition that discovered Tut's tomb in 1922, and he fell victim to the curse – "Death shall come on swift wings" and all that.

Sadly, for those of us who love a good juicy curse, that didn't happen. Darius Miller died on August 24, 1914, of appendicitis while on vacation in Montana. This was a full eight years before Tut's tomb was dug out from Egypt's shifting sands. To further dull the sheen of Miller's legend, he wasn't a curator at the Field, either. He was a boring old railroad president.

That hasn't stopped his afterlife from being pretty exciting. Darius Miller's beautiful crypt is home to a strangely predictable ghost light. In the early morning hours on the first of every May, the crypt lights up with an eerie blue glow.

MAY 2
A Quick-thinking Priest, Cookstown, Ireland (1819)

Thomas Meredith was a real Renaissance man, well-educated, and highly regarded by his friends. He was a distinguished mathematician who spoke before the Royal Irish Academy in Dublin. He was also a Doctor of Divinity, and served as rector of the parish church of Ardtrea, near Cookstown. He died young, on May 2, 1819. He was only 42 years old.

Thomas died of "apoplexy" – what we now know as stroke. There's a grand memorial to him at Ardtrea, which says that Thomas died as a result of "a sudden and awful visitation." While that is one way to look at a stroke, this is where we get to the weirdness.

The story goes that the manor house of Ardtrea was haunted by a ghost. (One version says it was a lady in white, possibly the fifth-century St. Trea. Another story just calls it a nasty ghost or even a demon.) Whatever it was, virgin saint or demon, it was so horrifying that everyone in the family had fled the house in terror. Thomas tried to shoot the ghost, but that had no effect. Someone suggested he use a silver bullet. That just seemed to piss the ghost off, because the next morning, Thomas was found dead on the floor. The demon-ghost was still loose in the house, gibbering and screaming out of the windows at the servant who found Thomas's body.

Neighbors advised the servant to fetch a priest to vanquish the ghost. At the man's request, the priest arrived, with a jar of whiskey in hand. The priest offered to pour the ghost a shot, which the ghost accepted. The priest kept pouring, and the ghost kept tossing them back, getting more and more chill by the shot. Soon the ghost was feeling no pain, and there was just one glass of whiskey left in the jar. The priest reached for the jar, pretending he was going to pour the last glass for himself. The ghost quickly made itself as skinny as an eel, and slipped into the jar to lick out every last drop. The priest grabbed the cork and slammed it into the neck of the jar, trapping the ghost inside. He made the sign of the Cross over the jar, and buried it in the cellar of the rectory. It's said that even now, the ghost can be heard in the cellar of the manor house, yelling to be let out of its glass prison.

MAY 3
A Prophetic Dream, London, England (1812)

John Williams sat up in bed, panting, his throat hot and tight from trying to scream in his sleep. This was the third nightmare he'd had that night, and the dreams had all been the same. He'd surface briefly, then get dragged back down into the same nightmare as it began again.

In the dream, he was standing in London at the House of Commons. He saw a man in a brown coat draw a pistol and shoot a small man who was wearing a blue coat. In each replaying of the dream, bystanders overpowered the assassin, but in each replay, the little guy in the blue coat was still lying on the floor, shot in the chest and bleeding out. John asked the same question all three times – who'd been shot? All three times, some faceless dream-actor gave him the same reply: it was the Prime Minister, Spencer Perceval.

When John finally clawed his way to wakefulness, his first thought was to warn Perceval. He wanted to set off for London immediately, but his family and friends talked him out of it. After all, it was only a dream.

A week passed. Then on May 11, 1812, John Bellingham, a grocer from Liverpool, walked into the lobby of the House of Commons and shot Spencer Perceval in the chest. He blamed the Prime Minister for the failure of his business. He sat quietly on a bench on the lobby as members of Parliament reeled in shock. Perceval was dead in minutes, blood soaking through his blue coat. A week later, Bellingham was hanged, and his body donated to the anatomists.

For the rest of his life, John Williams regretted not acting on his prophetic dream. Even stranger, Perceval himself had a series of strange dreams, ending by dreaming of his own death on the night of May 10, while he was spending the night at the house of the Earl of Harrowby. The next morning, he told the earl about his dream, and his friend tried to talk him out of attending Parliament that day. But Perceval refused to be scared. After all, it was only a dream.

MAY 4
Violence at Kent State, Kent, OH (1970)

The late 1960s in America were not always a time of flower children and free love. They were also a time of incredible social turmoil. The United States was still deeply involved in the Vietnam War, and young men lived every day with the knowledge that their names were on the draft list. Any day, they could be sent halfway across the world to kill or be killed, or wounded, or driven insane …

College students all over the country protested the war. Richard Nixon had won the 1968 election with the promise that he would get America out of Vietnam, but on April 30, 1970, Nixon ordered 20,000 American and South Vietnamese troops to invade Cambodia and destroy North Vietnamese and Viet Cong bases.

The unrest on college campuses boiled over into angry protests all that weekend. One of them, at a mid-size state college in northeastern Ohio, would resonate far beyond the end of the war.

At noon on May 4, several hundred demonstrators gathered on the Commons at Kent State for an anti-war rally. Several hundred more people were watching or cheering them on. A troop of National Guardsmen were also in attendance, to make sure things didn't get out of hand. They fired canisters of tear gas to break up the crowd. After clearing the Commons, the Guardsmen marched over to the practice field.

Protestors were gathered in the parking lot of Prentice Hall, still milling around. The Guardsmen fired more tear gas. The protestors responded by throwing stones and shouting obscenities. An officer ordered the Guardsmen to return to the Commons. Suddenly, without orders, a line of soldiers knelt and fired 67 shots into the gathered crowd, killing four and wounding nine.

The Guardsmen later claimed that they had fired in response to a sniper attack – but no one else reported a sniper on the roof of nearby Taylor Hall, or anywhere else. (Besides, why fire into a crowd on the ground if there's a sniper on the roof?) A soldier described the students in warlike terms: "We were surrounded and outnumbered ten to one. You should have seen those animals. They were trying to take our rifles away. Someone in the crowd yelled that we were only carrying blanks, so the students assaulted up the hill while others tried to outflank us by going around the rear of Taylor hill."

The Guardsmen's perceptions were seriously skewed – they swore that students were three feet away, brandishing rock as big as baseballs, and slabs of concrete. In reality, none of the rocks thrown were larger than golf balls. And the closest student, one of the nine wounded, was 60 to 70 feet from the line of fire. Some of the victims were as far as 700 feet away.

The deaths at Kent State sent the nation reeling, and the psychic echoes of that needless violence are still felt today. The young people who died – Jeffrey Miller, William Schroeder, Allison Krause and Sandra Scheuer – were barely out of their teens, all good students with promising careers ahead of them. Two of them, Schroeder and Scheuer, weren't even there for the protest. Sandra Scheuer was just on her way to her next class.

The bodies of the four students killed were taken to Stopher Hall (now demolished). Even though they were laid out together, the ghosts of Kent State are almost never seen together when they manifest. Their appearances are sporadic, and happen mainly in their former dorm rooms or apartments. Allison Krause lived in a room in Engleman Hall that now experiences significant paranormal activity. And reddit user Mach Elish posted that she may have brought the spirit of Jeffrey Miller back to her dorm room. She and her roommate would hear footsteps above them ... but they lived on the top floor. Mach Elish transferred to Kent State halfway through the year, as did Jeffrey Miller. Miller was 20 years old when he died, and at the time of her reddit posting, Mach Elish and her group of friends were all 20 years old.

What really creeped Mach Elish out, though, was the way Jeffrey manifested in her room. She and her roommate often heard heavy breathing in the room, as if someone invisible was breathing heavily through their nose. While doing research on Jeffrey's death, Mach Elish discovered that Jeffrey had been shot at a distance of 265 feet ... and the bullet had gone through his open mouth and through his skull, killing him instantly.

Could this be why Jeffrey's spirit now breathes noisily through its nose?

MAY 5
The Battle of the Wilderness, Fredericksburg, VA (1864)

In the spring of 1864, newly appointed General-in-Chief Grant began his Overland Campaign, aimed at Richmond, Virginia, the Confederate capital. Grant's goal was to keep Lee's Army of Northern Virginia busy defending Richmond, so that Lee couldn't send troops into Georgia to engage with Sherman's advance. Grant's Army of the Potomac crossed the Rapidan River on May 4, and Lee decided to face Grant in the dense Virginia woods known as the Wilderness. This was familiar terrain for the Confederates, and the heavily wooded landscape would reduce the advantage the Union troops had as far as numbers (there were 65,000 Confederates facing 115,000 Union troops). The battle was fought over two bloody, chaotic days, resulting in around 29,800 casualties.

The Battle of the Wilderness ended inconclusively, although Grant refused to order a retreat – he had promised Lincoln that he would not halt the army's advance, no matter what. Despite suffering more than 17,500 casualties over two days of fighting, the Union army pressed south to Spotsylvania Courthouse. Lee's army met them there on May 8, beginning the Battle of Spotsylvania, the third bloodiest engagement of the war. That battle lasted, incredibly, nearly two weeks, from May 8 to May 21, 1864.

The Wilderness Tavern was used as a makeshift field hospital, with bloody amputated limbs piled up outside the door. Only one outbuilding still stands today, but the area is still plagued with ghostly activity. Apparitions walk slowly around the area, and witnesses still hear the phantom moans and screams of soldiers who are forever undergoing amputations of mangled limbs.

MAY 6
The Death of Elenora French, ME (1865)

Mount Magunticook in Maine boasts miles of beautiful but strenuous hiking trails. The trails gain 1,000 feet in altitude, and the views at the top are amazing. It's the second highest mountain along the Atlantic Coast, and the tallest peak in Camden Hills State Park. The mountain is wooded, but there are two scenic lookouts, Maiden's Cliff and Ocean Lookout.

Maiden's Cliff is the rocky outcropping that brings us today's ghost story. These trails have been popular with hikers for many decades – a teacher took a group of girls up the trail on May 7, 1864, for a picnic. This group included 12-year-old Elenora French, her older sister, and some of her friends. They hiked up the trail to Maiden's Cliff. They crossed a small stream, then hiked up a steeper trail. The trail leveled off after a while, leading to the rocks at the top of the cliff.

No one really saw what happened to Elenora, but years later, Elenora's sister said that while her back was turned, a playful gust of wind snatched Elenora's bonnet off her head. Elenora automatically reached for the bonnet, not realizing she was right next to the edge of the rocky outcropping. She caught the bonnet, and sat on a rock to put it back on. While she was engrossed in this, another gust of wind knocked her off the cliff. She fell 300 feet down. She survived the fall, but she had suffered serious internal damage, and it took hours for rescuers to reach her. She died of her injuries that night.

Elenora was buried in French Cemetery in Lincolnville, but her story was not forgotten. A rich tourist named Joseph Sterna paid for a white cross to be erected on the ledge, a monument to the lost little girl.

Elenora's spirit still haunts the trails in the area, especially during the spring and summer months. She manifests as a warm breeze, or as an apparition hovering over banks of flowers in the park.

MAY 7
A Long Road to Death, Phoenix, AZ (1928)

The San Carlos Hotel in Phoenix, Arizona is home to more than one ghost. On May 7, 1928, the *Arizona Republic* reported the death earlier that day of pretty, 22-year-old Leone Jensen. Leone checked into Room 720, on the top floor of the hotel. Then she put on an evening gown, went to the roof of the hotel overlooking Monroe Street, and jumped. The death was considered to be a suicide, based on the note found, which pointed to trouble with Leone's boyfriend. The boyfriend, a bellhop at the nearby Westward Ho hotel, seemed to be abusing Leone, and was cheating on her with another hotel employee. There are other theories that Leone was pushed to her death, either by her boyfriend or by the other woman. Leone's spirit often appears as a white mist, but witnesses have also seen her apparition on the roof in her evening gown.

But Leone is not alone. The hotel had opened less than three months earlier, on March 19, 1928. Previously, the land had been the site of the first elementary school in Phoenix. The four-room adobe school began in 1874, and was enlarged several times over the decades. But in 1916, the building was condemned, with an eye towards building a luxury hotel on the land. The other ghost that haunts the San Carlos, according to employees, is a little girl between six and nine years old, who wanders into hotel rooms at night and sits crying. Three young boys are livelier, wandering the halls and bouncing balls to entertain themselves. Guests sometimes hear children laughing in empty rooms. Are they some of the school's students, mourning the loss of a place of learning and happiness? Or are they perhaps young victims of the 1918 flu pandemic?

In an even eerier turn of events, the school itself had a brush with the paranormal during construction. When the basement of the school was excavated in 1874, the contractors broke through and disturbed a spring that has been sacred to the Hohokam tribe for hundreds of years. Other stories claim that the school was built over the ruins of a Hohokam village. Is this how the disturbances here began? Supernatural occurrences often have a history going back decades. This may be the case at the magnificently haunted San Carlos Hotel.

MAY 8
The Churchyard Phantom, Hinxton, England (1885)

Alfred Bard was a gardener who lived in Hinxton. On the evening of May 8, 1885, he was walking home from work when at around 9:20 he passed through the cemetery in Hinxton. This wasn't unusual; it was his accustomed route home.

What was a bit unusual was that he saw a former employer, a Mrs. de Freville, in the cemetery. The lady was dressed in black, and was leaning against the fence near the vault in which her husband had been buried. Alfred thought it odd for the lady to be out alone so late at night, but he figured she simply wanted to visit the mausoleum.

Alfred walked up to the tomb, intending to see if it was open for Mrs. de Freville's visit. He walked around the outside of the crypt, keeping his gaze on old Mrs. de Freville. She turned and watched him as he came closer. He noted how pale she was, but assumed it was the wash of moonlight on her face. He was within five or six yards of her the whole time. He peered around the corner of the crypt to see if the door was open, and stumbled as his foot caught on a tuft of grass. He looked down to catch his footing, then looked up again.

Mrs. de Freville was gone.

Alfred assumed she had gone into the mausoleum, but when he got to the door moments later, he found it locked. This spooked him so badly that he rushed home.

The next day, Alfred heard that Mrs. de Freville had died the previous afternoon, in London.

MAY 9
The Sunshine Skyway Bridge Collapse, FL (1980)

Florida is known for beaches, sunny skies, and spring breakers gone wild. But the Sunshine State isn't always blue skies and bikinis. When it rains in Florida, it pours.

One of those torrential rainstorms pounded Florida on May 9, 1980 ... and led to tragedy.

It was the morning rush hour. Rain was sheeting down, and visibility was next to nil. Cars, pickup trucks, even a Greyhound bus full of college students, all picked their way carefully across the Sunshine Skyway Bridge over Tampa Bay.

Below them, another vehicle was struggling through the storm. The freighter *Summit Venture* was headed into port at Tampa to pick up 28,000 tons of phosphate. But at 7:30 in the morning, it was empty, riding high in the water and at the mercy of the squall. The wind lashed rain across the window on the boat's cabin.

Suddenly, *Summit Venture* hit one of the steel supports of the bridge, knocking down a chunk of road 1,260 feet long. Six cars, the pickup, and the Greyhound bus plummeted into the water fifteen stories below. Thirty-five people died. There was only one survivor. Wesley MacIntire, the driver of the pickup, only survived because the momentum of his truck was slowed when it hit the ship's prow. The truck later sank in 40 feet of water, but MacIntire managed to swim to the surface.

The harbor pilot, John Lerro, was unfairly blamed for the accident. He was trying his best to pilot the boat through a "hellacious" storm, keeping out of the way of oncoming boat traffic, in a ship that was so light, he described it as "like a sailboat, a giant steel, empty sailboat."

The loss of 35 people in the bridge collapse was a tragedy, but John has accepted his role in it. As he told a reporter for the *Miami Herald* twelve years later, "There is a reason why I'm here on earth. It wasn't to kill people."

Tragically, the May 1980 collapse is not the only reason the Sunshine Skyway Bridge is haunted. A boat collision earlier that year, on January 28, killed 23 men. And the bridge ranks fourth in the nation for jumps. Over 200 people have plunged from the 197-foot-high bridge.

The ghost stories of the bridge predate the two 1980 disasters. In the 1960s and 70s, people called the police quite often, saying that a young woman was getting ready to jump off the bridge, but investigation turned up neither jumper nor body. The bridge also has a phantom hitchhiker, a young woman who sobs as the car approaches the crest of the bridge, and vanishes before the car reaches the summit. Sometimes, early in the morning, people will hear screams and the shrill sound of squealing brakes.

Fishermen often sit on parts of the old bridge to cast their lines. According to one story, a group of men were fishing from one of the piers when they saw an older-model Greyhound bus drive past. The passengers all stared blankly ahead, except for one woman, who smiled and waved as the bus passed the men. After the bus had gone past, the fishermen realized that the date was May 9, 1990 ... the tenth anniversary of the bridge collapse.

MAY 10
A Ghostly Attack, Manila, Philippines (1951)

On May 10, 1951, police in Manila were called to pick up an 18-year-old girl who was found wandering the streets, shrieking that a black-caped monster was attacking her and biting her. Clarita Villanueva was taken into custody; the police figured she was either on drugs or an alcoholic suffering from delirium tremens.

The police medical officer, Dr. Mariana Lara, had a different opinion after his examination. He declared that Clarita had suffered an epileptic fit. He suggested that she be closely watched while in her cell that night, so she wouldn't injure herself further. He left Clarita huddled in fear behind the bunk in her cell. The police officer assigned to watch her reassured her that no monster could get her through the bars.

Clarita shrieked that the monster *was* coming, it was coming for her right through the bars!

As the police officer stared in stunned disbelief, angry red teeth marks began to appear on Clarita's upper arms and shoulders. He opened the cell door, rushed in, and helped Clarita to stand. She screamed again as more bite marks appeared. Blood was running down her arms as the policeman led her staggering from her cell.

Together they went in search of the police captain. Soon, Mayor Arsenio Lacson and the chief of police were there too, and the medical examiner had been summoned back to the station.

Dr. Lara arrived in a foul temper. He didn't appreciate, he said, being dragged out of bed in the middle of the night to look at a patient he'd already examined. The girl was epileptic, he repeated, and had obviously inflicted the bite marks on herself.

The chief of police and the mayor stared at Dr. Lara. Clarita had bite marks *on the back of her neck*, and still the doctor claimed they were self-inflicted?

Dr. Lara did another examination as the others questioned Clarita further. She told them that her attacker was a man dressed in a long, flowing black cape. He would rush at her with ugly fangs bared, sinking them into her flesh. The medical examiner admitted that the wounds did look like bite marks, and that Clarita didn't seem to be drunk or under the influence of any drugs.

Clarita spent the rest of the night on a bench in the front office of the police station, watched at all times by an officer. The next morning, she was taken to court on vagrancy charges. Everyone in the courtroom saw what happened next: the invisible monster attacked again.

Reporters swarmed to the front of the courtroom as Clarita writhed and shrieked from the pain of the bites. Everyone watched as bite marks appeared in Clarita's flesh, as invisible jaws tore at her. Dr. Lara told a police officer to send for the mayor again … and for the archbishop as well.

By the time Mayor Lacson got to the courtroom, Clarita was swooning with pain, her body a mass of blood, bruises, and bite marks. The mayor reacted with instinctive compassion. "You poor girl," he said, and took Clarita's hand in his. While he was holding her hand, red gashes appeared on either side of her index finger, as though teeth were trying to chew her finger off. Dr. Lara called for an ambulance, and he and Mayor Lacson rode with Clarita to the hospital.

Things got worse on the fifteen-minute ambulance ride. Clarita bucked in pain as she shrieked that now there were two vicious creatures attacking her. Invisible monsters still gnawed on her hands, and teeth marks appeared on both sides of her throat as she screamed.

Once Clarita was in the hospital, though, the attacks stopped. Clarita Villanueva was released after six weeks, almost completely recovered. She was never attacked by the invisible monsters again … but she bore the scars from May 10, 1951 for the rest of her life.

MAY 11
Murder at Sayre House, Morristown, NJ (1833)

The Sayre home, built in 1749 by the patriarch John Sayre, was a peaceful place, a place where generations of the Sayre family lived happily. But in 1833, someone arrived at the Sayre house who would throw everything into turmoil, and leave the Sayre home with the reputation of being one of the most haunted, infamous places in New Jersey.

Antoine LeBlanc was a French immigrant who came to seek his fortune. LeBlanc was from a good family, and he had plans to marry. He'd been in the country only three days when he was hired by Samuel Sayre to work the family farm.

At first, LeBlanc was thrilled. He had a job, even if it was just chopping wood and slopping hogs. Not bad for a guy who could barely speak English. But even with his limited communication skills, LeBlanc soon realized he had gotten a really bum deal. In exchange for his menial labor, he was to receive lodging in a small room in the dank basement of the Sayre house … and that was it. No wages, no cash, nothing.

LeBlanc was peeved. How could he afford to save his money to get back to Germany and marry his ladylove if he wasn't even getting paid for the work he did? And it was crap work, too. Even worse, since he was the low man on the household totem pole, he had to take orders from everyone – Samuel, his wife Sarah, even their servant Phoebe. Soon, LeBlanc had worked himself into a righteous fury. If he couldn't earn a decent wage, he'd steal it.

On May 11, LeBlanc took his revenge. He called Samuel Sayre out to the stable, saying there was a problem with the horses. Samuel, suspecting nothing, came out carrying a candle. LeBlanc met him with a shovel to the face, splattering Samuel's brains all over his coat.

Next, LeBlanc killed Sarah Sayre with another shovel blow. Then he went to tie up the loose end. Phoebe was asleep in her bedroom on the second floor when LeBlanc caved in her skull with one violent blow from a club.

After his killing spree, LeBlanc took whatever valuables he could find, stuffing them into pillowcases. He stole a horse from the barn and headed off into the darkness. What he didn't realize was that one of the pillowcases was leaking swag. LeBlanc left a trail of stolen goods behind him as he fled. Some of the items had Samuel Sayre's monogram on them. The next morning, a friend of the Sayres, Lewis Halsey, found the dropped items. Fearing the Sayres had been robbed, he rounded up some neighbors and they went to the Sayre farm to investigate.

The search party found the murdered couple in the barn, and Phoebe dead in her bed. Sheriff George Ludlow set off to look for the killer. LeBlanc hadn't gotten far. He'd planned to go to New York to find a ship bound for Germany. He got as far as the Mosquito Tavern in Hackensack Meadows when he got thirsty and stopped in for a mug of beer. LeBlanc bolted for the back door when Ludlow came in, but he was collared immediately.

The trial of Antoine LeBlanc for the murders began – and ended – on August 13. The jury took just twenty minutes to find him guilty, and there was no appeal. LeBlanc was sentenced to hang.

In the afternoon of September 6, LeBlanc was led to the gallows. He was to be hanged by a modern design, which jerked the condemned man upward, rather than dropping the floor out from underneath him. The counterweight dropped, and LeBlanc was jerked eight feet into the air. He twitched for two minutes or so, then was still.

Since 1833, the Sayre house has been crazy haunted. The house was eventually turned into a restaurant, which had many incarnations. In 1946, the house became the Wincerter Turnpike Inn. In 1957, a mysterious fire ripped through the building. In 1960, it was renovated and became the Wedgewood Inn. Over the years it has had many owners and many names: South Street, Argyle's Restaurant, Society Hill, Phoebe's Restaurant (yes, named after the innocent servant), and most recently, Jimmy's Haunt.

And through all the changes, the ghosts have been there. Doors opened and closed by themselves, and employees were spooked by the sound of footsteps on the second floor when no one was up there. One waitress saw a bloody hand reach out from one of the paintings on the wall. Other employees refused to go down into the basement alone after a bartender saw a lit candle moving around with no one holding it.

Sadly, the Sayre House no longer stands. Jimmy's Haunt was demolished in 2007 to make way for a Commerce Bank. Where the resident ghosts ended up is anyone's guess.

MAY 12
A Tale Told in Stone, Norfolk, VA (1823)

David Duncan, a sailor on a merchant ship, was relaxing in his quarters May 12, 1823. He turned the page in the book of poetry he was reading. His gaze skimmed the lines …

Suddenly his vision swam, and he saw his wife, Martha. But she was thousands of miles away, in Norfolk, Virginia. She was holding their two children, still babies, and she was screaming and begging for David's help as flames leapt up around the three of them. David reached for them as the vision wavered and faded …

Later, the shocking news arrived. On May 12, Martha Duncan and her two infant children had been killed in a house fire. They were buried in the graveyard at St. Paul's Church in Norfolk. David, the grieving widower, had to choose an epitaph. He had the stone carver chisel the words of poetry he'd been reading when he'd seen his loved ones begging for his help.

"Insatiate archer, could not one suffice? Thy shaft flew thrice and thrice my peace was slain."

MAY 13
A Strange Death, Winona, MN (1931)

On August 27, 1915, Bishop Patrick R. Heffron, founder of St. Mary's College, was shot while saying early morning Mass. The guy who shot him was Father Michael Lesches.

We'll take a look at this bizarre story on August 27. For now, though, just know that whenever something weird happened at St. Mary's College, it was blamed on Fr. Lesches.

And plenty of weird stuff happened. Faculty members died premature deaths in strange accidents after the attack on Bishop Heffron. The most bizarre of these was the death of Father Edward Lynch.

Fr. Lynch and Fr. Lesches had once been roommates, but since Lynch was good friends with Bishop Heffron, Lesches soon came to consider him an enemy. While they were roommates, Lynch had mentioned that he was a big sports fan. The unbalanced Lesches had snapped that Lynch would burn in hell for his sinful love of athletics.

On May 15, 1931, a nun cleaning rooms discovered Lynch's burned body lying face-up in bed. The bed wasn't even singed, but the priest's body had been charred, and a burned Bible lay nearby. The coroner, lacking any other explanation, ruled that Lynch had been reading his Bible in bed, and had been electrocuted by a faulty lamp when he reached up to turn off the light. But 110 volts of electricity is not enough to burn a body so completely.

The superstitious on campus swore there was a supernatural connection, that Fr. Lesches was somehow responsible. The explanation had to have a paranormal element … because at the time of Lynch's death, Michael Lesches was a patient at St. Peter Hospital for the Dangerous Insane.

MAY 14
An Accident, Santa Cruz, CA (1903)

The University of California, Santa Cruz, was founded in 1965. Much of the land on which the university sits, purchased in 1961, was once a massive ranch owned by the family of Henry Cowell. Cowell came to California in 1865 with the gold rush. He paid $100,000 for a partnership in a firm that produced lime. That investment made him a very wealthy man; by 1888 he was the owner of the firm and had built it into an international cement company. He began purchasing land as well. Henry Cowell, his wife Harriet, and their five children lived in San Francisco, but visited the Santa Cruz ranch often.

On May 14, 1903, Sarah Agnes Cowell, the headstrong youngest daughter of Henry and Harriet, unmarried at forty, went for a buggy ride. With her was her friend Evelyn George, whose husband was the superintendent of the Henry Cowell Lime and Cement Company.

The buggy's route took the women on a steep, rocky road near the upper kilns of the lime operation. The buggy's wheel hit a large rock and spooked the horse, which bolted. Both women were thrown out of the cart. Evelyn was injured, but Sarah had it worse. When she landed, her head struck a pile of rocks. Her skull was fractured, and she was dead by the time a doctor could arrive.

Henry Cowell died of grief soon afterwards. Sarah's sisters, Belle and Mamie, considered the ranch cursed after the accident.

Sarah's spirit still wanders the land, although she does tend to hang out in the meadows that the university has nicknamed the Pogonip, rather than at the rocky stretch of road that claimed her life. She is seen mostly in the late afternoon, as the shadows under the trees deepen into twilight. She wears a long, pale yellow dress and a bonnet.

MAY 15
Virginia Mourning Her Dead, Lexington, VA (1864)

Virginia Military Institute, in Lexington, sent a corps of cadets to fight in the Civil War. Since it was a college, these were college-age kids who fought. One of them, William Hugh McDowell, was only seventeen years old. His parents wanted him to have a military education, so his mother asked her cousin, who was married to Stonewall Jackson, to write a letter of recommendation for William. It was partly because of this letter from Mary Anna Jackson to General Francis Smith, the superintendent of Virginia Military Institute, that McDowell was accepted into the college.

McDowell and his classmates formed the corps of cadets. The young men, 257 of them, were organized into a battalion of four companies of infantry and one of artillery. The cadets fought fiercely at the Battle of New Market, allowing Confederate troops to regroup and push back the Union forces. The field where they fought had been freshly plowed, and after several days of rain, it was a morass of thick mud. Many of the cadets had the shoes sucked right off their feet by the clinging mud. That section of the battlefield became known as "The Field of Lost Shoes." Ten of those young men fell on the field of battle at New Market, either killed outright or dying later from their wounds. The oldest cadet killed was twenty-five; the youngest was fifteen.

On May 15, 1866, the second anniversary of the battle, the remains of five of those young cadets – Jones, McDowell, Wheelwright, Jefferson, and Atwill – were brought back to campus for reburial. The bodies were placed in the vault on the old Porter's Lodge. In 1878, the remains were moved to the cadet cemetery (which no longer exists).

In 1903, a monument was dedicated to the boys, a bronze sculpture of a woman leaning her cheek on her hand in pensive reflection. The sculpture was called "Virginia Mourning Her Dead". In 1912, the remains of the five cadets were brought to their final resting place at the monument. The boys have individual headstones – a sixth grave, that of Private Crockett, was added in 1960 – but their bones are buried in a copper box in the base of the statue. The other four cadets are buried elsewhere.

"Virginia Mourning Her Dead" comes by her name honestly. People have sometimes seen tears running down the statue's face, and witnesses standing nearby have heard eerie moans coming from the monument.

Inside Jackson Memorial Hall on campus, an 18-by-23-foot mural takes pride of place. Situated at the head of the hall, shaped like a church window with an arched top, bordered in scarlet, the mural was painted by 1880 VMI grad Benjamin West Clinedinst. It portrays the charge of the Corps of Cadets at the Battle of New Market. The painting is masterfully done, and the figures seem quite lifelike.

There are some who say that realism is more than just really good art. Supposedly, the mural comes to life at night. Cannons roar, rifles bark, and the soldiers move across the canvas, continuing their eternal charge.

MAY 16
Crisis Apparition, British Columbia, Canada (1985)

Mother's Day, 1985, was a happy occasion for Kathleen Belanger of Port Mellon, British Columbia. Her son Roger, his wife Myra, and their two little boys had come for a visit that morning. They'd all had a wonderful time … but after the family had left, Kathleen felt uneasy.

She decided to fill the time doing errands. In mid-afternoon she returned home from shopping, and found the garage door standing wide open. Not only that, every door in the basement was open too.

Puzzled, Kathleen went to shut the doors – and abruptly, Roger was right there in front of her, a big grin on his face. Kathleen was startled at her son's sudden appearance. She opened her mouth to ask Roger what was going on, when just as suddenly, he vanished.

The police arrived at around 9 pm that evening to tell Kathleen the bad news. Roger had been hit by a falling tree while logging. He had died instantly.

MAY 17
Airplane Hollow, Nelsonville, OH (1941)

On May 17, 1941, a twin-engine military plane crashed in a violent storm six miles north of Nelsonville, Ohio. The Beechcraft AT-7, a navigation training plane, was being flown by members of a squadron from Bartsdale Field, Louisiana, on a routine training flight to Cleveland. The plane ran into bad weather over Ohio. Buffeted by high winds and battered by torrential rain, the Beechcraft crashed in a wooded area. It rolled down a hillside, smashing trees as it went. It finally came to rest, embedding itself in a gravel drive, called Jacobs Road, that winds through the woods.

All five soldiers aboard were killed. In that area, now known as Airplane Hollow, witnesses have reported hearing screams and wails as the men relive their final terrifying moments.

MAY 18
The Vanishing Hitchhiker, WA (1980)

The eruption of Mount St. Helen's on May 18, 1980, was the most destructive volcanic event in United States history. Fifty-seven people and thousands of wild animals were killed when the volcano blew, sending millions of tons of ash and debris down the side of the mountain.

In the decades since the eruption, many people have reported a ghostly hitchhiker that seems to have some connection to the volcano. The hitchhiker is a woman wearing a white dress, who travels her way up and down I-5. When offered a lift, she gets into the back seat and sits there quietly for a while. Then she predicts that the volcano will erupt again between October 12 and 14. Then she disappears, often while the car is doing sixty miles an hour down the highway.

Interestingly, lava did erupt from the volcano's caldera on October 12, 2004. So maybe the vanishing hitchhiker did have some inside information.

MAY 19
Ram Tail Factory, Foster, RI (1822)

In 1799, William Potter came down Rhode Island's Ponaganset River to Foster. He bought up some land and founded the Foster Woolen Manufactory, which used the river to power the looms that wove wool into cloth. (During the weaving process, the stray pieces of cloth were trimmed from the finished product, and when they dropped to the floor, the curled bits reminded the workers of sheep's tails. Hence the mill's nickname: Ram Tail Factory.)

Potter expanded the operation in 1813, and soon the factory was surrounded by its own little community, with several houses, a warehouse for the finished cloth, and offices. William Potter's two sons managed the mill during the day, and Potter had also hired his son-in-law,

Peleg Walker. Walker was an irascible man, difficult to work with, but he found his niche. He worked as the night watchman, and didn't really have to interact with anyone much.

Walker's job was simple: he made the rounds of the buildings at night by the light of a lantern. Then at daybreak, he'd finish his shift by ringing the factory's bell to call the workers for the day.

Walker may have been family, but he was still temperamental, and there was tension between him and the Potters. Walker borrowed quite a lot of money from his in-laws; the debt eventually got to $500, well over $10,000 in today's currency. One day, there was a heated discussion, probably over the debt. Walker left the meeting dramatically, yelling one of the best parting shots ever: "You'll have to take the key to this mill from a dead man's pocket!"

On the morning of May 19, 1822, the factory bell did not ring to summon the workers. On investigation, it was soon clear why – Peleg Walker's body dangled lifelessly from the bell rope. Sticking out of his pocket were the keys to the mill. Cue mic drop.

Was it suicide? Could it have been murder? However he met his end, Peleg Walker was still dead. He was buried in the family plot.

But Walker did not let death stop him from making his rounds. The haunting of the Ram Tail Factory began almost immediately. Although Walker was no longer alive to ring the factory bell, it still rang every morning at the usual time. Creeped out by this, workers took the bell rope down. The bell continued to ring. That was even creepier, so they finally just took the bell down.

The haunting soon reached a new height. For several nights in a row, workers were woken up by the sound of the factory's machinery running all by itself. They stumbled from their houses to see the giant mill wheel, powered by the Ponaganset River, running at full tilt. Bizarrely, they realized it was spinning against the flow of the current.

This was too much for many of the mill employees, and they moved out. For the ones who remained, there was even more spookiness in store. People began seeing Peleg Walker's glowing ghost stomping around the place, checking each building, lantern in hand, just as he had in life.

The creep factor got to be intolerable, and by the 1840s, everyone had moved away and the community became a ghost town. In 1873, the old mill was destroyed in a fire. That didn't stop Walker's ghost from making his nightly lantern-lit rounds. In the 1885 state census, Ram Tail Factory was listed as haunted, making it the only officially haunted site in Rhode Island.

MAY 20
Edgar Allan Poe and the Mignonette *(1884)*

Edgar Allan Poe is unquestionably the master of the Gothic horror story. His tales of premature burial, gruesome murder, and other terrors have been giving readers delicious chills since the Victorian era.

An interesting thing about Poe's writing is that he took inspiration from the world around him, and from historical events. His story "The Cask of Amontillado" is loosely based on the 1817 death of Lieutenant Robert Massie at the army fort on Castle Island where Poe was stationed as a young man. And "The Masque of the Red Death" is a nod to the ravages of tuberculosis, a disease that claimed the lives of several people dear to Poe.

One of the most fascinating of these tales is Poe's novella *The Narrative of Arthur Gordon Pym of Nantucket*. The story involves three shipwrecked sailors who murder their cabin boy, then eat him to stay alive while adrift at sea. (Poe was never shy about going for the gross-out.) The details of the story are indeed gruesome, but nearly identical to an actual historical event.

One of the most sensational court cases of the 19th century involved the trial of three sailors, Thomas Dudley, Edwin Stephens, and Edmund Brooks. The men were accused of murdering their cabin boy, then cannibalizing the corpse, after their ship was lost in a hurricane.

Dudley was the captain. A wealthy Australian had bought a fifty-foot yacht, the *Mignonette*, and hired Dudley to sail it from Southampton to Sydney. Dudley hired a crew of three men: Brooks, Stephens, and Richard Parker, the 17-year-old cabin boy. The *Mignonette* left England on May 19.

It was smooth sailing until July 3. Somewhere in the south Atlantic, hundreds of miles from land, they ran into a hurricane. Slammed by the overpowering forces of nature's fury, the four men were forced to abandon ship. They piled into a flimsy dinghy in such a hurry that there was no time to provision the tiny lifeboat. When the skies cleared and the gale-force winds died down, the four were adrift. They had no drinking water, and their entire food supply consisted of a single tin of parsnips.

The men were adrift for nearly three hellish weeks. One day of rain saved them from serious dehydration, and they did manage to capture an unlucky sea turtle, which they pulled apart with their bare hands and ate raw. Nineteen days passed, and things were looking grim. The men couldn't say it aloud, but thoughts of cannibalism were beginning to creep through everyone's mind.

The men decided that they would draw straws to see who would be the one to die so that the others might live. But when three wolves and a sheep are deciding what to have for dinner, the sheep's not going to come out of it very well. Parker, the youngest and weakest, was killed. Poe writes that, "having by common consent taken off the hands, feet and head, throwing them together with the entrails, into the sea, we devoured the rest of the body…"

It was gross, but eating the cabin boy kept the others alive for a few more days. They were rescued by a German vessel, the *Montezuma*.

On board the *Montezuma*, the men shared the details of their harrowing experience – all of the details. But rather than agree that it was a case of simple survival, the crew of the German ship were horrified, and reported the situation to the authorities. When they reached port, Dudley, Brooks, and Stephens were promptly arrested.

The trial was sensationalistic, as can be expected. The judge, and the general public, weren't buying the killing as necessary, any more than the German sailors did. The three survivors were found guilty of murder and cannibalism, and sentenced to hard labor.

Poe went to great lengths to assure that the details in his story rang true. The number of men aboard, the violent storm, the eating of the turtle, the providential rain that gave them precious drinking water – all those incidents are included in Poe's story. The name of the cabin boy, Richard Parker, is the same. The supposed fairness of drawing lots to see who would be sacrificed, and the hint that the choice might have been rigged, that's all in there. But before you accuse Poe of lifting his story whole-cloth from actual events, remember that Poe published his story as fiction.

Also, please remember that the *Mignonette* sank in 1884 … 35 years *after* Poe's death and nearly 50 years after the publication of *The Narrative of Arthur Gordon Pym*.

MAY 21
The Murder of King Henry VI, London, England (1471, recurring)

Henry VI was the only child of Henry V, so it was pretty clear that he was next in line for both the English and French thrones. But the Wars of the Roses decreed otherwise. (The Wars of the Roses were English civil wars between two branches of the Plantagenet dynasty: the House of York had a white rose as its symbol, while the House of Lancaster was represented by a red rose.)

The House of York had Henry locked away in the Tower of London. With Henry out of the way, Edward IV seized the throne in 1471 after the Battle of Tewksbury. Shortly afterward, Henry was stabbed to death as he knelt at prayer around midnight in the King's Private Chapel in the Wakefield Tower.

Since then, every May 21 on the anniversary of his murder, the ghost of Henry VI appears just before midnight in the chapel. He paces and mutters for a while, then disappears at the final stroke of midnight.

MAY 22
The Joplin Tornado, Joplin, MO (2011)

Death dropped from the sky on May 22, 2011 when an F5 tornado ripped through Joplin, Missouri. It was the deadliest tornado in the United States since 1950, when modern record-keeping began. Up to a mile wide, with winds howling at more than 200 miles an hour, the Joplin tornado killed 161 people and injured over a thousand. It was on the ground for over 22 miles, and it left twisted rubble, shattered buildings, and devastating destruction in its wake.

It also left behind a few ghosts.

Bob Wilson was a first responder who helped with search and rescue after the tornado. Many Joplin first responders, including Wilson, noticed strange activity in their homes. Wilson invited paranormal investigators into his home. During the investigation, Bob asked if any of the victims of the disaster were there. When they played back the recording, they heard shuffling on the stairs, as well as a faint voice. Did a ghost, responding to Bob's compassion, follow him home?

Another strange thing that came out of the Joplin tornado is the story of the Butterfly People. The *St. Louis Post-Dispatch* reported that a mother was running for shelter, cradling her young daughter as she ran. The wind pushed them to the ground, and the mother saw a car lift from the pavement and hurtle towards them. The mother squeezed her eyes closed, bracing for the killing impact ... which never came. "Weren't they pretty?" her daughter asked. "Didn't you see the butterfly people?"

Reports came in from all over Joplin. All of the witnesses were children, and they all described the same thing – beautiful beings, with the resplendent wings of butterflies, protecting people from flying debris. A man and his daughter were pummeled by the wind as they sat in a car, but the little girl calmly told her father that Butterfly People were sitting in the car with them. A four-year-old boy was lifted by the howling wind and dropped in a field six miles away. He told rescuers that angels caught him and set him down so gently, he wasn't hurt.

So were these in fact angels? Or were these Butterfly People just a one-off, showing up in Joplin during the tornado and nowhere else? Butterflies are said to represent an angelic visit, but these beings, described by so many children, are unique.

MAY 23
The Hanging of Elizabeth Reed, IL (1845)

Backwoods Illinois in the mid-19th century was a really strange place. People got up to all kinds of weirdness in the hidden hills and hollows.

One of these areas was Purgatory Swamp. It doesn't exist anymore, but in 1844 it was part of Crawford County, in southern Illinois, on the eastern edge of the state almost due east of St. Louis. In this evocatively named corner of Illinois lived Leonard Reed and his wife Elizabeth.

During the muggy days of summer 1844, Leonard Reed "took sick". Elizabeth wasn't alone in caring for her ailing husband; a neighbor girl, Eveline Deal, came over to help. Eveline was at the Reed's cabin when the doctor was summoned, and she heard him say that Leonard was too ill to survive.

After the doctor left, Elizabeth brewed some refreshing sassafras tea for her husband. Eveline saw Elizabeth stir a white powder into the tea, and Elizabeth explained to the young girl that it was simply medicine. The doctor was to return the next day, August 15, but alas, before he even got there, Leonard Reed had died.

A funeral was held, and Leonard was properly mourned and properly buried. Everyone sympathized with Elizabeth at her loss … but Eveline couldn't get the image of that white powder out of her mind. She told someone, who told someone else, and soon, people in the area weren't so sure that Leonard Reed had actually died of a fever.

It must be said that Elizabeth Reed was quite a character, even for frontier Illinois. Legend says she suffered from some sort of facial disfigurement, and always wore a white cap. She never went out in public without a veil attached to the cap to hide her features. This secrecy alarmed her neighbors, who whispered that Elizabeth was a witch. The veil also proved to be her downfall.

The rumors that Leonard Reed had not died a natural death continued to spread. Finally, the sheriff of Crawford County was forced to launch an investigation. He didn't really think there was anything to find; he was just responding to the growing undercurrent of rumors and speculation surrounding Elizabeth Reed. But it soon became clear that the rumors had a solid basis in cold, hard fact.

Sheriff Thorn searched the Reed cabin, and found a scrap of brown paper, just like the paper Eveline Deal said she saw Elizabeth shake a white powder from, a powder she assured Eveline was "medicine". The sheriff traced the paper to a drugstore in Russellville, and that's where things began to look bleak for Elizabeth.

The druggist confirmed that the piece of brown paper found at the cabin matched the paper he routinely used to package various kinds of medicine. However, it was also the same kind of paper he had recently used to wrap up a portion of arsenic – purchased by Elizabeth Reed. Even worse, several witnesses came forward to say that they had seen Elizabeth in

Russellville making purchases from that druggist. They also said she'd been wearing a "disguise", which was why they remembered her. This could very well have been her usual veil and cap. The folks in Purgatory Swamp were accustomed to seeing her in this getup; people in Russellville, not so much.

This evidence was highly circumstantial, but it was enough to get Elizabeth arrested for the murder of her husband and thrown in jail. In September, a grand jury decided that the evidence was enough to charge Elizabeth with murder. She went to trial in April 1845. The trial lasted only a few days, and at the end of it, Elizabeth Reed was found guilty of her husband's murder. She was sentenced to hang on May 23.

Elizabeth's hanging was quite the social event. People showed up from all over the area, even from Indiana, across the state line. Some estimates say that nearly twenty thousand people showed up to watch the execution.

Elizabeth had found religion while incarcerated, and had been baptized after her conviction. The carrying out of a death sentence was a gala event in those days anyway, and Elizabeth gave the folks a show. She was brought to the gallows in a wagon, dressed in a long white robe, sitting on her coffin in the wagon bed. She was hollering prayers at the top of her lungs, and singing hymns in between the prayers.

Elizabeth was led onto the platform of the gallows, and Reverend John Sneed preached the funeral sermon. She kept up a running commentary – loudly – on everything the preacher said. The crowd just stood there, stunned into silence. They'd come to the hanging for some frontier entertainment, but this was just … weird.

When the sermon ended, Elizabeth stepped onto the trapdoor, and a black hood was placed over her head. The noose followed. Just after noon on May 23, 1845, Elizabeth Reed plunged through the trapdoor into eternity, and into history. She was the only woman ever hanged in Illinois.

Her body was buried in a shallow grave right underneath the gallows, but relatives soon moved her to Baker Cemetery just outside of Heathsville, to rest forever alongside the husband she had poisoned.

Leonard and Elizabeth Reed's graves are marked by one simple stone. Their epitaphs are cruelly blunt. Below Leonard's name, it says "killed by murder." Under Elizabeth's name are the words "killed by hanging." Whoever commissioned the gravestone was not one to mince words.

Perhaps in response to these bald statements of fact, it seems that Elizabeth Reed has remained bound to her final resting place. A woman dressed in a long white robe roams the small graveyard, and people have reported hearing the sound of a woman crying.

MAY 24
The Phantom Stagecoach, Winchester, VA (1862)

In 1862, Confederate General Stonewall Jackson was in Virginia, leading his troops to victory in fight after fight. Confederate forces were ranged along the 80-mile-long Valley Turnpike. This road was a marvel of construction, especially for the mid-19th century. Paved in crushed limestone, it was wide and easy to travel, and Jackson used it to his advantage. The

Turnpike connected New Market to Winchester. On May 24, the eve of the Battle of Winchester, Jackson had his troops in New Market, and was planning on attacking Union forces under General Nathaniel Banks at nearby Winchester.

A Union spy had also heard of Jackson's plans. Under cover of darkness, he stole a stagecoach, intending to use that well-paved road to reach Banks in time to warn the general of the impending attack. He had a good head start, but two Confederate officers discovered the plot and took off in pursuit of the spy.

A stagecoach really isn't the best getaway vehicle, and the Rebel officers soon had the spy in their sights. In the fitful glare of flickering lightning, they could see the spy on the coach's seat, hunched over, urging the horses to go faster, faster. The lightning continued to flicker, illuminating the road ahead. Near the crossroads at Mount Jackson, a flash lit the desperate scene. The Confederates were mere yards behind the lumbering coach when the spy turned on the seat and caught sight of them. He saw their drawn pistols, and fumbled his own revolver out, trying to get off a shot as the horses galloped and the coach jounced along the road.

Suddenly, a dizzying flash of lightning streaked down from the lowering clouds and struck the coach. The coach exploded into flames as though hit by cannon fire. The driver was incinerated where he sat, blasted into oblivion in an eyeblink.

The Confederate officers reined in their wild-eyed horses, stunned at the utter destruction they'd just witnessed. They wheeled their dancing mounts and rode back to New Market. The next day, Stonewall Jackson fell on Banks and the Union forces at Winchester with no warning. The Battle of Winchester was a Confederate victory.

Valley Turnpike is now Highway 11, and concrete has replaced the crushed limestone. But on nights when lightning splits the sky, the phantom of a stagecoach, painted red and pulled by four white horses, is sometimes seen thundering silently along the road. The driver, a blackened husk, cracks the reins along the backs of the laboring horses, still frantically trying to get to Winchester to deliver his message.

MAY 25
A Nightmare of Death, Chicago, IL (1979)

Do you remember your nastiest nightmare?

Think about it. Do you remember that feeling of creeping horror, that desperation to escape, that feeling of gasping yourself awake, the realization that thank *god* it was just a dream, because no one could survive that terror in real life?

Now multiply that ten-fold. Imagine waking up from the clutches of a nightmare – the *same* nightmare – ten nights in a row. Could you survive, and keep your sanity?

David Booth did. From May 15 to May 25, 1979, the 23-year-old Cincinnati man tossed and sweated through the same terrifying dream every night. In his dream, he saw an airplane crash just after takeoff, killing everyone on board. The dream was so vivid that he actually contacted the FAA on May 22, hoping desperately that they could stop whatever plane this was. He could see the American Airlines logo on the side of the plane, but beyond that, he couldn't identify the jet.

To their credit, FAA officials took Booth seriously. If this was some sort of precognitive vision, they wanted to stop it coming true just as much as he did. They figured out that the plane in Booth's dream was a DC-10. But that was all … they didn't even know where in the country this would happen, much less which flight number they should ground.

But on May 25, they stopped asking questions. That Friday afternoon, American Airlines Flight 191 took off from Chicago's O'Hare airport. Immediately after takeoff, the engine on the left wing detached, flew straight up into the air, and slammed into the tarmac. As the engine detached, it sheared through the hydraulic lines in the leading edge of the left wing. It also crippled the control panel in the cockpit. The captain, Walter Lux, a highly experienced pilot, could do nothing as the plane went down. Thirty-one seconds after takeoff, the plane plunged from the sky and crashed in a strip of land between the Chicago K-9 training area and the Des Plaines Mobile Home Park. Everyone on board was killed, as well as two people on the ground. The death toll was 273 (258 passengers, 13 crew, and the two bystanders.) The plane was loaded with jet fuel for a nonstop cross-country trip from Chicago to Los Angeles. The black smoke from the fireball was visible for miles.

If the tragedy could be said to have a silver lining, it was this: the plane crashed into mostly vacant ground, although a few mobile homes were damaged in the explosion and the resulting fire. It narrowly missed fuel storage tanks on Elmhurst Road, and the nearby I-90 Expressway.

Ghost stories soon began circulating about the crash site. Most of these involve people at the trailer park. They'll hear a knock on the door, and open it to find a disheveled, harried-looking traveler on their doorstep. The stranger mutters something about looking for their luggage, or needing to catch their flight, then they turn and wander away. Electrical disturbances aren't uncommon. And in the months following the crash, people driving past the crash site reported spook lights in the field. Investigators at the crash site have captured several interesting EVPs, including *"Almost made it"* and *"Need power."*

MAY 26
Fact or Faked?, Cambridge, England (1960)

What does a ghost look like?

I dressed up as a ghost for Halloween the year I was in kindergarten. (I know, super original. Hey, I was five.) I wore the stereotypical white sheet with holes cut out for eyes, the bog-standard ghost costume.

And it's bog-standard for a reason. For centuries, the image of a ghost has been a floaty white thingie. That's because for a very long time, people were buried wrapped in white cloth: the shroud. During the winter of 1804, a neighborhood of London was terrorized by "the Hammersmith ghost", a white figure that came out of a cemetery to wander the streets. One woman even died of fright after seeing the apparition. Some would-be ghostbusters decided to try and catch the spook. They hid in the cemetery for three nights, and didn't see a thing. But on the fourth night, they saw a white figure in the darkness. One of the vigilantes fired at the ghost … which fell to the ground. Coming up to the body, the ghostbusters discovered they had shot a bricklayer named Thomas Milwood. He usually took a shortcut through the cemetery coming home from work. His clothes, covered with cement dust, were powdery-white.

But that was 1804, I hear you say. Surely we've gotten more sophisticated since then. What would happen if someone in modern times dressed up as a ghost? What kind of reaction would they get? Tony Cornell, a member of the Society for Psychical Research, decided to find out.

At 10 pm on May 26, 1960, Cornell had his friends drape him from head to foot in butter muslin, a gauzy kind of cloth. Then he hung out for a while in the cemetery of St. Peter's Church in Cambridge.

The results were underwhelming. During the twenty minutes he was there, Cornell spent about half his time wandering among the trees, and half the time just standing motionless. And in that twenty minutes, about 90 cars, 40 cyclists, and 12 pedestrians passed the cemetery, but only four of them gave any sign that they'd seen a ghost. Only one person decided to investigate the "phantom" – a young man leaned over the fence and asked Cornell what he thought he was doing.

Perhaps Brits in 1960 were blasé about a ghost in their midst, but things are looking up for the spookiness of the spectral community. During the COVID-19 pandemic, every country in the world was encouraging social distancing as a way to combat the spread of the disease. In one village in Indonesia, a youth group had a brilliant idea. They dressed up as ghosts and hung out on the streets. "Pocong" are eerie figures, wrapped in white sheets, with powdered faces and eyes outlined in black kohl. The fake pocong did a fabulous job of keeping people inside. No one wanted to risk a run-in with these creepy spooks.

MAY 27
Off With Her Head!, London, England (1541, recurring)

One of the many ghosts of the Tower of London is that of Margaret Pole, Countess of Salisbury. Her crime? She was the 72-year-old mother of Cardinal Pole, who argued against Henry VIII's position as head of the Church in England. Cardinal Pole was in France, safely beyond Henry's reach, when he spoke against the king. His mother, though, suffered the spiteful royal revenge.

Margaret Pole was a staunch Catholic. When Henry VIII dissolved the monasteries and cracked down on the Catholics, she continued to practice her chosen religion. She was stripped of her lands and title by royal decree. In 1539, she was accused of attending a Catholic protest called the Pilgrimage of Grace. She swore she hadn't, but she was arrested anyway and spent two years in the Tower.

Margaret was frail to begin with, and her imprisonment was rough on her. She was finally executed on May 27, 1541.

The execution was a horrific show. We read of someone having their head cut off, but really, it's harder to do than it sounds. There are a lot of muscles in the neck, to hold the head erect. There's the spinal cord, protected by bony vertebrae. There are rings of cartilage that make up the throat. It takes real effort to chop off a head.

The executioner assigned to Margaret Pole was inexperienced, and he took a couple of swings at her before connecting. She was struggling the whole time, too, so his aim was off. He finally landed a hacking blow – on her shoulder. Margaret lunged to her feet and tried to stagger away, shrieking the whole time. The executioner had to follow her and chop at her blood-spattered body until she finally quit moving. It took eleven blows to separate Margaret's head from her body.

The countess swore she was innocent, and she died a gruesome death, so it's no surprise that she is now a ghost wandering the Tower. On the anniversary of her botched execution, Tower Green echoes with her screams of terror as her bloody ghost relives the grotesque scene.

MAY 28
The Death of Kickisomlo, Seattle, WA (1896)

Pike Place Market in Seattle is a bustling, thriving place to shop. Locals and tourists alike love the funky artisan vibe of the market. More than 200 shops offering everything from honey to fresh fish to bouquets of flowers to handmade books to pottery abound – it's a shopper's paradise. The market also hosts around 250 street performers. And there are a few folks in the crowd who are very good at being invisible.

There's the "Fat Lady Barber", a zaftig woman who used to run a barber shop in the 1950s. She would croon lullabies to her customers, who would often doze off right there in the chair. (Then she would pick their pockets.) She weighed around 300 pounds, and one day in the early 1970s she crashed through a weak floor on her balcony in the market, and died from the fall. She still sings her lullabies, but now they are only heard by the market's nighttime cleaning crews.

Another ghost is the young boy who haunts a bead store. During renovations, a basket of colorful beads was found in a space behind a wall. This caused a lot of conversation, as the last time the space had been accessible, the bead store didn't exist. There was simply no natural way for these beads to get into that hidden space. Paranormal investigators theorize that the ghostly little boy has squirreled away the beads one by one to play with.

The most famous – and respected – spirit of Pike Place Market is Kickisomlo, eldest daughter of Chief Seattle, for whom the city is named. She was called Princess Angeline by white settlers.

The 1855 Treaty of Point Elliott decreed that the Duwamish Indians had to give up their land and move to reservations. But Kickisomlo, born in 1820, simply didn't move when the government told her to. She just stayed where she was, in a small waterfront shack on Western Avenue. To support herself, she took in laundry and sold handwoven baskets.

She was friends with Catherine Maynard, who suggested one day that "Kickisomlo" was quite a mouthful, and wouldn't she be happier with a more easily pronounceable name, like Angeline? Maybe Princess Angeline, to denote her status as a chief's daughter. So Angeline it was, for the rest of her life.

The unassuming little old lady was a familiar figure in the city, and by her quiet example, she became somewhat of an ambassador. Chief Seattle was very friendly and helpful to the white settlers, and his daughter felt the same way. She provided a gentle, valuable link between her people and the settlers. In being kind to her, the citizens of Seattle realized that yes, it was possible to play nicely with the natives. Angeline became a well-known figure in Seattle. When she died on May 31, 1896, she was buried from the Church of Our Lady of Good Help. The church was magnificently decorated, and Angeline lay in state in a canoe-shaped coffin as the people of Seattle filed past to pay their respects.

Angeline died more than a decade before Pike Place Market opened, but she is often seen there because the market covers the spot where she used to live. Angeline's ghost appears much as she did in life, shuffling slowly along with the aid of a cane, dressed in layers of clothing and sporting a red kerchief on her aged head. But now, she doesn't touch the ground as she makes her rounds, and her ghost changes color, from white to blue to lavender.

Angeline's legacy lives on. Pike Place Market also houses eight buildings that contain 300 apartments, many for low-income elderly. The YWCA in Seattle has a shelter named after Kickisomlo, the Angeline's Day Center for Women. More than a century after her death, Princess Angeline is still keeping the American Indians alive in the minds of the people of Seattle.

MAY 29
All In The Family, Beverly Hills, CA (1942)

The acting family of the Barrymores has a long, proud history reaching back 400 years. Drew Barrymore's fourth-great-grandfather Thomas Haycraft and his wife, Louisa Rouse Lane, were both traveling actors. The family tradition continued, and Drew's grandfather (John Barrymore), great-aunt (Ethel Barrymore), and great-uncle (Lionel Barrymore) were considered some of the best actors of their time. All three siblings have stars on the Hollywood Walk of Fame. Lionel and Ethel won Academy Awards, and John won a Rudolph Valentino Medal in 1925, for artistic accomplishment in film. (Valentino's early death the next year made it the only Valentino Medal ever given out.)

John Barrymore was a leading man, a well-regarded actor of stage and screen. He loved doing Shakespeare, and his striking good looks earned him the nickname "The Profile." Unfortunately, another nickname he picked up was "The Monster" for his legendary drinking binges. His drinking made him erratic and prone to memory problems. By the end of his career, he could barely remember his lines. He died in 1942 of cirrhosis of the liver and kidney failure. He was only 60 years old.

One of John's most treasured possessions was an old cuckoo clock. The clock hadn't run in years, but John's friend Gene Fowler had a plan. Knowing that John was close to death, Fowler intended to set the hands of the clock to the exact hour of the great actor's passing, as a memorial.

John Barrymore died on May 29, 1942. The morning following his death, Fowler went into the den to set the hands of the clock. He reached for the clock – then stopped, dumbfounded. When the clock had stopped, two years earlier, the hands had frozen at 10:20 pm, the exact moment of the actor's death.

MAY 30
Johnsons Island, Sandusky, OH (1862-1865)

At the beginning of the Civil War, both sides realized the need for prisoner of war camps. One of these was Johnsons Island, built to house Confederate soldiers.

When the Federal government authorized the construction of a camp in northern Ohio, several sites around Lake Erie were considered. Unpopulated Johnson's Island was eventually chosen. Trees were felled, a stockade and several buildings went up, and the camp opened in April 1862. Over 11,000 Confederate prisoners of war, mostly officers, would pass through the camp.

Life at this particular camp was better than at most prison camps, Union or Confederate. Johnsons Island was near Sandusky, Ohio, which was served by rail lines. This made it easy to supply the camp. Also, many of the men imprisoned there were officers. They were from wealthier families, and had money sent to them so they could purchase supplies at the sutler's store. And Northern officials believed that officers deserved more lenient treatment than enlisted men. The prisoners were allowed to shop, and they had a lively social life, including putting on amateur theatrical productions.

But it was, in the end, a prison camp. The Southerners suffered during the Great Lakes winters. The buildings had been constructed from green lumber, from trees felled on site, and when that wood dried, chinks appeared in the walls and the wind whistled through. The prisoners made many attempts to escape, including trying to walk across the frozen lake to Canada, but only a few of these escapes were successful. Disease took its toll. The Confederate cemetery on the island holds the remains of over 200 prisoners. Ground penetrating radar has identified 267 sets of remains, of which 253 have been identified.

The cemetery is guarded by a bronze statue, erected by the Daughters of the Confederacy in 1910, called The Lookout. The statue faces north, towards Canada, because facing south could be seen as admitting defeat. It's said to change position at midnight. Confederate soldiers are seen wandering through the cemetery, and it's said that when it storms, the sound of screams and gunfire echo around the island.

The weirdest story from Johnsons Island comes from 1915. There are actually two stories, both involving a group of Italian laborers who were working in a quarry on the island.

The first story simply says that the Italian workers, who spoke little English, suddenly started singing "Dixie." Another, more detailed story holds that the workers saw The Lookout turn to face the cemetery, and that it blew a bugle. Ghostly soldiers straggled to attention and appeared through the mist, lining up for a spectral roll call. They stood at attention in rotting gray uniforms, then melted away into the darkness.

MAY 31
Death of Joseph Sellis, London, England (1810)

Ernest Augustus, Duke of Cumberland and Queen Victoria's uncle, was one of the most feared men in England. He was, to begin with, fearsome to look at. He'd been terribly wounded by a blow to the head in battle in May 1794. He had gruesome scars on his face, and he'd lost an eye. He had a reputation for being unscrupulous, overbearing, and sexually adventurous. He was generally considered the black sheep of an already weird family.

In the early morning hours of May 31, 1810, it seemed that fate had caught up to Cumberland. He was attacked with his own sword as he slept. Although the weapon was razor-sharp, the assailant used the flat of the blade, not the newly-sharpened edge. Even so, the first blow split Cumberland's skull wide open, cutting so deeply it exposed his brain. Three more blows fell as he stumbled from his bed. With a rush of adrenaline, Cumberland yelled, "Neale! Neale! I am murdered!"

Cornelius Neale, the duke's valet, came rushing in, but found Cumberland alone in his room. His attacker had fled, leaving the bloody sword on the floor. Neale made sure Cumberland was safe, and called for a doctor. Then he went in search of the would-be murderer.

The only member of the household unaccounted for was Cumberland's valet, Joseph Sellis. His slippers, though, were found in the duke's bedroom closet – the place where, it was thought, the attacker had hidden before slinking out to attack Cumberland. Sellis had to be found.

Two servants were sent to Sellis's room. As they approached, they heard a disgusting gurgling sound. They threw open the door and found Sellis lying on his bed, drowning in his own blood. His throat had been slashed with a straight razor so deeply that only his spine had stopped the blade.

An inquest was thrown together, and it was decided that Sellis had tried to murder Cumberland. Failing at that, he had retreated to his room and committed suicide. Court gossip, though, said otherwise. Sellis's head had been nearly severed from his body. There was no way, people muttered, that such a wound could be self-inflicted.

To add to the confusion, they pointed out that Sellis's hands were clean, but there was a basin filled with bloody water on his nightstand. So, did Sellis almost cut his own head off, then stop to wash his hands?

The straight razor found at the scene was nowhere near Sellis's hand. But a policeman had an explanation for that. Sergeant Joseph Creighton admitted that he'd picked it up to look at it, then had set it down several feet away. The crime scene hadn't just been contaminated; it had been rearranged.

If Sellis hadn't committed suicide, who had killed him? The alternative scenarios were varied and imaginative. Sellis had found Cumberland in bed with his wife. Or Cumberland had seduced Sellis's daughter, who had killed herself when she discovered she was pregnant. Or Sellis and Cumberland had been lovers, and when the other valet, Neale, had been hired, Neale had taken Sellis's place in the duke's bed. Or, or, or … the mystery has never been solved.

Maybe that's why Joseph Sellis haunts St. James Palace. His shadowy figure still roams the halls, accompanied by the coppery stink of fresh blood. Palace staff often report feeling as if they're being watched, and small objects get moved or go missing. The haunting is particularly severe in the room where Sellis was killed. A few unfortunate witnesses claim to have seen the specter of Joseph Sellis sitting in his bed, propped up on the edge of death, his mouth hanging open over a grisly wound in his neck, his head nearly severed from his body.

JUNE

JUNE 1
Death of Theresa Schumacher, Mount Pleasant, MI (1937)

Central Michigan University is yet another campus that is home to several ghost stories. Funnily enough, they all involve female students.

Carolyn Corey, a freshman, died in her sleep on May 6, 1951. She hadn't been feeling well the night before, and complained of stomach pains before heading to bed. She haunts Barnard Hall. Another girl is said to haunt Woldt Hall, but the details on that story are sketchier. This is because the story isn't actually true. The girl was rumored to have been murdered by a jealous boyfriend, but it's just an urban legend. In these two residence halls, the hauntings are subtle. Books will fall off shelves, lights will turn on and off.

A music student is reportedly buried under a piano-shaped garden in the courtyard of Powers Hall, although many agree that the garden is simply a memorial to the lost girl. Another girl is said to have hanged herself in one of the second-floor suites of Barnes Hall. Again, this is one of the sketchier stories, with hardly any details, but people have reported poltergeist activity.

There's the urban legend about a girl who froze to death under the Central Michigan University seal in front of Warriner Hall while waiting for her lover, who was delayed due to car trouble. But Warriner Hall does have a bona fide ghost too, the only other documented death in this campus's collection of ghostly tales.

Theresa Elizabeth Schumacher was a 19-year-old student who worked in the cafeteria. On June 1, 1937, she was bringing food down the building's central elevator when she stuck her head out of the little window on the elevator door. Unfortunately, the elevator moved before she got her head out of the window. She suffocated when her head was pinned.

Theresa's ghost is the only one on campus that people have actually seen. In 1969, students working at the college radio station saw Theresa's ghost on the fifth floor. And Keith Voeks, a university employee, had his own tale to tell. In the early 1980s, he and a friend were working late in the Warriner Hall auditorium. It was about 2 am, and they were locking up the building. Both men happened to look up, and saw someone walking across the auditorium's stage. They finished locking up and left quickly.

Theresa's spirit is responsible for disembodied footsteps on the central staircase in Warriner Hall. She most often manifests as a glow of blue light.

JUNE 2
Dew Shadows, Crete (1828, recurring)

The Greek War of Independence was waged by Greek revolutionaries against the Turks from 1821 to 1830. One of the engagements was the Battle of Frangocastello. This castle was built by Venetians in 1371 to protect Venetian nobles in the area. They called it the Castle of St. Nikitas, but the locals contemptuously named it the Castle of the Franks (meaning Catholic foreigners). The local name stuck.

On May 17, 1828, hundreds of Greeks were besieged at Frangocastello by the Turks, and 350 of them were massacred. The soldiers now make an annual return to the place where they fell. The ghost army, a mass of black shadows, appears armed and either walking or riding. The specters move from the monastery of Agios Charalambos towards Frangocastello. The phantoms appear yearly, either on the battle's anniversary or in early June.

The phenomenon seems to be tied to weather conditions. The locals have named the ghosts Drosoulites ("dew shadows") because they appear when the day is quite young, when the sea is calm and before the sun has risen very high. The ghosts form out of the sea, and march towards the castle, fading as the day grows brighter. The apparition lasts about ten minutes.

The appearance of the Greek ghost army is apparently pretty lifelike. In 1890, some Turkish troops saw the ghosts and ran away, thinking they were actual Greek rebels. And during World War II, a German patrol saw the ghosts and opened fire.

JUNE 3
Ghost Ships, Reykjavik, Iceland (recurring)

The Vikings arrived in Iceland in the 9th century, and have never left. Modern Icelanders are direct descendants of the Vikings … but there are other Norsemen who still prowl that frozen land.

If you stand on the beach at Reykjavik on June 3, you may be lucky enough to see a pair of ghost ships. Carved wooden dragons rear their proud heads over the waves, looking eagerly to a new land. Two Viking longships appear off the coast of Iceland every year and begin their annual trek. Every June 23, twenty days later, those same ships appear off the coast of L'Anse Aux Meadows, Newfoundland.

JUNE 4
The Black Abbess, Ireland (15th century)

Carlingford Castle and Abbey stand ruined against the blue Irish sky. The abbey was founded by the Dominicans around 1305, and the castle was built in the late 12th century by Hugh de Lacy. The ruins stand on a rocky bluff overlooking the harbor. There's not much left of the buildings, but they still hold a sad sort of romance.

They're home to a ghostly romance, too. Two shadowy figures, looking like a man and a woman in love, have been seen in the chapel. There's little left of the abbey, barely more than stone walls and a few arches. The chapel, though, is fairly well-preserved. There's no roof or floor, but the walls still stand. A niche in one of the walls once held a statue of the Virgin Mary, an object of devotion for the nuns who once lived and prayed at the abbey. And thereby hangs a tale …

In the first part of the 15th century, a female pirate named Henrietta Traviscant decided to retire. She gave up the sea to become a nun at Carlingford Abbey. She gave her ship, the *Black Abbess*, to Henry V to serve in the war against France. In honor of her vessel, when Henrietta was put in charge of the abbey, she called herself the Black Abbess as well.

Henrietta had a very personal reason for wanting to retreat from the world. During one of the voyages, her lover, Nevin O'Neal, had been lost at sea. She was at the abbey to mourn her loss.

One night, while Henrietta was praying on front of the statue of the Virgin in the chapel's niche, she heard a voice that seemed to float on the evening mist. She could have sworn it sounded like Nevin's voice …

But she was a no-nonsense woman, a pirate. She spoke aloud, demanding proof that it was indeed Nevin calling to her. The voice fell silent.

Later that night, perhaps driven by memories of the life she'd shared with Niven, Henrietta wandered down to the beach. Again, she heard Niven's voice calling to her. Overcome with loss and longing for him, she ran close to the edge of the beach, where the sea met the sand. A huge wave broke over the beach and swept Henrietta into the black water. Her body, like that of Nevin O'Neal, was claimed by the sea.

Sybil Leek, the famous psychic, visited Carlingford with ghost hunter Hans Holzer. Sybil reported that she did sense the presence of the two lovers, and that their spirits weren't frightening or unhappy. She called the haunting a "love imprint" of the past.

The ghosts of Carlingford are most often seen on summer nights.

JUNE 5
Explosion at Joliet Arsenal, Elwood, IL (1942)

The Joliet Arsenal was an ammunition plant that opened in 1940, when war was already raging in Europe. When the United States entered the war in 1941, the plant became even more vital. The "homefront heroes" that worked at the plant had a keen awareness of their importance in the war effort. The Kankakee Ordnance Works produced TNT – 1 billion pounds of it – and the Elwood Ordnance Works manufactured 926 million shells, bombs, and mines.

On June 5, 1942, workers on the night shift at the Elwood plant were busy loading anti-tank mines into railroad cars. The mines were packed five to a box, with an extra tetryl fuse booster for each mine. (Used in blasting caps, tetryl sets off the rest of the mine.)

At 2:41 am, two of the boxcars were already full, and another one was nearly full. The mines contained about 57,000 pounds of TNT. No one knows exactly what happened next. One account says that there was a small bang – then the earth shook from a devastating explosion.

The blast was felt in Waukegan, 60 miles away. It would take days to sort out how many men had died. The final count was forty-eight. Many remains had to be identified by fingerprints. Two fingers were all that was left of Lawrence McCawley. They were buried in a child's casket.

The arsenal continued to produce munitions during the Korean and Vietnam wars. It closed in the late 1970s, and the area where the arsenal was located is now the Abraham Lincoln National Cemetery, and the Midewin Tallgrass Prairie.

Witnesses report seeing the ghosts of the workers killed in the blast still going about their jobs. One of the victims, Roy Tighe, had been asked just that day what would happen if lightning struck the plant. His answer? "We'd never know it." Patriotism is a strong motivator, and these guys were doing something they were proud of, something they knew was vitally important to America's war effort. These ghosts are probably perfectly happy haunting the grounds – I expect they don't even know they're dead.

JUNE 6
The Gurkha Ghost, Kashmir (1948)

Khamba Fort is nestled in the mountains of Kashmir, between India and Pakistan. It is manned by Indian troops, and it has a reputation for the discipline of the soldiers stationed there. No sentry ever falls asleep on duty – if he does, he gets a slap and a stern dressing-down from … the resident ghost.

The spirit is said to be that of a Gurkha sergeant who basically captured the fort single-handedly during the 1948 war between India and Pakistan. The fort was held by Pakistani soldiers, who had been fighting Indian troops for weeks. Finally, this Gurkha sergeant had had enough. He found a crack in the fort's stone walls, and snuck in one June night. Armed only with a knife and a few grenades, he killed all the defenders, but he himself was fatally wounded.

The sergeant doesn't tolerate shirkers. Corporal Ram Prakash was making his rounds on the fort's wall one night. He was coming up to a turret when he heard a terrifying voice thunder, "I have given my life for this post. Why are you so slack?" The shouting was followed by the crack of palm against cheek. Later, he found out that a sentry in the turret was nodding over his rifle, and got a reprimand from the ghost.

The Gurkha ghost invariably appears wearing only one shoe. Apparently, he lost the other one in his one-man assault on the fort. The soldiers aren't afraid of their resident ghost, but they do respect him. To stay on the spirit's good side, they leave tea and sweets out overnight, to satisfy the sergeant as he keeps watch over the fort all night. They say the treats are always gone by dawn.

JUNE 7
A Ghost In The Form Of A Mongoose, Isle of Man (1931)

One of the absolute weirdest cases in paranormal lore is the delightfully obnoxious creature that appeared in the United Kingdom in 1931.

James Irving lived on a farm in an area of the Isle of Man called Cashen's Gap with his wife, Margaret, and daughter Voirrey. In September 1931, they began to hear strange rustling and growling in the walls of their house, and James and Voirrey caught quick glimpses of a mysterious creature, a little larger than a rat, with a flat snout and a small face.

James discovered that the creature was quite intelligent. The family members would call out the name of an animal, and the creature would imitate that animal. But it kept up the random snarling at night, too. One night, Voirrey made a startling discovery. She was reciting nursery rhymes aloud, in an effort to bore herself enough to fall asleep despite the creature's growls. To her astonishment, the animal started repeating the nursery rhymes. Their mysterious visitor had learned to talk.

Over the next several years, the thing that lived in the Irving's house made itself at home. It familiarly called its hosts "Jim" and "Maggie". It was perhaps the rudest, most obstreperous houseguest ever. In addition to the all-night scratching, the entity started moving things around, like a poltergeist. It presented itself as a mongoose, and said it had come from India. James began calling the critter "Gef", and the entity seemed to accept that.

Gef was quite the character. He'd shamelessly beg for food, yelling, "Hey, Jim, what about some grubbo? I'm hungry!" The Irvings would give Gef cookies, chocolate, and bananas, which he usually snarfed down with his mouth full. One day, Gef woke Jim up at 5 am whining, "Jim, Jim, I am sick," then Jim heard Gef vomiting behind the paneling. (I can't even imagine what a ghost mongoose whorfing up a hairball would sound like.) Another time, Gef yarked up some carrots under Jim's bed.

Gef had his moments, though. He took on the job, in his own way, of guarding the Irvings' house. He'd warn them of the approach of guests or of an unfamiliar dog. If someone had forgotten to bank the fire at night, Gef would do it. He also woke family members up if they overslept. And when mice got into the house, Gef would catch them – although he preferred to scare them into leaving, rather than kill them.

Gef was not so lenient with rabbits, though. During the years he stayed with the Irvings, he left more than fifty rabbits on the kitchen floor. Oddly, they had all been strangled – a mongoose would have used its teeth on its prey's throat.

As much as he professed to like the Irvings, Gef didn't confine himself to their house, and he got up to mischief around the neighborhood. He harassed a group of men repairing a road, by stealing their lunches. Several of the workers even said they saw their lunch sacks being carried off by something invisible.

Gef had his quirks, but he was very intelligent. One day at the end of March, 1934, James was reading the front page of the newspaper. Gef called out to him, "I see something."

"What?" James asked.

"I see a name that makes me quake, that makes me shake," Gef replied. He told James to look in the obituary column. James flipped to the page – and found a death notice for someone named Jeffrey – aka Jef.

Ghost hunter Harry Price sent a colleague to investigate the entity. Gef tormented the guy without mercy. As Gef hid in the wall, the investigator tried to coax him out so he could take a picture. Gef squirted water at him instead. Then he threw a needle at the investigator, and cussed him out. James tried to console the man, assuring him that Gef often threw things at the family.

Later, Gef was spotted sitting on a wall in the yard. The investigator asked Voirrey to take his camera to see if she could snap a photo of the entity. She was as calm and quiet as she could be, but as she raised the camera, Gef disappeared. The investigator still had better luck than Price did, when he came to see Gef for himself. When the famed ghost hunter visited Cashen's Gap, the capricious Gef refused to speak, throw things, or even scratch behind the wall. Price left the house never having experienced the entity.

Gef considered himself the family's guardian, but he shunned any attempt at affection. Once, Margaret put her hand into Gef's hiding place in the wall. She touched soft fur, and began to stroke it. Immediately, Gef nipped her and drew blood. Harry Price, intrigued that

Margaret had made physical contact with Gef, asked the family to try and get a hair sample for analysis. Gef woke the family up late one night, and told them he had a special surprise for them. He told them to look in a particular bowl in the kitchen. They did, and found a tuft of fur. They sent it off to Price, who had it analyzed by the London Zoo. Unfortunately, Gef had skunked everyone again. The fur was from the Irving's dog, not from a mongoose.

So what on earth *was* Gef? He told the Irvings different things during his stay with them. He said once, "I am not a spirit; if I were I could not kill rabbits." Another time, he called himself an "earthbound spirit", and said, "I am a ghost in the form of a mongoose, and I will haunt you." Once, feeling particularly squirrely, Gef roared, "I am a freak. I have hands and I have feet, and if you saw me you'd be petrified, mummified, turned into stone or a pillar of salt!" And another time, he chortled, "I am a little extra, extra clever mongoose."

Whatever Gef really was, he certainly made himself unforgettable. And why is he in this book, on this page? Because today is Gef's birthday. He told James Irving that he'd been born on June 7, 1852. In Harry Price's book *The Haunting of Cashen's Gap*, Price noted dryly, "It was his 83rd birthday on June 7, 1935, but nothing appears to have been done in the way of celebrating it."

JUNE 8
Alfie, Massachusetts (1888, recurring)

When Peg and Joe Roberts moved into their home in 1965, Joe had a few reservations about the place. Oh, it was a great house, sitting on five acres with lovely landscaping and beautiful old trees. It was huge, with plenty of room to raise a family, and the price was right. But something just felt "off" about the house to Joe. As they toured the house, Joe grumbled, "The damn place is haunted." The real estate agent brushed off his comment with a smile, but admitted that she was afraid to be there after dark.

Joe's instincts were right. The house is haunted. After all, the New England farmhouse was built in 1831, and many people have lived and died within its walls. But the spirits are gentle. They flit like shadows, watching Joe work in the basement. He just sees quick movement out of the corner of his eye.

After they moved in, one of their sons said that a little boy had come into his room in the middle of the night and had looked at his trains. Only the boy's upper half was visible, and it glowed in the dark.

Curious about their ghostly visitors, Joe and Peg invited several psychics to their home. One was able to identify the young ghost. His name was Alfie, and he was nine years old when he fell down the back stairs and broke his neck. He'd possibly been born in the house on June 15, 1888, the same day that an eccentric old lady named Mary Morgan died there. She may have been Alfie's great-grandmother, but there's no documentation for this.

At another séance, everyone felt a dog under the table, rubbing up against their legs. (The Roberts family didn't own any pets.) One psychic said it was Alfie's beloved dog Dodo, which went everywhere with him. (Even, apparently, into the afterlife.)

Every year on June 15, the haunting in the house got really intense. Soccer-ball-sized globes of light glided back and forth across the ceilings of the children's rooms. Wind-up toys in the toybox started up by themselves. And one night, Joe was woken up at 3 am by an odd thumping noise, like something falling down the stairs one at a time. When he got up the next morning, he discovered that Alfie had been rolling his marbles down the stairs.

The Roberts family chose not to have any of the psychics try to cross Alfie's soul over. They figured that a home filled with the love of a large family was a wonderful place for a lost little boy and his devoted dog.

JUNE 9
The Canfield Hotel Fire, Dubuque, IA (1946)

In 1925, William Canfield bought the Paris Hotel in Dubuque, Iowa. The hotel, a wood-frame building, had been built in 1890. He changed the name of the hotel to the Canfield, and in 1927 he built on an addition. This brought the capacity to 200 rooms. The addition was built of concrete rather than wood, and was advertised as fireproof.

This was one instance where a hotel touted as fireproof actually lived up to the hype. Unfortunately, the blaze that ripped through the Canfield on June 19, 1946 started in the wooden part of the hotel. The fire is believed to have started in a closet near the cocktail lounge on the ground floor. Some years before, Canfield had decided to modernize the hotel with a facelift, which included installing dropped-ceilings made of fiberboard. Fiberboard is highly combustible, and the fire raced through the four-story building faster than the hotel guests could run. One woman in the cocktail lounge died five feet from the barstool she'd been sitting on. When firemen arrived on the scene, they spent the first fifteen minutes just rescuing people with nets and ladders, before even attempting to fight the fire.

Most of the fatalities were from smoke inhalation, but some people died jumping from windows. One woman jumped into a net and hit her neck on the rim, which killed her and dented the net's iron frame. In a third-floor window, a woman stood with her grandchild, holding the kid up on the windowsill. Firemen begged her to throw the child down, then jump into the net herself. She slumped back into the room, defeated at the thought. She and the child both died. A man and his wife were sitting on the windowsill of their fourth-floor room. The man pushed his wife off, and she was safely caught. Then he threw his suitcase down and immediately jumped. He landed on the suitcase in the net, and broke his back. (He lived.)

Twenty-six people were rescued using the one net the firefighters had brought. Only one person died: the woman whose neck hit the rim. Another twenty-one were rescued with ladders. But nineteen people perished in the fast-moving flames, including William Canfield and his wife. (She died of her injuries at the hospital.)

People say the Canfield is haunted, but they can't put their finger on any distinct evidence. They just hear footsteps and strange sounds in the hallway, and when they go to look, there's no one there. Rather than an actual haunting, this may be a case where so much psychic energy was released so quickly in the panic of the fire that some of it seeped into the concrete of the building.

Oh, by the way, the six-story "fireproof" part of the building did actually live up to its billing. The first floor and some upper rooms were damaged, but the concrete construction didn't burn.

JUNE 10
The Villisca Axe Murders, Villisca, IA (1912)

Sometimes, the awfulness of a crime can leave a lasting impression on even the most pleasant place. That's what happened in Villisca, Iowa.

Villisca is a sleepy place even today. On June 10, 1912, it was just another small Midwestern town. Josiah Moore had squired his wife Sarah to the Presbyterian Church that evening. Sarah had coordinated the Children's Day program at the church, and the Moores' four children – Herman (11), Katherine (10), Boyd (7), and Paul (5) – had accompanied their parents. The Stillinger family was also at the program that night, and since they lived out in the country, Katherine invited Ina and Lena Stillinger to spend the night at the Moore house. Lena was twelve, and Ina was eight, so they were friends to ten-year-old Katherine. With three brothers, Katherine relished the chance to spend time with girls close to her own age.

The program ended at 9:30, and the Moores and the Stillinger girls walked home around 9:45 or 10 pm. They went to bed soon after, with Ina and Lena taking the bed in the guestroom.

At 7 am the next day, the Moores' neighbor, Mary Peckham, realized that the Moores hadn't come outside yet to do the morning chores. She knocked on the door, but got no answer. She tried to go inside, but the door was locked … odd for a small Iowa town in 1912. Mary, a good neighbor, let the Moores' chickens out to forage in the yard, then called Ross Moore, Josiah's brother. Ross came over with his key, and unlocked the door. While Mary waited nervously on the porch, Ross went into the too-quiet house.

Nothing could have prepared him for what waited for him inside. Ross went through the parlor and opened the door to the guest room. There was blood everywhere. Lena had cuts on her arm, and was lying crossways on the bed. Her face had been bludgeoned. Ina was just dead, her face another smashed-in horror.

Ross backed away from the sight, then realized that the deathly silence of the house hadn't changed. He went out onto the porch and told Mary to call the sheriff. Deputy Marshall Hank Horton arrived shortly, and went into the house. He went up the narrow staircase to the second floor, the wooden steps creaking loudly under his weight.

At the top of the stairs, another gruesome scene awaited him. Josiah and Sarah lay in their bed, their faces pulped by countless blows from an axe. Horton gulped, and continued on to the children's room.

Blood soaked the bedsheets, the pillows, and the pajamas of the four Moore children. They had also been murdered in their beds; their faces, too, had been obliterated with the blunt side of an axe.

The theory is this: someone snuck into the Moores' home, possibly while they were at the church. They hid in the attic, and waited until everyone had gone to bed. Then, when all was still, whoever it was crept out of the attic … and the slaughter began. The crime was never solved.

The activity at the Villisca Axe Murder house is intense. Witnesses hear the sound of children playing, and many investigators have caught ghost voices of children. Adult voices show up too. Ghost children peer out of windows – and some of these photographs are on display in the barn behind the house, where investigators can regroup while taking a break from the house's activity. People can get overwhelmed by the intense emotion that sometimes pervades the home.

JUNE 11
Grandpa Says Goodbye, Indianapolis, IN (1923)

Sometimes, loved ones will make a final encore appearance as they're on their way off of life's stage. At about 3:30 am on June 11, 1923, Gladys Watson experienced one of these visits.

She woke up to someone calling her name. She sat up in bed, and saw her grandfather standing there. He said, "Don't be frightened, it's only me. I have just died."

Gladys burst into tears, as she was very close to her grandfather. He told her calmly that he had been just "waiting to go" since his wife had passed. He gave her a reassuring smile, then disappeared.

Gladys' husband woke up then, and Gladys told him of her grandfather's visit. He said that it must have been a dream, and he called Gladys' parents to prove it. His mother-in-law, Mrs. Parker, answered the phone. She had been up most of the night, she said, because her husband's father had been suddenly taken ill. He had died about the time Gladys claimed to have seen him.

JUNE 12
House Call, New York State (1910)

Carol Ann Charles had been feeling ill for a couple of weeks, but she kept it to herself. Everyone had been so kind when her husband had died two weeks before. She didn't want to trespass too much on their sympathy. The cough was annoying, but surely it would go away on its own.

Half an hour past midnight on June 12, 1910, Carol came awake feeling like someone was in her room. She sat up and saw her husband standing beside the bed. He had been a doctor for thirty years, and he looked just as she remembered him – his stethoscope was in his ears, and his medical bag sat at his feet. His face was lit up with a warm smile, the smile she'd fallen in love with so many years ago.

But seeing him there in the darkness, when she knew he was dead, scared her some. She couldn't move to tell him hello; she just sat there petrified. Finally, she fell asleep.

When she woke up, she was startled to find a piece of paper on the bed that hadn't been there the night before. It was a sheet from her husband's prescription pad. On it was a note in her husband's familiar scrawl: "See Dr. Norton, State Street, Albany – urgent."

That was strange. It was obviously a reminder her husband had written to himself before he'd passed. Odd for it to show up on her bed. She threw it away and put it out of her mind.

The following night, she woke again at half past midnight. Her husband was again standing next to the bed, but now he wasn't smiling. He was wearing what Carol used to call his "doctor face", an expression of fear, concern, and anxiety that he reserved for his most stubborn patients.

When he saw her watching him, his gentle smile came again. He wrote something on a piece of paper, dropped it onto the bed, and vanished.

This time, Carol turned on the light. She grabbed for the paper. It was another sheet torn from his prescription pad. The message was the same. And this time, she'd seen him write it.

The next morning, Carol went to Albany for a visit to Dr. Norton, who had been a dear friend of her late husband. She told him about the notes, her husband's midnight visits, his expression of concern.

As Carol spoke, Dr. Norton's face paled. When she was finished, he had a strange tale of his own, one that mirrored hers. He, too, had had visits from Carol's dead husband, in which his friend had begged him to examine Carol as soon as possible. He did ... and discovered Carol had tuberculosis.

Luckily, the disease was in its early stages. Carol started treatment immediately. Within a few months she was cured.

Her husband's ghost never returned.

JUNE 13
Mark Twain's Prophetic Vision (1858)

Henry Clemens, Mark Twain's brother, the baby of the family, was a quiet, studious boy. (In fact, Twain modeled Sid, Tom Sawyer's annoyingly well-behaved brother, on Henry.) Henry worked at the same newspaper Twain did, and the brothers were close.

Twain even got Henry a job. Twain was a cub pilot on the steamboat *Pennsylvania*, which ran on the Mississippi River. Twain arranged a job for Henry as a "mud clerk". Mud clerks did anything that needed doing aboard the steamboat. They ran errands for the crew, carried messages, and did any job they were assigned. This was an unpaid position, but one from which Henry could work his way upward.

Around that time, in May or early June 1858, Twain had a deeply disturbing dream about his brother. He was in the sitting-room of his sister Pamela's house. A metallic coffin was supported on two chairs. Twain went closer, and was horrified to see Henry in the coffin, wearing one of Twain's suits. On his chest was a bouquet of white roses, with one red rose in the center. Twain woke from the dream convinced that it was real. It had *seemed* real.

Thankfully, Henry was alive and well. But there was trouble in the air. A pilot named William Brown accused Henry of not delivering a message, and hit him. Twain leapt to Henry's defense and beat the paste out of Brown. The captain broke up the fight, and offered to fire Brown. Twain arranged to return upriver on another steamboat, the *A.T. Lacey*. He told the captain he'd rejoin the *Pennsylvania* as soon as Brown was replaced.

It was a fateful decision. At 4 am on Sunday, June 13, the *Pennsylvania* was headed upriver, six miles below Memphis. She was pulling a flatboat loaded with wood. Many of the crew and most of the passengers were asleep when the boilers exploded, demolishing the front third of the boat.

Around half of the 500 people on board were killed instantly. Henry was blown off the ship, and suffered burns and internal injuries. Some stories say that the good-hearted Henry swam back to the ship and helped some victims escape the burning wreck. They were loaded onto the flatboat, which was then cut loose to escape the flames.

The *Imperial* was the first boat to arrive on the scene, and she took some victims to New Orleans. Others, including Henry, were rescued by the *Diana*, which took them to Memphis. People continued to die from the terrible injuries they'd suffered. Henry had inhaled superheated air, and his lungs were scorched.

Twain rushed to his brother's bedside. Henry fought his injuries for six days, aided by the attentive care of Memphis doctors. He seemed to be out of danger. But at 11 o'clock on the sixth night, a doctor told Twain that if Henry woke and couldn't get back to sleep, to ask the attending physician to administer 1/8 grain of morphine.

Henry did wake that night. The other victims moaned aloud in their pain, and Henry couldn't sleep. Twain told the medical student who had the overnight shift what the doctor had said. The student measured out the dose, but he may have gotten it wrong. Henry sank into a deep sleep. He died before dawn.

Word of Henry's heroics in the disaster had spread. Most of the wreck victims were being buried in plain wooden caskets, but the ladies of Memphis took up a collection to buy Henry a fancy $100 metal coffin. When Twain walked into the room where Henry was laid out, he felt a chilling sense of familiarity. Henry was in his metal coffin, which was laid across two chairs. He was dressed in Twain's clothes – Twain hadn't realized that Henry had borrowed one of his suits, and the undertaker simply used the best clothes Henry had. On Henry's chest lay a bouquet of white roses. That was the only detail the dream had gotten wrong – there was no red rose among the white blooms.

But as Twain stood there in his grief, an old woman came into the parlor and tucked a single red rose into the middle of the bouquet. The dream was complete.

JUNE 14
The Whispering Woman in Black, Columbus, IN (1895)

The *Columbus Republican* had an odd story for its readers in the June 14, 1895 edition. After assuring its readership that there were no such things as ghosts in Columbus, Indiana, the newspaper immediately cast doubt on that bold statement.

People on Franklin Street had been haunted by the mysterious figure of a woman, dressed in black, who would hang around houses at night, whispering ominously. Her words could never quite be understood, but her appearance was unnerving. In the article, the paper reported that the strange apparition had moved to another part of town. An elderly woman on Mechanic Street had finished her evening reading, and was closing up her house for the night. As she went to lock the front door, she saw a creepy woman in black staring at her through the screen. The peeping Thomasina scurried away, but the old woman was quite shaken.

Sounds like your average creeper, but apparently there was something "off" about the woman. The newspaper wrote, "It is said that even a policeman feels a strangeness come over his power of locomotion, and that he finds himself able to walk backward as well as forward when a woman in black approaches." We don't know much about this phantom, but she must have been a real weirdo to make a policeman backpedal.

JUNE 15
The Pink Lady, Yorba Linda, CA (1910, recurring)

Yorba Cemetery in Yorba Linda is home to a ghost with some unusual habits. The Pink Lady is said to be the spirit of Alvina de los Reyes. Alvina was the daughter of Bernardo Yorba. She was killed in a carriage accident on December 2, 1910. In some versions of her story, she was coming home from a dance at Valencia High School. (The problem with this version is that the school didn't exist in 1910.) Another story claims that Alvina was riding in a carriage with her husband, who was driving. He either swerved and tipped her out, or straight-up pushed her. She either died in the fall from the carriage, or landed on railroad tracks and was killed by a train before she could scramble to safety.

The story gets more of an urban legend flavor the more you look at it. The real Alvina de los Reyes actually died in childbirth at age 31. But some young woman's ghost still makes a regular appearance at Yorba Cemetery. She shows up on June 15 of even-numbered years. Witnesses say she materializes out of an oleander bush, then walks to the rear of the cemetery, perhaps to visit family members buried there. She has light brown hair and dark eyes, and wears a pink dress. The ghost became more active in the 1970s after renovations on the cemetery began.

She doesn't always show herself when scheduled, but even when she doesn't appear, strange things happen. Electrical equipment malfunctions. One year, a large crowd that had gathered to wait for the Pink Lady saw several lampposts flicker, then go out. They came back on moments later … glowing pink.

It seems she can have an effect on the living, too. One even-numbered year, a paranormal investigation group was at the cemetery. The Pink Lady didn't show herself that year, but one of the investigators found herself saying aloud: *"Por favor espera, que voy."* Later she discovered that the words meant, "Please wait, I'm coming."

She had to ask the meaning of the words because she didn't speak Spanish.

JUNE 16
The Death of Superman, Beverly Hills, CA (1959)

The television show *Adventures of Superman* enthralled viewers from 1953 to 1958. The star, George Reeves, was a solidly handsome middle-aged actor in need of a comeback. He'd done movie acting – he played one of the Tarleton twins in *Gone With the Wind* – but World War II put his big plans on hold. He languished in walk-on parts until 1951, when he was asked to play Superman in a TV pilot. The producers shot thirteen half-hour episodes, then sat on them for two years because no network was interested in the show.

But when the show finally aired in 1953, Reeves' career took off. Reeves appeared as Superman at celebrity galas and department store openings, and was mobbed by fans. Lots of the fans were kids, who could sometimes be unclear on the difference between fantasy and reality. Reeves often got punched in the stomach by overenthusiastic boys wanting to take their best shot at the Man of Steel. Reeves knew his career as a serious actor was virtually over. He burned his Superman outfit at the end of every season.

On June 16, 1959, Reeves went up to the bedroom of the house he shared with his fiancée, Leonore Lemmon. He took off all his clothes and shot himself in the head. When the police arrived, Lemmon and three friends were downstairs in the house, pickled with booze.

LA police and the coroner quickly agreed that it was an open-and-shut case of suicide, even though the bullet casing was found under Reeves' body – a ballistic impossibility for a suicide. An autopsy was done, but only after the body was thoroughly washed. There were unexplained bruises on the face and chest. And the coroner didn't check either Reeves' hand or the grisly wound in his head for traces of gunpowder.

The ruling was suicide, but questions remained. Maybe that's why George Reeves still haunts his old home. A young couple rented the home, and had several run-ins with the Man of Steel. One evening, they were entertaining friends in the living room when everyone heard noises coming from upstairs, in the room where Reeves had died. The couple always kept the room neat, but when they opened the door that night, the room had been trashed. Sheets were torn off the bed and clothes were scattered on the floor.

Later, they found their German shepherd at the door to that room. He was barking savagely, but suddenly cowered and ran, tail tucked. When they opened the door, they found that the bed had moved across the room.

The room had one more surprise for them. Around 3 am one summer morning, they saw Reeves standing in his old room, wearing his Superman costume. That was too much for the couple. They moved out that day.

Other renters claimed to hear a single gunshot in the middle of the night. Some smelled the tang of gunpowder in the room. Renters came and went. Two sheriffs were called out to the home because there were so many complaints from the neighbors. They were worried about the gunshots and screaming they heard in the night hours.

There was no one renting the house at the time.

JUNE 17
The Kansas City Massacre, Kansas City, MO (1933)

Thirty seconds on a June morning. That's all it took for a legend to be born.

Frank Nash was a criminal mastermind, with connections to gangsters all over the Midwest. He was likeable, charming, and charismatic. He knew how to get what he wanted.

In 1913, Nash and a friend, Nollie "Humpy" Wortman, stole about $1000 from a store in Oklahoma. Nash told Wortman that they needed to hide the money fast. As Wortman was burying the loot, Nash shot him in the back. Nash was arrested hours later.

He was found guilty of murder, and sentenced to life in the Oklahoma State Penitentiary. Five years later, Nash found a way to reduce his sentence to ten years. (I told you the guy had the golden touch.) He buddied up to the warden, and convinced him that if released, he'd enlist to fight in World War I. He got himself sprung, and immediately went back to a life of crime.

Nash worked with the Spencer gang, which terrorized Oklahoma in the 1920s. In March 1924, he and three Spencer gang members were convicted of mail robbery and assaulting a mail custodian. They were sentenced to 25 years in Leavenworth. By 1930, Nash had again cozied up to the deputy warden, and got himself appointed a general handyman. On October 19, 1930, he left the prison on an errand, and just never returned. He didn't forget his buddies, though. On December 11, 1931, Nash helped seven prisoners escape from Leavenworth.

The FBI really wanted to capture Frank Nash. Nash managed to dodge the manhunt for three years, but in 1932, agents arrested Francis Keating and Thomas Holden. The two gangsters were close friends with Nash, and they told the agents that Nash was hiding out in Hot Springs, Arkansas. He was arrested there on July 16, 1933, and taken to Fort Smith. There, FBI agents Joe Lackey and Frank Smith, along with police chief Otto Reed, would take Nash to Kansas City, Missouri by train.

News of Nash's capture spread quickly in the gangster underground. Nash was a pivotal figure in his world, and plans were made to rescue him from the clutches of the Feds. Vernon Miller, a renowned gunman, was joined by Pretty Boy Floyd and Floyd's sidekick, Adam Richetti.

Nash's train rolled into Union Station in Kansas City at 7:15 am on July 17, 1933. As Nash and the agents got into the car that would take Nash back to Leavenworth, the gangsters opened fire. When the machine guns fell silent, thirty seconds later, five men were dead: two police officers, a federal agent, the Kansas City police chief … and Frank Nash, who'd also caught his rescuers' bullets.

Nash has apparently not paid much attention to his own death. He is seen at Union Station by paranormal investigators and station staff alike. One night, a security guard saw something strange on the camera covering the Union Station Historical Room. A figure was sitting on a bench. The guard sent a colleague in to investigate. When he got to the room, the second guard radioed back that there was no one there.

"Yes, there is, I can see them on the monitor," the first guard insisted. And indeed, the figure was still on the screen. The guard in the room just couldn't see it. In the dispatch room, the first guard stared at the screen in growing horror. The figure on the bench didn't have a head.

Which makes sense, because Frank Nash's head was nearly severed in the storm of machine gun bullets that ended his life.

June 18
Murder of Cassandra Marinoni, Parma, Italy (1573)

The Rocco di Soragna is a palace in Parma, Italy, once home to the Marquis Diofebo di Soragna and his wife, Cassandra Marinoni. Lady Cassandra was a wise mistress, beloved by the people of Parma. Cassandra' sister Lucrezia also valued her advice. Lucrezia was married to Giulio Anguissola, a violent man who had squandered her fortune and tried to poison her.

In June 1573, Cassandra traveled to Lucrezia's castle in Cremona to comfort her sister while her husband was away. But on the night of June 18, Giulio and a gang of thugs broke in. They killed Lucrezia, and attacked Cassandra, stabbing her twenty-seven times. Rescuers brought Cassandra back to Soragna, where she died the next morning.

Cassandra's ghost is out for revenge, and with good reason. As it turned out, Diofebo was in on the plan. With both sisters dead, Giulio would inherit a fortune and split it with Diofebo.

Almost immediately after her death, Cassandra's furious spirit began haunting her faithless husband. She haunts all throughout the palace, but is seen most often in the Hercules Room. She wears a red dress, and she's been given the nickname Donna Cenerina (Ashen Woman) because of her long, ash-colored hair. She still harasses Diofebo's descendants. She takes particular glee in announcing the impending death of a Soragna family member. She rattles the furniture in savage celebration, filling the old palace with a cacophony of noise.

JUNE 19
Moundsville Picnics, Moundsville, WV (1931)

West Virginia State Penitentiary has the reputation of being viciously haunted. In operation from 1876 to 1995, the prison held the worst of the worst — a violent population of rapists, murderers, and serial killers. Overcrowding meant that while two prisoners in a cell had bunks, a third would get a mattress to put on the floor. In 1986, prisoners rioted, in part because of a leaky sewer pipe that ran under the cafeteria floor. During the last decade of operation, the prison became the scene of turf wars between gangs like the Aryan Brotherhood and the Avengers.

But it wasn't always like that. The prison was once its own little community. Prisoners raised their own food, and even mined their own coal. Residents of Moundsville could hire an inmate for day labor, paying around 25 cents a day.

The prison provided entertainment for area residents as well. The prison had an orchestra, and put on plays and minstrel shows. A dinner invitation in the warden's apartments was prized.

And then there were the executions. People could come and watch them too. These were jocularly known as "Moundsville picnics". Of the men executed, 85 were hanged and nine were electrocuted. Hangings were a popular public event … for a while.

Frank Hyer had been convicted of murdering his wife. He was scheduled to hang on June 19, 1931. Prisons used the long-drop method, using height and weight to figure out how long a drop was needed to break the condemned man's neck. Someone decided to hang Hyer from a twenty-foot drop. This turned out to be overkill. When Hyer's body hit the end of the rope, his head just popped right off. After that, executions were by invitation only.

The ghosts of Moundsville still walk the dingy halls of the prison. Some people say there are over 100 souls that don't realize that death has freed them. People have heard disembodied voices and footsteps. And they've noticed that one of the figures is missing his head.

JUNE 20
What Happens In Vegas, Beverly Hills, CA (1947)

By the time he was a teenager, Benjamin "Bugsy" Siegel had started his own gang in New York City with his friend Meyer Lansky. His exploits caught the attention of higher-ups in the

Mafia, and soon Bugsy was sent off to Los Angeles to keep an eye on gambling operations there.

On one of his trips to LA, Siegel stopped in at a dusty cow town called Las Vegas. He fell in love with the place. For one thing, the workers constructing the Hoover Dam were making very good money for the Depression, and spending it in Las Vegas. Siegel wanted a piece of that. But it had another draw for Siegel. Las Vegas was glamorous enough for a flashy gangster lifestyle, but also, it represented a chance for Siegel to reinvent himself. If he could buy a hotel and casino in Vegas, he wouldn't have to stay a lowlife gangster. He could be a respected businessman instead.

Siegel bought a half-finished hotel and named it the Flamingo. (His girlfriend, Virginia Hill, had long, lovely legs, and "Flamingo" was her nickname.) He convinced Meyer Lansky, Frank Costello, and Lucky Luciano to give him money so he could get the Flamingo finished. $1 million became $3 million, then $5 million … until Siegel had borrowed $16 million to pour into his pet project.

The Flamingo opened December 26, 1946. The opening was rushed, and the hotel wasn't quite finished. Siegel invited his Hollywood friends to come and gamble at his new casino, but very few of them came. Also, it rained that night, a rarity in desert Vegas. The casino lost $215,000 that night.

Siegel shut the Flamingo down in late January. He made some changes, and reopened March 1, 1947. The casino started making money, but the Mob had lost patience.

On June 20, 1947, Siegel and Virginia Hill were on vacation at Virginia's house in Beverly Hills. Siegel was reading a newspaper in the living room. Someone snuck up to the picture window with an M1 carbine, aimed at Siegel, and pulled the trigger. Of the nine shots fired, four hit Siegel, including two shots to the head. One round went through his right cheek. The other struck the bridge of his nose by the right eye socket. The pressure caused by the bullet passing through Siegel's skull blew his left eye out of its socket. It was later found across the room.

Bugsy Siegel still haunts Virginia Hill's house. Witnesses see a shadowy figure run across the mansion's living room, duck for cover, then vanish – what Bugsy probably wishes he could have done, if he'd had any warning. Bugsy and Virginia both haunt the Flamingo hotel site (it was demolished in 1993). They are seen in the casino.

Bugsy also haunts the courtyard garden at the casino. There's a monument to him in the garden, with begonias planted at the base of it for a pop of color. Even in that warm desert environment, groundskeepers are continually replanting the flowers, because every few days, the tender plants are blasted by some withering cold spot around the monument.

JUNE 21
The Tomb of Tamerlane, Uzbekistan (1941)

The Mongol warlord Tamerlane (great-great-grandson of Genghis Khan) took the throne in 1369, and set about proving his own bloodthirstiness. He's widely considered one of the greatest military tacticians in history, and he was a great patron of art and architecture. But his armies were feared throughout Asia, Africa, and Europe. His military campaigns led to the deaths of 17 million people – about 5% of the world's population at the time. Tamerlane was no one to mess with.

When he died in 1405, he was buried in what is now Uzbekistan. Legend says his tomb is covered by a huge slab of jade inscribed with a curse: "When I arise from the grave, the world will tremble." Another variant of the story says that if Tamerlane's grave should ever be disturbed, a "great battle" would be the result.

In 1941, Josef Stalin sent a team of archaeologists to look for Tamerlane's tomb. Uzbek leaders were furious when they heard of this, and pointed to the curse. Terrible things would happen if the ancient chieftain's bones were moved.

On June 21, 1941, the tomb was opened, and Soviet scientists removed Tamerlane's body for study. The next day, Hitler's forces crossed into the Soviet Union, starting the most ambitious German military operation of World War II. For over a year, scientists studied the ancient bones, and for over a year, the German campaign raged on. Hitler's army tore apart the Soviet Union; all told, 26.6 million people died in the invasion.

In November 1942, Soviet scientists decided they were done with the Mongol chieftain, so they reinterred his bones in his tomb, complete with proper Islamic burial rites. Days later, the German invasion was turned back at Stalingrad. The Germans began their retreat, and the Soviets marked the turning point of the war. Had the curse of Tamerlane been lifted? I'll let you decide.

JUNE 22
Admiral Sir George Tryon (1893)

Admiral Tryon was the Commander-in-Chief of the Mediterranean Squadron of the Royal Navy under Queen Victoria. Tryon was sailing the fleet off the coast of Lebanon when he had an idea. It was time for some water aerobics.

Tryon's flagship, the *Victoria*, was at the head of one column of ships. At the head of the other column was the *Camperdown*, helmed by Rear Admiral Markham. Tryon had his signalman send a message. He wanted to turn the two lead ships towards each other and sail past, doing an aquatic about-face. But the ships were too close together to do the maneuver safely. Markham could see this, and he waited for better orders, thinking Tryon had simply made a mistake. But he got another signal from the *Victoria*, essentially asking, "What are you waiting for?"

Markham took a deep breath and gave the signal to turn to meet the other line of ships. And it turned out exactly how he'd envisioned it: the *Camperdown*'s ram buried itself in the *Victoria*'s starboard bow. The *Camperdown* reversed and pulled clear. She had a hole in the port bow and some other damage, but she was in no danger.

The *Victoria*, on the other hand, was mortally wounded. Water poured in at 3,000 tons per minute through the jagged hole. Admiral Tryon gazed at the damage and murmured, "It is entirely my fault." His fault resulted in his own death and the loss of 321 other men.

That night, June 22, 1893, Admiral Tryon's wife was entertaining guests at their London home. At the moment of impact, and afterwards, when Tryon and his men were plummeting to the ocean floor, Lady Tryon's guests were astonished to see the admiral himself, in full regalia.

Over 100 guests saw Tryon stroll across the room, then vanish. Lady Tryon didn't see the apparition, and she was stunned when her guests told her that he'd just made an appearance. The next day, news of the wreck reached London. Lady Tryon realized that her guests had all seen the admiral's ghost.

JUNE 23
Hachioji Castle, Tokyo, Japan (1590)

The ruins of Hachioji Castle stand in quiet green woods. The peaceful atmosphere belies the terror that stained this building centuries ago.

The castle was built in 1570 by the feudal lord Hojo Ujiteru. He set out from Hachioji in 1590 to help lift the siege at Odawara Castle, leaving only 1,300 men at Hachioji to guard it.

On June 23, 1590, the shogun Toyotomi Hideyoshi attacked the castle with 50,000 men. He quickly overran the defenses and captured the castle. Rather than be taken prisoner and suffer rape, torture, and dishonor, the women of Hachioji Castle leapt from the battlements and died on the rocks below. It's said there was so much blood in the ravine below the castle that it ran like a stream, creating waterfalls of gore.

The castle immediately began replaying the sounds and emotions of the tragedy. Anyone who came to the site heard the screams and the sickening thud of bodies hitting the rocks. Soon the castle was deserted … and it remained empty for 350 years. In 1951, the castle was named a historical site, and archaeologists have been studying it since 1977.

There's not much left to study; Hideyoshi ordered the castle's destruction, and all that's left after centuries is a few stone walls, some roads, and a reconstructed bridge. But the sounds of the haunting – thuds, screams – still echo in the green woods. Locals consider all of Mount Fukazawa to be haunted. Every year on June 23, they cook a dish of *azukimeshi* (red beans cooked with rice) to commemorate the anniversary of the castle's capture.

JUNE 24
The Skridla-Reed Murder, Oregon, IL (1948)

A first date on a hot summer night. The warm June air is redolent with possibilities. But for two young people, their first date on June 24, 1948, ended in unsolved murder.

Mary Jane Reed and Stanley Skridla both worked at DeKalb/Ogle Telephone Company. Skridla, 28, was a lineman, and Reed, 17, was a switchboard operator. Reed was excited about their date, in spite of their age difference. She wouldn't let that bother her.

Their first date took them to several bars in Oregon, Illinois that night. At the end of the evening, they drove out to County Farm Road in Skridla's Buick for a little action on the popular lover's lane. They were never seen alive again.

Stan Skridla's body was found the next day on County Farm Road, lying face down in a ditch. He had been shot and dragged into the grass. Police later found five .32-caliber casings. About an hour later, his Buick turned up roughly a mile away. Except for a lipstick-smeared cigarette in the car, there was no sign of Mary Jane.

Skridla was buried on June 28. The next day, a man found Mary Jane's body in a patch of weeds along Silica Road. That area had been searched several times; Mary Jane's father passed the site every day on his way to work. She was found by a truck driver – the height of his cab meant that he could see over the weeds. She had been shot in the back of the head with what looked like the same caliber of gun used to kill Skridla.

The case has never been solved. Robbery didn't seem to be a motive, as Skridla still had his wallet and Mary Jane was wearing her mother's wedding ring. Investigations didn't get very far; they mostly led to dead ends.

The case went cold, and in spite of being reopened in early 2006, is still a mystery. One of the people interested in seeing justice done is Mike Arians. He owned a restaurant in Oregon, and was elected mayor of the town in 1999. He was led to the case by Mary Jane herself.

Arians owned the Roadhouse, which in a previous incarnation as the Stenhouse, was possibly the last place Mary Jane Reed stopped before she and Skridla were killed. He said that his employees had seen the ghost of Mary Jane, and that drafts of cold air would sometimes take people by surprise. He also pointed to the strange case of the flower delivery.

One day, a flower arrangement showed up at the Roadhouse – for Mary Jane. No one knew where the arrangement had come from. Arians later learned that it was Mary Jane's birthday.

JUNE 25
The Battle of Little Bighorn, Montana (1876)

The Battle of Greasy Grass, near the Little Bighorn River in Montana, was one of the most memorable engagements in the Sioux Wars. It took thousands of Sioux and Cheyenne warriors less than an hour to massacre 210 men of the 7th Cavalry. It's become famous as "Custer's Last Stand", but there was little that was noble or heroic about it.

George Armstrong Custer went to West Point, where he graduated dead last in his class of 1861. He fought in the Civil War, and was promoted several times. Despite his abysmal performance at West Point, he was a pretty good soldier. He showed competence, resilience, even bravery. He led his men from the front, and some accounts say he had eleven horses shot from under him. (He was only wounded once.) In fact, his stubborn pursuit of Lee's Army of Northern Virginia may have helped to end the war. His forces blocked Lee's final retreat, and when Lee sent a messenger with the white flag of truce, Custer was the guy who accepted it.

In February 1864, Custer married Elizabeth "Libby" Bacon. In 1866, he took her to Kansas with him to his new posting: fighting in the Plains Indian Wars. It was at this time when Custer began to screw up a little. At the end of his first campaign, he deserted to join Libby at Fort Riley. He was court-martialed and suspended without rank or pay for a year. His rashness and disregard for rules would be his downfall.

However, the army still needed him to fight Indians. Before his year's sentence was up, he retook command of the 7th Cavalry. He led a raid on Chief Black Kettle's Cheyenne village, and killed every warrior. Custer had gotten back in the army's good graces, but it wasn't to last.

The Plains Indians were in serious trouble by that point. At first, not many whites settled in the Great Plains, because the dry weather wasn't great for farming. But after the Civil War, whites realized that land in the far West wasn't unlimited, so they turned their eyes to the Plains.

The Plains Indians, for their part, knew that most of their people were on reservations by that time. Vowing to avoid that fate, they resolved to put up a fight against the settlers.

The government went after the Indians' livelihood, letting railroad companies slaughter buffalo wholesale as they went across the country laying track. In retaliation for this incredible loss, natives began attacking railroad workers and other settlers. By the time Custer arrived in 1866, the war between the Plains Indians and the government was going strong.

In 1868, the government assigned the Black Hills, in South Dakota, as part of the Great Sioux Reservation. Of course, when gold was discovered in the Black Hills in 1874, all bets were off. Custer was given his orders: relocate all natives in the area to reservations by January 31, 1876. Any Indian who resisted would be considered hostile.

Indians from all over the area were furious at this new deception by the United States government. The forces of Sitting Bull and Crazy Horse grew stronger by the day as more warriors joined the resistance. Eventually, several thousand natives settled on the banks of the Little Bighorn River.

The army dispatched three groups of soldiers to round up the Indians and herd them back to their reservations. One group was Custer's 7th Cavalry. The plan was for Custer's cavalry to meet up with Brigadier General Terry's infantry, then rendezvous with more troops. They'd find the Indians, surround them, and force them to surrender.

Custer met with Terry and Colonel John Gibbon in mid-June (the other commander, Brigadier General Crook, was delayed). They all decided that Custer's troops should surround the Indians at the Little Bighorn camp, then wait for reinforcements.

That's not exactly how things went down.

Around midday on June 25, 1876, Custer's scouts found Sitting Bull's camp. But instead of waiting for reinforcements as planned, Custer impetuously decided to attack the next day. Then he changed his mind and decided to attack right then.

Custer divided his 600 men into four groups. He left a handful of soldiers to guard the supply train. Then he told Captain Frederick Benteen and Major Marcus Reno to take their troops and attack to prevent the Indians from escaping to the south. Custer took the remaining 210 men for an attack from the north.

Reno's group attacked first, but quickly realized they were vastly outnumbered. Discretion being the better part of valor, after losing thirty men, they pulled back to what is now known as Reno Hill. There they were joined by Benteen's troops. And there they stayed, despite a message from Custer telling them to join him as soon as possible. They heard heavy gunfire coming from Custer's position, but they held their own ground. (Was this cowardice on their part? Or just good common sense?)

No one knows when Custer realized he was in trouble, because every single soldier in his group was slaughtered. (Custer took family down with him too. His 18-year-old nephew, Henry Reed, his brother-in-law James Calhoun, and his two younger brothers, Boston and Thomas, were all killed in the battle.) Custer and his men were armed mostly with single-shot Springfield carbines and Colt revolvers. The Indians, on the other hand, had not only bows and arrows, but also Henry, Spencer, and Winchester repeating rifles. They had a distinct advantage when it came to firepower.

DAYS *of the* DEAD

When Custer's group had been wiped out, the Indians rode for Benteen's and Reno's troops. The soldiers fought hard, and managed to hold out until General Terry's reinforcements arrived. Still, the army's losses were catastrophic. As the troops were leaving Fort Abraham Lincoln on the way to Little Bighorn, an optical illusion made it seem to those watching that half of the 600 men just rode off into the sky and vanished. Some said that was a bad omen. And when the final tally was made, Custer and 264 of his men – about half – were dead.

At the fort later, Libby Custer fainted without warning at 4 pm, at the time her husband was killed. She seemed to have had prior warning of the tragedy. Dr. Porter was the physician attending the wounded, who were taken to Bismarck on the steamship *Far West*. When Dr. Porter brought the news of the massacre to the military at Fort Abraham Lincoln, Libby's reaction was quiet acceptance. When Porter arrived to speak with her, she said, "You don't have to tell me. I know."

The American reaction to the massacre did not bode well for the natives. Within a year, most of the Plains Indians had been rounded up and forced onto reservations, or just killed outright.

Custer's Last Stand went down in Old West history mostly because of his wife. Libby Custer paid no attention to the critics who said Custer had led his men to certain death just because he wanted the glory. For the rest of her life, she promoted Custer as a brave hero who died with honor while defending his country.

Libby's devotion to her husband's memory did not go unnoticed. Custer had been at Appomattox for Lee's surrender. General Phil Sheridan later bought the table on which Grant wrote up and signed the terms of the surrender. He gave it to Libby Custer as a memento. When Libby died in 1933, she willed it to the Smithsonian.

The place where Custer and so many others met their grisly end is now a national monument. The cemetery, with its neat rows of white headstones, stands as witness to the lives lost. In 1894, Stone House was built as a residence for the cemetery caretakers. Many ghost stories have their origin here. One early employee saw a horrifying apparition – the dismembered torso of a soldier, missing arms and legs, sitting on the edge of his bed.

Government soldiers don't have a monopoly on the hauntings. Indian warriors have been seen arrayed on a blufftop, sitting silently on horseback, lances and shields at the ready, feathers waving in a breath of air. But no hoofprints remain as a sign of their presence.

The natives have no illusions about the paranormal activity on the battlefield. The Crow Indians even had a wry nickname for the first caretakers of the battlefield and its cemetery – they called them "ghost herders". When the caretaker raised the flag over the cemetery at dawn every morning, the Crow figured that was the signal for the ghosts to stop haunting the battlefield for the night, and return to their graves.

A few people have gotten lost as they wander the riverbanks and prairie of the battlefield. Search parties are rustled up, and the fields are scoured for the missing. No trace of them is found, but they return on their own, bedraggled, exhausted, and terrified. They all have a strange tale to tell: they were exploring the battlefield, and suddenly found themselves in the middle of the dust, blood, and screams of conflict. The scene vanishes, and they stumble back into the present.

The spirits of Little Bighorn have their helpful moments. A woman picnicking at the battlefield was just about to bite into her sandwich when she was startled by a loud screech, as though a phantom teakettle had just reached the boil. The noise was so jarring that the woman interpreted it as a warning. She took another look at her lunch, and realized that the leftover chicken she'd packed was spoiled. She threw it away, and said a quiet thank you to whatever spirit had just saved her from food poisoning.

JUNE 26
The Vanishing Riverboat, Vicksburg, MS (1882)

The *Iron Mountain* was a monster of a boat, 180' long, 35' across the beam. In June 1882, she was making her usual run up the Mississippi from New Orleans to Pittsburgh. She'd stopped off at Vicksburg, and was headed upriver, carrying 55 passengers and crew and a load of cotton and molasses. She was also towing a string of four barges.

The Vicksburg passengers were settled in when the *Iron Mountain* pulled away from the dock. Sparks and steam flew from her twin smokestacks as she got underway. She headed north, rounded a bend in the river, and disappeared into legend.

A while later, the steamer *Iroquois Chief* had to swing wide to avoid a loose string of barges that was drifting unattended downriver. Their crew snagged them and investigated. They had come from *Iron Mountain*. What's more, the barge rope wasn't frayed or broken – it had been cut. Someone had set the barges adrift on purpose. This wasn't uncommon: if a steamer ran into trouble, and it was lose the barge or save the boat, cutting the barge adrift was a viable option.

But barges aside, there was no sign of *Iron Mountain* – no wreckage, no floating cargo, no bodies, no fire, no explosion. The ship had simply vanished into the lore of the river.

Or had it? According to a pamphlet put out by the Army Corps of Engineers in 1977, *Iron Mountain* hit a submerged snag in the river, and all passengers and crew made it to safety before it sank. When the boat's officers went to check on the wreck the next day, it was gone – they couldn't locate it.

A couple of months later, *Iron Mountain* turned up … in a field next to the river. In 1882, when *Iron Mountain* sank (or disappeared, depending on who you believe), the Mississippi flooded. The floodwaters carried the wreck through a break in the levee, and dumped it into a field.

So *Iron Mountain* wasn't lost forever. But on the river, it's best not to let the truth get in the way of a good story.

JUNE 27
John Daniel, Dorset, England (1728, recurring)

St. Mary's Church in Beauminster is a neat little parish church that has served the congregation here for centuries. In fact, its ghosts date back to 1728.

The ghost of a young boy named John Daniel haunts the gallery of the stone church. At the time of his death, that part of the church was used as a schoolroom. John appeared to his classmates not long after he'd passed. They were so freaked out that they threw stones at the apparition, which obligingly disappeared. (The kid who suggested they throw stones was John's brother. What a brat.)

But John's ghost kept coming back. The spirit appeared so often that his coffin was dug up and blessed, in the hope that would satisfy the little ghost. When the coffin was opened to bless the corpse, a coroner examined the body.

John Daniel had been found dead in a field near his house. His mother Hannah told investigators that John had been prone to fits, so the coroner hadn't held an inquest at the time of death. But on examination, John was found to have been strangled. No one was ever accused of the crime, much less punished.

John is not the only ghost at St. Mary's. He usually shows up on June 27, and sits at a desk with a school cap on. Another ghost, a woman, is usually seen in the church doorway. She wears a dark gown, a straw hat, and a flowered kerchief around her neck, and is generally thought to be Hannah Daniel, John's mother.

The ghosts don't restrict themselves to the church, either. A dairy farmer saw two figures standing near his herd in a nearby field. They appeared to be a woman in a long white gown and a boy in a dark suit. The figures moved off into the graveyard, and disappeared at the Daniel plot.

JUNE 28
The Cursed Limo, Sarajevo, Yugoslavia (1914)

The luxury car company Graf and Stift made vehicles that were not just cars, but works of art. So when Archduke Franz Ferdinand wanted to make an impression on a state visit to Bosnia, he took his red Graf and Stift limousine.

While his driver was maneuvering the big car through the crowded streets of Sarajevo, the archduke didn't notice that one of the men in the crowd was getting a little too close to the limo. Gavrilo Princip worked his way through the crowd, then reached into his coat and pulled out a pistol. He fired into the limo, killing both Archduke Ferdinand and his pregnant wife Sophie. The assassination touched off World War I, and the world would never be the same.

It seems the momentous event left its mark on the stately car. The violent killing of the archduke and his wife may have stained the limo with a psychic residue, because after that, it was a death car.

The limo was purchased after the archduke's death by General Potiorek. He developed mental issues and had to be committed to an asylum, where he later died. An army captain bought it next. He hit and killed two peasants on the road, then died in an accident. Then it was purchased by the governor of Yugoslavia, who had four accidents in four months. One of the wrecks resulted in his arm being amputated. He sold the car to a doctor, who was killed in a rollover.

Everyone who owned the red car was either injured or killed while it was in their possession. In all, the cursed automobile was responsible for the deaths of thirteen people before it was taken off the road. The gorgeous limousine is now safely tucked away in the War History Museum in Vienna.

JUNE 29
Jayne Mansfield, Los Angeles, CA (1967)

Blonde bombshell and Playboy model Jayne Mansfield didn't appear in many movies, but she definitely made an impression. A statuesque blonde with a dazzling smile, Mansfield played the part of a desirable movie star off-screen as well. She spoke five languages and was classically trained in both violin and piano, but she knew people cared more about her body than her brain.

Mansfield was only thirty-four and had been in about a dozen movies when fate caught up to her ... fate, or something darker. On June 29, 1967, the starlet was riding in a car from Biloxi, Mississippi, where she had a standing engagement in a nightclub, to New Orleans, where she had a television appearance scheduled. Ronald Harrison, a driver for Gus Stevens Dinner Club, was driving Stevens' gray Buick Electra. His passengers were Mansfield, her lawyer Samuel Brody, and Mansfield's three children with ex-husband Mickey Hargitay – Mickey Jr. (Miklos), who was eight, Zoltan, six, and three-year-old Marie, also called Mariska.

The children were asleep in the back seat for the overnight drive. The car was purring down a narrow country road at about 2:15 am when tragedy struck. A truck had gone past the area earlier, spraying for mosquitoes, and the road was still foggy with bug dope. Without warning, the Electra came up on a slow-moving tractor-trailer. It rear-ended the other vehicle, then slid underneath it.

All three adults, as well as Jayne's little dog, were killed. Thankfully for fans of *Law and Order: SVU*, the children were banged up, but survived. Hollywood legend holds that Jayne was decapitated; she wasn't, but the top of her skull was shorn off in the crash.

So was it fate, or was it something darker? The year before, Mansfield had joined Anton LaVey's Church of Satan. Another rumor says that Jayne was the victim of a curse laid through the church. One story says Jayne was personally cursed by one of LaVey's consorts. Another version holds that the curse was placed by LaVey, but intended for Jayne's boyfriend Samuel Brody for being disruptive during church ceremonies.

According to this story, LaVey laid the curse on Brody because he was abusing Jayne, then asked Jayne to stay away from Brody. She didn't take LaVey's advice, and when the curse took hold, she suffered from the fallout as well. In Japan, her jewelry was stolen from her hotel room. Jayne's son Zoltan came with her to Jungleland in Thousand Oaks, California, where Jayne was doing a photo shoot. There, Zoltan was mauled by a supposedly tame lion. Jayne was charged with tax evasion in Venezuela, mugged in Las Vegas, and attacked and stripped naked by a Carnivale mob in Rio de Janeiro.

Jayne's death actually led to a change in federal law. In the wake of the tragic accident, highway officials recommended that tractor-trailers have "underride guards" installed – a bar under the trailer to prevent cars sliding under in a rear-end collision. These safety features are still known as "Mansfield bars".

When she hit it big in Hollywood, Jayne bought Rudy Vallee's LA mansion. She had her new home painted a garish pink, and it became known as the "Pink Palace". Jayne has been seen lounging in a bathing suit, near where the heart-shaped swimming pool used to be, in the backyard. Ringo Starr bought the house and had it painted white when he moved in, but legend says that the pink would seep through no matter how many times it was painted over. (The white did eventually take. It's just that hot pink is hard to cover with white.)

Jayne's spirit has been restless from the moment of her death. After the accident, Linda Mudrick, Jayne's longtime personal maid, was caring for Miklos, who'd been injured in the crash that had taken his mother. Linda often heard Miklos talking to someone when she knew he was alone. Jayne seemed to haunt the Pink Palace, too. Pipes burst, ruining furniture, and plumbers called in to fix the damage were scared off. Objects moved without explanation. People heard eerie moaning, and hired help refused to stay, often leaving after only a few days in the house.

Many people theorize that Jayne was still in the house keeping watch over her children. Fighting over her estate was fierce, and she may have been worried that her kids would be cheated out of their inheritance. She was right to be concerned: her third husband and his lawyer locked the children and Jayne's parents out of the mansion, then sold it.

The Pink Palace was demolished in 2002, and the intriguing starlet seems to have moved on.

JUNE 30
The Strange Case of Ceely Rose, Lima, OH (1896)

Late in the 19th century, there was a girl named Celia Rose, who lived in Ohio. With a pretty name like Celia Rose, you might be picturing a dainty girl with porcelain skin and cascades of curls, a demure damsel whose greatest joy would be to sit and work on her embroidery.

You would be wrong.

Celia Rose, or Ceely as she was called, was a big, ungainly farm girl. She lived with her parents, David and Rebecca Rose, and her brother Walter, who was much older. Ceely was probably an "oops" baby, as her parents were well into middle age when she came along. Rebecca often wondered if that's why Ceely seemed simple.

Ceely wasn't what that age considered an imbecile. She was just a bit slow, and had zero ambition. She was an avid reader, and had devoured all the books the family owned, reading them several times. But she never did anything with that modicum of intelligence. She made her way through school, and that was it. Her father and brother worked the family's grist mill, and her mother did a lot of canning to keep the family fed. Ceely helped if she felt like it.

Ceely wasn't dainty or even attractive, but people in the neighborhood treated her with kindness when they weren't ignoring her. Nobody really disliked her; she just wasn't popular.

The Roses were neighbors with the Berry family, but the families weren't close at all. George Berry lived close to the Roses with his wife, two sons, and his elderly father. Even though the Berry's front door was just twenty yards away from the Roses' mill, the two families barely spoke.

All that changed in 1896. Since Ceely only did housework when she felt like it, that gave her plenty of time to wander the woods and fields around the house. One fine spring day, Ceely spied Guy Berry plowing in his father's field. The 24-year-old Ceely became infatuated with the good-looking teenager (Guy was 17).

Guy, like everyone else, was polite to Ceely, but he really wasn't interested in a relationship with her. But to Ceely, Guy's friendly chatter was the next best thing to a marriage proposal. For several months, she met Guy as often as she could, her simple mind awhirl with romantic possibilities. Guy politely endured her visits, which just gave Ceely more fantasy-fodder.

Eventually, other Berry family members realized the depth of Ceely's feelings for Guy. Claude, Guy's 12-year-old brother, came right out and told Ceely bluntly that Guy wasn't going to marry her, and that in fact he had a girlfriend. Ceely brushed off the unwelcome news, saying she'd marry Claude instead. He begged off, telling her he was too young to get married.

"I can wait until you grow up," was Ceely's placid response.

This was really too much for the Berrys. Guy went to his father and told him he was tired of Ceely hanging around all the time. George Berry paid a visit to David Rose and asked him to control his daughter. Embarrassed, Rose yelled at Ceely for disgracing the family. Rebecca and Walter chimed in too. Everyone was sore at Ceely for her indiscretion.

Ceely's mind worked slowly, but it worked. In late June, 1896, Ceely's revenge began. In retaliation for the reprimand, Ceely took arsenic that her mother had bought as rat poison, and filled a pepper box with it. Then she sprinkled the arsenic on the cottage cheese her family liked to have for breakfast.

David, Rebecca, and Walter Rose all died of arsenic poisoning. David died June 30, and Walter died a week or so later. Rebecca began to recover, as she hadn't eaten as much of the poisoned cheese. But she told Ceely they had to move. Ceely was not about to be separated from her crush, so she retrieved the pepper box from under the dock plant where she'd hidden it, and dosed Rebecca's bowl of bread and milk with more arsenic.

Suspicion for the deaths fell on Ceely, as she was the only family member not taken sick. The prosecutor wanted to be sure Ceely had committed the crime before he took her to court. He asked Theresa Davis, who had been friends with Ceely when they'd been at school together, to try and worm a confession out of her.

Ceely opened up to her former friend, saying at first that Guy had suggested she poison her family so they could run off and get married. The next day, though, she admitted that Guy had nothing to do with the killings.

Celia was arrested and tried for the three murders. She was found not guilty by reason of insanity. The prosecutor didn't ask for any punishment; instead, she was sent to the Toledo Asylum. She was committed to the Lima State Hospital for the Criminally Insane in 1915. She died there in 1934, the day after her 61st birthday.

Ceely's house still stands in what is now Malabar Farms State Park. On quiet nights, people still sometimes see Celia Rose looking out of the windows by the light of the full moon. Perhaps she's hoping for one last glimpse of Guy, plowing the fields with his shirt off.

JULY

DAYS *of the* DEAD

JULY 1
The Phantom Rider, Chester, PA (1785 – recurring)

Many times, a recurring haunting is created by a failure of justice. This is exactly what happened with the tragic tale of William and Elizabeth Wilson.

The brother and sister were born in Pennsylvania before the Revolutionary War. When William was sixteen, he was apprenticed to a stone carver. When Elizabeth turned sixteen, she, too, was sent off to earn her living. (The family had been prosperous before the war, but father John Wilson had sided with the British, and had lost his land as well as his good name as a result.)

The Wilsons had relatives that managed the Indian Queen Tavern in Philadelphia. Elizabeth was sent to work as a barmaid there. It was there that Elizabeth's life began to unravel.

Both William and Elizabeth had been raised with strong Christian values, but Elizabeth met a man at the tavern who led her astray with promises of marriage. One thing led to another, and Elizabeth found herself pregnant. When she told her lover this, he dumped her. Heartbroken, she made her way back to her parents' house in Chester. There she gave birth to twin boys.

Her reputation ruined, and responsible for the raising of two infants, Elizabeth had no idea where to turn. A couple of months after the babies' birth, Elizabeth walked into the woods near Chester carrying her sons. She walked out alone. The twins were found dead just a little while later. Elizabeth was arrested for the murder of her children.

The trial began in late June, 1785. Elizabeth refused to say even one word in her own defense. Judge William Atlee had to enter a "not guilty" plea on her behalf, because she wouldn't even answer the question "How do you plead?". On July 1, Elizabeth was sentenced to death for the murder of her twins. The execution was set for December 7, 1785.

When William heard the news, he raced to be by Elizabeth's side. Growing up, the two had been exceptionally close, and William wasn't about to desert his sister in her hour of need. When he arrived, Elizabeth broke her silence. In her jail cell, she poured out the whole sorry tale to the person she trusted most in the world: her brother.

She told William that she had gone to the woods to meet the father of her children. When he'd seen the boys, he'd slipped into a cold rage, telling her that he had no intention of marrying her. Then he'd put the babies on the ground and stepped squarely on their chests, killing them. Destroyed by her lover's rejection and the sudden, violent loss of her babies, Elizabeth had wandered out of the woods. The arrest and conviction had followed.

The truth was out. William begged the court for more time, which was granted. No one wanted to hang this bereft young woman. The execution was pushed back to January 3, 1786. William intended to use the time to track down his sister's lover and make him face justice.

William did some detective work, and managed to track down the man who had seduced Elizabeth. William confronted the man, who denied the whole affair. Undaunted, William turned his efforts to tracking down witnesses who could link the man to Elizabeth. He soon had a sizeable list.

But with all these efforts, William took sick around Christmas, before he could bring the list of witnesses to the Supreme Executive Council in Philadelphia. When he recovered, he was horrified to discover he'd lost track of time. Instead of January 1, it was now January 2 – and Elizabeth was scheduled to be executed the next day.

William raced to Philadelphia to meet with the council. Benjamin Franklin was the president of the council, but after William had waited hours to meet with him, he decided that the vice president, Charles Biddle, would be better suited to handle the case.

William found a better reception with Biddle. Biddle knew that everyone in the court was sympathetic to Elizabeth, so he granted a postponement of the execution – something that really amounted to a reprieve. He knew the court eventually intended to pardon Elizabeth; it just had to be done through legal channels. He gave William a message for the court: "Don't execute Wilson until you hear further from council."

With the reprieve in hand, William set out on the fifteen-mile ride back to Chester. The winter travel was tortuous – the roads were bad, streams and rivers were swollen with rain, and the Middle ferry over the Schuykill River was closed. Determined to save his sister, William urged his horse into the frigid water to swim to the other side. The horse drowned fifty feet from the opposite shore, so William had to swim for it himself. The current carried him over two miles downstream, but he eventually made his way across the river. He found another horse, and continued on to Chester.

Word traveled fast in the small town, and people lined the roads hoping for a glimpse of the heroic William riding hard to save his sister's life. Even the authorities were rooting for the young siblings. The sheriff stationed flagmen along the Queen's Highway between Philadelphia and Chester in the hopes of receiving William's message.

Elizabeth sat silent and disconsolate in a wagon under a wild cherry tree. The rope had been tied to a horizontal branch, and the noose was around her neck. She could see the crowds of people lining the streets leading into Chester, eagerly waiting for William's arrival, but she had resigned herself to her fate.

The sheriff delayed his grim duty until the last minute, but noon arrived with no sign of William Wilson. By law, the sheriff could wait no longer. He gave the signal. The wagon moved forward, and moments later, Elizabeth's body swung from the branch.

At that moment, a signal came from one of the flagmen. A few minutes later, William thundered up on a lathered, mud-stained horse. He waved a crumpled piece of paper, screaming "Reprieve!"

His frantic gaze fell on the limp form hanging from the cherry tree. He ran to Elizabeth as the sheriff cut her down. They tried heroically to revive her, but in vain. Elizabeth was gone.

Devastated, William retreated from the world. He wandered the area for several years, and settled in Indian Echo Caverns. He lived a hermit's existence in the caves until his death in 1821, 36 years later.

The community of Chester was haunted for years by the tragic miscarriage of justice. The story was kept alive by the appearance of William's ghost. Every year, on July 1, the anniversary of the sentencing in 1785, William makes his desperate ride again, hoping that this time, he'll make it to the jail in the nick of time.

As for Elizabeth, her spirit sadly seems to have given up on hope of rescue, as she isn't seen on the road waiting for William. Instead, her ghost wanders the woods near Chester where her children's bodies were found, looking for something beneath the leaves.

DAYS *of the* DEAD

JULY 2
Lady Lindy, West Lafayette, IN (1937)

Purdue Airport was built in 1930, and opened in 1934. University president Dr. Edward C. Elliott was justifiably proud: this was the first university-owned airport, and Elliott was particularly interested in aviation.

He was also committed to excellence in higher education for women. Those two passions came together in the fall of 1935, when famed aviatrix Amelia Earhart spoke at Purdue. Dr. Elliott had a brainstorm. Who better to be a career counselor for young women, especially those interested in aviation, than Amelia Earhart? He pitched the idea to her over dinner that night after her talk. He offered her a position at the school, and she accepted. In November 1935, she became the advisor to the aeronautics department, and a visiting faculty member in the women's careers department.

Earhart spent several weeks each semester on campus, giving lectures and hanging out with the students. She used her popularity to promote progressive causes such as women's rights, while presenting herself as down-to-earth and approachable. She loved Purdue, and Purdue loved her right back.

Dr. Elliott volunteered to have the university supply Earhart with a "flying laboratory". He collected $80,000 in donations, and presented Earhart with a Lockheed Electra in July 1936.

The next year, in June, Earhart and her navigator, Fred Noonan, attempted to fly around the world. At 10 am on July 2, 1937, Earhart and Noonan left New Guinea on their way to tiny Howland Island. They never arrived. Instead, Earhart flew her Electra into legend.

But Earhart's spirit remains at Purdue University, a place where she found fulfillment and unwavering support.

While she was at Purdue, Earhart lived in a residence hall, and her ghost still hangs out there. The phantom of a petite women with short hair is seen in the hallway outside her former dorm room. Windows open on their own, and students feel cold drafts. But the most exciting evidence is the clickety-clack of an old-fashioned typewriter that drifts from the empty room late at night. Earhart spent her late-night hours writing. She devoted herself to inspiring others to find their calling in life. It's said she spent more time writing inspirational pieces about her flights, and about the ways she hoped to encourage others to follow their dreams, than she actually spent in the sky.

Besides the dorm, the other building at Purdue that feels Earhart's presence is Hangar One. Witnesses have seen a slightly-built woman in pants and an aviator's jacket, a scarf draped around her neck, in the hangar. It makes sense. Not only did Earhart feel at home in Hangar One, it was also where she made the preparations for her round-the-world flight. She poured a lot of emotion into the Electra as it sat in the hangar.

Hangar One has been renovated since Earhart's time. It now houses classrooms for Aviation Technology. It's quite possible that Earhart pops in from time to time to check up on the students.

JULY 1-3
Ghosts of Gettysburg, Gettysburg, PA (1863, recurring)

The Battle of Gettysburg marked the turning point of the Civil War, and turned a sleepy Pennsylvania town into a pilgrimage site for history buffs and paranormal enthusiasts alike. The violence that permeated the battlefields and the town over three hot days in July was incredible: 7,500 men killed, and over 40,000 wounded. The third day was the worst. Almost one-third of the men in combat that day fell on the field of battle.

This outpouring of emotion – terror, grief, panic, maybe even a little survivor's guilt – that swept over not only the soldiers but the civilians of Gettysburg too, left its mark on what may be the most haunted place in America. Authors have filled books with tales of the ghosts of Gettysburg. Here are just a few.

On July 2, Confederate Brigadier General William Barksdale was wounded while leading a charge on Cemetery Ridge. He was brought to Hummelbaugh House, where he faded quickly. A Union officer saw Barksdale lying in front of the house, delirious, calling out for water. A young boy was giving the general sips of water from a spoon, but the general was in such pain that he ignored the fact that he was being helped. He died soon afterward.

After the battle, Barksdale's wife came to Gettysburg to bring the general's remains home to Mississippi. The general's favorite hunting dog came with her. When Mrs. Barksdale was led to the general's grave, the dog collapsed on the grave and began to howl. Mrs. Barksdale tried to pull the dog away, but she couldn't. He mourned at the grave all night.

The next day, the exhumed coffin was loaded onto a wagon for the sad journey home. The dog, however, refused to leave the empty grave. Mrs. Barksdale tried once more to coax the dog away, but he refused to budge. She eventually had to leave him there, still grieving for his lost master.

Over the next few days, people tried to offer the dog food and water. There were many people willing to give the heartbroken dog a good home, but he refused all offers of comfort. Every so often, he would lift his head and let loose with yet another soul-rending howl of grief. The dog was found dead of hunger and thirst near the empty grave a while later. The faithful dog still mourns his lost master, because on July 2, the anniversary of Barksdale's death, people still hear the unearthly howls of the sorrowing dog.

The fighting affected the civilians of Gettysburg too. For weeks after the battle, the air around the town was thickly redolent with the stench of bodies rotting in the July sun. After the battle, people had to navigate the streets of the town with scented handkerchiefs pressed to their noses to combat the reek of decaying corpses. On Baltimore Street, witnesses can smell peppermint and vanilla, phantom wisps of long-ago scents.

The sights, sounds, and smells of battle were unforgettable. Around midnight on July 3, Maine private John Haley was on picket duty on Cemetery Ridge. He later wrote of the experience in his journal.

"The dead lay everywhere, and although not half a day has passed since they died, the stench is so great that we can neither eat, drink, nor sleep. Decomposition commences as soon as life is extinct … The dead are frightfully smashed, which is not to be wondered at when we consider how they crowded up onto our guns, a mass of humanity, only to be hurled back an indistinguishable pile of mutilated flesh, rolling and writhing in death. No tongue can depict the carnage, and I cannot make it seem real: men's heads blown off or split open, horrible gashes cut; some split from the top of the head to the extremities, as butchers split beef."

Haley's journal entry refers to the carnage wrought during Pickett's Charge, where

Southern troops attacked Union forces and were turned back at a decisive point in the war. Susan Carpenter is a member of a civilian reenactor group that visited Gettysburg. The group started at the point known as the High-Water Mark, which marked the farthest North the Confederacy ever reached. (And they were turned back there in defeat – another source of extreme emotion that still resonates today.)

As soon as Susan stepped onto the path, she felt cold seeping up from the ground. Soon her feet and legs were sheathed with chill. Then she began to hear men moaning, and she smelled the heavy odor of blood. When she looked down, there was nowhere to step – dead and dying soldiers lay all over the ground. Susan knew she was seeing a scene from the past, and the bodies were just images of corpses, but it felt so real. She just kept walking, and repeating "I am sorry, I am so sorry" in her head. When the group reached the point where Pickett's Charge began, and turned to walk back, the phantoms were gone, and the ground was clear.

Reenactors camping on the battlefields have had eerie experiences straight out of the past. In October 1966, Union reenactors camping near Devil's Den were awakened late at night by music floating on the night air. John Rushoe, one of the reenactors, recognized it as a Civil War tune. Thinking that another group of history buffs was approaching, the guys roused themselves to welcome their fellow reenactors to their camp. No one was there – but the music still filled the air.

Right above Devil's Den is the rocky hillside of Little Round Top. Delicia Wallnofer had an encounter on the hill in 1998. She was visiting with some relatives, and they went to the summit around sunset. They'd taken a few pictures with a reenactor who was portraying Robert E. Lee. The group was picking their way down the big rocks, when a young gentleman showed up. Delicia remembered him, because she'd admired his authentic uniform on the way up the hill.

The young soldier told the ladies of the group good evening, complimented them on their beauty, and offered to hand them down the rocks so they wouldn't fall. After he did so, Delicia looked up to see her uncle coming down the rocks, but no soldier. When asked, a few others standing around replied that the only person they'd seen near the group of women was Delicia's uncle. It seems that Southern etiquette lasts a lifetime – and beyond.

JULY 4
School's Out Forever, Middletown, OH (1910)

Poasttown Elementary School has probably hosted as many paranormal investigators as it has students. It opened in 1937, and after over sixty years of readin', writin', and 'rithmetic, closed its doors in 2000. Unlike many other historic and haunted buildings, this school has had only one purpose throughout its working life. Now, though, it hosts those who come searching for ghosts.

Even former students have said that they've felt strange sensations in the old building's hallways. People have been touched by invisible hands. Witnesses have heard the laughter of children at play. Doors open and close with no human hands on the doorknobs. Shadow figures inhabit the hallways.

There's never been any death in the building – it's always been a place of learning and encouragement for the future. So why is it so amazingly haunted?

The answer lies in the land. A flood forged a path of destruction through Butler County in 1913. And Middletown was the site of two deadly train crashes. On July 25, 1891, workers at National Cash Register were taking a train back to Dayton after their company picnic. Their train collided with a freight train, causing four deaths and injuring fifty people.

It was the crash on July 4, 1910, that made the biggest impression on the area. The wreck involved a passenger train and a freight train that should have been on separate tracks, miles apart. The northbound freight train was exactly where it was supposed to be. The southbound passenger train, the *Cincinnati Flyer*, had been detoured from its usual route by a crash earlier that day. The dispatcher mixed up his information, so both trains ended up on the same stretch of track. The *Cincinnati Flyer* was flying along at 50 to 60 mph when it hit the stationary freight train.

All the passengers in the two cars closest to the engine died or were seriously injured. There was no hospital in Middletown at the time, so a field was used for triage. That field, which saw 36 people dead and 50 injured, was where Poasttown School was built twenty-seven years later.

Darrell Whisman and his wife – who both attended the school – bought the old building in 2004, and repurposed it into a community center of sorts. The 54 rooms in the school have been rented out for police and fire training, a weightlifting club, massage therapy, even a nail salon. There's a room set up with a couple of beds, with room on the floor for an air mattress, so investigators can spend the night.

It's well worth a visit to experience the haunted hallways – Poasttown School's official motto is, "When you leave, you believe."

JULY 5
Incident at Jersey Bridge, Downieville, CA (1851)

California's Gold Rush is a rich source of history, adventure, and ghost stories. One of the most famous spirits of this area is the ghost of a young Mexican woman. She is known only as Juanita, but her tale is an integral part of California's history.

Juanita was a proud, graceful Spanish-Mexican woman who lived in a mining camp. Unlike most of the women there, she was not a prostitute, and she was damned proud of that fact. She was majestic, self-possessed, and did not take crap from anyone.

On July 5, 1851, Juanita and her boyfriend Jose were both at home when another miner, Fred Cannon, fell against the door of their house and knocked it askew on its flimsy hinges. Juanita's Spanish temper was roused, and she came charging out to confront Cannon. Jose followed, and told Cannon he had to pay for the damages. As Juanita let loose a torrent of furious, quick-tongued Spanish, Cannon lost his patience with the couple. He told Jose to "take [his] whore inside and shut her up."

This was a fatal mistake. Juanita shrieked in outrage, grabbed a knife and stabbed Cannon in the chest. As he bled out, other miners surrounded Juanita and Jose and locked them in a small cabin. Within an hour, thirteen men had gathered to form a judge and jury. Witnesses testified (falsely) that Fred Cannon had quietly tried to defuse the conflict, and that Juanita was a screaming madwoman who refused to calm down. The jury deliberated only fifteen minutes before finding Juanita guilty of murder.

Juanita was taken to the Jersey Bridge over the Yuba River and hanged. According to an article in the *Pacific Star Newspaper*, Juanita was very calm as she contemplated her approaching death. Once more, she was the regal beauty, sure of her place in the world. She shook hands with her executioners, and even placed the noose around her own neck. By four o'clock that afternoon, her lifeless body was swinging from the bridge. In the space of one day, Juanita had killed a man while defending her honor, stood trial in front of hundreds of miners, was found guilty, and executed. She was just 24 years old.

The grave digger had to dig two graves that day, but hacking away at the hard California soil in July proved too much for him. He scraped away enough dry dirt to form one large grave, and buried Juanita and Fred Cannon together.

As if the indignity of being buried with the guy who called her a whore wasn't enough, less than twenty years after her burial, Juanita's body was dug up. Bad: digging up everyone in the Downieville Cemetery and moving them so the prospectors had another place to look for gold. Worse: stealing Juanita's skull to use as a drinking cup. Yes, Juanita's body was moved to another grave (and presumably she had that one to herself), but her skull was stolen by members of a Gold Rush-era fraternal organization called E Clampus Vitus. This society had many secret rituals, and Juanita's skull may have been used in initiation ceremonies as a drinking vessel.

This may be why Juanita's spirit returns to the scene of her hasty death and slipshod burial. Since 1870, when her skull was taken, Juanita's ghost has been seen on the Jersey Bridge. The original bridge that served as the gallows was destroyed in a flood, and the current bridge was built in 1958. Nonetheless, her ghost haunts the bridge, appearing sometimes as a full-bodied apparition, sometimes as a human-shaped mist, and sometimes simply as a face surrounded by billowing waves of hair. She appears out of nowhere on the bridge, walking towards witnesses as if trying to tell them something.

JULY 6
Terror Under the Big Top, Hartford, CT (1944)

A hot summer day. The warm air is filled with an intoxicating mélange of smells: buttery popcorn, the beefy tang of roasting hotdogs, the sweet yeasty aroma of funnel cakes, and underneath it all, the wilder scent of sawdust and animal sweat. The circus is in town! And it's not just any circus. This is the big one, the granddaddy of them all, the Ringling Brothers and Barnum & Bailey show.

And on that afternoon in July 1944, people needed a show. War was raging in Europe, and those on the home front were in the mood for some entertainment. President Franklin Roosevelt gave circuses, who mostly traveled by train, a special dispensation to use the nation's rail system.

The afternoon show on July 6 was a special occasion. There had been a mix-up on the rails the day before. The circus usually ran like a well-oiled machine – an outfit that big had to be organized – but wartime shortages of both employees and equipment were causing mishaps. The flat cars used to transport some of the equipment were too long to comfortably manage some of the curves in the track between Providence, Rhode Island and Hartford, Connecticut. The train eventually made it to Hartford, but it pulled in so late that one of the shows had to be canceled.

This made the circus performers and other employees very nervous. The circus, like other performances, is a hotbed of superstition. A late show is bad; a missed show is catastrophic. The evening show for July 5 went smoothly, but the circus folk were on edge, waiting for the other shoe to drop.

To apologize to the good citizens of Hartford, circus management decided to add an afternoon show on July 6 to make up for the missed show. Grateful circus fans swarmed into the Big Top, filling it nearly to capacity: nine thousand people could fit around the tent's three rings. On this Thursday afternoon, the audience was mostly women and children. The best estimate of the crowd size is about seven thousand.

The Ringling Brothers Circus was quite the show. It was renowned for having the largest circus tent in the country. The massive tent had cost over $60,000, and was carefully maintained by the roustabouts. The canvas had been waterproofed the previous April with a coating of 1,800 pounds of paraffin wax dissolved in 6,000 gallons of gasoline.

The wild animal act, always a crowd-pleaser, opened the show. The big cats roared and preened, delighting the audience. While the lions were being escorted out, the Flying Wallendas, the famous trapeze artists, were climbing the poles and preparing to take the high-wire stage. Emmett Kelly, America's favorite hangdog clown, was keeping the crowd entertained with his antics. His character, Weary Willie, would spread a handkerchief below the high wires to catch the performers if they fell.

Suddenly, the circus band struck up the energetic notes of "The Stars and Stripes Forever". Performers and crew froze for one bare second. Then the Wallendas scooted back down the poles. That cheerful tune meant only one thing in the circus world: trouble. That song, also known as The Disaster March, is only played to alert circus personnel that something is very wrong.

A Hartford police officer was on duty at the main entrance. A dot of flame, no bigger than a cigarette burn, ate away at the canvas, traveling up the wall. Merle Evans, the bandleader, saw the fire at about the same time the policeman did, and swung the band into the warning song. Before that, the audience and most of the performers weren't even aware there was a problem.

Several buckets of water were sitting around in case of such an emergency. Someone tossed the water onto the flames, which were climbing steadily up the canvas. The water vanished in puffs of steam.

May Kovar and Joseph Walsh, the big cats' trainers, tried desperately to hurry the animals along, while ringmaster Fred Bradna urged the audience not to panic. The fire was still growing, but the audience milled about aimlessly. The fire was small, and circus staff had everything under control – didn't they?

Just then, a strong wind whipped through the massive tent. The fire devoured canvas, raining gobbets of hot paraffin down on the panicked crowd. The support ropes began to burn through as people rushed to the exits, stumbling over metal folding chairs. As each rope snapped, more of the burning canvas dropped, trapping more of the audience. Children were separated from their parents, and either ran in a blind panic or froze, wailing, where they stood. Women, their hair and dresses on fire from the falling chunks of flaming canvas, screamed in agony. Hundreds of bodies piled up at the exits. At least two people were actually found alive later, under those corpses, shielded from the heat by the bodies of the dead.

One by one, the support beams failed and crashed to the ground as the ropes and canvas burned. The sixth and final pole fell, bringing the tent down with a roar of destruction, the burning canvas smothering everyone left in the Big Top. Every person trapped and screaming under that fiery shroud was doomed. Just eight minutes had passed – eight minutes that, for some, turned into eternity.

Fire trucks and ambulances raced to the scene. The fire trucks could only put out the flames – by that point, there was no rescuing to be done. But ambulances rushed victims to a hospital in Hartford, which was actually prepared to treat burn victims in case of wartime air raids. Victims were given morphine and injections of plasma to replenish fluids.

Then came the horrifying task of identifying the dead. There were 168 victims, one hundred of them children. Fifty-nine of those children were nine years old or younger. Nearly seven hundred more were injured, some scarred and disfigured for life. None of the circus people fell victim to the fire, although the Wallendas barely escaped. Emmett Kelly acted quickly when the fire broke out, first dumping buckets of water on the fire, then pulling up the canvas to shoo children out under the side of the tent.

Two years after the fire, a temporary housing project for soldiers returning from the war was built near the site of the tragedy. Residents of the apartments claimed to hear weeping and screams, and spoke of seeing apparitions of people on fire. One man, while unlocking his door one evening, looked up to see a little boy go running past him in the hallway. The boy left a trail of smoke behind him, as though his clothes were ablaze. The man dropped the bag of groceries he was carrying, and ran down the hall to see if the boy needed help. But when he rounded the corner, no one was there. The man had moved to Hartford only recently, and had no idea that his new home was so close to the site of the fire.

A few years later, the housing project, no longer needed, was torn down. A school was built on the site, and the ghost stories continued. Today, a memorial to the fire victims stands witness at the place where so many young lives were tragically cut short.

JULY 7
A Traitor Hangs, Washington DC (1865 – recurring)

When a shot rang out at Ford's Theater April 14, 1865, followed closely by the cry of "Sic semper tyrannis!" and a thud as John Wilkes Booth crashed to the stage in a bungled escape attempt, the landscape of American history was changed forever. Lincoln was dead, and the aftermath of the Civil War was blown violently off-course.

But Booth didn't act alone. The assassination of the president took a lot of planning, and Booth took a few people down with him when he was cornered in a tobacco barn in Virginia and shot. After fracturing his leg in the jump from the presidential box to the stage, Booth paid a visit to Dr. Samuel Mudd to have his broken bone set. Before that, the assassination was planned in detail. And the conspirators met at the boarding house owned by Mary Surratt.

Mary Jenkins married John Surratt when she was about 17 years old. Before her marriage, she had attended a Catholic girls' boarding school. In 1853, the Surratts bought 287 acres of land in Prince George's County, Maryland, about a two-hour ride from Washington DC by horse. John Surratt built a tavern and a post office, and the community became known as Surrattsville. The couple had three children: Isaac, Anna, and John Jr.

The Surratts were rabid Secessionists, and during the Civil War, the tavern was used as a safe house for Confederate spies. But John Surratt was no businessman, and the war further eroded his fortunes. He died in 1862.

In 1864, Mary Surratt moved to a three-story townhouse she owned in Washington, and rented the tavern in Surrattsville to John Lloyd. She turned her Washington home into a boardinghouse. Mary's son John served as a Confederate secret agent in the war, and was friends with many of the key players in the assassination conspiracy, including John Wilkes Booth, George Atzerodt, Lewis Powell, and David Herold.

Some say that Mary Surratt was simply the hostess at the boardinghouse, but others are convinced that she had a hand in planning some details of the assassination. Whatever her involvement, on April 17, 1865, a team of military investigators showed up at the Surratt home to interview Mary and other residents about the assassination. The investigators found incriminating evidence in the home, evidence that pointed to Mary as one of the conspirators. She was arrested and taken to the Old Capitol Prison, then to the Washington Arsenal.

From then on, Mary Surratt was watched by two armed guards at all times. Her cell, although larger and airier than those of the other prisoners, was sparsely furnished with only a straw mattress, a table with a wash basin, a chair, and a bucket. The other conspirators were shackled and forced to wear padded canvas bags on their hands to prevent suicide attempts. Mary didn't suffer either of these indignities.

On May 9, an Army military commission was formed to try Mary Surratt, David Herold, Lewis Powell, George Atzerodt, Edman Spangler, Michael O'Laughlin, Samuel Arnold, and Dr. Samuel Mudd for their parts in the conspiracy to kill Lincoln. The cases against Mary and Dr. Mudd were flimsy and circumstantial, but under the law of conspiracy, if one person commits a crime, all conspirators are guilty.

On July 5, all eight of the prisoners were found guilty. Herold, Atzerodt, Powell, and Mary Surratt were given the death penalty. The others were sentenced to life in prison.

Five of the nine judges on the commission signed a letter to President Andrew Johnson, suggesting that given Mary's age and the fact that she was a woman, her sentence should be reduced to life in prison. Johnson refused to grant clemency; he said that Mary had "kept the nest that hatched the egg."

On July 7, the morning of the hanging, Anna Surratt pushed her way onto the White House grounds in an attempt to speak with Johnson. She made it all the way to the front door, where she banged and sobbed in a heartrending plea to save her mother's life. Security guards pulled her away, and she never did get to see the president.

Surratt, Herold, Powell, and Atzerodt were led through the courtyard of the Washington Arsenal to the gallows, and hanged at 1:15 pm. Mary Surratt didn't struggle much, and seemed to die quickly. The bodies hung for about half an hour before being cut down. They were placed in pine coffins, with the name of each person written on a piece of paper and put into a glass vial, which was placed in the coffin. The bodies were buried in shallow graves against the prison wall, just a few feet from the gallows. Four years later, Mary's body was released to Anna, her daughter. She was buried in Mount Olivet Cemetery.

Mary Surratt's spirit haunts her boardinghouse in Washington with sounds of weeping and groaning. Since 1965, the Surratt Tavern has been open to the public as a historic site, run by the state of Maryland. Museum staff regularly hear footsteps in the upstairs hallway, and the facial expression on Mary's portrait seems to change. She also haunts the Washington Arsenal, where she and the others were executed, and the Old Capitol Prison, where she was first held.

After the British torched the halls of Congress during the War of 1812, the legislature met for several years at the Old Brick Capitol. The building later became a residence, then during the Civil War, it became the Old Capitol Prison. The building was demolished in the early 1900s. The building now on that site is the home of the United States Supreme Court. When the Old Capitol Prison building still stood, there were reports that every July 7, Mary's ghost could be seen in the window of her jail cell, crying bitterly as she gripped the iron bars.

The Washington Arsenal is now Fort McNair. Mary's spirit is seen here too, walking across the courtyard to the site of the gallows where she and the others were executed.

One year, when a major snowstorm blanketed Washington with a foot of snow, a cleared path about 300 feet long appeared on the parade ground of the fort. The path was the exact route taken by the condemned prisoners across the courtyard. No one on the base had cleared the snow away, and there were no underground pipes or steam tunnels that could have melted the snow.

On Lincoln's birthday one year, an officer at the fort heard the voice of a woman outside his window, alternately pleading softly for help and screaming.

And every year on July 7, the ghost of Anna Surratt appears on the north portico of the White House, banging on the door to plead for her mother's life.

JULY 8
The Wedding Ring (1923)

Eileen Chapman and her daughter, Christine, were sitting in a local café enjoying an afternoon coffee. They'd spent the morning at the church rummage sale, wandering past tables piled with clothes, dishes, and all sorts of tchotchkes. Eileen had bought a gorgeously carved wooden jewelry box. Judging from the style of the costume pieces inside, the box had to be an antique.

Eileen and Christine had emptied the contents of the box onto the table, and Eileen was examining the satin lining of the box. She noticed a small envelope tucked into one of the pockets of the lining. She fished it out and opened it.

The envelope held a woman's wedding ring, engraved with the initials M.B. and the date 7/8/23.

"Well, this isn't a piece of costume jewelry," Eileen said, tucking the ring back into the envelope. "I wonder who M.B. is?"

The bell on the café door chimed, and Eileen's elderly neighbor, Frank Burrows, walked in. He stood for a bit, his gaze scanning the room. Then he saw the two women and his face brightened. He threaded his way through the tables to where Eileen and Christine sat.

"Thank God I found you, Eileen. I stopped in at the church, and I was told you might be here." There was an unmistakable note of relief in his voice.

"Frank, what is it? What's going on?"

Frank gestured to the jewelry box on the table. "When I donated that to the church for the rummage sale, I'd forgotten I'd put my wife's wedding ring in it for safekeeping. I was happy to give the box, along with Mary's clothes, but I didn't mean to donate the ring along with it!"

"Of course not!" Eileen smiled. She opened the box and took the envelope out of the inside pocket. "Here you are. I'm glad it was me who bought it and not some random stranger."

"Thank you, Eileen. This means a lot to me." Frank tucked the envelope into his pocket and gave the pocket a pat with arthritis-swollen fingers. He smiled at the women, then left the café.

Eileen picked up her coffee and took a sip. "What an amazing coincidence! I'm so glad I was able to return Mary's ring to him. He's been so lost without her. I can't believe it's been nearly a year since she passed."

Eileen and Christine walked home from the café, each of them carrying a bag from the church sale. When they turned onto their street, they saw a police car and an ambulance idling in front of Frank Burrows' house. Eileen's husband, John, was standing on the porch, talking to the woman who had been caring for Frank since Mary had died.

Eileen hurried to join them. "What happened? Is Frank alright?"

John grimaced. "No. He's gone. It looks like he had a massive heart attack last night."

Eileen stared at him, astonished. "But … that's impossible. He can't be dead. Christine and I just talked to him at the café."

Christine nodded. "Yeah, it was like an hour ago, maybe?"

The caregiver shook her head slowly. "I found him late this morning, and he was already cold. He was clutching his wife's wedding ring in his hand." Eileen felt a cold shiver run down her spine as the woman took the ring from her purse and showed her. "I knew Frank would want me to keep it safe."

Eileen looked at her daughter, who stared back at her. Frank Burrows had been at their table. He'd talked to them. And he had asked them for Mary's wedding ring.

Now, thanks to Eileen, Frank was at peace.

JULY 9
A Series of Unfortunate Events (1945-1949)

We all love a good coincidence story. But sometimes coincidence stretches itself so far that it moves from cool, to bizarre, to downright creepy.

Take the strange story of a particular plane, a Lockheed Constellation. The Constellation was developed in World War II as a troop transport, the C-69. After the war, that model morphed into commercial use, and it was an enormous success. A dolphin-sleek body soared through the air, propelled by four powerful engines. Pilots loved flying the Constellation because her graceful lines made her a dream to handle. The Constellation aircraft was popular the world over.

But there was one particular Constellation, registration AHEM-4, that seemed to be dogged by bad luck, the worst kind of bad luck … the killing kind. The AHEM-4 was built in the final months of World War II, and swung into service immediately.

On July 9, 1945, a mechanic working on the plane lost his footing and stumbled into one of the propellers. The whirling metal hacked his body into pieces in mere moments, a spray of blood and meat marking his demise.

On July 9, 1946, Constellation AHEM-4 was making an Atlantic crossing. The flight was going incredibly smoothly, the plane cruising along at altitude, cleaving the sky like a silver dart. The passengers in the comfortable cabin sipped their coffee and flipped through their magazines, blissfully unaware of the drama unfolding in the cockpit. Captain Arthur Lewis slumped over the controls, dead. The copilot took over the controls for the rest of the flight, bringing the Constellation in for a safe landing.

On July 9, 1947, AHEM-4 underwent a regularly scheduled maintenance inspection. She had flown for several thousand hours of flight time, and she was due for a "spa day" – parts were repaired or replaced, keeping the aircraft in top condition. Among other upgrades, AHEM-4 got a new engine to replace one of the four that was starting to lose efficiency.

On her next flight, the Constellation lifted off from the runway smoothly and beautifully. As the gear was folding up, though, the new engine exploded into flames. Running on only three engines, the aircraft was still only at the end of the runway, rising, but slowly. Captain Robert Norman immediately engaged the engine fire extinguisher system. Chemicals poured in to smother the flames, and the blaze was put out. But the remaining three engines were churning furiously as Norman desperately tried to gain enough height to clear the buildings looming in front of him.

Captain Norman saw an apartment building directly in the Constellation's new, significantly lower flight path. He shoved the throttles forward in an attempt to urge every ounce of power from the laboring engines. The Constellation's nose lifted, and the plane cleared the building by inches.

Captain Norman and his crew heaved sighs of relief. Against the odds, they'd made it. The plane was starting to pick up speed, and Norman planned to ease off the throttles, giving the engines a smooth burst of power rather than overheating them at maximum operation.

But the throttles were jammed into position, a result of Norman's heroic clearing of the building. Engine temperatures were climbing steadily. Flying a plane takes skill – not brute force. But brute force was called for in this situation. Norman and his copilot both manhandled the throttles back into a safe position.

Captain Norman radioed the tower and declared an emergency. He brought the airliner around, back to the airfield, and set the Constellation down safely.

On July 9, 1948, everyone having anything to do with AHEM-4 held their breath all day … and nothing happened. At the end of the day, people breathed a sigh of relief. The hex was broken.

On July 9, 1949, Constellation AHEM-4 crashed near Chicago, killing everyone on board, including the pilot … Captain Robert Norman.

JULY 10
The Haunted U-Boat (1918)

Let's go from the wide blue sky to the deep blue sea. Here's another story of a haunted craft, a German submarine.

The Germans found submarines extremely effective during World War I. In 1916, the German Navy was building twenty-four U-boats in the shipyards at Bruges, in occupied

Belgium. Construction went smoothly for twenty-three of the boats, but for U-65, nothing seemed to go right. Several workers were killed in accidents during construction.

U-65 was finally launched in October 1916. During the launch, one of the officers was swept overboard and drowned. The first underwater test nearly ended in disaster. The submarine dove ... then was unable to surface for nearly twelve hours. The crew was deeply freaked out by this, especially since when the sub was examined, technicians couldn't find any reason for the malfunction.

The very next day, there was another accident. A torpedo exploded on deck, and a second lieutenant and five crewmen were killed. The second lieutenant soon became the boogeyman blamed for later accidents on the boat – and there were plenty.

A rumor started going around that the dead lieutenant was haunting the ship. One man even admitted it: "We saw him come aboard and walk slowly to the bow. He stood there, staring at us, with his arms folded across his chest."

The U-boat captain tried to downplay the rumors, saying that it must have been the men's imagination working overtime with the stress of war. He asked the men to put the whole incident out of their minds. But at least one of the crewmen who reported seeing the ghost had a hard time forgetting the experience. He deserted, and was never found.

U-65 was repaired after the tragic accident, and put out to sea. For several months all was well – then the ghost showed up again. This time, the captain saw it too. The ghost sighting seemed to bring disaster. The sub docked at Bruges for routine maintenance, and the crew was allowed shore leave. While the men were ashore, the Allies bombed the city, and the captain of U-65 was killed.

This was absolutely horrible for morale. But the German Navy needed every U-boat it had. The boat was thoroughly checked, on the theory that some kind of fumes were causing hallucinations. Again, no reason for any malfunction was found.

Admiral Schroeder, head of U-boat command, derided the talk of ghosts as "superstitious nonsense". To prove to the U-65's crew there was nothing to fear, he spent a night on board, and reported that he hadn't been bothered by any ghosts at all; in fact, he'd had a peaceful night's sleep. He did call in a priest to perform an exorcism, just in case.

Admiral Schroeder chose a tough new captain for U-65, Lieutenant Commander Gustav Schelle. As soon as Schelle took command, he laid down a new rule: anyone who reported seeing ghosts would be severely punished. For the next year, there were no ghost sightings on the U-65 – at least, no one admitted seeing anything strange.

But one day, one of the most trusted officers cracked. Master Gunner Erich Eberhardt rushed into the control room screaming, "I've seen the ghost – an officer standing near the bow torpedo tubes. He brushed past me and disappeared." Eberhardt was so hysterical that he had to be locked up. After several hours, he had calmed down, so his shipmates let him out. That was a mistake: Eberhardt grabbed a bayonet and stabbed himself to death.

A while later, Chief Petty Officer Richard Meyer was swept overboard. His body was never recovered.

After a year of peace, these two deaths hit the crew hard. They started avoiding any enemy contact, but even so, they were struck by enemy fire and had to return to Bruges for repairs. Admiral Schroeder was livid at the crew's mutinous behavior. He had every officer, including Captain Schelle, removed from U-65. When she set to sea again in the middle of 1918, she had a new crew, as well as an entirely different set of officers.

On the morning of July 10, 1918, an American submarine patrolling off the southern coast of Ireland saw the U-65 lying on its side on the surface. The weirdness of the situation was not lost on the Americans, so they watched the German sub for a good long time. They saw no signs of life. The American captain decided to blow up the enemy boat, just to be safe.

The Americans readied their torpedoes, but before they fired, the U-65 exploded in a spray of metal, flames, and seawater. Was it really a decoy filled with explosives that detonated prematurely? Or was there something else going on? Just before the U-65 was blown apart, the American captain said he thought he saw someone standing on the ship.

The figure appeared to be a German officer wearing a Navy overcoat. It stood, arms folded, unmoving, near the bow.

JULY 11
Not Throwing Away My Shot, Weehawken, NJ (1804)

The bitter rivalry between Alexander Hamilton and Aaron Burr ended in an early-morning duel on July 11, 1804. Hamilton had spent his life going for all the gusto he could grab, while the more cautious Burr hung back. Hamilton's political star outshone Burr's, and Burr stewed in resentment until the tension exploded into the famous duel in Weehawken, New Jersey.

After the duel, the mortally wounded Hamilton was taken to the house of Dr. John Francis, his physician, at 27 Jane Street in Greenwich Village. When it was clear that treatment would be futile, he was taken to his friend William Bayard's house, a short distance away, to die.

The house where Alexander Hamilton was treated has since been demolished, but he apparently haunted the house at 27 Jane Street for quite some time. Jean Karsavina lived in the house for many years beginning in 1939, and experienced footsteps, blurry shadows, and the chain on the toilet swinging.

Many paranormal investigators, and fans of the musical *Hamilton*, believe that the incredible energy stirred up by the smash hit has given Hamilton's spirit new life, so to speak. Paranormal activity at 71 Jane Street has been particularly strong. Joe Hamilton (no relation) bought the house in 1994, and since then, she and her family have experienced loads of activity, including crashes so loud they had to wear ear plugs. A previous owner, Irene Connors, actually saw a man in the house, a slim man who wore light-colored knee-length trousers and a white powdered wig.

The *New Yorker Radio Hour* sent reporter Becky Cooper to a séance that attempted to communicate with Hamilton's ghost. The medium didn't sense Hamilton himself, but picked up on a child. Using a Ouija board, she asked the child what their mother's name was, and got the answer "*Eliza*". The spirit said its own name was "*Phillip*".

Now, Alexander and Eliza Hamilton did have a son named Phillip – in fact, they had two. Phillip number one died in a duel, in 1801, three years before his father would die in the same place. And Phillip number two, a baby in 1804, was brought into the room where Hamilton lay dying, to give his father a kiss goodbye. But neither of them died as a toddler. Maybe the spirit had reverted back to that traumatic time in his life. Maybe it was a different Phillip altogether, who just happened to have a mother named Eliza. 71 Jane Street has had many people pass through its doors in its history. I'll let you decide.

JULY 12
Shooting at Pollak Library, Fullerton, CA (1976)

We tend to think of school shootings as a modern phenomenon, but unfortunately, tragedies like this have struck in the past as well. In what's widely considered the first major school shooting, custodian Edward Charles Allaway came into the basement of the Pollak Library at Cal State Fullerton on July 12, 1976. Armed with a .22 caliber semiautomatic rifle, he shot nine staff members, killing seven of them. Allaway was mentally ill, and was convinced that his fellow employees were making pornographic movies with his ex-wife. He was found criminally insane, and is now in Patton State Hospital.

The university memorialized the victims with a plaque in the Quad, where seven trees were planted in their memory. But they are remembered elsewhere, too. In the basement of the Pollak Library, the women's restroom has an excess of paranormal activity. The motion-sensor paper towel dispenser will sometimes come on all on its own, maniacally shooting out paper towels until it's completely empty. And a student assistant reported that she once followed a girl into that restroom, but found the room empty.

JULY 13
The Death of John Rowan, Bardstown, KY (1843)

Cemetery monuments are an impressive way of memorializing those who have gone before. They can be as simple as a name and two dates, or they can be grand pillars of carved stone, cementing the deceased's reputation for the ages.

John Rowan was one of Kentucky's most prominent men in the early 19th century. Rowan served his state as both a senator and a representative. He had a long, distinguished career as a judge, eventually serving as Kentucky's secretary of state and chief justice. (His fondness for the rule of law may have stemmed from his early brush with it. In 1801 he fought a duel with Dr. James Chambers over a drunken dispute. The men were playing cards, and an argument ensued, possibly over which of the men was better at speaking Latin and Greek. Rowan ended up killing Chambers in the duel, but a judge declared that there was insufficient evidence to convict Rowan of murder, so he was released.)

In spite of this brilliant career, John Rowan expressly forbade his family to mark his grave with *any* monument, not even a simple stone. His will stated: "There is to be no monument nor placed over my grave any tombstone. In this sentiment I am emphatic and it must not be violated. When my venerated and beloved father and mother died, they, like the multitude in that day, were interred without tombstones. My children have been buried in the same way -- neither of them has a tombstone, nor shall I have one." A reasonable argument, one would think. He also pointed out that there's no place for pride among the dead. But when he died on July 13, 1843, his relatives and friends promptly ignored his last wishes and put up a graceful obelisk in his honor. The pure white stone is covered in carved text that extols his distinguished career.

It's a beautiful monument, and apparently, John hates it. Within a few months, the obelisk started falling off its base for no reason. Stonemasons were called in so often to repair the marker that they started getting deeply freaked out, and refused to come to the cemetery. Ever since, cemetery workers have had to periodically pick up the obelisk from where it has toppled off its base yet again.

JULY 14
Monument to Murder, Glamorganshire, South Wales (1822)

We'll turn from a stone the deceased didn't want, to a stone nobody wanted to put up.

Margaret Williams lived in Wales in the early decades of the 19th century. A pretty 26-year-old, she worked on a small farm near the village of Cadoxton. Her cheerful, straightforward personality and hard work made her well-liked in the community. The farmer's son also noticed Margaret, and they were soon an item.

But sadly, their relationship didn't last. Margaret accepted the situation with as much grace as she could muster; she quietly gave notice to the farmer and found work caring for an elderly gentleman who lived nearby. She was soon back to her cheerful self. But she couldn't stop herself from complaining to her new neighbors that she had left the farm pregnant, and that the farmer's son was the father.

On the morning of Sunday, July 14, 1822, Margaret's badly beaten body was found in a ditch near town. She had been strangled to death. An autopsy confirmed that she had been pregnant at the time of the murder.

A warrant was immediately issued for the arrest of the farmer's son, and he was locked up to await trial. The inquest went on for two days, but the coroner couldn't find any solid evidence to bring judgment against the young man. He was released, and the inquest jury's verdict was returned as "willful murder by some person or persons unknown."

The suspicion that fell heavily on the farmer's son was too much for him, and he moved away and was never seen in the community again. It wasn't only the whispers and the side-eye. A memorial to Margaret Williams was erected in St. Catwg's churchyard. The stone gave the particulars of the murder, and expressed a desire that even though the murderer had escaped worldly justice, there was to be a divine reckoning.

"Although the savage murderer escape for a season the detection of man yet GOD HATH SET HIS MARK UPON HIM either for Time or Eternity and THE CRY OF BLOOD will assuredly pursue him to a certain and terrible, but righteous JUDGMENT." (You can tell these folks were serious because of the all-caps.)

Now, this sounds like a dramatic one-off, put up to memorialize a young woman who found herself in trouble and paid the ultimate price. Actually, "murder stones" were quite common in England. It was popular in the 1820s to erect memorial stones like Margaret's; they are all found in the country, never in urban areas. Margaret's stone, besides being the only murder stone in Wales, is unusual in a couple of other respects. Her stone is in a churchyard – most were erected at the site of the violence. (You can see parallels in our modern custom of placing flowers, candles, and other mementos at the scene of a violent death.)

There's another reason Margaret's stone is unusual. It commemorates an unsolved crime. Most of the other memorials are to people whose killers were found and executed. But Margaret's is a cry for justice – justice that wasn't served in this lifetime.

Because it marked such a ghastly event, Margaret's stone soon became a focal point for ghost stories. People were afraid to go past it at night, and several villagers said they had seen two ghostly figures near the stone, most likely Margaret and her lover reunited. (Whether or not this absolved the farmer's son of Margaret's murder in popular opinion is unclear.) The ghost sightings continued into the 1920s, a century after the murder.

JULY 15
The Blue and the Gray, Shohola, PA (1864)

We're going to take a look at one more cemetery monument. This one is at Woodlawn National Cemetery in Elmira, New York. It marks the final resting place of about seventy Civil War soldiers. This is believed to be the only place in the United States where both Union and Confederate soldiers are buried together in a mass grave. The Confederate soldiers hail from at least eight North Carolina regiments, six Virginia units, and six Georgia regiments. They are joined by seventeen members of the Federal Eleventh Veteran Reserve Corps. So how did they all end up in a mass grave in New York?

On July 15, 1864, an 18-car train was transporting 833 Confederate prisoners of war from Point Lookout, Maryland to Elmira, New York. Guarding them were 128 Union soldiers. Locomotive 171, headed westbound, was classified as an "extra", meaning it ran behind a scheduled train. This scheduled train gave Engine 171 the right-of-way, but 171 was delayed at Jersey City, New Jersey, while the guards searched for several missing prisoners. It arrived at Port Jervis four hours behind schedule.

Telegraph operator Douglas Kent was on duty at the Lackawaxen Junction station. He saw the scheduled train come through, heading west, with the flags warning of a following "extra" displayed. Kent was supposed to hold all eastbound trains until 171 had gone through. But at about 2:30, a 50-car coal train stopped at the junction and asked if the track was clear.

Kent said yes.

The train continued on its eastbound path. At 2:45, Engine 171 blew through headed west. The two trains met on a blind curve with only fifty feet of visibility. Both trains were going about twenty miles an hour.

The collision was titanic, forcing the two locomotives up against each other so that they were practically standing on end. The wooden passenger cars telescoped into each other, killing soldiers with flying glass, splintered wood, and jagged metal. Thirteen soldiers of the 51st North Carolina Infantry were killed instantly. At least 51 Confederate prisoners and 17 Union guards died either on the spot or within a day of the wreck. Five prisoners escaped during the chaos and were never accounted for.

Confederate corpses were laid out in rows. The most hideously mangled were hurriedly covered with grass and leaves. The Union dead were wrapped in blankets. Two Confederates, John and Michael Johnson, were taken to the nearby home of a Mr. Hickok. They died overnight and were buried in the cemetery of the Congregational Church. The other bodies were buried throughout the night, until dawn of the 16th.

The Confederates were buried without much ceremony. Workers nailed crude boxes together using wood from the wreckage, and the Rebels were put in them and buried four at a time. The boxes were lowered into a 75-foot-long trench. Toward midnight, pine coffins arrived for the Union dead, who were buried in individual graves. By 9 am on July 16, four more men had died. Their bodies were added to the mass grave near the railroad tracks. (Also at 9 am on July 16, Douglas Kent, the telegraph operator at Lackawaxen Junction station, left his post and was never seen again. According to community gossip, Kent was a habitual drinker and may have been under the influence. He didn't take the wreck very seriously, and after the wreck, he went out of town to a dance. When he came back, he found the public furious at him over his actions. He left town and never came back. An inquest jury found him negligent, but he had vanished, and was never brought to justice.)

In 1911, the train crash victims were exhumed and brought to Woodlawn National Cemetery where they were reburied in a common grave. Their names – those that were known – were inscribed on two bronze plaques on a single stone monument. The names of the Union dead are on the north side of the stone, and the names of the Confederate dead face south. The two Johnsons, buried at the small church in Barryville, were left where they were.

JULY 16
The Monkey Hill Crooner, Joliet, IL (1932)

One fine summer night in 1932, a woman named Mrs. Dudek was enjoying the peaceful quiet of the evening. She was sitting out in her backyard, which was next to the burial ground for Joliet Penitentiary. The paupers' graveyard went by the whimsical name of Monkey Hill. Mrs. Dudek didn't mind that her backyard butted up against Monkey Hill. At least the neighbors were quiet.

But not tonight. As Mrs. Dudek listened to the sounds of a summer night, another sound joined the crickets … a man's gorgeous baritone. Someone in the graveyard was singing.

Mrs. Dudek called to her daughter. "Genevieve? Come on out here. And bring a flashlight." Mother and daughter shone the flashlight into the cemetery. The beam played over the stones, but they couldn't see the singer, who was treating them to what sounded like Latin hymns from the Catholic Mass.

The next night, Mrs. Dudek's husband George and her son Stanley heard the mysterious singing too. The men went into the graveyard to search for the singer – but there was no one there.

Well, of course the Dudeks had to share this wondrous circumstance. They invited their friends, who invited *their* friends. All who heard the beautiful singing agreed that there could only be one explanation.

A ghost was singing Latin hymns in the prison cemetery.

Obviously.

News of the singing ghost spread, first through the Dudeks' neighborhood, then in the town of Joliet. The ghostly concerts would begin around midnight, and folks would show up every evening to listen to the ethereal music. Within ten days or so, the curious descended from all over the Chicago area. The story was featured in local newspapers, then was picked up by papers in Chicago, Indiana, and all across the country.

Monkey Hill became a destination for people as far away as Wisconsin, Missouri, and

Kentucky. Hundreds of visitors traipsed around the cemetery when the singing began every night, searching for either the singer … or the source of the trickery. They searched for hidden speakers, transmitters, even a telltale wire – but all they found were the weathered gravestones of forgotten prisoners.

The skeptics were unable to prove that the voice was a hoax, so an agreement was reached: people just decided to enjoy it. Thousands of people spread blankets on the grass and opened picnic baskets for the nightly concerts.

But as the nights passed, the spectral performer began to miss his nightly shows. When he did sing, curtain time could be as late as 4 am, rather than the predictable midnight of mid-July. Still, the singer had an audience. After all, the ghost was singing hymns! They couldn't miss *that*.

In late July, prison officials debunked the situation. The phantom singer, they said, wasn't a ghost at all. He was William Lalon Chrysler, a prisoner who had been convicted of larceny. He'd served four years of his sentence, and had recently become eligible for parole. He was so happy about this … that he was singing for joy. Chrysler, it seemed, was responsible for late-night inspection of the water pumps at the nearby quarry, where prisoners worked limestone. Prison officials insisted that it was Chrysler's voice, resounding off of the bare limestone walls and echoing in the hilltop cemetery, over a quarter mile away, that people were hearing. They claimed that Chrysler, an Irish-German, was singing Lithuanian folk songs in English, to fight the boredom of being in the quarry on pump inspection duty by himself.

If this sounds like a reach to you, you're not alone. Some folks were convinced by this explanation, but others found it a little far-fetched. But the prison staff *really* wanted to debunk the ghostly singing. Thousands of people had been – let's face it – trespassing on prison property for half of July. The cow pasture, also owned by the prison, had been turned into an impromptu parking lot, and the barbed-wire prison fence had been knocked down and trampled by the press of the crowds. The local criminal element was drawn to the gathering of out-of-towners. Pickpockets roamed the grounds, preying on the oblivious. Some of the local teens had started their own protection racket, threatening motorists with broken windshields if they didn't pay to keep their cars "safe".

Now that they'd come up with an explanation, prison officials soon closed off the field, ordering the trespassers to go home. The voice seems to have stopped its nightly devotionals after the closing of the cow pasture to visitors, and Chrysler's "confession". The mystery had been solved … or had it?

The curious still had questions. If Chrysler really was the person singing, to relieve the monotony of late-night pump inspection, why did people hear only his voice, and not the chug and whine of the pump machinery? And why was he working in the dark of the bottom of a quarry at midnight without any source of light? People had peered into the quarry, and had never reported seeing a light down there.

Here's another good question: how could the sound of one human voice, without amplification, rise from the bottom of a quarry, and seem to be originating from a graveyard on a hilltop a quarter-mile away? Chrysler would have had mad ventriloquism skills to pull that off. Ventriloquists interviewed at the time said that the trick would have been extremely difficult, if not downright impossible, for someone without proper training. Chrysler admitted he'd never been trained to throw his voice.

The mystery that began on that warm summer night in 1932 has never been truly solved. It's said that the voice wasn't heard after prison officials explained it away. But that could simply be because the crowds were shooed off the property. If a tree falls in the woods, and no one is there to hear it, does it still make a sound?

And if a ghostly voice wanders a prison graveyard singing Latin hymns at midnight, does someone living have to be there to listen?

JULY 17
Phantom Ships of Devils Lake, ND (1893)

J. Morley Wyard was a passenger on the steamship *Minnie H.*, traversing Devils Lake in northeastern North Dakota, when he saw something quite extraordinary. The ship was making the crossing from the old Chautauqua grounds to Fort Totten on the south shore. The shoreline of Devils Lake is twisty and varied, some of it with meadows stretching miles away from the lake, some of it steep and rocky, some of it sheer bluffs several hundred feet high. The water is crystal clear, and on that day, July 17, 1893, it was calm as well. The *Minnie H.* cruised along under a cloudless blue sky.

When the *Minnie H.* was in the middle of the lake, Wyard looked out toward the southern shore. A bit west of Fort Totten, he saw the hull of a large ship, without masts or sails. The ship hung motionless in the water, and Wyard watched it until the path of the *Minnie H.* carried him around a shoreline outcropping called the Point of Rocks, which hid the ghost ship from sight.

Wyard reached Fort Totten and did his errand there. On his way back across the lake a few hours later, he saw something even more amazing.

Wyard saw a ship coming out of a cove near the shoreline. Later, in an article he wrote for the *Gazette Witness*, he said that even though there wasn't a breath of wind that day, the ship "swept along with wonderful rapidity until it might have covered ten miles in about as many minutes." (I'll do the math for you. That's a ship moving at sixty miles an hour. In 1893.) Again, Wyard watched the ship until it disappeared behind the Point of Rocks near Fort Totten.

JULY 18
The Wandering Bones of J. Dawson Hidgepath, Alma, CO (1865)

Pity poor J. Dawson Hidgepath. He was a miner in a camp called Buckskin, just two miles from the town of Alma, Colorado. The ratio of men to women in mining camps was woefully skewed, and Buckskin was no different. But Hidgepath wasn't about to let this tarnish his mojo. A born romantic, he fell in love with every woman who came through the camp – young, old, single, married, it didn't matter to Hidgepath. He adored them all. When he wasn't mining, he was busy writing sappy poems, picking wildflowers, and delivering the droopy bouquets and crumpled pages to his ladylove of the week.

Surprisingly, Hidgepath did not get shot by a jealous husband. His end came in a much tamer way – an accident, really. On July 23, 1865, Hidgepath was on the west side of Mount

Bross. Maybe he was prospecting, maybe he was picking flowers. Whatever he was doing, he lost his footing and fell over a precipice, landing several hundred feet below. His fellow miners found first his distinctive hat, then his broken body. His remains were gathered up and buried in the cemetery in Buckskin.

But Hidgepath didn't let death curtail his pursuit of love. He continued his visits to the ladies of Buckskin. But he didn't manifest as a cold spot, or a misty figure, or a whisper on the night breeze.

Hidgepath himself visited the ladies. Or at least, his body did.

The dead miner's bones started showing up in women's beds. They were always accompanied by his distinctive hat – presumably so the lady would know whose bones were in her bed. Sometimes the lucky woman would find a few decaying flowers or a love poem scribbled on a scrap of paper clutched in the bony fingers.

Every time Hidgepath's bones showed up, folks reburied them. They were undoubtedly his – each time the bones appeared, his were missing from his grave. The people of Buckskin tried burying the bones deeper, and even put a large rock on the grave to keep the wandering bones buried, but nothing worked.

The camp town of Buckskin eventually dried up, and people moved away, but Hidgepath continued his visits to local ladies, seeking out female company in Alma, and even venturing as far as Fairplay. His bones made their trips through the rest of the 1860s and all through the 1870s. At the end of the decade, someone finally got tired of reburying the peripatetic bones, and dumped what was left of Hidgepath into an outhouse in Leadville.

The traveling bones didn't travel after that. (There's a rumor, though, that a lady using the privy heard words of woo whispered to her from the depths.) Perhaps Hidgepath, finding his bones disposed of in such a gauche manner, decided not to subject his amorous interests to the stink of an outhouse. He fancied himself too much of a gentleman to be so uncouth.

JULY 19
Crash of United Flight 232, Sioux City, IA (1989)

United Flight 232 took off from Denver, Colorado, headed for Chicago, on July 19, 1989. The plane was a McDonnell Douglas DC-10, an aircraft plagued since its beginning with a poor safety record and bad press. (American Airlines Flight 191, which crashed outside O'Hare Airport on May 25, 1979, killing everyone on board, was a DC-10.)

The flight left Stapleton International Airport in Denver at 2:09 pm and climbed to cruising altitude. At 3:17, just over an hour later, the plane banked in a shallow right turn, and the DC-10's crew heard a loud bang. The number two engine had exploded, and shrapnel shredded the hydraulic lines. The plane settled into a descending turn to the right, and the crew fought to save an aircraft that had suddenly lost its hydraulics.

The crew had to slow the increasing right bank before it turned into a roll – if that happened, the plane could never be recovered. The crew closed the throttle on the number one engine and throttled up the number three engine. The difference in thrust forced the DC-10 to yaw left, and the wings leveled out.

The plane was still flying without a hydraulic system, and a glance at the wings proved that the inboard ailerons on both wings were locked up and the spoilers were locked down. The crew radioed air traffic control, who directed them to the airport at Sioux City, Iowa.

Runway 22 had been closed for about a year, but it was the best option for the wounded aircraft. Using the asymmetric thrust, the crew lined up with the runway as best they could. With all three hydraulic systems gone, the flaps for slowing the plane wouldn't work. Neither would the brakes, once the plane touched down. The landing gear would have to be lowered manually, using a handle in the floor of the cockpit.

At 4 pm, the stricken plane approached the runway, traveling at around 215 knots (250 mph). (The DC-10's normal landing speed is around 140 knots.) As the plane landed, the right wing suddenly dipped and hit the runway. The aircraft cartwheeled and burst into flames. Despite the heroic efforts of Captain Al Haynes and his flight crew, 111 of the 296 people on board died in the crash.

The Sioux Gateway Airport is still haunted by the apparitions of those who perished in the fiery crash. Passengers arriving at the airport are sometimes greeted by the sounds of people screaming in pain. Inside the airport, people sometimes hear strange moans. Some witnesses even report seeing nearly transparent figures wandering through the airport, then disappearing into the walls.

JULY 20
The Fading Ghost of Highway 93, Denver, CO (1881)

As much as we might like them to, some ghosts don't hang around forever. Here's a story of a phantom that started off strong, only to fade away over the decades.

On July 20, 1881, a man was walking along the Ralston-to-Golden tracks near Van Bibber Creek. Maybe he was a tramp, maybe he was just some ordinary guy out for a stroll. Whoever he was, he was struck by a Colorado Central locomotive.

The violent impact knocked the man far into the bushes. Despite an intensive search along the tracks, his body was never found. The only sign of him was a derby hat lying next to the tracks.

Probably because his body was never laid to rest, the man began haunting the scene of the accident within the month. And he did it with gruesome style, too. Wearing a derby hat and stinking of rotting flesh, the ghost appeared along the tracks, spooked people passing through the area, and even showed up in trains that ran along that route.

The landscape is different now than in 1881, and the phantom's ferocity has faded. Highway 93 now runs where the tracks once crossed the land. The nameless man's presence is still felt, but instead of appearing as a horrifying corpse, he now manifests as an oddly-shaped dust cloud, a wisp of vapor, or simply a lingering sense of dread.

JULY 21
Papa Hemingway, Oak Park, IL (1899)

Ernest Hemingway, smoker of cigars, big-game hunter, macho man extraordinaire, began life in a dainty Queen Anne-style house in Oak Park, Illinois.

The Hemingway Birthplace is graceful and elegant, with Victorian gingerbread and a wraparound porch. It was built in 1890 by Hemingway's grandfather, Ernest Hall. Hemingway was born in a second-floor bedroom on July 21, 1899. He only lived in the house for the first six years of his life. When Hall died in 1905, the family moved to a Prairie-style house a few blocks away.

In 1919, Hemingway left Oak Park and began the life that would take him to fame as one of the most beloved writers of the 20th century. But it seems that Hemingway has never forgotten his roots. His spirit is seen near his birthplace in the summer months. Witnesses have seen a husky man in his late thirties, wearing light summer clothes. The phantom even sports Hemingway's bushy mustache. The ghost pauses on the sidewalk, gazes at the beautiful home for a moment, then strides briskly away. Papa Hemingway doesn't seem to be much for nostalgia.

JULY 22
Bridget McCaffary's Ghost, Kenosha, WI (1850)

John McCaffary left Ireland and came to America in May 1837. He liked America so much, he applied for citizenship in 1846. In August 1847, he reached another milestone: he bought a plot of land in Kenosha, Wisconsin (then known as Southport), from Charles and Caroline Durkee. Not long after, he built a two-story brick house on the lot. And on May 2, 1848, he married Bridget McKean at St. James Church in Southport.

Two years into their marriage ... something happened. Around midnight on July 22, 1850, neighbors awoke to a woman's screams. The cries of "Oh, John, spare me!" and "Oh, John, save me!" were heard over a block away. Neighbors rushed to the McCaffary house, and found John coming out of the backyard. Some people said they heard faint splashing sounds coming from an abandoned well in the backyard, but those sounds soon stopped.

The neighbors, concerned, asked John if Bridget was in the well. He replied vaguely that *someone* was in the well. The neighbors rushed over, but it was too late. A look into the murky water revealed a body dressed in a white shirt ... a bruised body that was indeed Bridget McCaffary.

Bystanders also found John's hat and one shoe in the well. The other shoe was between the well and the house, and was slimed with muck from the stagnant well. There was only about 18 to 20 inches of water in the well. Investigators put the picture together pretty quickly: John McCaffary had tried to drown his wife in the well. When that didn't work, he stomped on her head until she died. And then he chucked her into the well.

John was tried for murder in July 1851. He was found guilty and sentenced to death by hanging. He didn't testify in his own defense. And he never gave a reason for his heinous attack on his wife.

According to local stories, somewhere between two and three thousand people witnessed the hanging. But the hanging wasn't the traditional "drop the guy through the trapdoor" affair. It was much less humane than that – the victim was raised into the air, meaning that instead of (hopefully) a nice clean snap of the neck, the condemned slowly strangled to death. After McCaffary had hung suspended for eight minutes, doctors checked his pulse. It had only slowed slightly, not stopped, so they let him hang ten minutes more. The execution of John McCaffary was the first and last capital punishment carried out in Wisconsin.

Bridget McCaffary did not rest easily, even though her husband paid for his crime. John told a newspaper reporter that Bridget had visited him on several occasions during the days leading up to his execution, to taunt him with his impending doom.

The McCaffary house, and the house next door to it, are haunted by the unfortunate Bridget. The story goes that John chased Bridget around the yards of both houses before grabbing her and throwing her into the well on the McCaffary property. One owner told the *Kenosha News* in 1999 that he had been sitting in the neighboring house with a friend when the friend saw the startling sight of a woman's face in the window – a window that was ten feet off the ground.

Later, in the McCaffary house, the former owner was sitting with friends when one person saw an apparition in the living room doorway. Another time, he clearly heard footsteps in the upstairs rooms when he was alone in the house. The house had been divided for a while into upper and lower apartments, and none of the tenants stayed very long, explaining that disturbing noises kept them awake all night. The paranormal activity doesn't seem to be threatening in nature; people just say the house has a "bad feel" to it.

The McCaffary house has recently been restored to its original function as a single-family residence. The new owners haven't reported any activity ... yet.

JULY 23
Montgomery Clift, Hollywood, CA (1966)

The Roosevelt Hotel in Hollywood was the site of the very first Academy Awards. Far from the glamorous spectacle of today, that early awards show (held in the hotel's ballroom, the Blossom Room, on May 16, 1929) was a simple banquet for fewer than 250 people. The awards part lasted just twelve minutes.

But that's not the Roosevelt's only claim to fame. Many of Hollywood's brightest stars have stayed at the hotel, some for several months while rehearsing for movies. Among them was Montgomery Clift, a darkly handsome actor nominated for several Academy Awards, who was known for his portrayal of moody, sensitive young men. He stayed in Room 928 for three months while shooting the 1953 movie *From Here to Eternity*. Clift started acting on Broadway before making a very successful switch to the movies, earning Academy nominations for Best Actor for *The Search* and *A Place in the Sun*.

As he'd started his career in New York at the Actors Studio, Clift was a devotee of the Stanislavski Method, which trains the actor to use his or her own experiences as fodder for their emotions during performances. During his preparation for his role in *From Here to Eternity*, in which he played a young soldier, Clift decided he should learn how to play the bugle, so it would seem natural on film. While living at the Roosevelt, he could often be heard practicing. He would also pace the ninth-floor hallway as he ran his lines. This hard work resulted in his fourth Best Actor nomination.

In 1956, Clift accidentally crashed his car into a telephone pole. He suffered internal injuries, but recovered. However, his face was badly damaged. The accident left him with an addiction to alcohol and painkillers that would last the rest of his life.

He continued to act after the accident, and did well, despite his struggles with substance abuse. He died of a heart attack at age 45 in his home in New York City on July 23, 1966.

Montgomery Clift's spirit prefers to haunt his old room at the Roosevelt Hotel. Dozens of guests staying on the ninth floor over the years have called down to the front desk to complain of someone playing a trumpet in the hallway. The blatting music can usually be traced to Room 928 – even if no one is staying in it at the time. Hotel staff know exactly who the amateur musician is, and nonchalantly tell guests that it's just the ghost of Montgomery Clift, still putting in his practice time.

Celebrated paranormal researcher Brad Steiger and his wife had their own experience with the actor. They were staying at the Roosevelt in 1992, in preparation for filming the Halloween episode of HBO's *World Entertainment Report*. The night before filming, Kelly Green, a staff member at the hotel, had put the Steigers in the room next to Clift's haunted room on the ninth floor. The investigators planned to get an early start the next morning, filming in the haunted room. They were disappointed, and a little irked, to hear rambunctious noises coming from the room all night, as if someone was very inconsiderately having a raucous party. They could even hear kids running around creating a ruckus.

The Steigers couldn't believe that the helpful Ms. Green would book guests – especially a family – into a room the night before they were scheduled to film in that very room, and with an early start, too. In the end, though, they decided not to mention it. They were grateful to have the opportunity to film in the haunted room, no matter the circumstances.

Brad and Sherry went to bed sincerely hoping that their next-door neighbors would be checking out early the next morning. But the people in Room 928 showed no inclination to pack it in and head for bed themselves. The noises of a party in full swing continued through most of the night.

The next morning, the investigators learned that the conscientious Ms. Green had indeed left orders at the desk for the Clift room to remain unbooked so they could film at their leisure. It gave even those two seasoned ghost hunters a chill to realize the loud sounds of partying were coming from an empty room.

That wasn't all. Later that day, Sherry Steiger remembered that she had been woken up the night before by what sounded like one of the rambunctious kids tooting on a horn. The irritating blat had drawn her from sleep, but she and Brad were recovering from giving a seminar at the Los Angeles college. She was dog-tired, and her sleep-addled brain didn't register the significance of the bugle music she was hearing.

DAYS *of the* DEAD

JULY 24
The Eastland Disaster, Chicago, IL (1915)

Fate has a way of turning on a dime. A happy outing can turn tragic in an instant, changing lives forever.

Saturday, July 24, 1915, dawned cloudy and cool, with scattered thunderstorms predicted for the Chicago area. Despite the lowering skies, it was a holiday for many families – employees of Western Electric Company, along with their friends and families, were going to the annual company picnic in Michigan City, Indiana. To bring the 7,500 guests to the picnic, the company chartered five steamers: *Petoskey, Eastland, Missouri, Theodore Roosevelt,* and *City of South Haven.* These craft would take the picnickers from Chicago across the southern edge of Lake Michigan.

The boats were moored in the Chicago River between the Clark Street and LaSalle Street bridges. Since *Theodore Roosevelt* and *Eastland* were the newer of the steamers, most employees wanted to board them, instead of the older boats.

Eastland was built in 1903 to haul passengers and fruit across Lake Michigan. She was a fast ship, but she had a tendency to roll. Before the 1915 season, two inches of concrete were poured over her deck to keep the wooden planking from rotting. And since the *Titanic* disaster three years earlier, all passenger vessels were required to carry a full set of lifeboats. This made *Eastland* even more top-heavy. Even so, starting at 6:40 am, more than 3,200 people climbed aboard the steamer, which had a capacity of 2,500.

Passengers rushed to the starboard side, near the dock, to claim the best spaces for the trip. This made *Eastland* list to starboard. No problem – the chief engineer just flooded the port ballast tanks, and *Eastland* righted herself. At 6:51 am, she was level again. Many passengers went belowdecks, out of the cool morning air, hoping to warm up.

A passing fireboat, in the river on the port side of *Eastland*, fired off its water cannons to give the crowd a thrill. Passengers rushed to the port side of the deck, causing *Eastland* to list again. The engineer filled the starboard ballast tanks and righted her. Then she overbalanced and listed toward the dock. The engineer pumped out both the port and starboard tanks, leaving no ballast in the steamer at all. Top-heavy with passengers, *Eastland* rolled to port again. The captain started the engines, but the steamer didn't move forward. Instead, she righted herself, then counterbalanced yet again, continuing her ponderous list to port, into the river.

Cargo shifted; passengers panicked. River water started pouring in through the lower viewports on the port side. Moments later, *Eastland* succumbed to gravity. She rolled over onto her port side and came to rest on the bottom of the Chicago River, in eighteen feet of water.

Passengers who had been on deck when the steamer capsized were thrown into the water. They struggled there, the women's long dresses pulling them below the murky water. People inside the boat fared even worse. Many were crushed by furniture that fell to one side of the boat. Those who weren't immediately killed were drowned moments later.

First responders cut holes in the boat's exposed hull above the waterline. They began pulling survivors from the water – and bodies from the boat. Corpses were lined up along the dock, or arranged on the deck of *Roosevelt*. Bodies were later taken by wagon to funeral homes and morgues.

Contemporary sources reported that 844 bodies were pulled from *Eastland* that day. That number isn't necessarily accurate – it could be much higher. The sinking of *Eastland* was the worst disaster in Chicago history. The death toll outstripped other Chicago tragedies like the Iroquois Theatre fire and even the great Chicago Fire.

Grieving survivors went to makeshift morgues to identify the remains of their loved ones. In order to keep the process of identification moving, the coroner's office had a rubber stamp made up: "Drowned. July 24, 1915, from steamer EASTLAND, Chicago River at Clark Street." Many families, intending to enjoy their holiday together, were simply all wiped out. On Friday, July 30, the last body was identified as the remains of 7-year-old Willie Novotny. Willie's immediate family, his parents and older sister, had also perished.

Such a horrific tragedy was bound to leave its mark on the surrounding area. Pedestrians between the Clark and LaSalle Street bridges still tell of hearing cries of terror near the riverbank. Others hear a sudden splash, then hundreds of screaming voices. A look at the river's surface reveals not even a ripple of disturbance, but still the voices plead for rescue. Some unlucky witnesses even see the apparition of people flailing around in the water. One good Samaritan even jumped in to save someone he thought was drowning, only to find himself alone in the river.

Two of the buildings used as temporary morgues were the Reid Murdoch building and the National Guard armory. The Murdoch building is now a traffic court. After several repurposings, including being used as a stable and a bowling alley, the armory was purchased by Harpo Studios, Oprah Winfrey's production company.

Harpo Studios is rife with stories from security guards, maintenance staff, and others claiming that the building is still haunted by victims of the *Eastland* tragedy. The most well-known of these lingering spirits is the ghost of a woman in a gray dress, who wanders the corridors before vanishing through the wall. Staff also report moaning and sobbing, phantom footsteps, and doors that open and close by themselves.

JULY 25
A Shipyard Full of Ghosts, Norfolk, VA (1967)

The United States Naval Shipyard is almost ridiculously haunted, with spooks in several different buildings.

The drydock facility was built in 1767, and the buildings where phenomena occur all have parts of old sailing vessels in them. Also, there's been plenty of time for the shipyard to collect a whole crew of ghosts.

The apparition who haunts Buildings 29, 31, and 33 had been nicknamed John Paul by employees, because he manifests dressed like Revolutionary War hero John Paul Jones. In 1918, a sailor broke his leg trying to get away from the ghost.

Drydocks 1 and 2 are haunted by three British soldiers whose graves were unearthed near the docks in 1971. The old sailmakers loft boasts ghostly voices, misty white shapes, and the sound of sewing machines.

The *Forestal* often docks at Norfolk, and that's handy, because the ship is also haunted. The aircraft carrier is the stomping ground of a ghost that sailors have named George. He haunts Number 1 and Number 3 holds, and delights in moving objects, slamming doors, tapping sailors on the shoulder, and turning lights off for no reason. Once, George grabbed the leg of a sailor who was climbing a ladder – and wouldn't let go. Another sailor had to pull his terrified friend to safety.

So why is the shipyard so active? Besides its rich history, the shipyard at Norfolk was also the scene of a terrible accident. On July 25, 1967, a torpedo from an F-4 Phantom was sitting on the deck. Somehow, it got fired, and hit the fuel tank of a nearby plane. The resulting explosion and fire killed 134 men.

JULY 26
The Shelton Gang, Peoria, IL (1948)

Chicago in the 1930s was known for its rampant gang activity, but the Windy City by no means had a monopoly on organized crime. Farther south in the state, Peoria and southern Illinois were ruled by crime figures such as the Shelton gang and Charlie Birger. Peoria in particular, being the second-largest city in the state, and the largest metropolitan area south of Chicago, became a gambling mecca by 1940. The Depression was over, and people once again had money to blow. Gambling was regulated and taxed in Peoria, so it was tolerated by city officials – and welcomed by gangsters.

For a while, that is. By 1945, Peorians were getting tired of the town's reputation as a "sin city". Mayor Woodruff was voted out, and Carl Triebel, who ran as a reform candidate, took office. The new mayor met with Carl Shelton, the oldest brother of the Shelton gang and its leader, and told him that gambling in Peoria would be shutting down. Carl shrugged, saying that now he'd have time to farm. He moved down to southern Illinois.

However, gambling was still available outside the city in Peoria County. Bernie Shelton, the youngest brother, stayed to oversee this operation. Bernie was a big, brawny guy, known for his toughness and his temper. He was the gang's enforcer.

But the Shelton gang had made many enemies in their Peoria career. Also, gangs in Chicago and St. Louis saw this as their chance to take over gambling operations in southern Illinois. Between February and October of 1946, three gangsters involved in the Shelton gang were killed in Peoria. On October 23, 1947, Carl Shelton was killed near his farm in southern Illinois.

And on July 26, 1948, Bernie Shelton was shot through the chest with a large-caliber rifle as he was leaving the Parkway Tavern on Farmington Road outside Peoria. The assassin fired from the woods near St. Joseph Cemetery behind the tavern. Bernie died in the hospital about half an hour later.

Earl Shelton was the last of the gang. Between 1950 and 1951, he survived three attempts on his life. He decided he'd had enough. He packed up his relatives and moved to Florida, thereby ending the era of the Shelton gang in Illinois.

The gang was gone from Peoria, but the belligerent ghost of Bernie Shelton remained. For the next fifty years, Bernie haunted his old bar. Many customers and staff reported encounters with Bernie's angry, powerful presence. Restroom doors slammed, jars of hot sauce were thrown, and lights turned on and off when Bernie was around. Bar patrons felt breathing on their necks, or an icy hand on their arm. People heard the sound of gunshots in the parking lot. Gusts of wind would blow through the tavern, slamming open the front door where Bernie crawled after being shot. (This happened even on days when there was no wind, not even a breeze.) In 1998, investigators held a séance at the tavern. After fifty years, they finally convinced Bernie's restless spirit to move on.

But did he? The Parkway Tavern became Kenny's Westside Pub in 2013. The bar has been renovated, but current employees report that paranormal activity, though subtle, still happens – lights flicker, things move. Perhaps Bernie Shelton's ghost didn't go all that far.

JULY 27
Murder of Jane McCrea, New York State (1777)

Life during the Revolutionary War wasn't all battles and bloodshed. Ordinary people still lived their ordinary lives. Some of them even made plans to get married.

Jane McCrea, a black-haired beauty of 23 years, was engaged to David Jones, an officer in British General Burgoyne's army. On July 27, 1777, Jane went to the home of Sarah McNeil. She planned to leave from Sarah's house to meet up with David, as it was their wedding day.

But before the women left, the house was attacked by a patrol of General Burgoyne's Indian allies. Sarah and Jane were forced from the house, separated, and taken down different roads. Sarah eventually made it safely to a nearby Loyalist camp … but Jane was not so lucky.

General Burgoyne's Indians fought over which of them should be Jane's guard for the trip. During the argument, one of the warriors dragged Jane off her horse and shot her. Then he scalped her, using his tomahawk to cut off her long black hair. Her body was later discovered tossed into a ravine.

General Burgoyne refused to punish the warrior who had killed Jane, fearing that such an action would cost him the support of his Native American allies. This, interestingly, turned the Loyalist Jane McCrea into a martyr for the Revolutionary cause. If Burgoyne would allow his own people to be killed without consequences, the colonials argued, he was manifestly not to be trusted. Burgoyne arrived at Saratoga to find the patriots stirred up and itching for a fight. The ensuing battled turned the tide of the American Revolution.

Jane McCrea is buried in the Fort Edward cemetery, not far from the house where her ordeal began. The Jane McCrea House still stands, and some people have reported footsteps in the attic and lights turning on and off. Others tell of hearing screams coming from a closet. However, the present owners never heard the closet screams. For a while, they thought they heard someone walking up the stairs to the second floor, but that was a while ago. As for the attic noises, after they had the heating system serviced to get air out of the lines, the mysterious footsteps stopped. So maybe Jane McCrea is resting in peace after all.

JULY 28
A Helpful Spirit (1895-1898)

Captain Joshua Slocum was an adventurer extraordinaire. He was the first man to sail single-handedly around the world, making the 46,000-mile journey in a 36-foot sloop called the *Spray*.

Slocum was also a noted writer, and realized that people would be keenly interested in tales of his seafaring adventures. He wrote a book about his solo circumnavigation, calling it (naturally) *Sailing Alone Around The World*.

He set sail from Boston on April 24, 1895. More than three years later, on June 27, 1898, he made port in Newport, Rhode Island.

The book is considered a classic of travel literature, and with good reason; it's well-written and engaging. Here's the start of the trip: "I had resolved on a voyage around the world, and as the wind on the morning of April 24, 1895 was fair, at noon I weighed anchor, set sail, and filled away from Boston, where the *Spray* had been moored snugly all winter … A thrilling pulse beat high in me. My step was light on deck in the crisp air. I felt there could be no turning back, and that I was engaging in an adventure the meaning of which I thoroughly understood." Kinda makes you want to join him, doesn't it?

By the time July rolled around, Slocum was well into the Atlantic Ocean, between the Azores and Gibraltar. There, he had a very strange experience.

A storm had battered the *Spray* for three days. In addition to fighting the bad weather, Slocum was stricken with vicious stomach cramps from food poisoning. Feeling utterly wretched, Slocum was lying on the bottom of the boat when he looked up and saw a tall, heavy-set man standing at the helm.

The man was wearing 15th-century clothing, the cap of which he doffed to Slocum, then smiled. He introduced himself as one of Columbus's crew, the pilot of the *Pinta*, and said he'd come to help. "Lie quiet, señor captain," he said, "and I will guide your ship tonight."

The phantom gave Slocum a bit of grief for eating white cheese of dubious freshness. Then it sang while steering the *Spray* through the storm. The sloop, and Slocum himself, survived, and after the storm had passed, the phantom sailor vanished.

So was this a hallucination brought on by an upset tummy? Or did a sailor from the *Pinta* come to Slocum's rescue in the middle of the Atlantic?

JULY 29
Dining With Spirits, Twin Cities, MN (1892)

Joseph Forepaugh seemed to have the world by the tail. He came to St. Paul, Minnesota, in 1858, and started a dry-goods business called Forepaugh and Justice. On October 19, 1862, Joseph married Mary Lanpher, and they had five children. His business ventures continued to prosper over the years. In 1888, he retired from business and started investing in real estate. In 1889, Joseph had a gorgeous Queen Anne-style house built in the swanky part of St. Paul. Joseph, Mary, and their children moved into the house in 1891.

But that just wasn't quite enough for Joseph Forepaugh. Legend has it that he began a hot-and-heavy affair with one of his housekeepers, a woman named Molly. Apparently, Joseph and Molly weren't very discreet at all. It didn't take long for Mary Forepaugh to get wind of the affair, and when she did, she forbade Joseph from ever seeing Molly again.

Joseph was broken up about losing his mistress. He was also a product of his times – he was a successful, wealthy businessman in the 1890s, a time when social conduct of rich people was highly scrutinized by other rich people. Facing the loss of his mistress, the scorn of his wife, and the harsh judgment of his social circle, Joseph left his home on the morning of Friday, July 9, 1892, without telling anyone where he was going. When he didn't return by suppertime, his family feared the worst, and organized a search party. Police questioned the family, and Forepaugh's only grandchild told them she'd seen her grandfather leaving the city by streetcar.

This clue led searchers the next morning to Joseph's lifeless body. Shortly after 11 am, the body was found along the Milwaukee railroad tracks. Joseph had shot himself in the head with a revolver.

He didn't leave a suicide note, so his motives were never really clear. People said Forepaugh was facing bankruptcy, but when his will was read, his estate was valued at nearly half a million dollars. Then people began to whisper that Molly was pregnant with Joseph's illegitimate child. These rumors were never proven either. After Joseph's suicide, Molly took a rope up to the third floor of the Forepaugh mansion and hung herself from a chandelier.

Over the decades, the beautiful mansion Joseph had built for his and Mary's enjoyment fell into disrepair. But in 1974, it was renovated and turned into a restaurant, fittingly named Forepaugh's.

The revitalization brought back to life not only the stately mansion, but also the spirits that linger there. Customers and staff happily share their many encounters with several ghosts that inhabit the restaurant. Some people see an arrogant-looking man who strides around the place like he owns it. Well, he does – that's Joseph Forepaugh.

Another spirit is a woman dressed in Victorian garb. Witnesses theorize that this may be Molly's ghost. It's *someone's* ghost, all right, because whenever she appears, she is nearly transparent.

Some of the experiences at Forepaugh's are simply puzzling. One long-time employee was straightening the hangers in the coat closet, making sure they were neatly spaced an equal distance apart. Finished, she turned to leave, and heard the clash of the hangers being pushed together. When she spun back, all of the hangers had been moved to one side of the closet. She decided she was done straightening that particular closet for the night.

Cold spots abound at Forepaugh's. Silverware, laid out for a big event, has been found rearranged, as though someone wasn't quite satisfied with its placement. And employees have arrived at work to find dining room chairs moved, even flipped upside-down.

The most haunted spot in Forepaugh's is the third-floor chandelier, the place where Molly is said to have committed suicide. People who don't know the story have reported hearing the sound of rope creaking when they stand near the spot. Many employees refuse to work upstairs at night. Some say, in all seriousness, they would rather be fired than work alone at night on the third floor.

If you visit Forepaugh's, you can request the table that is directly under that chandelier. If you do, don't forget to look up once in a while. People who sit there regularly report seeing the chandelier swing back and forth on its own … just as if something is hanging from it.

JULY 30
Misty Friends, Crescent City, CA (1865)

There are several spirits who inhabit Battery Point Lighthouse. Jerry and Nadine Tugel served as lighthouse keepers for twelve years, retiring in the mid-1990s. Nadine is a wealth of information on the hauntings at the lighthouse, and even wrote a booklet collecting the many ghost stories. She refers to the lighthouse ghosts as the Misty Friends – an apt description.

Battery Point Lighthouse was constructed in 1856, one of the first lighthouses on the California coast. In 1855, the ship *America* had burned in the harbor at Crescent City. Three cannons were salvaged from the wreckage and put at the entrance to the harbor. The cannons were often fired during Fourth of July celebrations, and gave the area the name Battery Point.

The lighthouse served the area for decades, and even survived a tsunami. On March 27, 1964, the strongest earthquake ever recorded in the northern hemisphere struck Alaska, generating waves that raced south at nearly 600 mph. Crescent City was slammed with waves that reached up to twenty feet high, causing the worst tsunami damage ever suffered on North America's west coast.

The following year, the Battery Point lighthouse beacon was turned off, and harbor navigation was done by a flashing light at the end of the breakwater. But on December 10, 1982, the lighthouse light was restored. This is when Nadine and Jerry Tugel served as the lighthouse keepers.

They had many paranormal experiences during their tenure there. One day before going to the mainland, they closed the door to the upstairs (so their cats couldn't get into their bedroom or the museum room), locked the front door, and set the alarm. When they came back late that evening, everything was just as they'd left it. When they climbed into bed, though, Nadine discovered a toasty-warm spot right by her feet. She told Jerry about the anomaly, and he jokingly said, "Well, why didn't they warm my side?"

The next night, there was another warm spot on the bed – on Jerry's side.

Many people have seen the antique rocking chair rock by itself, and noticed that when it does, the distinctive scent of pipe smoke fills the room. Visitors to the lighthouse's museum sometimes feel a gentle touch on their arm, as if someone is politely asking them to move aside. They do – then discover there's no one there.

Keepers beside the Tugels have had experiences at the lighthouse during its 145-year history. One of the most persistent of these phenomena is that during stormy weather, keepers will hear footsteps in the tower. These occur every hour on the hour as long as the rough weather lasts, as if someone was assiduously checking to make sure the lighthouse beacon stays lit.

One stormy night, the footsteps woke both the lighthouse keeper and his wife. An alarm was set up to ring if the light went out. The alarm hadn't sounded, but the keeper had the feeling the light was out nonetheless. He went up the tower stairs to check, and sure enough, the bulb had burned out. He replaced the bulb, went back downstairs, and went back to bed. Neither he nor his wife heard the footsteps again that night. A check of the alarm system the next day found it to be in perfect working order. The keeper never did figure out why the alarm didn't go off … but if he hadn't been woken up by the phantom footsteps, he wouldn't have known the light had burned out.

Investigators have pinpointed three spirits at the Battery Point lighthouse: two men and a child. Who are they?

Captain John Jeffrey became the second keeper in 1875 and served for almost forty years.

His wife Nellie was employed as assistant keeper. Together, they raised four children at the lighthouse, and their son George became assistant keeper at nearby St. George Reef lighthouse in 1894.

Captain Samuel DeWolf never lived at Battery Point lighthouse, but he died within sight of it. He was captain of the steamship *Brother Jonathan*, which crashed at St. George Reef in a storm on July 30, 1865. The ship was carrying almost 200 passengers and crew. Only nineteen people survived the wreck.

Captain DeWolf and Captain Jeffery may be the two male spirits inhabiting the lighthouse. But what about the child? There's no record of a child dying at the lighthouse. Maybe it's one of the Jeffrey children – perhaps even George – who has chosen to return at an age that held their happiest memories, growing up in a lighthouse.

Nadine and Jerry Tugel think this is a good theory. They even named their two cats Captain Samuel and Captain Jeffery, in honor of those two men of the sea.

JULY 31
Hungry Ghosts, China

In the West, we think of the days in late fall as belonging to the dead. October 31 is Halloween, November 1, All Saints' Day, and November 2, All Souls' Day and Dia de los Muertos. But in the Far East, the Hungry Ghost Festival is celebrated on the 15th day of the seventh month. The entire month is called Ghost Month.

Ghost Month is when spirits come out of the lower realm to visit the living. During Ghost Month, the realms of heaven and hell are opened, and spirits can move freely around the earth. They usually spend this time looking for food and entertainment. It's the duty of the living to provide this for them.

The ghosts are believed to be those of people who didn't get a proper funeral or ritualistic send-off, or the ancestors of people who forgot about them after they died. (And it doesn't have to be *your* ancestors. It's considered polite to honor all of these hungry ghosts even if they weren't related to you, so they don't interfere in your life and bring you bad luck.)

The hungry ghosts have long, needle-thin necks, either because their family hasn't fed them properly, or as a punishment making it impossible for them to swallow. (Some of them came from hell, remember?) They wander the streets during the month, seeking sustenance. Shops are closed, to keep the streets clear, so the ghosts can move around freely. Altars are set up in the middle of every street, with incense, fresh fruit, and other sacrifices.

Taoists and Buddhists perform rituals to ease the suffering of the dead. Elaborate meals are prepared and served, setting places for family members who have passed on. They are served and greeted as though they are still there. Other activities include burning incense and making offerings of food. Priests and monks hold ceremonies in the afternoon or early evening, as it's thought that the ghosts are released from hell when the sun sets. Monks throw rice or other small bits of food into the air to distribute to the ghosts.

The ghosts need entertainment as well as food. Celebrations during Ghost Month include live performances of Chinese opera, drama, even burlesque shows. Everyone is invited, but the first row of seats is left empty – that's where the ghosts sit, and for a living person to rudely take a ghost's seat is very bad luck. The shows are performed at night, and always at full volume, as the sound is believed to attract the ghosts.

A surefire way to make sure a ghost gets your offering is to burn it. So, in addition to incense, people burn paper representations of material goods, such as clothes, jewelry, and money, on up to cars, houses, and servants.

On the last night of the festival, people light paper lanterns and set them afloat on paper boats to help the ghosts find their way back to the afterlife. When the light goes out, the ghost is safely home.

AUGUST

DAYS *of the* DEAD

AUGUST 1
An Angry Young Man, Austin, TX (1966)

They say everything's bigger in Texas. Even universities have veritable skyscrapers on campus. Consider the Main Building at UT Austin, nicknamed the Tower. At an impressive twenty-seven floors, it's one of the most recognizable symbols of both the university and the city of Austin. Perhaps it was this landmark status that drew Charles Whitman to the observation deck on August 1, 1966. Whitman, an architectural engineering student and former Marine, brought with him a scoped Remington 700 rifle, as well as other weapons.

Whitman, a solidly built young man whose blonde hair bristled in a military crewcut, had been admitted to the university in 1961 on a scholarship from the Naval Enlisted Science Education Program. For a short while, Whitman thrived. He met Kathy Leissner, and they got married in 1962.

Whitman had been a good student and an Eagle scout, and had left home to join the Marines as soon as he turned eighteen. But college life didn't seem to be his strong suit. In 1963, his grades were suffering, and he was called back to active service in the Marine Corps. But his service record was littered with courts martial and demotions. He made it as high as Lance Corporal, but was busted back down to private. A couple years later, he was honorably discharged, and in the spring of 1965, he gave the university another try.

Whitman's father was a domineering, overbearing perfectionist who drove his son away. Whitman's mother left her husband in 1966. She found an apartment in Austin, not far from her son. She had escaped her abusive husband ... but it took her to something far worse.

By 1966, Whitman was suffering from severe headaches, and was seriously concerned about his mental health. On the evening of July 31, 1966, Whitman lost the battle against his inner demons. He went to his mother's apartment and shot her. Whitman returned home, and sometime after his wife went to sleep, he killed her too. He stabbed her four times – once for every year they'd been together.

The next day, Whitman took an assortment of guns and a machete to the observation deck of the Tower on the UT Austin campus. He also packed a trunk with enough food to last him several days. On his way up to the deck, he killed a receptionist and two others. Once up on the observation deck, he started shooting. Eleven people fell to his bullets, including the unborn son of Claire Wilson, one of the 32 wounded. (One of those wounded, David Gunby, died of his injuries 35 years later.)

Two police officers and a deputized civilian managed to make their way to a balcony above the deck. From there, they shot Whitman twice in the head, ending his hour-and-a-half reign of terror.

Whitman had some idea that something in his brain was wired horribly wrong. In several notes, he requested that an autopsy be done on him to see if there was any physical sign of mental illness. The police did oblige him with an autopsy, and found a brain tumor. Experts disagreed, though, whether this actually did affect his behavior.

Whether it was the tumor or his father that made him snap, it seems that Charles Whitman still haunts the Tower. His ghost is sometimes seen on the observation deck, sometimes as a misty figure, sometimes just a dark shape. He also plays with the security guards at the Tower, turning lights back on after they've been shut off for the night. He does this so often that the guards sometimes have to call him out on it. "Charlie, let's get along," they'll chide, and the lights will turn themselves off.

Since the 1966 shooting, there have been nine suicides that have jumped from the observation deck. And the very first death was a worker who fell twelve stories during construction in 1937. The Tower was closed for 24 years to prevent further suicides, but in 1998 university president Larry Faulkner recommended reclaiming the Tower. He said that if the Tower stayed closed, the university community would constantly be reminded of its tragic history, without the opportunity to create new, positive experiences. After the installation of high fences to discourage jumpers, the observation deck was reopened in 1999. The Tower's carillon bells still play every morning at 8 o'clock.

Life goes on.

AUGUST 2
Little Boy Lost, Albuquerque, NM (1951)

The KiMo Theatre is a showplace of Old Town, in downtown Albuquerque. The first owner, an Italian immigrant named Oreste Bachechi, built the theater at a cost of $150,000, then spent another $18,000 to install a magnificent Wurlitzer pipe organ to accompany silent movies. The theater opened on September 19, 1927, and soon became renowned not only for its movies, but also for its vaudeville and variety shows. Headliners included Gloria Swanson, Tom Mix, Vivian Vance, and Mickey Rooney.

Tragedy struck on a hot summer day in 1951. On August 2, Bobby Darnall, six years old, was enjoying a movie with friends in the cool darkness of the balcony. A loud siren in the movie's soundtrack startled the boy, and he scrambled out of his seat and ran for the door, tearing down the staircase from the balcony. He was halfway across the lobby when a hot water heater underneath the concession stand exploded, showering the area with debris and scalding water. At least seven people were severely injured in the accident, and Bobby was killed.

The theater struggled along after the disaster, but the era of the opulent silent film palace was quickly fading. After a fire in 1963 that destroyed the original stage and damaged the rest of the building, the theater fell into ruin. It closed in 1968, and was scheduled to be demolished.

Fortunately, before the wrecking ball swung, the city purchased the building and restored it. It now hosts a variety of live entertainment. And the spirit of little Bobby Darnall has chosen to make its home there as well.

When he is seen, he is dressed in a striped shirt and blue jeans. He usually plays on the staircase that leads from the balcony to the lobby. He's fairly well-behaved for a perpetual six-year-old, but sometimes he likes to trip actors or make noise backstage during performances.

To calm the spirit down, actors started putting out doughnuts for him. To keep them out of the way, they threaded the treats onto a cord, and hung them on a pipe that runs along the wall backstage. According to theater lore, doughnuts left out overnight were usually gone by morning. Any that were left had tiny bitemarks on them.

In the 1980s, a no-nonsense director tried to do away with the superstition, and ordered the cord taken down and the doughnuts thrown out. Almost immediately, trouble started. Actors forgot their lines, windows opened on their own, then slammed shut, lightbulbs blew out, and the soundboard malfunctioned. The actors replaced the hanging doughnuts with a small backstage shrine. There, they started leaving coins, candy, small toys, and of course, Bobby's doughnuts. The young ghost was satisfied, and the technical difficulties stopped.

AUGUST 3
The Hanging of Peter Johnson, Ste. Genevieve, MO (1810)

Would you live in a haunted house?

There are plenty of people who do. And as is the case with any roommate, sometimes these folks get along with their ghostly companions, and sometimes they don't.

Bob and Stacy Browne live in the historic town of Ste. Genevieve, Missouri, in a house that is well over a hundred years old. And a house with that kind of history has every right to be haunted. It's a gentle haunting, mostly a touch on the shoulder, a tug on a pants leg, or footsteps from upstairs when nobody's there.

Records show that in 1805, the house belonged to Dr. Walter Fenwick, who used it as both home and office. He lived there with his wife and son, Zenon. Dr. Fenwick and Zenon both died in the house, and seem perfectly content to stay. But they may not be the only spirits in the house.

When the Brownes realized they were sharing their home with spirits, they did a little practical investigating. In addition to combing the historical records, they also did some digging in the dirt floor of their basement. Bob found tools and medical supplies buried beneath the house.

They also found human bones in the basement dirt.

The Brownes welcome investigators to their home, and it's been explored by a team from St. Louis under the auspices of TAPS. The team captured a voice that came through the spirit box, and identified itself as Peter Johnson.

And in 1810, Peter Johnson was the first person in Ste. Genevieve to be executed for murder.

Johnson killed John Spear in Big River Township on May 25, 1810. He was tried and found guilty, and was hanged on August 3 on the hill near Ste. Genevieve Academy. His body was given to – wait for it – Dr. Fenwick for scientific study. And when the good doctor was done with the corpse, it's entirely possible that he buried it in a handy place – the dirt floor of his own house, where Bob Browne dug up human bones 200 years later.

AUGUST 4
The Battle of Dieppe, France (1942, 1951)

The seaside village of Puys, near Dieppe, France, is a lovely place to go for a restful vacation. In 1951, two British women visited Puys in search of a quiet stay.

They didn't find it.

At 4 am on August 4, the women were startled awake by a horrendous racket coming through the open windows of their hotel room. They looked out, but even in the faint light of dawn, they couldn't see anything amiss. Then they remembered that Dieppe was the site of an Allied "practice invasion" of the French coast, and that Puys was one of the landing beaches.

On August 19, 1942, a joint operation of British and Canadian forces attacked the German-occupied port of Dieppe, in Normandy. The Allied troops would have more success on June 6, 1944, but this was no D-Day. The Allied forces weren't intending to land and then strike inland, like they would in 1944. They were just doing a practice run. Unfortunately, it was a complete disaster. The attacking force consisted of 6,086 troops. The Germans killed or wounded 3,623 of them.

The British women had lived through the war, which had only ended six years before. They knew the sound of bombers flying in formation. When they were jolted awake by the sound of men shouting, they had the presence of mind to note the time, and write down what they heard.

1951: Around 4 am, the women heard the shouts of men trying to make themselves heard. Immediately after that, they heard gunfire, exploding shells, and the scream of dive-bombers.

1942: At 3:47 am, the lead ships began to exchange shots with German ships patrolling the French coast. On shore, German soldiers shouted to each other as they got into position.

1951: At 4:50 am, the thunder of battle abruptly stopped. For seventeen minutes, the women listened to utter silence.

1942: At 4:50 am, the ships stopped shelling the beach. The attack was 17 minutes behind schedule. The gunfire was stopped, so that the invasion fleet wouldn't fire on its own men.

1951: At 5:07, the 17-minute silence was broken by the rolling crescendo of explosions and the shriek of airplane engines. Under this cacophony the women heard the faint screams of wounded men.

1942: The first wave of landing craft slammed onto the beach at Puys at 5:07 am. Fighter planes and light bombers attacked buildings along the water's edge believed to shelter German troops. Meanwhile, the 17-minute delay was proving disastrous, as men scrambled to get ashore and escape enemy fire. British ships pounded the beach in a barrage of shelling, trying to give the Allied troops some protection.

1951: At 5:40 am, the hotel room fell silent again.

1942: The British bombardment ended at 5:40 am.

1951: At 5:50 am, the women recognized the thunderous approach of many bombers flying in formation. Beneath this, they heard the sounds of desperate battle.

1942: At 5:50 am, a relief force of British bombers, flanked by heavy fighter escorts, came screaming into Dieppe to give the Allied fighters support. By now, the Luftwaffe had taken to the air, and the skies over the beaches were exploding with conflict.

1951: At 6 am, the sounds in the hotel room began to fade. By 6:25, even the thunder of shelling and the whine of aircraft engines were down to a whisper, and the moans of men were all but inaudible. By 6:55, it was all over.

1942: By 8:30 am, it was all over. The Germans were in control of the battle. Any British and Canadian troops who had survived the carnage surrendered to the German army.

Here's the weirdest thing: although the thunderous roar of aircraft engines, the shouts of fighting men, the near-deafening blast of explosions seemed to shake the entire hotel, the two women were the only people in the building who heard anything at all.

AUGUST 5
Marilyn Returns, Los Angeles, CA (1973)

Bob Slatzer, a journalist, was walking through the lobby of Twentieth Century Fox Studios one summer day in 1946 when he struck up a conversation with a pretty girl. She told him her name was Norma Jean Baker. The friendship that began that day lasted until August 4, 1962. By that time, Norma Jean had transformed herself into the Hollywood superstar Marilyn Monroe. And on August 4, 1962, she died of an overdose of barbiturates.

Slatzer mourned his friend's death, but believed that her spirit was still around him. In 1973, he participated in an experiment that brought Marilyn's spirit back for a brief moment.

Slatzer was also friends with Anton LaVey, author of *The Satanic Bible*. He discovered that LaVey was fascinated with Marilyn Monroe. One night, LaVey told Slatzer that on August 4, the eleventh anniversary of Marilyn's death, an astrological "dark moon" would occur. LaVey wanted to use the phenomenon to make Marilyn's spirit manifest, and he needed someone who knew the actress well to help him. Slatzer agreed to go along with the plan.

The two men, with Mrs. LaVey in the back seat, drove to the house in Brentwood where Marilyn had lived. They parked in the cul-de-sac outside the locked gate that led to the home.

At around 11:45 pm, LaVey started a tape running with songs from Marilyn's movies. Meanwhile, Slatzer was looking around the cul-de-sac. No one was in sight, and the night was perfectly still, without a breath of wind. LaVey had written down some sort of chant, and was reading it aloud by the soft glow of a penlight. By 12:15 am, nothing had happened.

All of a sudden, the leaves of the eucalyptus tree at the corner of the house began to toss, the branches flailing as if buffeted by high winds. The tree shook for three or four minutes, while everything else remained completely still.

Then, from nowhere, a woman appeared. Slatzer claimed that one moment she wasn't there, and the next moment, she was. She wore white slacks, a black-and-white patterned top, and white loafers. Wavy platinum-blonde hair crowned her head. The woman started to walk slowly towards the car, stopping about thirty feet away.

LaVey was sweating heavily and looked stunned, and Mrs. LaVey was white with shock and fear. Everyone in the car recognized the late Marilyn Monroe. The ghost clasped her hands in front of her, and seemed to look past the car. It was as if she wanted to go through the gates and go up to the house, but didn't want to pass the car. Then she turned to her left and started to walk down the street.

Slatzer couldn't bear it – he had to get out and talk to his friend one more time. He wrenched his door open, got out, and followed the ghost. As he came closer to her, she turned, then vanished in front of his astonished gaze.

AUGUST 6
The Happy Hollow Horror, Greensburg, KY (1932)

One August day in 1932, the Ragland family had some very unexpected visitors for breakfast.

Mr. and Mrs. Ragland and their three children lived in Happy Hollow, near Greensburg,

Kentucky. They were renting the old Blakeman place, about a mile outside of town. On that hot morning, Mrs. Ragland had just called her family to the breakfast table. Everyone had just sat down and pulled up their chairs, when there was a commotion at the door.

Mr. Ragland paused, the coffeepot hovering over his cup. Who could be at the front door at this time of the morning? Any friend or neighbor surely knew to come to the back door instead of standing on ceremony.

Then the front door was flung open with a crash, and several pairs of heavy footsteps came with a measured pace down the hardwood floor of the hallway. The intruders seemed to be headed for the back of the house, straight to the kitchen, where the Raglands sat at their rudely interrupted breakfast.

The family looked towards the kitchen door – and saw who was making the ominous footsteps. Six men, dressed in black, were marching through the hallway carrying a coffin on their shoulders. On top of the coffin was a snow-white lamb ... missing its head. Blood, shocking red against the white wool, dripped from the ragged stump of the neck. The six pallbearers stared straight ahead as they marched right past the Raglands. The back door swung open on its own, and the procession continued out the door and into the backyard. The Raglands, stunned at the bizarre sight, rose from the breakfast table and looked out the back window.

There was no sign of the six men, or the coffin, or the headless, gory lamb.

That broke the spell. Mr. Ragland ordered everyone into the car, and they roared to Greensburg to report the strange incident to the county sheriff.

Sheriff J. W. Thomas listened to the fantastical story as it came tumbling out. He grabbed Sam, his deputy, and the two men went out to the Blakeman place to check it out. They found ... nothing. There was no sign of forced entry at the front door, and the only footprints in the backyard were those left by the Raglands as they scrambled to get into the car. The neighbors hadn't seen a thing. The folks in Happy Hollow all knew each other, and someone would surely have noticed six somber strangers carrying a coffin.

The Blakeman house became a place for legend-trippers, people eager to see the house where such a bizarre event had happened. The Raglands moved out as soon as they could, and the landlord had no end of trouble getting tenants after that.

The phantom pallbearers were never seen again.

AUGUST 7
The Griffon, *Green Bay, WI (1679)*

There have been many ships lost to the Great Lakes. Between 1878 and 1898 alone, nearly 6000 shipwrecks were reported. The waves on these lakes are sharper and more unpredictable than in the ocean, and the storms can rival those on the open seas for ferocity.

Lake Michigan is particularly deadly. There are few natural harbors for a ship to find refuge. North winds sweep across the lake, stirring up dangerous winds, and currents from the Straits of Mackinac combine with the shifting sands of the coastline to make sailing very hazardous indeed.

But the early French explorers knew that the Great Lakes would someday be vital to shipping and commerce in the area, so they accepted the risks. Rene de La Salle built ships for exploration and trade. His shipyard was the bank of Cayuga Creek in the Niagara River, several miles north of the American side of the falls. His ships were made from local materials, hewn from the forest around them. Two of his ships, the *Frontenac* and the *Griffon*, would be remembered forever in maritime history.

The *Frontenac*, a 10-ton, single-decked ship, was the first European ship to be lost to the Great Lakes. She went down in Lake Ontario on January 8, 1679.

The *Griffon* has the distinction of being the first full-sized sailing ship on the Great Lakes. With a keel forty feet long, the 45-ton ship was the largest vessel ever seen in that part of the world. This really bothered the Native Americans, who considered the huge ship an insult to the Great Spirit. The Iroquois prophet Metionek reputedly warned La Salle that *Griffon* would sink.

La Salle ignored the prediction, and on August 7, 1679, he sailed from Niagara to Detroit, where several men joined the crew. The *Griffon's* maiden voyage, with La Salle, Fr. Louis Hennepin, and 32 crew members aboard, took the ship through Lake Erie, Lake Huron, and into Lake Michigan. She anchored off the shore of Green Bay, Wisconsin, where traders had collected 12,000 pounds of furs while they waited for her arrival.

La Salle decided to take four canoes and explore the area, and sent *Griffon* back to Niagara. On September 18, the pilot and five crew members set sail for the Niagara River. The *Griffon* carried a cargo of furs valued from 50,000 to 60,000 francs ($10,000 to $12,000), and the rigging and anchors for another ship La Salle planned to build.

He never saw *Griffon* again.

Some blamed the loss of the ship on an attack by the Ottawa or the Potawatomies, or even the Jesuits. Fr. Hennepin wrote that *Griffon* had been lost in a storm. This theory seems the soundest. The *Griffon* rode out a four-day storm at anchor before she left, and the day after she departed, it's recorded that a terrible storm lashed the area. Even September storms can be vicious on Lake Michigan.

Whatever the reason, La Salle had good cause to remember Metiomek's warning. The prophet had given La Salle another prediction: he'd said that La Salle's blood would cover the hands of those he trusted. In 1687, La Salle's men mutinied, and he was murdered by Pierre Duhairt.

The *Griffon* was not only the first full-size ship to sail the Great Lakes. She is also the first ghost ship to be recorded on those haunted waters. For centuries, sailors have reported seeing the lost *Griffon* in the fog in Washington Harbor, off Green Bay. The ghostly ship nearly collides with the modern vessel, vanishing at the last second. Unsurprisingly, a sighting of the *Griffon* is considered a bad omen.

AUGUST 8
Helter Skelter, Los Angeles, CA (1969)

Before Sharon Tate married Roman Polanski, she dated Jay Sebring, a wealthy hairstylist. In 1966, Sebring bought a home in Beverly Hills. The mansion had been owned, in the early 1930s, by Paul Bern, the agent who was married to movie star Jean Harlow. Bern committed suicide in the house on September 5, 1932. He and Harlow had been married two months.

Sebring invited Tate to stay at his new house while he traveled to New York on business. Tate jumped at the chance to explore the expensive home. But her stay there would be memorable for other reasons.

Sharon awoke to strange noises one night. She turned on the bedside lamp, and saw a spooky figure creeping into the bedroom – a figure that looked like descriptions she'd heard of Paul Bern. Strangest of all, the figure didn't act like either a burglar or a ghost. It bumped around the room, crashing into furniture and generally making a racket. (Bern shot himself in the head – maybe his spirit was disoriented?)

Sharon bounded out of bed, struggled into a robe, and started to go downstairs … but what she saw on the staircase was far more horrifying than a bumbling ghost.

An apparition was lying on the stairs, someone Sharon "knew" was either herself or Jay Sebring. This ghost, whoever it was, was bleeding copiously from a slashed throat.

Sharon edged past the specter, made it downstairs, and tossed back a stiff drink. Then she steeled herself and went back up the stairs, avoiding the still-bleeding corpse and dodging the other phantom, who was still clumsily navigating the bedroom. Exhausted and terrified, Sharon collapsed into bed and let the alcohol take her away.

In 1968, Sharon married director Roman Polanski. They rented a house at the end of Cielo Drive, only a mile or so from Sebring's home in Benedict Canyon. On the night of August 8, 1969, four members of the Manson Family broke into the home. They murdered Sharon Tate, Jay Sebring, and three others who were in the house.

AUGUST 9
The First Ghost in America, Sullivan, ME (1799)

It's hard to say when people started telling ghost stories. One of the first recorded ghost tales comes to us from the ancient Roman pen of Pliny the Younger. But in the New World, we Americans had to wait until 1799 for our first documented ghost sighting.

The story starts on August 9, 1799, with a banging sound coming from the cellar – an appropriate beginning. Abner Blaisdell lived in Sullivan, Maine, with his wife Mary and their seven children. The banging was so insistent that Abner went down to check it out. But he couldn't see who it was that was knocking. Thoroughly freaked out, he raced back upstairs. He was a religious man, so he fell to his knees, asking for a sign that would let him know if the knocking was benign or demonic.

The answer came the next January. Along with the knocking, the phantom of a young woman began appearing in the Blaisdell's cellar. She introduced herself as Nelly Butler, daughter of David Hooper, and the deceased wife of Captain George Butler.

Here's where things get super weird – yup, weirder than a ghost showing up in the basement. George Butler had indeed lost his wife Nelly in childbirth a few years earlier. Now, he was dating Lydia Blaisdell, Abner's second-oldest daughter. She was 15 years old. He was 29. Abner was understandably reluctant to have George sniffing after his teenage daughter. Moses Butler, George's father, was none too pleased about it either. One of the main reasons the ghost appeared, so she said, was to make sure the wedding happened.

Abner Blaisdell invited David Hooper to his home, and the two men went down to the cellar. There, Nelly Butler showed herself, and convinced David that she was his deceased daughter. She continued to appear in the Blaisdell's cellar for quite some time, giving predictions that later came true, preaching, and generally hamming it up. She appeared as a glowing, beautiful spirit dressed in white, sometimes holding her dead newborn. Once, knowing that his father was ill, Abner asked Nelly how he was doing. She replied, "He is in Heaven praising God with the angels." He had actually died the week before, and Abner hadn't yet gotten the news.

Nelly was a considerate spirit. She always knocked to announce her presence, just as a polite human visitor would. She only answered when spoken to, as she said she didn't want to startle anyone by just talking to them. She only appeared in the Blaisdell house in the cellar; she left the rest of the house to the living, respecting their privacy. (She did appear outside the Blaisdell house at times.)

By August 1800, Nelly's activity had really ramped up. She manifested on at least 29 occasions that month, eventually appearing to over a hundred people. Oddly, she wasn't always visible to everyone at the same time. Sometimes she was invisible, just a disembodied voice. Sometimes she appeared to just a few people, while those standing nearby saw nothing. She let George Butler touch her, but as witnesses watched, his hands went right through her.

Nelly made it quite clear that she wanted her former husband George to marry Lydia Blaisdell. She encouraged everyone involved, including the bride and both fathers-in-law, and she pulled it off. George and Lydia were married May 29, 1800. And in a scene straight out of a horror novel, Nelly visited the newlyweds the very next day with a prophecy: she told George he must be kind to Lydia because within the year, she would die in childbirth. Ten months later, after a complicated pregnancy, Lydia gave birth. Neither she nor the child survived.

The Nelly Butler haunting is a complicated story, and interesting in that it predates the era of American spiritualism by fifty years. A traveling evangelist named Abraham Cummings refused to believe the story, dismissing it as a hoax, until Nelly appeared to him herself. The experience changed his life. After that, he collected all the eyewitness accounts he could, and published a pamphlet about the haunting.

Over two hundred years later, all we have is circumstantial evidence – both sides, hoax or heavenly visitor, have nothing to offer but hearsay. I'll let you decide.

AUGUST 10
Petit Trianon Time Slip, Versailles, France (1901)

When we visit historic places, we can sometimes feel swept away by the tides of history. If we use our imagination and squint a little (or a lot), we can almost trick ourselves into believing that we have gone back in time to see the place in its heyday.

On August 10, 1901, two British tourists had this very experience at Versailles. Only in their case, they believed they really did go back in time.

Eleanor Jourdain, a headmistress at a college, and Anne Moberly, the principal of the school, were on vacation on France, visiting Versailles. They found the main palace boring, so they decided to visit Petit Trianon. The chateau was built in 1762 during the reign of Louis

XV. Later, Louis XVI gave it to his 19-year-old wife, Marie Antoinette, as a kind of clubhouse where she and her serving ladies could play at being rustic milkmaids.

When the two got to the gates of the Grand Trianon Park, the park was closed. They decided to try and find their way to the chateau using their guidebook. They missed the main street, and mistakenly turned down a small alley.

That was when things got weird.

Moberly saw a woman shaking a dustcloth out a window. Jourdain saw an abandoned farmhouse with a rusty plow in front of it. Neither of these sights fit their expectations of an elegant French chateau.

The women both suddenly felt a sense of dreary oppression. Everything they saw felt artificial, flat, lifeless. No wind stirred the trees. Even the people – a woman and young girl standing in front of a cottage – seemed fake somehow. They pressed on, and asked two men who looked like palace gardeners for directions. The men told them to go straight.

Moberly and Jourdain saw a man sitting near a garden shed. He was dressed in a cloak, and his dark, rough face made both women nervous. They scurried past him.

The women finally reached Petit Trianon, and Moberly saw a woman sitting on the grass, drawing in a sketchbook. The woman wore a light summer dress, and a white hat was perched on her long hair. Moberly figured the woman was a tourist, but her appearance felt odd, somehow misplaced in time.

Jourdain said she never saw this woman at all.

The women made it back to their tour group, but neither of them could shake the weird feeling. After a week, Moberly cautiously brought up her theory that maybe Petit Trianon was haunted. Jourdain agreed.

So why did the women experience their time slip on August 10? Being academics, they couldn't let the odd occurrence go without doing some research. They discovered that on August 10, 1792, the Tuleries Palace was surrounded by revolutionaries. The king's guards were all killed, and Louis and Marie Antoinette were hauled off to prison. Louis was beheaded in January 1793, and Marie followed him to the guillotine later that year, in October.

AUGUST 11
Murder in the Red Barn, Suffolk, England (1827)

It's an old story. Poor girl catches the eye of son of well-to-do family, the two fall in love and make plans to elope, guy gets cold feet and dumps the girl. But in the case of William Corder and Maria Marten, there are a few interesting wrinkles.

Murder, for a start.

Maria Marten was 24 when she started seeing 22-year-old William Corder, a son of the local squire. William wanted to keep his relationship with Maria secret, but that proved difficult – she gave birth to their child in 1827. Even with all William's flaws, she wanted to marry him.

William was not so keen on the idea. To keep Maria quiet, he suggested (in front of Maria's stepmother, Anne Marten) that he and Maria should elope. He asked her to meet him at the Red Barn.

After that, both Maria and William disappeared.

Maria's stepmother began telling people she'd had dreams that Maria had been murdered and buried in the Red Barn. In 1828, she convinced her husband to investigate. He dug in one of the grain storage bins and discovered Maria's dead body in a sack. William's handkerchief was around her neck.

The officials quickly tracked William to London. He was brought back to Suffolk and, because of the wounds on Maria's corpse, was charged with her murder. It took the jury just 35 minutes to find William Corder guilty. He was hanged on August 11, 1828.

Corder's body was taken from the gallows and given to the anatomists for dissection. His skin was tanned and used to cover a book containing an account of the trial. His skeleton was disassembled, boiled clean, then put back together to go on display at the West Suffolk Hospital.

But it was Corder's skull that had the most adventures after his death. A Dr. Kilner stole Corder's skull and put a spare skull from the anatomy lab in its place. Dr. Kilner had Corder's skull polished, and he enshrined it in a fancy box which he kept in his drawing room.

This was a bad idea. People who came into the drawing room felt a sense of unease ... then the noises started. Doors slammed violently. Hammering and sobbing sounds were heard coming from the box that held the skull.

Kilner knew he had to get rid of the skull, but how? If he brought it back to the anatomy lab, someone would surely notice that the skull was polished, and the rest of the skeleton wasn't. He decided to give the skull to F.C. Hopkins, a retired prison official.

Dr. Kilner and Mr. Hopkins both suffered a run of bad luck, and in a few months, they had both gone bankrupt. Hopkins finally gave up and bribed a gravedigger to bury the skull in consecrated ground. That decision turned out to benefit Kilner, too. Both men's bad luck eased up after that.

AUGUST 12
The Radiant Boy, England (1822)

One night in the early 1800s, Viscount Lord Castlereagh was hunting in Ireland when he was caught in a sudden storm. Through the pounding rain, he saw the lights of a manor house. He urged his horse forward, splashing through puddles on the road, until he reached the house. Sheltered from the worst of the rain by the portico, he knocked on the front door.

As it turned out, Castlereagh wasn't the only traveler caught unawares by the violent storm. The house was crowded with impromptu guests. After a good dinner, the butler showed the viscount to a bedroom, large enough, but bare of furniture, with only a mattress pulled up on the floor in front of a roaring fire. Castlereagh was too exhausted to question the odd arrangement. He lay down and fell into a deep sleep.

A few hours later, he woke suddenly. The light in the room was even brighter, and at first, the viscount thought the room was on fire. On second glance, though, he saw that the fire had gone out.

The light was coming from the apparition of a beautiful young boy. The boy glowed with an unearthly yellow light. He stared at the viscount for several long moments, then faded away.

When Castlereagh got up the next morning, he sought out his host and told him he was leaving immediately. When the host asked why, Castlereagh – who had no sense of humor – grouched that someone had played a trick on him during the night.

The host listened to Castlereagh's story, then gravely told him what it was he'd seen. The ghost, he said, was the spirit of a boy who'd been killed centuries before by his mother in a fit of madness. He admitted that the sight of the glowing ghost was a sign of terrible things to come. Whoever saw the Radiant Boy would first come into great prosperity ... then die violently.

Castlereagh brushed off the warning. He was the second son of the marquis of Londonderry, so he wasn't the heir. Also, he was in the military, so the prospect of a sudden, violent death didn't surprise him.

But fate had other plans for Lord Castlereagh. His older brother drowned in a boating accident, leaving him the heir. With this change in fortune and responsibility, the viscount left the army and went into politics. He was soon one of the most powerful men in England.

This didn't make him popular, though. He was cold and arrogant, and nobody really liked him – they just feared him. By 1822, he had become suspicious and paranoid of everyone around him. His family had him confined to his country home, and hid all of the razors and other sharp objects in the house.

But they'd overlooked what was in the viscount's desk. On the night of August 12, 1822, Lord Castlereagh went into his study, took the double-edged penknife from his desk drawer, and slit his own throat.

AUGUST 13
Abigail West, New York State (1811)

Summer storms can be things of awesome beauty and ferocity. One August afternoon in 1811, a storm blew into the area of West Mountain, west of Glen Falls, New York. Abigail West, seeing the approaching downpour, rushed to get her family's washing off the line before the rain hit. As she wrestled the last flapping sheet off the line, half-blinded by the driving rain, lightning struck – but Abigail didn't hear the crack and roll of thunder. She was killed instantly by the lightning strike. Two days later, she was buried in a small cemetery nearby.

Abigail joined the spirits who wander the mountains of rural New York State. In the late 1800s, hunters told of meeting a woman in the forest, and of hearing a strange wailing in the woods, especially in August, and most especially during storms.

Of course, in the forest, the bark of a fox or the shriek of a bobcat can sound like a woman screaming. But that doesn't explain the strong scent of perfume that witnesses have smelled in the vicinity of the West's old farm.

In the early 1970s, a local radio station sent a crew to West Mountain to see if they could record any ghostly wailing. The crew sat in a van, waiting out the rain that poured down for hours. After two hours, the crew recorded a scream coming from the woods behind West Cemetery. To those who cried "hoax", the radio show host pointed out that the crew hadn't told anyone they were headed out in search of Abigail. Who, then, would have hid for hours in the dark, rainy woods?

AUGUST 14
Haunting at the Old Fort, Fort Yates, ND (1876 – recurring)

Fort Yates, North Dakota, is the tribal headquarters for the Standing Rock Sioux tribe. The fort was established in 1863 to oversee several bands of Sioux.

In 1868, the land was given to the Sioux under the Fort Laramie Treaty, but the army retained a military presence at the fort. In 1878, the fort's name was changed from the Standing Rock Cantonment to Fort Yates, to honor Captain George Yates, who was killed at the Battle of Little Bighorn. (You have to wonder how the Sioux felt about this.)

The fort is home to a residual haunting. On the 14th day of every month, Captain Yates returns to show his appreciation for the army naming the fort in his memory. He appears in the north section of the original fort. He walks a short distance, turns, walks back, and vanishes. Short, sweet, residual.

AUGUST 15
The Fort Dearborn Massacre, Chicago, IL (1812)

Chicago is known for its rich ghost lore. And the stories begin far back in the city's history.

Many people who walk through Chicago's bustling Loop don't realize that they're hurrying through what was once terrifying wilderness. Fort Dearborn was carved out of the frontier forest in 1803. It sat on a hill that is now the south bank of the Chicago River at Michigan Avenue.

As part of the Treaty of Paris, which ended the Revolutionary War, Britain gave the Northwest Territory – Ohio, Indiana, Illinois, Michigan, and Wisconsin – to the United States in 1783. The Native Americans were not okay with this. The powerful Shawnee chief Tecumseh formed a confederation of tribes to block westward expansion. The British considered the natives their allies, as they formed a buffer between the new United States and Britain's Canadian colonies, so they provided them with arms.

By 1811, it was clear that the United States and Britain would soon be at war again. Tensions between settlers and natives in the Fort Dearborn area increased. On June 18, 1812, the United State declared war on the British. General William Hull ordered Fort Dearborn evacuated. He told the fort's commander, Captain Nathan Heald, to destroy all the arms and ammunition, and give the rest of the supplies to the local Potawatomi tribe. Hull hoped the Potawatomies would agree to escort the settlers to Fort Wayne.

Heald thought this was a good idea – but in talks with the Potawatomies, he gave them the impression that he'd be giving them the fort's guns, ammo, provisions, and whiskey. Actually, Heald ordered the guns, ammo, and booze destroyed. A Potawatomi chief named Black Partridge warned Heald that his warriors were furious at the deception, and wanted to attack.

At 9 am on August 15, 1812, the garrison left Fort Dearborn. Fifty-four soldiers, twelve militia, nine women, and eighteen children headed to Fort Wayne, accompanied by about thirty Miami natives. They got about two miles south of the fort, picking their way across the lakefront sand dunes, when 500 Potawatomies attacked. Within fifteen minutes, sixty-eight people lay dead on the sand. Twenty-eight soldiers, seven women, and six children were taken prisoner.

The fort was burned to the ground. The site of Fort Dearborn is where Wells Street now runs. Tourists taking pictures in the area sometimes capture ghostly images. It's said that phantoms dressed in early 19th century clothing still wander the area.

AUGUST 16
The Fire Goddess, Hawaii (ongoing)

We tend to think of gods and goddesses as dim, dusty figures, white marble sculptures out of mythology. But for some cultures, their gods are very real.

Take Pele, the fire goddess of Hawaiian folklore. She is one of the seven Hiiake sisters. Beautiful and imperious, she demands respect. In the olden days, she wandered the islands of Hawaii until she reached the Big Island. She dug day and night until she reached fire. This pleased her, and she stayed at the cozy hearth. Now, Kilauea Crater on the side of Mauna Loa is officially Pele's home. The Volcano House Hotel, built on the crater's rim, is spared destruction only because the owner regularly pours gin into the volcano to keep Pele happy.

The fire goddess is capricious, but she rewards those who show her respect. Once, two girls whose families lived in opposite ends of the same house were roasting breadfruit over a campfire. An old lady came up to them, and one girl offered her some breadfruit, while the other girl ignored her. The old woman told the generous girl to mark her door that night. The girl told her parents what had happened. Realizing that the girl had seen Pele, the parents tacked a tapa leaf to the door. That night, a slow stream of red-hot lava crept quietly down from the mountain above the village. It spread out as it went, and when it reached the village, it oozed over the end of the house where the selfish girl and her family lay sleeping, and incinerated them. The other end of the house, where the generous girl and her family lived, was untouched.

This story from folklore might seem fanciful, but there have been plenty of times when a flow of lava has mysteriously diverted itself around a building, leaving it unharmed. This happens after the inhabitants have prayed to Pele. In 1960, the lighthouse at Kapoho was in the direct path of flowing lava. People in the lighthouse prayed frantically to Pele to spare them as the flaming lava poured down the mountain. Just before tragedy struck, the lava flow diverted from its path and flowed into the sea, sparing the lighthouse.

Sometimes, Pele appears to her people, manifesting as a beautiful woman in a fiery dress. She's usually accompanied by a small white dog. On August 16, 1959, a woman of ethereal beauty, in a red dress, asked for help finding her room at Hilton's Hawaiian Village Hotel. As an employee walked the woman to her room, she abruptly vanished, leaving the employee convinced he'd had a brief encounter with the inscrutable goddess.

AUGUST 17
The Great Boat Race, Mississippi River, Iowa (1858)

When you were a kid, did you ever try to cheat a little when running a race with your brother or sister, by not telling them the two of you were actually racing until it was halfway through? No? Just me?

That's exactly what happened on the Mississippi River on August 17, 1858. The steamboat *Itasca*, with David Whitten as her captain, ran on the upper Mississippi between St. Louis and St. Paul. One of her rivals was the *Grey Eagle*, captained by Daniel Smith Harris. Captain Harris had built the *Grey Eagle* with $60,000 of his own money, and he was proud of owning the fastest boat on the upper river.

On August 16, 1858, the first transatlantic telegraph message was sent from Queen Victoria to President Buchanan. The next day, the message was given to the *Itasca*, to be delivered to St. Paul (which had no telegraph line). Captain Harris, though, decided *he* wanted to deliver the Queen's message ahead of anyone else.

Telegraph lines ran to Dunleith, where the *Grey Eagle* was loading cargo bound for St. Paul, and to Prairie du Chien, where the *Itasca* was also being loaded, also headed for St. Paul. Both boats were scheduled to depart at 9 am. Captain Harris, at Dunleith, had 65 miles farther to go than Captain Whitten did – but here's the thing: Whitten had no idea he was in a race.

Harris grabbed copies of the Dubuque and Galena newspapers, containing the Queen's message and President Buchanan's reply. Then he poured on the coal – and pitch, grease, anything combustible, even butter – steaming madly north for St. Paul. He didn't even stop to deliver the freight he was carrying, but left those stops for his return trip. The *Grey Eagle* carried the mail, just like *Itasca* did, but the mail sacks just got thrown onto the shore as the boat ran along. Since the *Grey Eagle* was so far ahead of schedule, there weren't any mail sacks ready for her, so she didn't even slow down. The passengers were offered free meals and berth to stay on board without complaint. They knew they were about to be part of a record-breaking feat, so they agreed.

Meanwhile, the *Itasca* went steadily along at her usual pace. Captain Whitten stopped at every scheduled landing, loaded and unloaded cargo, and paused to chat with the stationmasters about the momentous message he was carrying.

Just a few miles from St. Paul, Whitten happened to glance behind him, and recognized the *Grey Eagle* churning up the river almost ten hours ahead of schedule and getting closer all the time. He realized that Harris was trying to beat the *Itasca* to St. Paul and be the first to deliver the Queen's message. Whitten ordered "full steam ahead". The *Itasca* was not a slow boat, and if Whitten had known from the beginning that Harris wanted to race, she would probably have won. As it was, the boats were neck and neck at the end, and *Itasca* won by less than a length. But Harris wrapped the newspapers around a piece of wood, tied them securely, stood on the *Grey Eagle's* roof, and threw the message to shore. He had won.

But Harris was to discover that being a jerk doesn't pay. A few years later, in 1861, the *Grey Eagle* collided with the Rock Island Bridge and sank in less than five minutes. Captain Harris got the karma that was coming to him. He retired to his home in Galena, broken-hearted by the loss of his beautiful ship. It was the only accident Harris was ever involved in, but it was the last. He never commanded a steamboat again.

But on some foggy nights on the Mississippi, people say they can still see the two ships battling in a race only one of them knew about.

AUGUST 18
Haunted Loras College, Dubuque, IA (2004)

The motto of Loras College is "achieve more than a degree." As with many institutes of higher learning, this small Catholic college in Dubuque offers more than just classes in its educational experience. Students can also run across a ghost or two on campus. Or even off-campus.

In the fall semester of 2009, a group of students who lived in a residence house on Belmont Street began to experience strange noises. Students watching television on the first floor would hear footsteps on the second floor, even when no one was up there. Soon, the footsteps were joined by phantom voices in empty rooms. The students complained to the Student Life Office, which promised to send a priest to bless the house (although nothing ever came of that).

Light was shed on the mystery when the next-door neighbor told the residents that a student had killed himself in the building a few years before. An employee of the college who had some psychic abilities said that the young man's soul was trapped, and that he didn't mean any harm; he just wanted to be remembered.

A ghost that just wants to be acknowledged is still a ghost, and that freaks some people out. When a television came on by itself in a locked room, and the students saw unexplained tears in the eyes of a picture of a child, they were unnerved enough to try to resolve the haunting.

Research into the neighbor's story pointed them to Saroj Simkhada. The biochemistry major had killed himself in August 2004 when his girlfriend broke up with him. The students contacted a paranormal investigator, who suggested a sensible approach: since Simkhada, who was Nepalese, had been Hindu, and since one of the house's current residents was also Hindu, why not hold a Hindu funeral ceremony? The students took this advice, and it seems to have worked. The building is no longer haunted.

AUGUST 19
Geysers of Dirt, Fish Lake, MN (1940)

MANY ARE MYSTIFIED BY SOIL-BLOWING IN FISH LAKE CORNFIELD
Manifestations First Noticed on Monday, August 19
Hundreds of People Have Visited Mrs. Effie Snell Farm and Wondered

Marvin Oldenburg was a teenager in 1940. His job was to collect raw milk from farms and bring it to Minneapolis for processing. The Snells only had a half-dozen cows, enough for half a can of extra milk, but Oldenburg still stopped to collect it.

One morning in late August, Roland Snell rushed out to meet Marvin's truck when his friend drove into the farm's lane. The boys were about the same age, and had been friends for years. Today, Roland had something weird to show his friend.

Roland, Marvin, Roland's three sisters, and a brother all walked down to a cornfield where twisted stalks, thinly spaced, were struggling to grow. The field was more dirt than corn, it seemed. That was what Roland wanted to show his friend.

"Goddammit, here came the dirt," Marvin recalled seventy years later. "I don't know who threw it or how it got out there, but it came … falling out of the sky. How it got up there I couldn't tell you. It was just coming down." Dirt was geysering up from the ground and pattering down in a shower of rocks and dust.

When he got back to town, Marvin shared the weirdness with another friend. They both came back out to the farm, and saw the flying dirt again. Marvin then told another friend, Herman Schultz, who also wanted to see the anomaly. Back out to the farm Marvin went, Herman in tow.

"We walked through the doggone corn again, and I told them I wanted [everyone] ahead of us so we can watch everything they're doing," Marvin said. "We walked in there a little way, and the dirt started flying. We walked a little farther in, and Herman said that's enough; let's get out of here."

As it turned out, Herman had a theory about the dirt explosions. He suggested they were the work of a poltergeist.

Roland Snell's father, Fred, had died young not too long before, leaving Effie and the children to fend for themselves. Before he died, Fred and the pastor of the local Lutheran church had gotten into a disagreement. The children had been going to a confirmation class, which Fred pulled them from. He also forbade the family from going to weekly services.

On his deathbed, though, Fred accepted a visit from the pastor. Afterwards, he made Effie promise to take the children back to church. But after Fred died, Effie let the promise slide. The Snells didn't attend church, and Effie didn't send the children back for catechism classes.

Herman told Marvin he would ask the pastor to visit the Snells, which he did. The children were enrolled in religion classes again, and the family started attending church every Sunday.

Soon afterwards, the mysterious eruptions of dirt stopped.

AUGUST 20
The White Stallion, Drawbridge, MD (late 19th century)

The roads of Dorchester County in Maryland are haunted by the apparition of a white horse and the two riders it carries. Late in the 19th century, a gypsy man fell in love with a beautiful local girl. The two were to be married, but the girl's seven brothers were against the union. They killed the groom, leaving their sister heartbroken.

But with the murder, the brothers brought a gypsy curse on themselves. Every year for seven years, one of the brothers suffered a mysterious death. In the eighth year, the young woman herself fell into a coma and died.

Several years later, in the early 1900s, a ghost began to wander the roads around Drawbridge. To be accurate, three ghosts appeared: the ill-fated young woman, her gypsy lover, and the white horse that carries them through eternity.

AUGUST 23
The Angel of Mons, Belgium (1914)

One of the most famous battles of World War I was the Battle of Mons, which pitted French and British troops against the German army. The battle was one of a heartbreaking series of struggles during that global conflict, as British and French forces desperately tried to keep the Germans from reaching Paris. However vital the battle is to military history, though, it's also famous for its supernatural aspect. It was during the retreat from the battle that the British Expeditionary Force got help from an unexpected source.

The British were badly outnumbered, but they fought valiantly, dropping many German soldiers as they retreated step by hot, muggy step. The Brits were facing four-to-one odds, and the August heat was taking its toll. By August 26, the battle had been raging for three days, and some of the British soldiers hadn't eaten in 24 hours. A division commander, watching the fighting withdrawal, commented tearfully, "The Germans may be able to kill them, but by God they can't beat them."

Supernatural help was on the way. Tall, unearthly figures materialized in the gloom over the battlefield. Through the smoke of the incessant shooting, both German and British soldiers saw heavenly beings joining in the battle, defending the British as they fell back. Some soldiers said they saw St. George, patron saint of England, wearing golden armor and sitting astride a huge white horse. Others said they saw the warrior angel St. Michael, his divine sword drawn for action. Still others saw angels, their massive wings outspread, hovering in the gathering darkness. Phantom bowmen, English archers from the Battle of Agincourt centuries before, sent volley after volley of ghostly arrows into the German lines, buying time for the British troops' escape. German officers, finding hundreds of soldiers dead on the battlefield with no apparent wounds, concluded that the British had used poison gas.

Several soldiers shared their experiences with Red Cross nurses, and later with magazine and newspaper reporters. Some of the witnesses were regular rank and file, but others were officers, men who weren't prone to hysteria or delusion.

Was it exhaustion, or delusion, or just plain wishful thinking? Battle fatigue can mess with soldiers' perceptions, no doubt about it. Skeptics pointed out that it was impossible to authenticate these fanciful stories, which was true. But keep in mind that the spectral vision of phantom archers, St. George, and St. Michael were reported at different times and in different places. The soldiers telling these tales were tough, no-nonsense men, experienced fighters who had no time for fairy tales. Maybe they were hallucinating.

And maybe they weren't.

AUGUST 22
Ghosts of Katrina, New Orleans, LA (2005)

The city of New Orleans has long been the home of countless ghosts, haints, and phantoms. With the coming of Hurricane Katrina, the spectral population jumped considerably.

Over the course of less than a week, Katrina went from a gentle breeze over the Atlantic to a towering dervish of destruction, causing more than $125 billion in damage, and snuffing out over 1,200 lives.

The hauntings began almost immediately. Thousands of people sought refuge in the Superdome. The huge stadium already had a reputation for being haunted, as it had been built over the abandoned Girod Street Cemetery. But the sheer human misery that drenched the Superdome in the days after Katrina shone a supernatural magnifying glass on the place that became a makeshift refugee center, hospital, and morgue rolled into one. People in desperate need of life's basics – food, water, shelter – could only sit and mourn their lost loved ones while chaos raged around them. With the natural disaster came a breakdown of society: rape, robberies, and murder were rampant in the damaged, reeling city. The Superdome still feels the stain of those terrifying days; there's still a general feeling of wrongness in those corridors.

It can be hard to put a human face on such an overwhelming tragedy. But New Orleans has a human face: Vera Smith. Vera, 66 years old, ventured out to find supplies for herself and her partner, Max Keene. She was hit and killed by a drunk driver. Her body lay on the street for days, as authorities had far more pressing problems. Caring neighbors covered the body, and eventually made a makeshift grave. Vera's body was eventually cremated and taken to her parents' gravesite in Texas.

A restaurant, Deanie's Seafood Kitchen, now stands on the site where Vera was killed. The restaurant is plagued with strange encounters. Another restaurant, Charcoals, that predated Deanie's was also said to be haunted. Lights would flicker, ghosts appeared in the windows, and at times the temperature would plummet to freezing within moments. The folk-religion-minded citizens of New Orleans have taken Vera's spirit under their wing, and regularly cast spells to help the desolate ghost.

AUGUST 23
Death of a Legend, Hollywood, CA (1926, recurring)

Rudolph Valentino was one of the early superstars of the silver screen. The lithe, handsome Italian came to New York City around 1912 and began his career at Maxim's as a "taxi dancer" – he was paid by club patrons to dance with them. He found his way into the theater, and soon moved to California.

There, he started off as a movie extra, then moved up to bit parts. Screenwriter June Mathis saw Valentino perform in 1919's *The Eyes of Youth*, and cast him in the lead role in her next film, *The Four Horsemen of the Apocalypse* (1921). From there, Valentino was cast in the movie that would catapult him the immortality: *The Sheik*.

Valentino became a megastar of the 1920s. Women drooled over his dark good looks; men scorned him as being unmasculine, but copied his smooth-as-butter appearance, hoping to attract the ladies just as the Great Lover did. Over the next seven years, Valentino made fourteen movies, and had the world on a silver platter.

On August 15, 1926, Valentino collapsed at the Hotel Ambassador in New York City. He underwent emergency surgery for a perforated ulcer, but developed peritonitis. Eight days later, he was dead. He was only 31, and at the height of his fame.

Women (and a few men) all over the world were plunged into mourning. Pola Negri,

Valentino's actress girlfriend, collapsed sobbing in front of his casket. After a week's worth of services in New York, Valentino's body was shipped back to California. June Mathis, who'd given him his first break, had Valentino laid to rest in her family crypt in Hollywood Forever Cemetery. (It was supposed to be a temporary arrangement, but he's still there.)

The Great Lover's giant personality couldn't be dimmed by death. His ghost has been seen in the costume department at Paramount Pictures (whose lot, conveniently, is next to the cemetery). He's also been seen at his beach house, in the suite of his favorite hotel, at an apartment building called Valentino Place, and at Falcon's Lair, his palatial Hollywood home. His spirit hangs out in the stables at Falcon's Lair, and one of the stable hands quit after seeing Valentino petting his favorite horse at sunset one evening. An animal lover, Valentino seems to have company in the afterlife. His Great Dane, Kabar, haunts the pet cemetery where he is buried. Visitors to Kabar's grave have heard a large dog panting and barking, and a few have even been licked.

Valentino and his faithful dog are not the only ghosts in this story. For many years, a mysterious veiled woman, dressed in mourning black, brought a bouquet of flowers to Valentino's temporary-permanent resting place on August 23. The click-clack of her heels on the mausoleum's floor would announce her annual visit.

Of course, this devoted fan no longer visits her idol in the flesh. The mysterious woman is believed to have died in 1955. The unmistakable click of her heels no longer echoes along the Cathedral corridor. But she is still seen moving silently through the mausoleum's hallways.

And every year on August 23, a bouquet of flowers is left at Valentino's crypt.

AUGUST 24
The White House Burns, Washington, DC (1814, 1953)

Tensions between England and her former colonies hadn't completely subsided after the American Revolution. A generation later, the War of 1812 flared. The British took this opportunity to invade the capital and on August 24, British troops burned the White House. Dolley Madison famously saved a portrait of George Washington and a copy of the Declaration of Independence.

In 1953, the ghost of a British soldier carrying a torch appeared in a White House bedroom. The couple staying there while they visited the Eisenhowers said that the spirit spent the entire night trying to set their bed on fire. Apparently, the soldier didn't realize he was 141 years late to the party.

AUGUST 25
A Helpful Ghost, Mobile, AL (1852)

In the early hours of August 22, 1852, rain began to fall in Mobile, Alabama. Strong winds started to pummel the area. The Great Mobile Hurricane had begun. Winds pushed waters from the Gulf of Mexico into Mobile Bay, causing the worst flooding the city had ever experienced. Eighteen inches of rain fell, and streets flooded to depths of ten to twelve feet.

Captain Hugh Barlow was no stranger to the perils of hurricanes. He designed and built his house to be able to float in case of a flood. Being a responsible dog owner, he built his dog's house to float too, just in case. The doghouse was even fitted with a weathervane and a ship's bell.

Captain Barlow – and his dog – are still warning other sailors of approaching storms. When a hurricane threatens Mobile Bay, boaters have seen two strange crafts out on the water. First, a doghouse appears, with a dog – a cocker spaniel, by the looks of him – standing in the doorway. The ringing of the bell on the doghouse presages the appearance of the second phantom: a two-story house, also floating in the choppy water. A white-bearded man in the uniform of a sea captain dances on the porch, waving a lantern as he dips and reels, keeping his footing against the pitch of the waves.

A sighting of Captain Barlow means a hurricane is coming: he's been seen before storms in August 1950 and in 1932 and 1926, and in 1906 and 1893. The captain and his dog were seen in September 1979, and three days later, on September 12, Hurricane Frederick struck. The storm damaged three out of every four buildings in Mobile, and caused over $2.2 billion in damage. But because of Captain Barlow's warning, more than 100,000 people were evacuated. In that incredibly destructive storm, only one person was killed.

AUGUST 26
Wreck at Bostian Bridge, Statesville, NC (1891, recurring)

It doesn't pay to get in a hurry. Around 2:30 am on August 27, 1891, the Richmond & Danville Railroad Engine Number 9 left Statesville, North Carolina, pulling six cars: a tender, a baggage car, a first-class coach, a second-class car, a Pullman sleeper, and the R&D's superintendent's private car. Engineer William West was 34 minutes late leaving the station, so he poured on the steam.

Less than five minutes later, the train came off the rails as it crossed Bostian Bridge. The train, traveling 35 to 40 mph, was literally airborne when it derailed. The sleeping car hit the ground 153 feet from where it left the bridge. All seven of the cars smashed into Third Creek, sixty feet below.

Nearly thirty passengers were injured – nine seriously – and 23 of them were dead. Dazed passengers pulled themselves from the wreckage. Others sat on top of the train cars until help arrived. A few walked back into Statesville to report the accident. Statesville had no hospital, so the injured were taken to private homes for treatment. The dead were laid out in the Farmer's Tobacco Warehouse for identification.

Such a tragic accident was bound to have repercussions, and the wreck regularly replays itself on the anniversary. In 1941, fifty years after the accident, a woman was waiting on the side of the road near the tracks when she saw a phantom train drive right off the bridge. She was waiting for her husband to return after their car got a flat tire, but a train wreck was much more urgent. She ran to the edge of the embankment and looked over to see a steaming, twisted mass of metal. But when she dragged her husband to see the wreck, no trace of the mangled train could be seen. The woman, confused, made her husband drive to the Statesville train station to ask if any crashes had been reported. When the station agent told them about the 1891 wreck, the woman screamed and fainted.

Since this is a recurring haunting, Bostian Bridge is a favorite site for ghost hunters. Unfortunately, in 2010, on the 119th anniversary of the crash, a trespassing pedestrian was hit and killed, and two others were injured, when they mistook a real train hurtling toward them for the ghost train.

AUGUST 27
Rivals, Winona, MN (1915)

Morning Mass in the Catholic Church is normally a peaceful time, an opportunity for quiet reflection. But in the chapel on the second floor of St. Mary's Hall, Bishop Patrick Heffron had his private time rudely interrupted. On August 27, 1915, Father Louis Michael Lesches came into the chapel and shot the bishop twice as he knelt in prayer.

Father Lesches had been aching for an assignment to his own parish for years. But Bishop Heffron, his superior, refused to give him a posting. He found Fr. Lesches "eccentric, peculiar, and unreliable", unfit to serve as a pastor. The mentally unstable Lesches seethed under this slight. Bishop Heffron was a man of strong character and iron will, someone who did what he thought was best for his flock whether others liked it or not. Once he'd made up his mind, he could not be swayed.

Years of conflict between the two men finally boiled over into violence. Lesches came into the bishop's private chapel armed with a Smith & Wesson revolver. He fired four times, and two of those shots found their mark. The second round smashed into the bishop's thigh. The third shot hit the tabernacle, but by the fourth shot, Lesches was close enough to aim directly at Heffron's heart. Heffron threw out his left arm to deflect the shot. The final shot, delivered so close that the bishop's vestments had powder burns on them, lodged in Heffron's chest. Lesches fled the chapel and retreated to his room, where he was arrested shortly after the attack.

Bishop Heffron, tough old goat that he was, survived the shooting, and testified at Lesches' trial. Father Lesches was acquitted by reason of insanity, and spent the rest of his life in the State Hospital for the Dangerous Insane at St. Peter, Minnesota. He died there in 1943 at the age of 84. He'd spent almost 28 years in the asylum. (Being locked up didn't stop his vindictive streak. Remember the story for May 13? Go back and revisit it, if you like. I'll wait here.)

Heffron, 56 years old at the time of the shooting, recovered quickly and lived another twelve years, dying of cancer at the age of 68.

The ghost of Fr. Lesches, still bitter and insane after death, still haunts Saint Mary's College. He is especially active in Heffron Hall, the dormitory built in 1921 and named in honor of his arch-nemesis. The antagonistic phantom concentrates his energy on the third floor, causing cold spots and anomalous breezes. There have also been a few face-to-face confrontations. One student, startled by the priest's sudden appearance, threw a punch – and broke his hand when the punch hit the wall behind the ghost.

AUGUST 28
The Haunting of Esther Cox, Amherst, Nova Scotia (1878)

There was nothing particularly special about 19-year-old Esther Cox. In fact, she was often described as plain, chubby, and unpleasantly sulky. But the fact that she was available seemed to be enough for Bob McNeal. He asked Esther to join him on a buggy ride, and she accepted his invitation. The date was August 28, 1878 … a day that marked the beginning of one of the strangest, most violent hauntings in Canadian history.

The outing did not go well. McNeal picked Esther up at the home of her sister and brother-in-law, Olive and Daniel Teed. They drove out of town, and McNeal stopped the buggy along a dirt road halfway through a stand of forest. He tried to force Esther to go with him into the woods, but she sensibly refused. He pulled a pistol on her, and threatened harm if she didn't go along with his wishes. Luckily, another wagon happened along the narrow road, and Esther was saved from rape by the appearance of potential witnesses.

McNeal, furious at having his fun spoiled, whipped his horse into a gallop, throwing Esther back against the buggy seat. To add insult to injury, it started pouring rain, and McNeal didn't stop to put the buggy's top up. He just drive Esther home, fuming all the way.

When he dropped her off at the Teeds', McNeal barely stopped the buggy long enough for Esther to clamber out. Then he raced away, leaving Esther to make her way inside, dripping and humiliated. She crept up to the bedroom she shared with her sister, Jane, changed out of her sodden clothes, crawled into bed, and cried herself to sleep.

One look at Esther's red eyes and puffy face the next morning told the family that Esther's date had not gone well. They prudently gave her space, and didn't pry. This white-glove treatment lasted four days – but on the fourth night, something happened to take everyone's mind off of Esther's fizzled love life.

Jane and Esther were drifting off to sleep, when Esther hopped out of bed, shrieking that she'd felt a mouse. She and Jane stripped the bed, but found nothing. As they were making the bed, Jane noticed movement under the mattress. She pointed out that the mouse was inside the mattress, so it couldn't crawl on them. The girls went to bed.

The next night, they woke everyone in the house with their screams. When Daniel Teed burst into the room, he saw Esther and Jane crouched on the floor, a pile of quilt squares in front of them.

Babbling in fear, the girls tried to explain – they'd heard more scratching, and thought the mouse had gotten into their quilting supplies. Daniel couldn't understand what had the girls all worked up – until they pointed to the corner of the room.

The box that held the quilt squares was floating in mid-air. It swooped and danced, suspended by an invisible force. It soared around the room for hours, while the family watched, stunned.

The next night brought even more excitement. Jane was sound asleep when she was woken by Esther's terrified scream. She lit a lamp – then let out a shriek of her own. Esther's skin was hot to the touch, and blood-red, nearly glowing. Her eyes bulged, and her hair was standing on end as if electrified. As Daniel came into the room to see what all the screaming was about, Esther's body began to swell to almost twice its size.

Olive, Esther's older sister, followed on Daniel's heels. She gasped as she saw Esther's grossly swollen features, and shrieked, "She's going to burst!" Just then, three loud bangs came from under the bed, and Esther suddenly deflated.

In the morning, Daniel Teed sent for Dr. Thomas Carritte. The doctor, of course, didn't believe a word of Daniel's story, but agreed to examine Esther.

It didn't go well.

The doctor watched, stunned, as Esther's pillow slid back and forth under her head. Then, the family heard scratching coming from the wall above Esther's head. Letters nearly a foot high appeared as if being scratched into the plaster by an invisible hand: ESTHER COX, YOU ARE MINE TO KILL. After the chilling message had been delivered, a chunk of plaster threw itself across the room.

The poltergeist activity continued, stunning in its inventiveness and ferocity. Dr. Carritte was pelted with a torrent of potatoes that appeared out of thin air. Lit matches materialized and dropped onto furniture – and onto people's clothes. A neighbor's pocketknife was wrenched from his hands and stabbed into Esther's back. Forks would whiz through the air and embed themselves in the walls. Reverend Temple, the family's Methodist minister, saw a bucket of cold drinking water, which had been set on the kitchen table, come to a rolling boil.

Trying to protect the majority of his family, Daniel sent Esther away to live elsewhere, but her hosts sent her back in pretty short order, as the poltergeist phenomena followed her from place to place. This ended up getting Esther into serious trouble. Daniel found Esther a job working on Arthur Davison's farm. Soon after her arrival, some items belonging to the family with whom she had last stayed appeared in Davison's barn. Esther was accused of theft. Then, before an investigation could get underway, the barn caught fire and burned to the ground. Esther swore it was the poltergeist who'd done it, but the fact remained that she was the last person seen near the barn. A skeptical judge sentenced her to four months in prison.

This seemed to break the poltergeist's hold on Esther. She was released early, and met someone and got married. She didn't have any more paranormal trouble for the rest of her life.

So what was going on in the Amherst poltergeist case? Was it true poltergeist energy, released by the troubled Esther? She lived in close quarters with a large family, and may have sensed that she was very much a fifth wheel. She may also have experienced repressed sexual desires, a sure recipe for poltergeist activity around adolescent girls.

Did Esther just create the phenomena herself? She could have simply wanted attention. But it was generally agreed that while she was hysterical, flighty, and unpopular, she also wasn't terribly bright. She certainly couldn't have pulled off the spectacular manifestations around her.

There's another theory to examine in the Amherst case. Bob McNeal may have been responsible for the poltergeist activity. His attempted rape may have knocked some repressed sexuality loose in Esther, resulting in release of uncontrollable, unconscious energy. That's one possibility.

Here's something else to consider: no one ever saw or heard from McNeal after the night of August 28. Maybe, fearing retribution for the attempted assault, he just left town. But he could also have gone to some secluded part of the forest and committed suicide. In that case, it's possible that it was his ghost that came back to torment Esther for her refusal. There's an interesting postscript that supports this theory: at times, Esther and her family were able to communicate with the entities in the house. The entities claimed that there were three spirits involved in the haunting, and that the most violent of the three was "Bob Nickel" – which could be a pseudonym for "Bob McNeal". Food for thought.

AUGUST 29
Tragedy on Vacation, Ely, NV (1954)

In August 1954, Larry Exline took a two-week vacation to go fishing in Nevada with friends. His wife, Juliette, happily waved goodbye as he left. He'd been working so hard – he deserved a break.

On the night of August 29, Juliette was startled awake by the sound of Larry's voice calling to her. He sounded as if he was hurt. Juliette got out of bed and went into the hallway. Larry was at the end of the hall, sagging against the wall. His clothes were sodden with blood, and he could barely stand.

Juliette screamed and ran towards him, but he held up a bloody hand to stop her. "Don't touch me," he warned. "I must return." Juliette begged him to explain, but first she said she needed to call a doctor for him.

Before Juliette could pick up the receiver, the telephone rang. It was a sheriff from Ely, Nevada, calling to tell her that Larry had been in a car crash, and that he had died instantly. "No, you're wrong," Juliette insisted. "My husband's here."

She dropped the phone and rushed back into the hall – but Larry wasn't there.

AUGUST 30
A Faithful Friend, Edisto Island, SC (1862)

The story of the Civil War is a story of separation. Men, of both North and South, left their families to fight for a cause they supported. Some never returned.

John Beaujot Legare grew up on Edisto Island, the son of a wealthy rice grower. John's father died when John was quite young, but left the family well-off. John came of age learning the secrets of crop management from his uncles. He was a strong, sensible young man who took good care of the plantation he'd inherited, and of his widowed mother.

Soon after his father's death, someone had given John a puppy. John named the dog Moses, and the two became inseparable. Moses bonded with John in the way only a dog can, and followed John all over the plantation.

Edisto Island was an isolated marshland. A single one-lane wooden bridge connected it to the mainland. But the war touched the remote community nonetheless. As soon as the guns at Fort Sumter fired, John Legare enlisted in Company A of the First South Carolina Volunteer Infantry. He left behind his plantation, his worried mother … and his devoted dog.

Animals sometimes seem to have a sixth sense, knowing when something is about to happen before humans have a clue. Moses moped for weeks after John left, but one morning, he trotted to the end of the Legare's lane to the main road and sat there expectantly. Soon, the postman delivered a letter from John.

Mrs. Legare was overjoyed to get a letter from her son. Moses seemed comforted to hear from his master, but his blue mood continued. He wouldn't be truly happy, Mrs. Legare knew, until John came home safe and sound.

She knew exactly how Moses felt.

Moses always seemed to know when a letter from John would arrive, and he would go down the lane to meet the postman at the main road. But one day in late August, Moses changed his behavior. He went down and sat in the middle of the main road, and wouldn't budge. He ignored the wagon traffic around him, and didn't even look at the riders that had to steer their horses to miss him.

He stayed there all that night.

In the morning, Mrs. Legare walked down the lane to find Moses still sitting there. Her heart lifted, thinking that perhaps they'd get a letter from John. But Moses was acting strangely. He got up and walked down the road as Mrs. Legare followed him. He walked all the way to the bridge that connected the island to the mainland. There he sat, staring across the bridge, whining softly.

Mrs. Legare finally convinced Moses to come home, but the dog's steps were a dispirited plod as he followed her. She shivered despite the hot summer air. What news did Moses have about John, that she hadn't yet heard?

The next day, a man passed Moses as the dog sat at the end of the Legare lane. The man was coming from the grocery store, the hub of local news. This time, the news was bad.

On August 30, Private John Legare had fallen at the Second Battle of Bull Run. He'd survived the first day of battle, but on the second day, a bullet had found him.

John Legare was buried from the Presbyterian church, and laid to rest in the Legare tomb. A sister-in-law, Julia Legare, had passed in 1852, and John joined her in eternal sleep. Moses came into the mausoleum as his master was being laid to rest. He lay down next to the casket, growling and snapping at anyone who came near. John's mother, herself grieving her son's loss, insisted that the heavy marble door of the mausoleum be left open until the dog had finished his own mourning.

Moses stayed at John's side, refusing food and water, growing weaker and weaker. Within a week, the dog had died of a broken heart.

Mrs. Legare had Moses carried home and buried in the garden. Then she allowed the mausoleum door to be sealed.

A few days later, the door was found open again. The sexton closed it, but again, it was soon found open. Workmen secured the door with iron chains, but they were soon found lying on the floor of the open tomb.

Moses wanted to be with John. It didn't matter that a heavy marble door stood in his way. Eventually, Mrs. Legare, and the cemetery officials, acquiesced to the ghost dog's wishes. The sexton removed the door, and the Legare mausoleum stands open to this day.

(This is just one story to explain why there is no door on the Legare mausoleum on Edisto Island. Another story is not so charming. Remember Julia Legare, who died in 1852? She may have been buried alive in that very mausoleum. She died of a fever, possibly diphtheria, which can cause a very low heart rate and shallow breathing. She may have simply fallen into a coma. But as the story goes, when her family tomb was opened – probably to bury John in 1862 – Julia's skeleton was found crouched next to the door rather than in her casket. Since then, they say, Julia's spirit has forced open the marble tomb door, until, again, the sexton finally gave up and removed the door.)

AUGUST 31
Terror at White Lick Creek, Avon, IN (1907)

The early years of the twentieth century were a boom time for the railroad industry. Chicago was flexing its broad shoulders, and railways were needed to connect the big city with other Midwest commercial centers. In 1907 the Inter-Urban Railroad Commission began construction on a stretch of railroad connecting Indianapolis and Terre Haute, Indiana.

The often-dangerous work of railroad construction wasn't done by railroad employees. Instead, the railroad hired temporary workers from the surrounding areas, often farmers who needed something to do after the crops had been planted in the spring.

But in late August, many of these part-time workers had to return to their farms to bring in the harvest. The railroad, desperate for hands, posted in cities that there was work to be had in Indiana.

Since the work had to progress quickly, and these workers were only temporary, they were seen as expendable. Near the end of August, 1907, the unthinkable happened.

The workers were building a concrete bridge over White Lick Creek outside of Avon, Indiana. The process was this: build a form for the pylon, mix the cement, then fill a bucket with the cement and winch it up to the workmen on the platform above, who waited to pour the cement into the wooden pylon form.

One of the workmen on the platform was a huge Black man who went by the name of Dad Jones. He was a mountain of a man, six feet five inches tall, with a sullen, irritable disposition. He was no fun to work with, but he worked hard, and was reputed to be the strongest man on the crew.

Dad Jones waited on the platform for the second load of cement to be winched up. Impatient to get on with the job, he reached for the bucket and muscled it into place over the pylon form. Then he and another worker tipped the bucket, and the cement started to fill the form.

There was a crack, and before anyone could react, the platform collapsed, sending Dad Jones and the other worker falling. The other worker was tossed to the ground, but Jones fell directly into the wet cement. He struggled, screaming, but the cement from the tipped bucket was still flowing into the form. Jones was still screaming as the wet sludge oozed quickly and covered him. In a heartbeat he was entombed in solid concrete.

The foreman was shocked, but soon recovered his composure. Even if it was possible to scrape the cement out of the form and retrieve the body, he couldn't just stop work and tear up a newly-poured pylon just to find the corpse of a temporary worker, and a Black man at that. Some of the men argued that Dad's spirit wouldn't rest easy if he was denied a Christian burial, but their concerns were brushed aside. There was work to be done. Within a few hours, the upper platform was rebuilt, and more concrete was mixed and poured. Dad Jones was well and truly gone.

Then the screaming started.

A local farmer was the first to report it. He'd been out raccoon hunting one moonlit night, and was under White Lick Creek Bridge as a freight train went by overhead, heading for Indianapolis. Just before the train reached the bridge, the farmer swore he heard a man's loud cry. What unsettled him most, he said, was that the shriek seemed to come from inside the bridge pylon.

Several teenagers had an even eerier experience less than a month later. They were walking along the tracks late at night. A train came past, and they scattered into the bushes to let it pass. As the train came across the bridge, the teenagers heard a man's hoarse scream from inside the bridge. The scream stopped after the train thundered past – but then the teens heard dull thumping sounds coming from the bridge pylon, as if someone was inside, desperately beating his fists on the concrete, demanding to be let out.

The teens ran to town and woke the sheriff, who took them with him back to the bridge to investigate. All was quiet, but the sheriff noticed something odd about the condensation running in thin rivulets down the cement of the pylons. He touched a finger to the cold wet concrete, and it came away wet – with water the color of blood.

Since then, White Lick Creek Bridge has gained a reputation as one of the most haunted spots in Indiana. Engineers began to report a misty shadow that formed in the middle of the tracks. Even now, visitors to the bridge say they can hear the voice of Dad Jones bemoaning his sudden, unfair death, and hear the thump of his fists as he hammers to be let loose from his eternal prison.

SEPTEMBER

DAYS *of the* DEAD

SEPTEMBER 1
The Atkinson Spook Light, Georgia (1900)

Late in the summer of 1900, a railroad locomotive dropped some live coals as it trundled over the Satilla River trestle in southeastern Georgia. The coals landed on the wooden trestle and began to smolder. The fire burned its way through quite a bit of the bridge without anyone noticing. But the damage had been done. Later that same day, a train came along and wrecked, killing several crewmen.

I just pulled a bait-and-switch on you, though, because this section of track is not haunted by the men killed in the wreck. Here's what happened: the railroad company decided to hire a watchman for the trestle, to make sure nothing like that ever happened again. A Mr. T.B. Sceals was hired for the position.

For some reason, though, Sceals was replaced at the end of August by John H. Williams. Sceals was upset at being fired – anyone would be. But Sceals was upset enough to kill. On the night of September 1, 1900, he went to the trestle and hit Williams over the head, knocking him cold. Then Sceals put Williams's body across the tracks. A westbound train soon finished the job Sceals had started. Sceals was later convicted of murder and spent several years in prison.

Williams seems to have joined the ranks of folks killed on railroad tracks that wander looking for justice. The Atkinson Spook Light, said to be Williams's lantern, is a softball-sized red-orange ball of light. Interestingly, it has what looks like a grid of lines on its surface, like the wire guard on an old-fashioned signal lantern. It has another strange quirk: it looks exactly the same through binoculars as it does just looking at it.

SEPTEMBER 2
The Hamshall Haunting, England (1934-1938)

The lovely green countryside of England hides many haunted places. Rectories, or the houses near churches given by the parish for the use of the pastor and his family, seem to be favorite places for ghosts. Epworth Rectory was the scene of intense poltergeist activity from December 1716 to January 1717. British ghost researcher Harry Price called Borley Rectory "the most haunted house in England", and actually rented it for a year in 1937, opening it to fellow researchers.

Price's attention was drawn to another such place, Hamshall Ridware Rectory in Staffordshire. The rectory has gained a modest amount of fame as the home of Jane Austen's cousin, Reverend Edward Cooper. Much later, in March 1934, it became the home of Reverend G.S. Hewins and his family. It was Reverend Hewins who contacted Harry Price.

He told the ghost hunter that in September 1934, his young nephew came to stay with the family. He fell ill on September 10, and when the household went to bed that night, Mrs. Hewins left the doors to both bedrooms open – hers and the nephew's – in case he needed help in the night. About 4 am, she heard the shuffle of slippers on the landing. She sat up, expecting the nephew. But as the footsteps came closer to her bed, the air became icy cold. Mrs. Hewins shut her eyes tightly and clasped the small cross that hung around her neck. She felt the mysterious presence bend over her and the sleeping reverend. Then she heard a deep sigh, and the presence melted away.

Mrs. Hewins forgot about the ghostly visit until September 1935. After the first visit, she insisted on sleeping in a different wing of the house. The ghost followed her. One night she was awakened by three loud bangs and the sound of footsteps.

The next year, the family was on vacation in September. If anything happened at the rectory while they were away, no one told them about it.

In September 1937, the rector and his wife moved back into their old bedroom, thinking that whatever anniversary the ghost was marking had passed. But at 6:30 am on September 12, Hewins heard three loud thumps on the bedroom door.

Reverend Hewins wrote to Harry Price in August 1938. With September approaching, he decided to contact the famous ghost hunter for advice. Price couldn't get out to the rectory himself, so he arranged for another trusted researcher to spend the night of September 10 there. Unfortunately, the researcher got sick and couldn't make the investigation. It didn't matter, though, because that year's weirdness didn't happen until September 17. The manifestations for September 1938 consisted again of three loud bangs that woke Mrs. Hewins.

Price fully intended to visit Hamstall Ridware Rectory in September 1939, but war prevented it. Mr. Hewins did relate an incident that got Price thinking. The rector said that in autumn 1937, he and Mrs. Hewins were undressing for bed in the haunted bedroom. Hewins had forgotten something, so he took the candle with him for a few moments, leaving his wife in the dark. When he returned, she told him that as she'd lifted her petticoat over her head, it had burst into flames. She dropped it, and it fell to the floor in a shower of sparks.

This led Price to a theory of hauntings. He was familiar with static electricity, of course. Even Price admitted, though, that a petticoat, of whatever material, should not burst into flames just from pulling it over one's head.

But the electricity theory stuck with him. In his book *Fifty Years of Psychical Research*, Price theorized that the reason some ghosts appear on a schedule is that the spirit's energy accumulates like a battery. If the spirit's energy is strong, the battery will take just a few days or weeks to charge. If the energy is weak, it could take longer, maybe even a year.

SEPTEMBER 3
A Warning, Atlantic Ocean (1939)

One late-summer night, Mrs. Axel Wenner-Gren headed up the stairs on her way to bed. The only light still on was the one on the landing at the top of the stairs. Halfway up, Mrs. Wenner-Gren looked up to the landing – and gasped in terror.

There was a figure standing on the top stair; a man, drenched to the skin. In his arms, he held the limp body of a child. Blood oozed from a deep cut on the child's forehead.

Mrs. Wenner-Gren screamed, and the eerie figures vanished. She ran to find her husband. Shaking, she described the encounter. Her husband put it down to nerves – everyone was upset these days, what with the war going on. He suggested a getaway on their yacht, the *Southern Cross*. (Axel Wenner-Gren was a millionaire. Electrolux had made his fortune, so a yacht vacation was a perfectly reasonable suggestion.) Mrs. Wenner-Gren nodded, still trembling. A vacation might do her good.

Soon afterward, on the night of September 3, the *Athenia* was sailing between Glasgow and Montreal. The captain knew there were German U-boats patrolling the waters off northern Ireland, so he gave orders to extinguish as many lights as possible. Porthole curtains were drawn, and passengers were discouraged from even having a cigarette on deck, for fear the Germans would spot the tiny red glow. The *Athenia* took a zigzag route across the Atlantic, moving to avoid German subs.

Unfortunately, the commander of U-30 saw *Athenia* running without lights in a zigzag pattern, and assumed she was an armed merchant cruiser. At 7:40 pm, Fritz-Julius Lemp ordered four torpedoes fired at the *Athenia*. One of them hit her, and she began to sink by the stern. The *Athenia* carried 1,103 passengers and 315 crew. Of these, 117 civilians were killed. *Athenia* was the first British ship to be torpedoed in World War II. (As soon as Lemp realized he'd hit an unarmed passenger liner, rather than a troopship or an armed merchant ship, he swore his crew to secrecy and altered the ship's log to erase any connection with the attack.)

The *Athenia* took several hours to sink, and all 26 lifeboats were launched. Two ships nearby saw *Athenia*'s distress signals and came to help: the Norwegian *Knute Nelson* – and the Swedish yacht *Southern Cross*. Both ships began taking on survivors.

The first person to come aboard the yacht was a man, soaking wet with seawater, carrying the body of a dying child: the very same figures Mrs. Wenner-Gren had seen on the stairs. Ten-year-old Margaret Hayworth was hit in the head with a fragment of a torpedo shell. She was taken on board *Southern Cross*, then transferred to the American ship *City of Flint* for medical care. She died six days later.

SEPTEMBER 4
The Galveston Hurricane, Galveston, TX (1900)

The deadliest natural disaster in American history is the hurricane that leveled Galveston, Texas on September 8, 1900. Winds over 135 mph flattened over 3,600 buildings. Casualties were estimated between 6,000 and 12,000, although historians generally settle on 8,000 dead.

Cuban scientists, who had become very good at tracking storms in the Caribbean, said that a hurricane had gone north of Cuba and was headed to the Gulf of Mexico. But the Weather Bureau in Washington, only about ten years old at the time, predicted that the storm would pass over Florida and go up to New England.

The Bureau's director, Willis Moore, was irrationally jealous of the talented Cuban scientists. He basically shut off scientific communication from Cuba to the United States. At the same time, he told regional forecasters that they couldn't issue hurricane warnings without going through the bureau in Washington first.

Moore's petty jealousy and paranoia proved deadly. In the days before the hurricane struck, Isaac Cline, the Weather Bureau's chief observer in Galveston, began to suspect that the forecast from Washington was inaccurate. He tried to warn city officials, but his warning came too late. Cline's wife was one of those killed in the devastation.

Others lost included the nuns at St. Mary's Orphanage and many of their charges. When the hurricane struck, the nuns led the children to the newer girls' dormitory. Just a few yards away, the boys' dormitory splintered under the ferocious winds. The nuns, singing to distract the children from the destruction all around them, tied the kids to their waists in case the unthinkable happened and they were swept away by the rising waters. Sister Katherine held two of the smallest children in her arms, promising never to let go.

Just as the last knot was tied, the 135-mph winds smashed the boys' dorm to pieces. The debris pounded the girls' dorm, and the building collapsed, sending all inside into the raging water.

Three boys managed to grab a tree as they were swept along. They clung to the wet branches all night long. They were the only survivors from the orphanage. Over the next few days, the bodies of the nuns and the other children were found along the shore. The nuns' coarse, simple habits weighed them down. The bodies were found half-buried in the sand, still tied together in a hopeless bid for survival. Brave Sister Katherine still clutched the two little children. She had kept her promise not to let them go, even beyond death.

A Walmart now stands where St. Mary's Orphanage once was. The children of the orphanage seem to have returned to the home where the devoted nuns cared for them with such kindness. Toys in the store are regularly found out of place, and fall from shelves for no reason. The store's aisles echo with the laughter and running footsteps of children, even when no living children are there.

SEPTEMBER 5
Execution of Carl Panzram, Leavenworth, KS (1930)

Serial killer Carl Panzram was a thoroughly horrible person. Just before his execution at Leavenworth prison, he confessed to 21 murders, thousands of robberies and acts of arson, and over a thousand instances of sodomy. About these despicable acts, he said, "For all these things I am not the least bit sorry."

Panzram was the product of a horrific childhood. Born in 1891 in Minnesota, Panzram committed his first burglary at the age of twelve when he stole cake, apples, and a revolver from his neighbors.

This crime landed him in the Minnesota State Training School, where he was beaten, raped, and tortured by staff. When he was released, he ran away from home and started riding the rails. This furthered his sadistic education when he was gang-raped by a bunch of hobos. Panzram quickly moved from victim to predator, stealing and burning down buildings.

In 1915, Panzram was caught and sentenced to seven years at the Oregon State Penitentiary. He was an obstreporous prisoner, and he spent a lot of time in solitary confinement. While in solitary, he ate little besides cockroaches.

Panzram escaped in 1918 and continued his life of barbarism. He bought a yacht in 1920 with his ill-gotten gains and used it to lure drunk sailors, which he then raped, killed, and dumped in the Atlantic. After the yacht sank, Panzram made his way to Africa. He talked six guides into taking him crocodile hunting, but before leaving on the tour, he killed them all and fed them to the crocodiles.

He eventually went back to America, where his killing spree continued. He was a brute of a man physically as well as emotionally, and he easily overpowered his victims. Panzram was more skilled as a killer than as a thief, though, and in 1928 he was once again arrested for robbery. He was sent to Leavenworth, where his career began to come to a bitter, violent end.

Panzram tried to escape Leavenworth, but he was caught, and the guards beat him unconscious. Panzram bided his time, and a year later, he beat laundry foreman Robert Warnke to death with an iron. For this, he was sentenced to death. Carl Panzram had run out of second chances.

Amazingly enough, one of the guards on death row, Henry Lesser, befriended Panzram. He felt sorry for the murderer and gave him a dollar to buy cigarettes. Later, he smuggled in writing materials and encouraged Panzram to jot down his life story as he waited to be executed.

Panzram threw himself into the project with gusto. He wasn't shy about going for the gross-out; he included all the gruesome details of his crimes. Even though the writing was finished in 1930, *Panzram: A Journal of Murder* didn't see print until 1970. Publishers were just too squicked out by the graphic confession.

Carl Panzram was hanged on September 5, 1930. His last words were typical of his loutish impatience: "Hurry it up, you Hoosier bastard! I could kill a dozen men while you're screwing around!"

Execution Rocks Light is a lighthouse off the coast of New York, in Long Island Sound. It gets its name from its use by British soldiers to execute colonial prisoners, who would be tied to the rocks to await the rising tide.

Centuries later, in 1920, Carl Panzram arrived on the scene. He dumped ten of his victims in Long Island Sound, just 100 yards from the Execution Rocks Lighthouse.

Both the Revolutionary War-era executions and Panzram's body dumping have left their stain on the lighthouse. Enough strange voices and shadows have been experienced there that it drew the attention of Ghost Adventures. Of course, Zak Bagans challenged the dark energy of the place, and Panzram came through, freezing Zak's camera for a few moments after the taunt.

SEPTEMBER 6
Presque Isle Storm, Michigan (1992)

The lighthouse at Old Presque Isle is also haunted, although not for the terrifying reasons Execution Rocks Lighthouse is. Standing guard over Lake Huron's Presque Isle, it's small as lighthouses go, only thirty feet tall. But it was a welcome sight for more than 150 years. The light was decommissioned in 1871, when the taller New Presque Isle Lighthouse came "online".

Patrick Garrity served as the last keeper at the old lighthouse. Commissioned by Abraham Lincoln, he served there from 1861 to 1871. When the New Light opened, he moved up the road and served another thirty years, until 1903. Patrick's wife, Mary, served as assistant keeper, and four of their children also served as keepers. In 1903, their daughter Anna became keeper of the Range Light, one of the very few female lighthouse keepers on the Great Lakes.

The Old Presque Isle Lighthouse is now run as a museum. In 1977, George and Lorraine

Parris, a retired couple, served as caretakers.

In 1979, an interesting but disconcerting phenomenon occurred: the light started shining again. This was problematic. Once a light is decommissioned, it's removed from official lists. If it were to appear again, confusion would ensue – and possibly tragedy. The Parrises turned it off immediately. The Coast Guard came out and helped George disconnect it, removing the motor and gears so the light couldn't rotate. They even cut off the electricity to the tower.

But in 1992, the light came back on. Lorraine told a few friends, who agreed that the glow in the tower must be caused by the reflection of the floodlights that illuminated the tower – but turning off the floodlights made no difference to the glow.

The Coast Guard came out again, and not only changed the direction of the Fresnel lens, but also removed the old bulb in the tower. The windows of the lantern room still glowed.

It may be the spirit of Patrick Garrity, still keeping the light on. But Lorraine Parris has another theory. Her husband George died of a heart attack at the lighthouse just a few months before Lorraine saw the light reappear in 1992. George was a master electrician – perhaps he powered up the old light to let Lorraine know of his continued survival.

Lorraine also relates another strange encounter she experienced. On September 5, 1992, a bad storm struck the area. Lorraine was cozy enough in the keeper's house, but she decided to move her car closer to the lighthouse. She tried to get out the back door, but found two white chairs braced against the door from the outside.

Lorraine decided that maybe she just wasn't meant to go outside, so she sat back down at her desk and continued her paperwork. Moments later, a bolt of lightning struck just outside the building, exactly where Lorraine would have been standing had she gone outside.

SEPTEMBER 7
The Women in White, Gloucester, MA (1871)

Can ghosts warn us in our dreams?

John Nelson sure thought so. Nelson was the cook aboard the schooner *Sachem*, which set sail from Gloucester on September 7, 1871. The captain, J. Wenzell, was planning to fish the waters near Georges Bank.

Around midnight, Nelson awoke from a horrible dream. He couldn't remember all the details, but he knew the dream meant disaster. How? He'd had the dream twice before, aboard different ships. And each time he'd had the dream, the ship had foundered.

Nelson hunted up Captain Wenzell. "Captain, you have to turn the ship around. Take her back to port, or at least get her away from Georges Bank. She's going to run into a storm in there, or hole herself on one of the reefs, or something!"

"You can't possibly know that," Wenzell scoffed.

"But I do!" Nelson insisted. "I dreamed of the White Women."

He explained that the dreams were basically the same, but slightly different. In the dreams, he saw women dressed in white. The dreams always had something to do with water, too. Once, the women were standing in the rain. Once, they were near a waterfall. This time, they were trying to cross a stream.

"These ladies spell disaster, Captain, just see if they don't!"

Captain Wenzell looked doubtfully at the night sky, which was clear, with a light breeze freshening the air. It didn't seem like stormy weather – but Nelson was a reliable fellow, not given to tall tales. Wenzell ordered the sailors on watch to keep a sharp eye out for trouble.

Around 1:30 am, the wind picked up, and the *Sachem* was tossing on the waves. A sailor came panting up to the captain. "She's taking on water!"

Wenzell went down to the hold. Sure enough, about six inches of water sloshed in the ship's hold. He told his men to start bailing while he looked for the leak, but the *Sachem* was being tossed around so forcefully that it was impossible to tell where the water was coming in.

Wenzell knew when he'd been beaten. Luckily the *Pescador* was nearby, and took all the men off the *Sachem*. With all his sailors accounted for, Wenzell turned for one last look at his ship. The *Sachem* rose above the water a bit, then nosedived under the waves, rolling over as she sank.

John Nelson's dream warning had come true yet again.

SEPTEMBER 8
The Sinking of the Lady Elgin, Lake Michigan (1860)

Here's another tale of the sea for you.

The schooner *Augusta* was said to be haunted, a cursed ship. This is how it happened: in the early hours of September 8, 1860, the *Augusta* was maneuvering the storm-tossed chop of Lake Michigan. Near her was the palatial side-wheeler *Lady Elgin*, an excursion steamboat running from Chicago to Milwaukee, carrying nearly 400 passengers. *Augusta* was carrying a load of lumber, which shifted, throwing her off-balance. In the confusion of the tossing waves and the poor visibility, *Augusta* smashed into *Elgin*. *Augusta* suffered hardly any damage, and went on her way to Chicago.

But the damage to *Lady Elgin* was severe. *Augusta* had smashed a huge hole in *Elgin's* wooden hull, and she sank within half an hour. About 300 people lost their lives. It was said ever after that *Augusta* was cursed for this tragedy.

The ship's owners changed her name to *Colonel Cook* to try to escape her past, but the ruse was unsuccessful. Karma had her way with the former *Augusta*. It was claimed that with every trip she took, a man was lost overboard or otherwise injured. Sailors claimed she was plagued by the restless dead of *Lady Elgin*. During the long watches of the night, waterlogged corpses would appear on the ship's foredeck and stare vacantly, silently, accusingly at the living crew.

SEPTEMBER 9
The Battle of Sabine Pass, TX (1863)

It's been said that US Navy Lt. Frederick Crocker's attempt to invade Texas was one of the most one-sided victories in the Civil War. Unfortunately for the Union lieutenant, the victory went to the Confederates. Here's how it happened.

On September 8, 1863, Lt. Crocker sailed four gunboats up the Sabine River. His intention was to invade Texas and claim a Union victory. He was pretty confident about the operation: behind the gunboats were seven Navy transports full of soldiers. The gunboats got as far as Fort Griffin … and that's where Crocker's plan fell apart.

There were forty-six men in the fort, who'd been sent there for punishment (kind of like being thrown in the brig). With nothing else to do, the men had been practicing their artillery skills. The practice paid off when Crocker's boats came into view.

The first boat up the river was the *Sachem* – and the guys in the fort shelled the paste out of her. Next up was the *Clifton* – they pounded her too. The next two boats realized what was happening, and prudently hung back, instead of chugging into the same gunfire that had taken out the first two. Soon, they reversed course and backed away. A force of 46 Confederates had whipped 5,000 Union troops.

The men at Fort Griffin were lionized for their feat. Apparently whatever they'd been punished for was forgotten, and they were all given medals.

And now for the ghost story: one of the soldiers killed on the gunboats was decapitated by a cannonball. Locals say that on nights of a full moon, you'll feel a sudden chill in the air, and hear a low moan as he emerges from the river to search for his missing head.

SEPTEMBER 10

The Battle of Carnifex Ferry, Summersville, WV (1861, recurring)

The state of West Virginia exists today, in part, because of the battle that took place here in 1861. It was just a skirmish, but it drove Confederate troops from the area, and led to the creation of another state.

Confederate Brigadier General John B. Floyd crossed the Gauley River and attacked Union troops under the command of Colonel Erastus Tyler. But on September 10, the Union side was reinforced by three infantry brigades under Brigadier General William S. Rosecrans. Rosecrans also brought heavy artillery, and the Confederates were routed. As a result, West Virginia statehood proceeded without serious threat from the Confederates. Six weeks later, West Virginia joined the Union as the 35th state.

Every odd-numbered year, the Carnifex Ferry Battlefield State Park holds a reenactment of the battle. But the spirits who inhabit the area show up *every* September 10. Locals report hearing the sound of gunfire, the shouts of soldiers in battle, and the moans of wounded men. Sometimes unexplainable mists and glowing balls of light roam the battlefield. If you go ghost hunting there, you might want to go in an even-numbered year. That way, you can be sure that the soldier you see is an actual ghost, not a reenactor.

SEPTEMBER 11
The Tale of the Cenci Family, Rome, Italy (1599, recurring)

Count Francesco Cenzi ruled his family with an iron fist. A violent man, he made his wife and children's lives hell.

Beatrice was Francesco's daughter from his first marriage, to Ersilia Santacroce. He had a son as well, Beatrice's older brother Giacomo. When Beatrice was eight years old, in 1584, her mother died. Francesco remarried, taking Lucrezia Petroni as his wife and siring another son, Bernardo.

History tells us that Francesco abused his wife and sons, and raped Beatrice many times, adding incest to his atrocities. Beatrice sought help from the authorities, but found no one willing to listen to a young woman. Francesco, meanwhile, was jailed for other crimes, but was freed early because of his noble status. When he discovered that Beatrice had reported his abuse, he sent her and Lucrezia away from Rome to the family's castle.

The four (sane) members of the family, Beatrice, Lucrezia, Giacomo, and Bernardo, decided to take matters into their own hands. On one of Francesco's visits to the castle, they drugged him. Unfortunately, this didn't kill him. So Beatrice, her brothers, and her stepmother bludgeoned Francesco with a hammer, then tossed the body off a balcony to make it look like an accident. That did the trick.

But eventually Francesco's absence was noticed in Rome. The papal police were dispatched to investigate. The murder was discovered, and the four Cencis were arrested, found guilty, and sentenced to death.

The people of Rome protested the decision – they knew Francesco had it coming. But Pope Clement VIII didn't overturn his ruling. Francesco was the head of his family, and even though he was a despicable human being, patricide (especially of a nobleman) could not go unpunished. The verdict stood.

At dawn on September 11, 1599, the four Cencis were taken to Sant'Angelo Bridge. Giacomo was tortured in the cart on the way to the scaffold. At the bridge, he was quartered with an axe, and the pieces were hung in the four corners of the piazza in front of the bridge. The women were beheaded with a sword – first Lucrezia, then Beatrice. Bernardo, twelve years old, was spared, but he was forced to watch the execution of his whole family. Then he was returned to prison, and the family's properties were confiscated by the Pope.

The ghost in this story is that of Beatrice. She became a symbol of resistance against the arrogant aristocracy. The people who live in her old family home, the Palazzo Cenci, have seen her beautiful, melancholy spirit, and have heard her weeping for the loss of her family and for her own life cut short. Every year on the anniversary of her death, she appears on the bridge where she was executed, carrying her own severed head.

SEPTEMBER 12
The Bare Grave, Shropshire, England (1821)

Sometimes a ghost story, or some other unexplainable phenomenon, gets embellished in the telling. Romantic details are added to the bare facts, and the "new and improved" version gets passed down the ages.

In 1818, a young wanderer named John Newton showed up at the farm of widowed Mrs. Morris in search of a job. For Mrs. Morris, Newton's arrival was fortuitous. Oakfield, her home, had been a manor house on a prosperous farm, but her late husband's idleness had allowed the farm to fall to ruin. She had been almost at the point of selling the property to a Thomas Pearce, whose family had once owned it but had lost it years before. She took a chance and hired Newton to work the farm.

It was a good move. Newton was a diligent worker, and soon the farm was flourishing under his stewardship. He was cordial to Mrs. Morris and her daughter Jane, but reticent about his life before he'd come to Oakfield. Jane and her mother were content not to pry.

Newton had been at Oakfield for about two years, and was establishing himself comfortably. Mrs. Morris was delighted with his work, and Jane was growing fond of him as well.

But there were those in the community who were not so happy. Thomas Pearce, whose family had once owned Oakfield, saw the property slipping from his potential grasp. His neighbor, Robert Parker, was sweet on Jane Morris, but had never made his feelings known. He saw his unwitting rival's success, and it ate at him. Parker and Pearce, each with a bone to pick, egged each other on, and soon came up with a plan to lay John Newton low.

One November day Newton went to a farm fair at Welshpool, a few miles away. Business kept him late, so it was dark by 6 o'clock when he started the walk home. Pearce and Parker waited for him on the road, and sprung their trap.

No one knows what really happened on the dark road, but Pearce and Parker hauled Newton back to Welshpool and accused him of highway robbery with violence. The crime was punishable by death, but at his trial, Newton was strangely calm. He didn't ask for a lawyer, he simply stated his innocence.

Newton was still practically an unknown, and Parker and Pearce were respected members of the community. Newton was found guilty. When the judge allowed him to say a few words, he only said that he forgave the two men whose false testimony had led to his conviction. But, he added, he was innocent of that crime. And to prove it, he swore that if he was innocent, no grass would grow on his grave for at least a generation.

The execution was set for September 12, 1821. As the bell began to toll for the public execution, the sky became overcast. As Newton stepped onto the scaffold, the sky grew dark. When his body fell to jerk at the end of the rope, the heavens opened and thunder shook the air.

John Newton is buried in an unmarked grave in a remote corner of Montgomery Churchyard. The Reverend Richard Pryce wrote a pamphlet in which he told the (highly embellished) story of John Newton's arrival at Oakfield and his execution. Mr. Pryce claimed that many people had spread grass seed on the grave, but even with assiduous watering, the grass never sprouted. In 1852, the year Pryce wrote his story, someone laid sod over Newton's grave and tended it so carefully that it did grow, except at the head of the grave, which remained bare. But within a month, that grass died too.

Mr. Pryce embellished the story of John Newton to make a good tale. We can't know how much of it is true, and what came out of Pryce's romantic imagination. I will point this out, though: the *Salopian Journal* reported the news of the hanging. Elsewhere in that day's paper, they ran a weather report which confirms the sudden storm that blew up in the area on the day of the execution.

SEPTEMBER 13
Dickens' Ghosts (1861)

It may come as a surprise to those who love the four ghosts of Charles Dickens' *A Christmas Carol* to discover that Dickens was not a great fan of the supernatural. In fact, he was as unimpressed by ghost stories as was Ebenezer Scrooge confronted by the ghost of Marley.

Therefore, it may be even more of a surprise that Dickens wrote many ghost stories besides *A Christmas Carol*. (Some historians blame a nanny in his childhood who entertained him with hair-raising tales.)

In 1861, Dickens wrote four ghost stories that were published in the magazine *All The Year Round*. In one of the stories, a portrait painter is riding on a train, and strikes up a conversation with a young woman. The date is September 13. During their conversation, the woman asks the artist if it is possible to paint someone's portrait from memory. The artist's answer is a hedging "maybe, I guess so." She asks him to study her face carefully, just in case he ever has to paint *her* portrait. Humoring her, the artist gazes at her for a good while.

Two years later, a gentleman visit the artist's studio with a strange request – could the artist paint a portrait of the man's deceased daughter based only on the man's description? The artist does his best, but can't quite manage it. Finally, he casts his memory back two years, and draws on the features of the young woman on the train for inspiration. The client takes one look at the portrait and is thrilled with the result – it's the very image of his beloved lost daughter. Out of curiosity, and because it's a short story, the artist asks when the girl had died. The father answers: "Two years ago, on the 13th of September."

Well, *that's* good for running a chill down the spine. But someone was not at all pleased with the tale. The magazine had barely hit the stands when Dickens got an enraged letter from an actual portrait painter, who accused Dickens of stealing his story – a story he'd written, *based on an experience that had actually happened to him*. Every detail in the story – the meeting on the train, the grieving father's request for a portrait – was identical to this unpublished story. Dickens *had* to have stolen the story somehow, the artist accused. What baffled the artist most, he said, was how Dickens had come up with the date mentioned in the story. "How else was it possible that the date, the 13th of September, could have been got at? For I never told the date until I wrote it."

Dickens was just as flummoxed as his accuser. He later said that when he'd originally wrote the story, he hadn't even mentioned a date. But when he read the story for revision, he realized that the story would be much more effective and spookier with a date. So he jotted a random date – September 13 – in the margin.

SEPTEMBER 14
Battle of South Mountain, Boonsboro, MD (1862)

Robert E. Lee was feeling pretty fine on September 14, 1862. His troops had just finished a successful campaign at Second Manassas, and Lee decided the time was ripe to invade the North. He sent half his army with Stonewall Jackson to capture a Union arsenal at Harper's Ferry, and Lee looked to three passes within South Mountain: Crampton's Gap, Turner's Gap, and Fox's Gap.

Unfortunately for Lee, his orders were leaked to Union General George McClellan. McClellan moved quickly to counter Lee's forces. The fierce fighting led to 4,500 casualties and a Confederate defeat.

The whole area is rife with residual paranormal activity. The oldest report comes from the late 1800s, not long after the war. Guests at the South Mountain House in Turner's Gap heard the sounds of battle just over the hill – cannon fire, men yelling, the whole shebang.

Another tale comes from Fox's Gap. A group of hikers witnessed either a massive residual haunting or a time slip. Just down the hill, they saw an entire army making camp. They saw soldiers tending cooking fires, picketing horses, and generally milling around. Figuring they were seeing reenactors doing their thing, the hikers continued on their way. Later, they learned that there were no reenactors in the area. So, what did they see?

SEPTEMBER 15
The First EVPs (1952)

The idea of communication with the dead is a powerful one. One of the best ways we have (right now) to facilitate this is the study of EVPs, or "electronic voice phenomena". Simply put, this is when investigators pick up a "ghost voice" through electronic means. EVPs can be captured by using radio station noise, other white noise, or just out of thin air. For most researchers, the really exciting part is when they capture an answer in response to a question.

Thomas Edison was the first person, in the 1920s, to theorize that it might be possible to capture disembodied voices on a recording device. He never accomplished this, but other researchers continued experimenting.

Friedrich Juergenson, a Swedish film producer, was recording bird songs in 1959 when he heard something unexpected on playback. His mother's voice said, "Friedrich, you are being watched. Friedel, my little Friedel, can you hear me?" Juergenson was understandably fascinated by his inadvertent capture, and he went on to do much more recording on purpose. He eventually caught hundreds of ghost vices, earning the title "the father of EVP."

Of course, modern researchers are purposely looking to record the voices of the dead, but especially in the early days, it happened quite by accident. On September 15, 1952, two music enthusiasts, Catholic priests Father Ernetti and Father Gemelli, were recording Gregorian chants on a reel-to-reel tape recorder. The machine kept breaking. Frustrated, Father Gemelli looked to the heavens and asked his dead father for help. Later, both men were shocked to hear Gemelli's father answer his son's plea.

"Of course, I shall help you. I'm always with you."

SEPTEMBER 16
Suicide of Peg Entwistle, Los Angeles, CA (1932)

Picture the iconic "Hollywood" sign in Los Angeles. I sort of led you to a conclusion there, but did you know that it didn't always say "Hollywood"?

And did you know that it's haunted?

The sign, erected in 1923, originally said "Hollywoodland". It was put up as an advertisement for a real estate agency. (The "land" was taken down when the city of Hollywood bought it in 1949.) It stands as a symbol of the glitz and glamour of the entertainment industry. Countless aspiring actors, models, and musicians have arrived in Hollywood to seek fame and fortune. Most, of course, never find it.

Peg Entwistle was a British actress who did well for herself on Broadway in the mid-1920s to early 1930s. Buoyed by this success, she decided to make the leap from stage to screen, and move to Los Angeles.

She leapt – and missed.

She was cast in the film *Thirteen Women*, but her pretty face was lost in a sea of pretty faces. The film didn't test well with audiences, and Peg was left on the cutting room floor.

Distraught, probably drunk, Peg wobbled her way out to the Hollywoodland sign on September 16, 1932. She climbed to the top of the H and stepped off, falling fifty feet to her death. A hiker found her body the next day, along with one shoe, a jacket, a purse … and a suicide note.

"I am afraid, I am a coward. I am sorry for everything. If I had done this a long time ago, it would have saved a lot of pain. P.E."

The ghost stories started in the 1940s, when the H inexplicably fell over. People still speak of smelling Peg's gardenia perfume, and of seeing a disoriented blonde woman dressed in 1930s clothing disappear in front of them.

SEPTEMBER 17
Battle of Antietam, Sharpsburg, MD (1862)

In a war filled with violent superlatives, the title for bloodiest single day of the Civil War goes to the Battle of Antietam. On this deadly day, twelve hours of fighting resulted in 23,000 casualties, including around 3,650 dead. The battle was a virtual stalemate, but the Union didn't lose, so Lincoln took the opportunity to announce his Emancipation Proclamation a few days later. This changed the course of the war: with the Proclamation, France and Britain decided not to acknowledge the Confederacy. This made it harder for the South to re-supply its troops and citizens, as the Confederacy was no longer getting supplies from Europe.

Just a few days before, Lee had split his Army of Northern Virginia in half, sending half with Stonewall Jackson to attack Harper's Ferry, while Lee tried to invade the North through South Mountain. McClellan successfully defended the three passes, pushing Lee's forces down South Mountain to Sharpsburg. Lee planned to retreat, but heard that Jackson had indeed captured Harper's Ferry. This gave Lee the impetus to regroup at Antietam Creek.

As Union troops moved into the area Lee's army had vacated, two Union soldiers found something extremely interesting: three cigars. Wrapped around the cigars was a piece of paper – with detailed Confederate troop movements written on it. McClellan was ecstatic at the find. Knowing the movements of the enemy was a huge advantage.

The fighting began as the morning sun burned the dawn fog off the battlefield. Union forces outnumbered the Confederates two to one, although McClellan thought Lee's forces were much larger than they actually were. The two sides faced off over a 30-acre cornfield, and the carnage began.

Near the center of the battlefield was a lane that local farmers knew as "Sunken Road." Confederate Major General Daniel Harvey Hill stationed 2,600 men along the road. Soon 5,500 Union troops arrived, ready for a fight. The fighting here raged from 9:30 am to 1 pm. In those few short hours, over 5,000 men were killed or wounded just at this spot. (In the part of the area known as Cornfield Trail, the Confederate cause suffered the biggest number of casualties of any battle of the war. Between 6 and 7 am, they lost 82% of their force.)

An Irish regiment, the 69th New York, fought desperately to take Sunken Road, losing 60% of their men in the attack. After the battle, the dead lay so thick on the ground that it was said a man could walk the length of the road without touching the ground. Sunken Road got a new name that day: Bloody Lane.

The Battle of Antietam was one of the pivotal battles of the war, and the battlefield gets thousands of visitors each year. For school groups, it's a chance to see history come alive. A group from the McDonogh School in Baltimore took a field trip to the battlefield for a truly immersive experience. They learned how the soldiers drilled, and reenactors showed the students what a soldier's life was like in camp.

Toward dusk, the students had some quiet time at Bloody Lane, to gather their thoughts about this momentous day in America's history. As they walked back to the buses in the growing darkness, their teacher gave them an assignment: write an essay about what they'd learned, and what parts of the visit had impressed them the most.

Since the students had just come from Bloody Lane, that part of the battlefield was still fresh in their minds. Curiously, many students mentioned hearing Christmas carols as they walked along the lane – specifically, the chorus to "Deck The Halls". Intrigued, their teacher asked several students to repeat the strange sounds. They did the best they could, rendering it as "Fa-la-la-la."

The teacher was an expert on the Civil War, and the Battle of Antietam in particular. The boys' vocalizations stunned him. Many of the students who heard the "Christmas carol" were sitting at the section of Bloody Lane that was taken at such cost by the Fighting 69th …

… who were known to use as their war cry the call "Clear the Way", which in Gaelic is "Faugh a Ballagh", pronounced Fah-a-bah-lah. It seems the boys had heard the war cry of the Irish Brigade in the exact spot where 540 men of the regiment fell.

SEPTEMBER 18
Unlucky Thirteen, Augusta, GA (1780)

The Ezekial Harris House (formerly the Mackay Trading Post) is said to be the place where one of the atrocities of the Revolutionary War took place.

The city of Augusta, named after Princess Augusta, wife of the Prince of Wales, was founded in 1736. For a brief time in 1779 it was the capital of Georgia after Savannah fell to British occupation, but Augusta was then also captured by the British.

Just before the war began, the Sons of Liberty captured the Loyalist Thomas Brown. The colonists tarred and feathered Brown as an example to other Loyalists. Brown recovered from the ordeal, and vowing revenge, he returned to Augusta at the head of British troops in May 1780. He began a campaign of retribution against the colonists, expelling some families, confiscating the possessions of others, even arresting and executing patriots.

On September 14, 1780, colonists attacked an Indian village. The Americans also laid siege to Mackay's Trading Post for four days, harassing Brown's British troops and his Native American allies. It did not go well for the colonists.

Twenty-nine soldiers were captured by the British. Brown had been wounded, which probably pissed him off even more. On September 18, he ordered Captain Ashby and twelve other colonial prisoners to be hanged in the open-air stairwell at the back of the house, so he could enjoy the sights and sounds of their death agonies from his third-floor bedroom. He chose to hang thirteen men to represent the thirteen rebellious colonies. Two of them were just teenagers. Sixteen other prisoners were handed over to the natives for torture.

In 1946, the Richmond County Historical Society bought an 18th century house, thinking it was the Mackay Trading Post. Locals had been telling ghost stories about the thirteen hanged colonists for decades, so the historical society basically crossed its fingers and hoped that this was a building of historical significance. However, a 1975 study by the state of Georgia burst that bubble, confirming that the house was actually built in 1797. It was subsequently named the Ezekial Harris House, after the presumed builder. It's not the house where *that* history happened, but it was saved and restored because someone mistakenly identified it as the trading post.

Even if the Ezekial Harris House isn't the Mackay Trading Post, there are still a few ghostly legends attached to the property. It's said that if you stand in the stairwell and count to thirteen, you can hear the thud of falling bodies and the creak of taut ropes, or the moans of those being tortured.

Higher up, on the second floor, the ghost of a thin woman glides slowly around the rooms as if searching for someone. This is thought to be Mrs. Glass, mother of the two teenage boys who were hanged.

SEPTEMBER 19
Eagle Point Curve, Dubuque, IA (1887)

Two miles north of Dubuque, the early-morning stillness was shattered by the horrific crash of two passenger trains coming together in a head-on collision. Early on September 19, 1887, a northbound train was running late. The dispatcher ordered it to leave Dubuque to make up time. Conductor Wolcott and Engineer Winchester refused at first, saying they'd meet the southbound train in unfortunate circumstances. They usually passed the other train five miles north of Dubuque. The dispatcher insisted the train leave immediately.

At 5:30 am, the sharp curve at Eagle Point was shrouded in fog. The trains didn't see each other until they were just fifty feet apart. The engines both stopped abruptly; the cars behind them did not. Five crew members died in the crash, and many of the passengers were injured. For decades after the accident, locals spoke of hearing the sounds of the crash, and of seeing the lights of the doomed engines coming together in a fateful, inevitable crash.

SEPTEMBER 20
Death House, North Carolina (1866)

One of the most haunted places in North Carolina is a once-beautiful two-story house built in 1816 by Thomas Shannonhouse. He and his wife Elizabeth raised ten children there, blissfully unaware of the tragedies that would eventually blight the house.

Their son John, born in the house in 1824, inherited the property after the death of his parents. John loved all his children, but his daughter Ellanora was his favorite. She was a pretty, poised, charming child who grew into a lovely young lady. For her sixteenth birthday on August 7, 1866, John gave his treasured daughter the present of her dreams: a horse of her very own. Ellanora was delighted, and spent many hours riding her beloved pet.

On a Sunday afternoon six weeks later, Ellanora was thrown from the horse and critically injured. For two days, the girl clung to life as her heartbroken parents kept a vigil at her bedside. As John held his daughter on the night of September 20, she looked at him and whispered, "But Father, I can't die so young." Then she was gone.

John's face contorted as his grief turned to bitter anger. He shrieked a curse aloud: "I hope all who inhabit this house may know the pangs of death which so pained me!"

For more than a hundred years, that curse has stolen the lives of those unfortunate enough to live in the house. Soon after Ellanora's death, John moved his family out of the house and sold the property to Ephraim M. Stanton. Two of Stanton's young children soon contracted diphtheria and died. In 1870, Stanton sold the house to Elisha Lister. Three of Lister's children died of disease in the house.

A laborer working at the house died of tuberculosis in an upstairs bedroom. Just before his passing, he spoke of seeing a girl riding down the road on a white horse. The road was a dead end, and no horse or rider had gone down it that day.

In 1909, Lister's cousin was sitting on the front porch visiting when he suddenly pointed to the empty road, clutched his chest, and died instantly.

The Markham family moved into the house in 1920. Three years after they moved in, Mrs. Markham was sitting on the front porch swing with her baby son. She looked toward the road and saw a white horse ridden by an apparition of shimmering white. Mrs. Markham got up from the swing, still holding her baby, and went down into the yard to confront the rider – and both rider and horse vanished. The next day, her infant son fell ill. Within a week, he was dead.

In the late 1930s, another son took ill. The Markhams hurriedly moved, and the boy survived. Others who lived in the house were not so lucky, as the curse continued to claim the life of at least one person in every family who lived there.

The last death in the house was in 1969. Ellanora's death, and John's curse, had led to over a century of grief and loss. The house has been empty ever since. No one is willing to challenge the curse that may still lie dormant in the abandoned house.

SEPTEMBER 21
Old Julie Brown, New Orleans, LA (1915)

About half an hour northeast of New Orleans lies the Manchac Swamp, a lush, primeval place alive with gloomy cypress trees, alligators, and swarms of bugs. The swamp is also said to be the home of two unnerving personalities: the loup-garou (Louisiana's werewolf), and the ghost of voodoo queen Julie Brown.

Julie Brown was a cranky, reclusive old lady known for her magical charms and her curses. She would sit on the porch of her cabin at the edge of the swamp and croon eerie songs while playing her guitar. The lyrics of these weird tunes tended to freak people out – especially the one that went, "One day I'm going to die and take all of you with me." The creepy jam sessions didn't stop people from seeking Julie's help with voodoo spells and herbal healing, but it did give them food for thought.

Julie died in September 1915. She was feared, yes, but she was also deeply loved. Nearly 200 people turned out to say goodbye to their healer. On September 21, the day of her funeral, the area was hit by a Category 4 hurricane, battered by sustained winds of 145 mph. Three towns were wiped out by the devastating tidal wave, and hundreds of people perished. According to local lore, the bodies were buried, along with the old voodoo queen who'd predicted their demise, in a mass grave somewhere in the swamp.

Census records tell us that Julia Bernard was born around 1845, and married Celestin Brown in 1880. A modern New Orleans voodoo priestess, Bloody Mary, has done research on her colleague, and has a very different attitude towards the famously cranky old lady. She points out that Julie served as a healer and midwife, caring for the locals as the three towns in the area had no doctors.

Bloody Mary also doesn't believe that the devastation of the 1915 hurricane resulted from Julie's cursing the town. In fact, she suggests that Julie's famous ditty may have been, not a curse, but a warning to those who heard it.

SEPTEMBER 22
Tragedy on the Green, British Columbia, Canada (1936)

The Victoria Golf Club in Oak Bay is famous for its ghost, a classic Lady in White who screams for help. The unhappy spirit is Doris Gravlin, who was murdered by her husband on September 22, 1936.

Doris Thomson was born in England in 1906 and came to Canada with her parents. She became a nurse, and married Victor Gravlin in 1930. Victor was a sports reporter who enjoyed golfing with his brother.

The Gravlins' marriage deteriorated when Victor began to drink heavily. Doris left him and went back to her profession, finding work as a private nurse.

In mid-September 1936, Victor sent Doris a letter. No one really knows what it said, but apparently, he asked her to meet him on the seventh green of the Victoria golf course to discuss getting back together.

At about 7:45 pm on September 22, Doris left the house where she was staying. Victor met her on the golf course as planned. In his distress over their failed relationship, the only solution Victor could think of was murder-suicide. He threw a cord around Doris's neck and strangled her, then dragged her by the cord still wrapped around her throat down to the nearby beach. He left her body there, and walked into the water to drown.

Days later, Doris's body was discovered by a caddy looking for lost balls. A month after that, a fisherman found Victor's corpse floating in a kelp bed.

Doris still haunts the Victoria Golf Club. At first her apparition was just a faint ball of light, but she has gotten much stronger over the years. Now she appears much as she did in life, a graceful, 5-foot-tall woman, easily recognizable as she floats over the beach. She has also been known to fly through open car windows to startle motorists along Beach Drive, or shoot through windshields as a cold mist.

SEPTEMBER 23
A Rebel's Death Foretold, Los Angeles, CA (1955)

The actor Alec Guinness, already famous for his stage roles, arrived in Los Angeles in September 1955 to make his first Hollywood film, *The Swan*. While waiting for a table at a restaurant, Guinness struck up a conversation with a 24-year-old American in jeans. The kid invited Guinness and his companion, scriptwriter Thelma Moss, to join him for dinner. But first, he led them outside to see the car he'd just bought – a sleek silver Porsche Spyder. The kid, who said his name was James Dean, was over the moon about the car. He planned to race it, he said.

Guinness couldn't shake the eerie feeling he had as soon as he laid eyes on the car. Even looking at it made his skin crawl with a sick feeling of impending doom. As Dean chattered on about the plans he had for "Little Bastard", his affectionate nickname for the pretty little car, Guinness felt his gut twist.

Suddenly, Guinness found himself speaking, as if someone else was in his mind giving the orders to make his mouth move. He looked at his watch. "It is now 10 o'clock, Friday the 23rd of September, 1955. If you get in that car you will be found dead in it by this time next week."

Coming out of his reverie, Guinness shook himself, then apologized for his odd outburst. Dean brushed it off with a laugh.

Shortly before 6 pm on September 30, James Dean was killed instantly in a collision with a black limousine while driving his new silver car to a race at Salinas. "Little Bastard" had claimed its first victim.

SEPTEMBER 24
Death of Paracelsus, Salzburg, Austria (1541)

When we think of alchemists, we might picture some wizened old dude, maybe with a wizard's hat if we want to get fancy, holed up in a tower room surrounded by bubbling pots of potions, trying unsuccessfully to turn lead into gold. But the alchemist and prophet Paracelsus was a bit different. He was a pioneer of medical care in the Renaissance. Instead of prescribing leeches and toad ashes, he believed in the value of minerals, medication, and herbal tinctures. As a professor, he realized that doctors needed a solid education in science, especially chemistry. His revolutionary ideas became the basis for modern medicine.

Born in 1498 in Switzerland, his real name was Philippus Aureolus Theophrastus von Hohenheim. His father Wilhelm was a physician, and educated his son in botany, medicine, mineralogy, and other natural sciences. Paracelsus was hungry for knowledge, and his travels took him all over Europe. He worked for a while as an army surgeon, and all the while, he worked on his medical writings.

Paracelsus was an independent thinker whose ideas, revolutionary for the time, got him kicked out of every major university in Europe. He was offered a place in Salzburg, Austria, by the Prince Bishop of Salzburg. Paracelsus reluctantly accepted the offer, even though he and the Prince Bishop didn't get along, because at that point, he was flat broke. But shortly after Paracelsus arrived, some thugs hired by the medical faculty of the University of Vienna attacked him and beat the snot out of him. On September 24, 1541, he died alone in his small room at the White Horse Inn. He was hurriedly buried in the graveyard of St. Sebastian's Church.

Paracelsus may have been shoved into the ground with little ceremony, but his grave has become a pilgrimage site. Many ill or crippled people visit his grave hoping for a miracle cure from the great physician's spirit.

When he's not handing out cures from beyond the grave, Paracelsus's spirit is not at rest. Legend has it that the Prince Bishop, his old enemy, stole manuscripts from Paracelsus's room and hid them. Now, Paracelsus's ghost roams the grounds of Salzburg Castle looking for the missing papers.

SEPTEMBER 25
The Last Photograph, England (1915)

Lord Oliver Lodge was an eminent physicist who was knighted in 1902 for his service to science. Interestingly, he also served as president of the British Society for Psychical Research, the ghost-hunting group. His interest in the paranormal never interfered with his talent in conventional scientific circles. He and his wife, Lady Lodge, were both convinced of the possibility of life after death.

That conviction was put to a terrible test on September 14, 1915, when their son Raymond was killed in service. Although the parents grieved for their son, they believed they had the resources to contact him. On September 25, Lady Lodge visited the medium Gladys Osborne Leonard, in the hopes of speaking to Raymond.

Gladys told Lady Lodge of a photograph that had been taken of Raymond posing with a group of fellow officers. The Lodges had plenty of photos of Raymond, but none like the one Gladys described. Gladys insisted the photo existed, and said that Raymond had asked her to tell his mother about the photo. Gladys said that in the photo, Raymond was holding his walking stick under his arm.

On November 29, the Lodges got a letter from a Mrs. Cheves, the mother of a friend of Raymond's. She wrote that she had a photograph of a group of officers, including Raymond. She asked if the Lodges might want a copy of the photo.

The Lodges jumped at the chance, writing back immediately, but the photograph didn't arrive until December 7. In the meantime, the Lodges visited another medium. Contacting Raymond, this medium gave them further details about the photo. The spirit of Raymond relayed that the front row of men in the photograph were sitting. He said there were about a dozen men in the photo, some of whom he hardly knew, but he knew a couple of them. He also said that he was in the front row, sitting, and that a couple of officers were behind him. One was familiarly leaning on Raymond's shoulder, which Raymond said annoyed him.

When the photograph was delivered on December 7, the Lodges rushed to inspect it. It wasn't a great picture of Raymond, but it was excellent evidence that Raymond had indeed communicated with them from beyond the grave. The walking stick the first medium had mentioned was in the photo, although it wasn't under Raymond's arm. The fellow officers that the second medium had described were in the photo. The men were arranged just as both mediums had described.

But what really blew Lord Oliver's mind was this: one of the officers behind Raymond really did have a hand on his shoulder. Lord Oliver wrote about the experience for the *Journal of the Society for Psychical Research*.

"By far the most striking piece of evidence is the fact that someone sitting behind Raymond is leaning or resting a hand on his shoulder. The photograph fortunately shows the actual occurrence, and almost indicates that Raymond was rather annoyed with it; for his face is a little screwed up, and his head has been slightly bent to one side out of the way of the man's arm. It is the only case in the photograph where one man is leaning or resting his hand on the shoulder of another."

The Lodges still mourned Raymond's loss. But this photograph, and the evidence supplied by the two mediums, convinced them of the existence of life after death.

SEPTEMBER 26
The Hero Engineer, Sacramento, CA (1880)

Of such things are heroes made. Railroad engineer William Brown made the ultimate sacrifice on September 26, 1880, dying so that hundreds of lives would be saved. Someone had thrown the wrong switch, and Brown found his train headed onto a ferry wharf that led directly into San Francisco Bay. Thinking quickly, Brown managed to unhitch the passenger cars from his locomotive. The cars slid to a stop, but the engine plunged into the water. When the locomotive was pulled from the bay, salvagers were astounded to see Brown still grasping the controls, still trying to bring the engine to a stop.

Brown is now said to haunt Old City Cemetery in Sacramento.

SEPTEMBER 27
A Ghostly Warning, England (1777)

This chilling tale comes from 18th century England. Reverend James Crawford was out for a ride one day, his sister-in-law Hannah Wilson riding behind him. Their trip led them to a river, which Crawford realized they'd have to ford. This made Hannah nervous. Their horse was sure-footed, but Hannah thought that the river was too high and the current too swift. She was afraid that the horse would be swept away if they tried to cross.

Reverend Crawford pointed out that there was another rider, whose horse was even then picking its way across, paying no attention to the rushing waters. Hannah saw the other rider then, and relaxed a bit. Reverend Crawford called out to the rider to see how he was doing, if he felt he was in any danger.

The rider stopped and turned his face to them. Crawford gasped, and Hannah screamed. The rider's face was fishbelly white and almost glowed, and its eyes radiated pure hate. Crawford spurred his horse out of the shallows and headed back home.

In the next few days, Reverend Crawford shared their terrifying encounter. He learned that local folklore held that the ghostly rider appeared in that river whenever someone was about to drown. Crawford, an educated man of God, scoffed at the tale, saying he didn't believe in warning spirits.

But when he tried to cross the river again, on September 27, 1777, he was swept away in the attempt, and drowned.

SEPTEMBER 28
The Haunted Police Station, Ahmedabad, India (2007)

In fall 2007, about a dozen police officers in Ahmedabad, India, claimed they saw poltergeist activity in their station.

Constable Batuksinh Danbar said that an unseen force terrorized the Ramol police station for over a month. The entity overturned furniture, threw chairs around the room, and even assaulted officers. Some officers felt like they were being strangled. Others awoke to crushing chest pain in the middle of the night, which they blamed on the poltergeist. Officers on the night shift suffered more than the others.

Paranormal investigators theorized the poltergeist activity was the work of a female spirit, a woman who had died while working in a mill that had previously been on the site of the police station. Hearing this, some of the officers prayed to Meldi Mata, a Hindu goddess, when coming in to work. A tantric, similar to an exorcist, was asked to perform cleansing rituals at the station. After this, the poltergeist activity gradually tapered off.

SEPTEMBER 29
Still Racing, Saratoga Springs, NY (1960s)

The old groundskeeper bent to his task at the Eighth Pole at the Oklahoma Track. The fall afternoon held a chill in the air. The racing season had ended in August, and the horses had been moved to tracks farther south. Alone on the huge track, the groundskeeper was repairing the track rail.

Lulled by the repetitive work, he was deep in his task when he heard a horse galloping towards him. When the noise of hoofbeats registered in his mind, he looked up in mild surprise. It had just occurred to him that there were no horses currently training at the track. The hoofbeats grew louder, until he could have sworn the horse was thundering past right in front of him.

Then the air was split by the unmistakable shrill scream of a horse in frightful pain. Then – silence.

The tools dropped from the groundskeeper's nerveless fingers. He hadn't seen the horse, but he sure had heard it. He hoped never to hear a scream like that again. He stared across the empty track as the silence wrapped itself around him. He shook his head. He couldn't explain to anyone what had just happened.

Eventually, though, he was in conversation with a blacksmith who also worked at the track. He didn't expect the blacksmith to believe his crazy story, but the other man nodded.

The blacksmith no longer remembered the horse's name, but he told the groundskeeper what had happened at the Oklahoma Track in the 1940s. A horse was pounding down the track during a race. He had just rounded the corner for home, at about the Eighth Pole, when he stumbled, fell, and broke his leg. He had to be euthanized where he fell.

But it seems his spirit is still racing at Saratoga Springs.

SEPTEMBER 30
The Headless Horseman, Redington, NE (1883, 1913)

The town of Redington on Nebraska's western border was once renowned for being the site of a grisly murder – a murder that was said to result in a haunting.

On the night of September 30, 1883, Charles Adams was brutally killed in his cabin. Robbers broke in, sliced Adams's head clean off, then ransacked the place, stealing a large sum of money as well as other valuables.

A few years passed, and the murderers were never caught. The story gained new life when people began telling tales of seeing a ghost at the cabin. Adams was said to appear on the anniversary of his murder, riding a white horse and carrying his severed head in his hands.

The town of Redington continued to grow, and so did the legend of the phantom horseman. In 1913, the Redington School hired a new teacher, a pretty young woman named Maud DeVault. She heard the tales, and declared she'd like to go out to the Adams cabin sometime and meet the ghost. Some of the town's pranksters overheard this, and decided to make Miss DeVault's wish come true.

One young man agreed to play the part of the ghost. He draped himself and his horse with white sheets, and went to hide behind the Adams cabin. At a signal from his buddies, he was to ride out from behind the cabin and spur his horse down the road, hopefully scaring the paste out of Miss DeVault and anyone else who was there.

At 9 pm on September 30, 1913, a group of ghost hunters went out to the dilapidated cabin. It was the thirtieth anniversary of the murder, so everyone agreed that conditions for seeing Adams's ghost were ripe. Suddenly, the group was startled by the thunder of hooves, and the "ghost" tore around the side of the cabin, headed straight for them. Everyone panicked, nearly trampling each other as they scrambled to escape – everyone, that is, but Maud DeVault.

The intrepid young teacher stepped forward and grabbed the horse's reins. Then she unholstered a revolver – who knew the schoolmarm was packing? – pointed it, and asked the ghost why it haunted the cabin.

Then she popped off a couple of shots, just to make her point.

The poor horse was just as freaked out as everyone else. It bolted and crashed into the fence. Several white sheets floated to the ground. The teacher had killed the ghost!

The crowd pushed and shoved in confusion. One of the women, a formidable mountain of a girl at nearly 280 pounds, broke from the group and beat feet back to Redington to spread the news. Someone else hopped in a car to follow her, and just barely caught up to her. They brought her back to the cabin, and that's when she discovered that it was her brother that had been the prankster under the sheet. He'd survived both the shots fired and the runaway horse. His sister collapsed with the relief and stress, and a doctor had to be called.

When the kerfuffle died down, Maud explained that she had fully expected people to play a joke on the new-to-town schoolmarm, and had loaded her revolver with blanks. People looked at her with a new respect after that.

The town of Redington sputtered out in the mid-1960s, and the "haunted" cabin burned int 1974. But the story of the fearless ghostbusting schoolteacher remains.

OCTOBER

OCTOBER 1
Mob Justice, Bloomington, IL (1881)

There has only been one lynching in McLean County, Illinois, and it had nothing to do with race (the victim was white). Still, it was a vicious example of "justice" taken to barbarous extremes. The town of Bloomington has a proud, illustrious history, but the hanging of Charles Pierce on October 1, 1881, is a dark stain that can never be erased.

Pierce was accused of being a horse thief, and was being held at the McLean County Jail. He was being moved from one cell to another when he attacked his jailer, Henry Frank. Pierce grabbed Frank's Colt revolver and shot him in the shoulder, then fired a fatal shot into the jailer's chest.

Sheriff Joseph Ator heard the shots and came running. Pierce had probably not meant to kill Frank, because he looked shocked as he shouted, "I surrender, I surrender!" Ator disarmed Pierce and shoved him back into a cell.

Pierce picked the wrong guy to kill. Frank was a well-known, well-liked public official. When word spread that he'd been shot and killed in the line of duty by a low-down, no-good horse thief, it took only about half an hour for a crowd to gather at the jail, demanding their own justice for Pierce. By 8 pm (the murder happened at 6:30), there was a crowd of several thousand people milling around in front of the jail.

Then the mob started to lay siege to the building. It took them about two hours to break into the jail. When they did, they dragged Pierce out to face "Judge Lynch."

"Give me five minutes to pray," he begged, and someone yelled back, "This is not the time for praying." Pierce was repeatedly kicked as he was led to a nearby tree. "Don't kick me, boys," he pleaded. "I haven't but a minute more to live."

Someone snugged the noose around Pierce's neck and threw the rope over a limb. Helping hands tugged the rope tight, and Pierce was raised off the ground. One of his executioners climbed onto the stout limb and pulled on the rope to lift Pierce a few feet higher, then let him go so he fell with a jerk. The crowd laughed and cheered, so the joker did it a few more times.

This seemed to be the signal for the crowd to have its sick fun with Pierce. A Chicago newspaper later described the vicious scene.

"The pants were ripped from the body, and a lighted cigar was stuck in the gaping mouth. One plug-ugly, more atrocious than the rest, slid down the rope with great force to the shoulders of the struggling victim. Small boys hooted, yelled, and taunted [Pierce], calling him all manner of vile names." Pierce hung there for half an hour before McLean County Coroner William Matthews arrived to cut him down.

Pierce's degradation continued after his death. He was taken to the undertaker Montell Jeter, who put him on display for the edification of the hundreds of locals who traipsed past to gawk at the corpse. Pierce's body was covered with a sheet, but the rope was still tied around his swollen, discolored neck.

Charles Pierce, when his humiliation was finally over, was buried in the McLean County Poor Farm cemetery. The poor farm is long gone, but the cemetery is still there, a lonely, overgrown spot in a plowed field just south of the county's animal control building. It's a fitting resting place for Pierce and many other forgotten souls of the poor farm.

OCTOBER 2
The Battle of Saltville, Saltville, VA (1864)

The town of Saltville was named for the saltworks there. Because salt was used in meat preservation, the operation was vitally important. As the Union strengthened its hold on the South, Federal troops attacked strategic targets like ordinance centers, supply depots, and the saltworks.

There were actually two battles fought over Saltville, but it is the first one, on October 2, 1864, that brings us today's ghost story. The first battle, more accurately known as the Saltville Massacre, was one of the greatest atrocities of the Civil War. A combination of Union military ineptitude and Confederate racial hatred, the battle ended with the wholesale slaughter of colored troops. The fact that most of the victims' bodies were never recovered makes Saltville ripe for haunting.

Stephen Burbridge raised his own Union regiment for the war. He joined the army officially in 1864, and successfully repelled John Hunt Morgan's incursion into Kentucky. Lincoln was so impressed that he put Burbridge in charge of squashing other Confederate guerrilla actions. Burbridge threw himself into the assignment with gusto, imprisoning Southern sympathizers, declaring martial law, and earning himself the nickname "The Butcher of Kentucky." One of his enthusiasms was General Order 59 which stated, "Whenever an unarmed Union citizen is murdered, four guerrillas will be selected from the prison and publicly shot to death at the most convenient place near the scene of the outrages." Retribution at a four-to-one rate certainly counts as overkill.

Camp Nelson in Kentucky was home to 600 troops of the 5th US Colored Cavalry, commanded by Colonel Robert W. Ratliff. Ratliff and Burbridge were assigned to capture Saltville. Ratliff's untrained troops and Burbridge's 5,200 soldiers combined forces and began their march to Virginia in the fall of 1864.

(Of course, the colored troops were shamefully abused by the white soldiers along the way. Colonel Ratliff later wrote, "The 5th USCC were made the subject of much ridicule and many insulting remarks by the white troops, and in some instances petty outrages, such as pulling off the caps of the colored soldiers, stealing their horses etc. These insults, as well as the jeers and taunts that they would not fight, were borne by the colored soldiers patiently ... In no instance did I hear colored soldiers make any reply to insulting language used toward [them] by white troops.")

The Union forces approached Saltville on October 2, 1864, and came under heavy fire. This delayed their progress long enough for Confederate reinforcements to arrive. The Union forces made several futile attacks on the entrenched Confederates, losing several hundred troops in each advance.

Then the Confederates saw the colored troops, and went absolutely berserk. They jumped over their fortifications and charged towards the Union troops, bayonets fixed, howling and shrieking with rage. Burbridge and Ratliff fled the field, leaving behind hundreds of dead, dying, and wounded Union soldiers.

Over the next six days, the Confederates took out their frustrations on the Union soldiers left behind. The Southerners shot every Black soldier they found. They didn't only slaughter the troops they found on the battlefield, either. A Union surgeon working at a nearby Confederate hospital reported that many wounded colored troops were hauled off into the woods, never to return. Several white officers, too, fell to the wrath of the Confederates, who shot or stabbed them as they lay in their hospital beds.

There was, and is, no way to tell how many Union troops, Black and white, were massacred that week. Many of the dead or dying were dumped into a nearby sinkhole or thrown into the river, or stuffed into one of the mineshafts that dot the area. Local lore holds that some of the victims were buried in a mass grave, which then had a hog pen built over it.

Burbridge was removed from command for his failure, and was replaced by General George Stoneman. On December 20, 1864, Stoneman made another attempt to take Saltville. This time, the Union troops were successful. They captured the town and destroyed the saltworks.

The two battles combined resulted in more than 500 casualties, and they are a lively bunch. Reenactors say that the spirits like to join in when the battles are recreated. They see ghostly figures on the field, and hear the whiz of phantom lead zipping past them.

OCTOBER 3
Time Slip, Lincoln, NE (1963)

In 1963, Coleen Buterbaugh was working as secretary to Dean Sam Dahl at Wesleyan University in Lincoln, Nebraska. One morning her boss sent her over to the C.C. White Memorial Building, the university's music department, to track down a visiting professor from Scotland, Dr. Tom McCourt. Coleen made her way across campus, dodging students who had just gotten out of early class.

She reached the room in which she expected to find Dr. McCourt, and knocked on the door. There was no answer, so she knocked again. Still, there was only silence.

Knowing that some professors become engrossed in their work and ignore the world around them, Coleen opened the door and peeked inside. The room was dark, but she could see someone standing in the shadows near a filing cabinet.

Coleen came further into the room, wrinkling her nose. The building had been built in 1903, and that morning, its age was showing in the musty scent of mildew that permeated the air even with the window open.

"Dr. McCourt?" Coleen tried again. She flipped on the lights.

To her surprise, the lights revealed not Dr. McCourt, but a tall, thin woman in her mid- to late-thirties. Her dark hair was done up in an old-fashioned bun, and she wore a long-sleeved white blouse and a skirt down to her ankles. Ignoring Coleen, she reached into the open drawer of the filing cabinet.

"Excuse me, have you seen Dr. McCourt?" Coleen asked. The woman stayed silent, focused on her filing cabinet search. Coleen was about to turn her back on the rude woman, when she happened to glance out the window.

Instead of the trees and the building next door that should have been the view, Coleen saw only a bright sunny sky – no trees, no buildings. Now thoroughly disconcerted, Coleen looked back to the woman.

That's when the woman slowly faded. The scent of age and dust was almost chokingly strong. Coleen stumbled out of the room just in time to avoid being sick. She walked back to the dean's office in a daze.

When she got back, Dahl asked her if she'd found McCourt. Coleen was still so stunned at her strange experience that the truth came tumbling out of her.

Dean Dahl had an interest in paranormal phenomena, so he listened without judgment to Coleen's story. Together, they decided to do some research.

Coleen described the woman. They both realized she was too old to be a student, and was probably a faculty member. They worked back through yearbooks, searching for a picture. In the 1936 yearbook, they found their mystery woman.

Clara Mills taught music at the university from 1912 to 1936. The room Coleen had seen Clara in had been Clara's office – and it was where she had died, in 1940. The filing cabinet that Clara had been looking through was found to contain choral music dating back to the teacher's years at the university. Interestingly, Clara died shortly before 9 am in the office on October 3, 1940.

Coleen stepped into the office around 8:50 am on October 3, 1963, the anniversary of Clara's death.

OCTOBER 4
The October Curse, Christie, WI (1907)

October: the month of bonfires, trick-or-treating, thick cozy sweaters, and pumpkin spice. But for Charlotte Mills, October meant only heartache and death.

For years, the Mills family lived a perfectly normal life in the small town of Christie, Wisconsin. But in 1901, tragedy struck. Fay Mills, Charlotte's oldest son, was drowned on October 12 in Alaska when the ship he was working on was caught in a storm.

Not even a year had passed when Charlotte's second son Benjamin died on the job in Idaho on October 2, 1902. Charlotte was gutted by the loss of two of her sons in less than a year. She took comfort in the love of her husband and her youngest son, Claude.

But more sorrow awaited Charlotte. Her husband, John Calvin Mills, died suddenly of heart failure in 1905. Charlotte struggled along as best she could, but depression sank dull claws into her soul. In 1907, the October curse claimed one more victim.

On October 4, Charlotte told Claude that she was going to a friend's house for a visit. It wasn't unusual for her to spend the night on such a visit, so when Charlotte didn't return home that evening, Claude wasn't unduly concerned. But when he still hadn't heard from Charlotte the next morning, a worried Claude set off to find her.

Tracks near the bridge on the bank of the Black River made him fear the worst, and a bit more looking confirmed those fears. He found Charlotte's lifeless body floating near the shore. Medical examiners agreed that the cause of death was pretty apparent. Claude realized for himself that his mother's death was no accident when he got back home. There, he discovered that before leaving, Charlotte had laid out the clothes she wished to be buried in on her bed.

The story would have remained just a tragic family tale, were it not for the ghost. Only a few months after Charlotte's suicide, local resident Albert Neis told police that his horse had been startled near the bridge by a brilliant light that rose up before him, then disappeared. Another man, Lenwood Shaw, was returning from town with his wife when they saw the mysterious light on the bridge over the Black River. Before the year was out, eight people had witnessed the strange light. People assumed that the light was the ghost of Charlotte Mills. The light appeared so often that farmers began to avoid the bridge, saying that their horses refused to cross it. That was in 1907, but even today, people report feeling uncomfortable at the bridge.

OCTOBER 5
The Medium and the Maiden Voyage, France (1930)

Renowned British ghost researcher Harry Price was always on the lookout for evidence of the paranormal. On October 7, 1930, he arranged a séance with medium Eileen Garrett, hoping to contact Arthur Conan Doyle, who had recently died. Price didn't get to chat with the famous author. What did happen in the séance was far more intriguing.

Eileen went into a trance state and began speaking in a deep voice. She identified herself as Flight Lieutenant Irwin, commander of the R101, a British airship. Eileen had experienced premonitions of a disaster involving an airship for several years. In 1926, she'd had a vision of a dirigible in the sky over London. In 1928, she saw the dirigible again, but this time, smoke was coming from it. In 1929, she saw the ship again – and this time, it was in flames.

Also in 1928, while in trance, Eileen passed along a message from the deceased Captain Raymond Hinchcliffe. The message warned Hinchcliffe's friend, Ernest Johnson, who was the navigator of the R101, not to go on the ship's maiden voyage.

During the October 7 séance, Eileen (speaking as Lt. Irwin) spoke in a disjointed tone, saying that the airship was too heavy for the engine to lift, and that it had almost scraped the roof in a French town called Achy. She also said that the combination of carbon and hydrogen was completely wrong.

Two days before the séance, on October 5, the R101 crashed on its maiden voyage from France to India. The airship had passed over the village of Achy so low that it almost scraped a church tower. The impact itself, on a hill in Beauvais, France, was gentle and survivable, but the gasbag was filled with hydrogen. The engine backfired and the gas ignited, killing 48 of the 55 people onboard.

Ian Coster, a colleague of Price's, published highlights from the séance. Shortly afterwards, a man named Will Charlton contacted Price and asked for a complete transcript of the séance. Charlton worked at the base where R101 was built. He was amazed to find that Eileen Garrett had mentioned over forty highly technical details about the airship. Even stranger, she seemed to deliver information from the dead crew that explained why the airship had crashed. Unfortunately, due to its paranormal source, Eileen's "testimony" was not considered in the official inquiry into the crash.

OCTOBER 6
The Bells of St. James, Prince Edward Island (1859)

Early one Friday morning, the people of Charlottetown were awakened by a great clang. A man living near St. James Church recognized it as the voice of the church's bell, which tolled a second time. When the bell rang a third time, he and some neighbors went to see who was ringing the bell. The fourth toll sounded as they entered the churchyard, and by the time they got to the doors, the bell tolled a fifth time. With the sixth ring, the doors of the church flung themselves open. Inside the church, the men saw three women, all dressed in white.

The bell rang again, and the doors slammed shut and refused to open. Looking through a window, the men saw the three women drift through the church to the bell tower steps, then disappear. By this time, the minister had arrived. He unlocked the door, and the men headed for the belfry. On their way up the stairs, they heard the bell above them toll for the eighth time. Someone had to be up there.

When the men got to the bell tower, the great bell had fallen silent. There was no sign of anyone in the belfry.

Later that strange morning of October 6, 1859, the steamer *Fairie Queen* set off from Pictou, carrying mail, cargo, and passengers. The weather was fine, and the ship was scheduled to make the trip to Charlottetown in about seven hours.

She never arrived.

A few days later, word arrived that the steamer had sunk. There had been eight passengers on board – one for each toll of the church bell. Five men and three women had drowned ... and the three women were parishioners of St. James Church.

Was it their spirits the men saw as the bell tolled their loss?

OCTOBER 7
King's Mountain, North/South Carolina (1780)

The Battle of King's Mountain, fought on the border between North and South Carolina, marked the turning point of the Revolutionary War. The Overmountain Men, led by John Sevier, joined forces with other patriots to defeat Loyalist troops on October 7, 1780. The fighting was fierce, and the colonists suffered grievous losses.

Near the end of the battle, Robert Sevier, John's brother, was wounded in the side as he tried to reload. The British ball went into his kidney. A captured British surgeon tried unsuccessfully to extract the ball. He dressed the wound and told Robert he had two choices. The ball could be removed later – if he stayed put and recuperated for a while. But if he set off for home, the damaged kidney would become infected and kill him in nine days.

Robert was a frontiersman, fierce and independent. John, his brother and commanding officer, asked him to heed the doctor's warning and stay quietly where he was. But Robert was determined to get home. Barely able to mount his horse, Robert set off, accompanied by James Sevier, his nephew.

On the ninth day of their journey, the two men stopped for the night, at the same place the Overmountain Men had bivouacked on their march to King's Mountain. They made camp and ate a scanty meal. That night, Robert took a turn for the worse. Just as the surgeon had predicted nine days earlier, he died. James buried his uncle in the shade of an oak tree. Robert's horse, sensing the loss of his master, tossed its head and balked as James led it away to continue the sad trip home.

It's said that Captain Robert Sevier still walks the highway in that area. People walking along US 19E get the eerie feeling of being followed. And it seems Robert's horse is still waiting for its master. Witnesses have reported hearing the clip-clop of an approaching horse that never appears. One rider, Clark Stafford, encountered the invisible horse while out riding. His own horse was so terrified by the supernatural encounter that it threw him.

OCTOBER 8
Cities on Fire, Chicago, IL (1871)

The autumn of 1871 was very dry in the Midwest. Northern Illinois and Wisconsin baked in the heat, still sultry in early October. Chicago had only had about an inch of rain since the 4th of July. Firemen in the city had already responded to twenty fires in the first week of October.

On October 8, several fires broke out in the area. The town of Peshtigo, in northern Wisconsin near Green Bay, was destroyed, with 1,500 lives lost. But it is the Great Chicago Fire that most people remember today. The loss of life was not as drastic – it's estimated that there were between 200 and 300 fatalities – but it is the Chicago Fire that has given us the ghost stories.

The fire started in a barn behind DeKoven Street, just a few blocks east of the Church of the Holy Family. (Catherine O'Leary, whose cow is traditionally blamed for kicking over a lantern and starting the fire, was a parishioner there.) The second oldest parish in Chicago, it was founded in 1857 by Jesuit missionary Fr. Arnold Damen.

The fire that raged through the city devoured 28 miles of wood-paved streets, 18,000 buildings, and landmarks such as the first Chicago Historical Society, the newly-built Palmer House hotel, and the Tribune Building. The fire was finally doused by nature when it began to rain. Even then, the city was so hot that it took over a day for things to cool down enough for people to return. Business owners who were able to find their safes were often bitterly disappointed when they opened them; superheated contents often burst into flames with the rush of oxygen into the safe. William Ogden had a very bad day – he lost not only his Chicago home but also his lumber company in Green Bay to the flames.

One of the surprisingly few ghost stories that came out of the Chicago Fire involves the Excalibur nightclub, or rather, the building that stood where the Excalibur is today. The fire moved incredibly quickly, and many of the victims were trapped inside buildings and burned to death. Several women who were running down the street to escape the flames decided to take refuge in the building. The fire soon overran the building, and they were killed.

The activity at the Excalibur is intense. Candles light themselves after closing time. Glasses and beer bottles shatter for no reason. The women who burned to death are seen and heard in the club. Witnesses report hearing panicked screams coming from the restrooms on the first floor, even when there's no one in them.

One of the oddest quirks about the hauntings here is that things often appear on ledges that are well out of reach for someone without a ladder. Chairs and cases of booze are found stacked to great heights. Once, a teddy bear was found perched on a ledge 25 feet above the floor.

And what of the Church of the Holy Family, so very close to ground zero? When the fire broke out, Fr. Damen was in New York on a mission trip. A telegram warned him of the fire. Fr. Damen wired back, begging his parishioners to pray for the church to be spared. Fr. Damen himself prayed all that night, and pledged that if the church was spared, he would create a shrine to Our Lady of Perpetual Help. The wind shifted, carrying the flames away from the church. When Fr. Damen returned, he ordered seven candles to be lit on a side altar to commemorate the miracle. The candles were later replaced by gas jets. Now, seven lightbulbs keep silent, joyful vigil in the chapel.

OCTOBER 9
Boo!, Hattiesburg, MS (1959)

When a family builds a new house, they generally expect to be the only ones living there. This was not the case for the Howells of Hattiesburg, Mississippi. They built a ranch house in 1977, and soon realized they were not alone.

There seemed to be someone – an invisible someone – living in their attic.

The family routinely heard shuffling sounds coming from the attic. Eventually, whoever-it-was came down and began to rummage through the house. (Perhaps it was getting comfortable with the Howells.)

Things got really interesting the day their son Scott heard the ghost come down from the attic, go outside, and start up their riding lawnmower. Apparently, the ghost was unfamiliar with the controls, because soon the riderless mower smashed into the side of the Howells' Cadillac. Unfortunately, their insurance company refused to pay for the damage.

So, who is this reckless-driver spirit? The Howells have a theory about the identity of their invisible housemate. Harry Blosser. An Air Force pilot, died when his B-58 jet crashed on the property in October 1959. The Howells believe that Blosser's disoriented spirit wandered the woods until they built their house.

Then, he moved in with them. Hey, ghosts like company too.

OCTOBER 10
London Bridge Is No Longer Falling Down, Lake Havasu City, AZ (1971)

In the early 1970s, London Bridge was, indeed, falling down. More accurately, the centuries-old bridge was beginning to sink under the weight of modern traffic. The original wooden bridge was built in various stages between AD 50 and 1176. Stonework was added in the medieval period, and the Victorians added more stone in 1831. By the 1960s, the bridge was showing its considerable age. But you can't just tear down London Bridge. The City of London decided to auction off the historic landmark in 1968.

Robert McCulloch, an American entrepreneur, made the winning bid. The bridge was dismantled block by block, and each stone was numbered. The blocks were shipped via the Panama Canal to Long Beach, California, then trucked 300 miles inland to Lake Havasu City, Arizona.

It took three years of careful reconstruction, working from the coded diagram and from plans from 1824, but in 1971, the bridge was fully restored. It was officially dedicated on October 10, to great fanfare: fireworks, a parade, and a visit by the Lord Mayor of London.

Adorably, an English village was built next to the bridge. Exports from the UK abound – transplanted English grass, a red telephone box, an iconic double-decker bus, and a London taxi. City planners also added an English restaurant and a pub, Ye Hog In Armour.

Those aren't the only things that came over to keep the bridge company. London Bridge has its own complement of Old World ghosts.

The lamps on the bridge are made from melted-down cannons from Napoleon's warships, captured in the Battle of Waterloo. So, if you think about it, those lampposts have killed a lot of people. Other energy comes from victims of the Black Death in the mid-1300s. Corpses of plague victims were stacked on the riverbank to be picked up by a ferry for burial.

There are individual ghosts that haunt the bridge too. One is a London bobby, still patrolling his beat. People say the ghost of Jack the Ripper hangs out at the bridge too – he killed seven girls in 1888 in Whitechapel, which was within one mile of the bridge when it stood in London.

Other ghosts include a couple in Victorian dress who walk along as if enjoying an evening stroll. And why not? They probably think they're still in foggy London, not in the Arizona desert. Or maybe they do know where they are, and are glad for the change in scenery.

One lucky witness was thrilled to see four ghosts wandering the bridge in Victorian garb. She thought it was absolutely ingenious of the organizers to add a touch of London spooky to the bridge by creating realistic holograms, or projections, or … whatever …

After searching for a projector, and not finding anyone who could answer her questions about the ghosts, she realized that the Victorian "ghosts" that so enthralled her were not, in fact, projections for the delight of tourists visiting London Bridge.

They were real.

OCTOBER 11
Happy Birthday? Keokuk, IA (1934-1936)

A strange presence showed up at the Haines family's home in Keokuk, Iowa, every October 11 from 1934 to 1936. The annual visit was marked by poltergeist activity, mostly furniture being moved. The apparition of a young man would appear … but the ghost never fully materialized, usually manifesting just his lower torso. He made up for that shortcoming in other ways, like the time he rode a phantom bicycle through the house.

No one ever figured out who this young man was, or why he haunted the Haines family. The family did notice, though, that the ghost's annual visit coincided with the birthday of one of the Haines boys.

OCTOBER 12
Lieutenant Sutton, Annapolis, MD (1907)

Can a ghost, wronged, defend itself?

James Sutton was a lieutenant at the naval academy in Annapolis, Maryland. On October 12, 1907, Sutton attended a Navy dance, where he had a bit too much to drink. On the way home, he picked a fight with his buddies. He was pushed to the ground, and came up swinging. Enraged, he threatened to kill the others. When they all got back to base, Sutton went to his tent. Still fuming, he picked up two pistols, and went in search of his friends. Someone spotted the guns and arrested Sutton, but before the authorities could take him into custody, he started to fire wildly. The fight ended suddenly and dramatically when Sutton put one of the pistols to his temple and pulled the trigger.

At least, that was the official version of events. Lieutenant Sutton himself had a very different tale to tell.

Sutton's family lived in Portland, Oregon. Before they even heard of his death, his mother had a dreadful sense that something awful had happened to her son. When the news of Sutton's suicide reached her, she refused to believe that her son could have died by his own hand.

Sutton appeared to her in a vision, and confirmed her suspicions. She said later, "Jimmie stood right before me and said, "Momma, I never killed myself … My hands are as free from blood as when I was five years old."" He told her what had really happened – the others had shot him, and tried to make it look like a suicide.

Mrs. Sutton experienced this vision for several months. She was distraught over her son's death, of course. But she became convinced, through the ghost's insistence, that there was more to her son's death than the authorities were admitting. Sutton provided details of the fight that weren't in the official report, and told his mother about wounds he'd received before she found out about them.

In 1909, the Suttons contacted Arlington National Cemetery and requested that Sutton's body be exhumed. An examination revealed wounds on the body not mentioned in the navy doctor's report – wounds Sutton had described to his mother.

Unfortunately, this didn't take the case any further. The testimonies of the witnesses to the fight were inconsistent, and there was no reason for Sutton to have killed himself in a drunken brawl. Unanswered questions swirled around the case, but investigators were never able to agree on a resolution.

Sutton's ghost appeared less frequently, and then stopped visiting his mother entirely.

OCTOBER 13
Horserace With The Devil, Bath, NC (1813)

Jesse Elliot was a hard-drinking, free-spirited mane who loved to race horses. He often boasted that he owned the fastest horse in the county. He would race anyone, and day of the week. He'd even skip church on Sunday if there was a race to be run.

One sunny Sunday in mid-October, a stranger rode into town on a coal-black horse and announced that he wanted to race. Jesse leapt at the chance, and saddled his horse. Some other fellows who weren't big churchgoers gathered to cheer Jesse on. As the race began, a few of the men heard Jesse yell to his horse as he urged it down the track, "Take me in a winner or take me to Hell!"

At that moment, the riders were neck and neck, pounding down the track. Jesse's horse took the curve too fast, then balked, tossing its head and digging its hooves into the ground. Jesse was thrown from his mount, and went headfirst into a pine tree, hard enough to leave hanks of hair stuck in the bark. His neck broke on impact, and he died instantly.

The mysterious dark rider hauled his horse to a halt, stooped over Jesse's body for a moment, then rode off, never to be seen again.

Within days, the pine tree that took Jesse's life turned brown and rotted on the side where Jesse's head had struck it, while the other half stayed vibrant and green. His hair remained embedded in the tree for almost a year.

The hoofprints in the soil are still there, over 200 years later. In the 1950s, a news crew came to the field to investigate the prints. Locals told the crew that chickens and hogs would eat corn from all around the indentations, but wouldn't eat any corn that had fallen in the holes. The crew found this hard to believe, so they tried it for themselves. They scattered corn all over the hoofprints, then brought some chickens to the field. The birds ate every single kernel from the area around the hoofprints, but ignored any in the divots.

A 93-year-old man who'd lived in the area his whole life told the crew that when he was a boy, he and his brothers would place items in the prints on their way to school, and find the prints empty on their way home. This jibed with local lore, which held that nothing would stay in the divots for long – any forest debris would mysteriously vanish from the hoofprints. Intrigued by this, the crew conducted another experiment. They filled the indentations with dirt, leaves, and pebbles, then crisscrossed the hoofprints with black thread. They watched and filmed for a few hours, until it got dark. They came back at dawn to find that the holes were clean of all debris … but the nets of black thread were undisturbed.

OCTOBER 14
The Spirits of Cedar Creek, Middleton, VA (1864)

In the autumn of 1864, General Phil Sheridan was ordered to wage total war on the Shenandoah Valley, scouring it of anything that could be of use to the Confederate army. The residents referred to it as the Burning.

General Jubal Early, in command of 15,000 Confederates, was tasked with defending the valley as best he could. Early's army was vastly outnumbered, and Sheridan knew it. By

October 10, Sheridan's army was encamped beside Cedar Creek near the town of Middleton, Virginia. Sheridan had such confidence in his superior forces that he decided to take a little break from the field. He stayed for a while at the Logan house in Winchester, about twenty minutes away from the Union camp. Even the troops setting up camp were relaxed – the regimental band even found time to hold concerts in a nearby Episcopal church.

The morning of October 19 dawned slowly, with Cedar Creek shrouded in fog. Union soldiers yawned as they poked campfires to life and poured water into coffeepots. Gray shapes moved in the fog, but the troops went about their morning camp duties, oblivious.

Then the fog exploded in bursts of muzzle flash. The Union troops hadn't bothered to set up pickets to guard the camp. General Early sent some of his troops to surround the camp, and led the rest in a frontal attack. Surprise turned to blind panic. In just a few moments, three Union corps were routed and on the run.

The Confederates didn't press the fleeing Union troops. Seeing the breakfast preparations, the Southerners couldn't resist the chance to down some hot food and coffee. They sat down to enjoy what the Union soldiers had left behind.

Meanwhile, Sheridan heard the distant sound of gunfire, and realized that something was horribly wrong. He jumped on his horse and pelted toward Cedar Creek. He ran right into his own fleeing soldiers. Amazingly, Sheridan was able to halt the rout and gather his troops. He pulled his men together and talked them out of their panic. Soon, he had collected his troops into some semblance of order, and gotten them turned around to meet the Confederates, who by then had resumed their pursuit. The tables turned – the Rebels fled, and the Union troops took back the Cedar Creek camp.

The church where the band had played was turned into a field hospital. Casualties were buried in the churchyard. The battle was over … but the haunting of Cedar Creek was just beginning.

Workmen were detailed to dig up the bodies of the Union dead and put them in pine boxes to be shipped home. The boxes were stacked in piles next to the church. Locals said that late at night, a light would emerge from the church and wander over to the wooden boxes, as if someone was carrying a candle to search for something among the coffins. At other times, people would hear music coming from the empty church – the same tunes played by the regimental band.

Farmers in the area began to report the sounds of battle still being played out in their fields, and some even saw phantom regiments, led by ghostly officers, marching along the roads.

One farmer, Holt Hottel, leased an old barn that stood on the battlefield. One evening at dusk, he went into the barn to feed the horses. He was pitching hay down from the loft when he saw a dark figure in the shadows. Thinking a tramp had wandered into the barn looking for a place to sleep, Hottel yelled at the man to leave. When the figure didn't move, Hottel feinted at him with the pitchfork. The tines of the pitchfork went right through the shadowy figure. Terrified, Hottel dropped the pitchfork and fled the barn.

Nearby Belle Grove Plantation is also home to some spectral phenomena. Sheridan used the gracious mansion as his headquarters after the battle. But before that, Belle Grove was the scene of a bittersweet reunion between brothers in arms.

Confederate general Stephen Ramseur had commanded Early's advance guard during the initial attack on the Union camp. When Sheridan counterattacked, Ramseur's division was at the forefront of the fighting. Ramseur was mortally wounded, captured, and taken to Belle Grove.

Although he was in the hands of the enemy when he was taken to Sheridan's headquarters, Ramseur found himself surrounded by old friends. As Ramseur lay dying in the parlor, his classmates from West Point – Henry DuPont, Wesley Merritt, George Armstrong Custer, and others – gathered around him. Ramseur was conscious when he was brought in, and the Confederate general and his Union friends were able to have one last reunion before he died.

On at least one occasion, visitors to Belle Grove have seen a group of Civil War commanders gathered in the room where Ramseur died. They assume its a group of reenactors dressed in the blue and gray of officers' uniforms, until the staff tell them there are no costumed interpreters at the mansion.

OCTOBER 15
Murder and Retribution, New Orleans, LA (1890)

New Orleans Police Chief David Hennessy spent his career fighting the Stoppagherva, a Sicilian mob syndicate operating in the French Quarter. On the evening of October 15, 1890, as Hennessy walked home from the police station, he was ambushed by a group of gunmen on Basin Street. A light rain was falling as Hennessy left the station with Captain William O'Connor just after 11 pm. Hennessy turned up Basin Street, headed home. O'Connor walked in the opposite direction. For the past three years, Hennessy had been accompanied by bodyguards on his nightly walk home. But that night, he was alone.

Before he reached the home he shared with his widowed mother, Hennessy was shot several times. He drew his own revolver and returned fire, but his assailants melted into the night. O'Connor heard the shots, and ran several blocks to find his friend bleeding on the muddy ground. O'Connor asked Hennessy who'd shot him.

"Dagoes," he whispered.

Italians were loathed in New Orleans at the time, just as they were all over America. Sicilians were especially reviled in the skin-color-conscious Deep South. As it was well-known that Hennessy had been hunting the Sicilian mob, the New Orleans police immediately began rounding up Italians.

Within 24 hours, between 45 and 250 Italians were taken into custody. Pietro Monasterio, a shoemaker, was arrested because he lived across the street from where Hennessy was standing when he was shot. Antonio Marchesi, a fruit peddler, was arrested because he was friends with Monasterio. Emmanuele Polizzi, who was mentally ill, was identified as one of the men running from the scene of the crime. Eventually, eighteen men and a 14-year-old boy (the son of one of the accused) were charged with murder or as accessories, and held without bail.

The trial concluded on March 13, 1891. The lack of evidence was overwhelming, and all suspects were acquitted. Still, they were held in prison for a while longer.

Tensions in the city were running high. When the not-guilty verdict was released, New Orleans exploded into violence. The morning after the verdict was announced, a mob thousands strong met to demand vigilante justice. They broke down the prison door with a battering ram. Warden Lemuel Davis, helpless against the raging mob, let all nineteen prisoners out of their cells and told them to hide as best they could. Gasparo Marchesi, the teenager, hid under a box across the hall from his father Antonio. He undoubtedly heard the shot that killed his father.

Eleven of the eighteen men were killed by the mob. The mentally ill Polizzi was dragged outside, hanged from a lamppost, and shot. Nine others were shot in the head or clubbed to death inside the prison.

The Italians who were murdered that morning joined the plethora of spirits who walk the streets of New Orleans. A couple were on their way to a birthday party one December evening, and the woman stopped to record a bit of video of the Christmas lights decorating a house they were passing. When she played the video back, she realized she had captured a male voice saying something strange. It sounded like *"Ho freddo."* The couple played the video several more times, trying to parse the voice. Then, the boyfriend recognized the words.

"Ho freddo" means "I'm cold" in Italian.

OCTOBER 16
The Ghost of James Wormwood, Birmingham, AL (1899)

Iron smelting at the end of the 19th century was a dangerous job. Conditions in furnaces were best described as "hellish", and for good reason: the temperature inside a smelting factory could reach 120 degrees or more, the hours were long, the work was physically demanding, and the work environment was incredibly dangerous. Catwalks were suspended over an open cauldron filled to the brim with molten iron – not a place for the faint of heart.

Sloss Furnaces in Birmingham, Alabama, was such a place. The huge factory chewed up ore and spit out iron and steel. It also chewed up men and spit them out too. There was no such thing as workman's comp back then. If a man was injured on the job and couldn't work, he was simply fired. There were plenty of guys hungry and eager to take his place.

During the time the Sloss Furnaces Mill was in operation, fifty-five men were killed there. Forty-seven of those fatalities happened on the graveyard shift. The foreman on that shift was James Wormwood, and he was a hard man to work for. Iron workers had to be tough to survive their jobs, but Wormwood was sadistic.

Wormwood was foreman over about 150 men. Not much work was expected out of the graveyard shift; their job was mostly just to keep the furnaces hot enough to ensure full production on the daytime shifts. But Wormwood was ambitious, desperate to look good to management. He drove his workers much harder than he should have – and he was vicious about it. He made them take dangerous risks to speed up production, in an environment where shortcuts could be deadly. He abused his men verbally and physically. He was hated, but he was the foreman.

On October 16, 1899, Wormwood was standing on the catwalk above the cauldron of molten iron when he lost his balance and fell over the railing into the furnace. Death was almost instantaneous.

Almost.

That's what the official report said, anyway. But according to rumor, Wormwood's accidental death wasn't an accident. He had no reason to be up on the catwalk during the graveyard shift. And wasn't it odd that an experienced iron worker could suddenly lose his footing so carelessly? Factory gossip held that Wormwood didn't suffer at all when he fell into the molten iron ... because he was already dead. The scuttlebutt was that several workers ganged up on the hated foreman, murdered him, then dumped his body into the cauldron to cover up the beating.

After Wormwood's death, the workers on the graveyard shift should have been able to relax. But strange things began happening. The tough, burly iron men started complaining that an "unnatural presence" was following them around. Production on that shift dragged, and workers quit in droves. In 1901, the company discontinued the graveyard shift.

The weirdness slowed down, but didn't stop. In 1926, a night watchman was shoved from behind. Right before he was pushed, he swore he heard a rough voice snarl, *"Get back to work!"* In the 1940s, workers reported seeing the badly burned figure of a man, who yelled at them angrily. Over the years, nearly a hundred reports were filed that could be considered supernatural. Many involved physical assault. Most of them happened in September or October. Nearly all of them took place late at night, during what used to be the graveyard shift.

Sloss Furnaces eventually closed as an industrial site. In the 1970s it was reopened as a museum, and has been designated a National Historic landmark.

It's also a popular spot for late-night hangouts for adventurous local teens. Many people have reported encounters with the vengeful, mutilated ghost of James Wormwood.

One girl went to the site alone one night. As she explored the abandoned furnace, it seemed to her that all the machinery turned on. She heard the roar of the foundry, and felt the incredible heat. Men's voices rose all around her, although she saw nothing. Then she heard a scream, and men yelling "He fell in the furnace!"

On another occasion, a carload of teenagers visited Sloss Furnaces on a ghost-hunting expedition. As they made their way across a catwalk, a whistle shrieked, scaring the crap out of them. The farther they ventured into the factory, the more the night came alive around them. They heard footsteps behind them, and the clang of metal being worked. Nervously, they tried to explain the sounds away as their imaginations playing tricks on them.

But around 3 am, as they were leaving, something happened that was definitely not a trick of sound. A phantom came barreling up behind them, shoving one boy from behind. When the others turned around, they saw a man with melted skin that had been charred black. He glared at them with glowing red eyes, shook his fist, and yelled, *"Get back to work!"*

The boys bolted for their car, piled in, and burned rubber getting away. The boy who had been pushed soon started complaining that his back was sore. The driver stopped at a convenience store to regroup. The boy who'd been shoved pulled up his shirt, and his friends saw two large burn marks on his back – in the shape of handprints.

OCTOBER 17
Blackbird Hill, Decatur, NE (1849, recurring)

The Omaha Indian Reservation lies eight miles north of Decatur, Nebraska. The revered Chief Blackbird is buried here in a mound nearly 45 feet high, sitting upright on his favorite horse. In 1804, Lewis and Clark paid their respects to the honored chief, leaving offerings at the burial mound.

Blackbird Hill is said to be haunted, but it's not Chief Blackbird doing the haunting.

Instead, the ghost is that of a young woman who was murdered here.

The story begins, not here in Nebraska, but back east. In the early 1840s, a young couple fell in love and planned to marry. Their plan was for the boy to finish his education, go abroad for a while, then on his return, they would get married. The girl agreed to wait for her intended.

The young man left after graduation, but never returned from his travels. The girl was devastated. She waited for several years, but eventually accepted the fact that her fiance was gone. She married another man, and they emigrated west, settling in Nebraska on Blackbird Hill, overlooking the Missouri River.

On October 17, 1849, the young bride was working on the homestead when she saw someone walking up the path from the river. To her astonishment, it was her fiance. He, too, was stunned to find that she was the one living in the small cabin.

The lovers shared a joyful reunion, unbelieving that fate could be so kind as to bring them back together. The young woman confessed that she had only married because she'd thought him dead – she'd never stopped loving him.

The young man told her the tale of his travels. He'd been shipwrecked, and had made his way back home after five long years. When he reached home, he was gutted to discover that his mother had died, and that his fiancee had married another. Hearing that she'd moved West, he'd joined a wagon train and traveled to California. He had no luck finding his lost love on the west coast. Heartbroken, he began to make his way back East, following the Missouri River. At the foot of Blackbird Hill, he'd seen a path leading up the slope, and decided to follow it. He'd never imagined that his long-lost love was waiting for him at the top of that winding path.

The young woman told him that when her husband came home, she would explain the situation, and ask to be released from her marriage to him. Then the two of them would be free to begin their life together, the life that had been so sadly postponed. The young man agreed to wait in the nearby woods, as the couple discussed the situation.

When the husband returned home, the young woman told him that her true love had appeared, and that against all odds, they'd found each other again. The husband reacted badly to the news. At first, he begged his wife to stay. When she refused, he became enraged. He drew his hunting knife and lunged at her.

She fell to the floor, screaming. The husband gathered his bleeding wife in his arms and ran out of the cabin, heading for the cliff overlooking the river. Hearing his lover's shriek of agony, the young man burst from the woods just in time to see his rival jump from the cliff, taking the love of his life with him.

The young man collapsed with grief. Bereft, he wandered aimlessly, not eating, not sleeping, just mourning. Eventually, he was taken in by a band of Omaha Indians, who cared for the delirious, ragged figure.

The path from the cabin to the cliff edge can still be seen today, because even today, over 170 years later, no grass will grow there. Every year, on October 17, it's said that people can still hear the young woman's screams of terror as she plunges to her death.

OCTOBER 18
Two Last Goodbyes, Zurich, Switzerland (1940)

Mr. F was walking back to work after his lunch break. It was around 1:45 pm on October 18, 1940. As he walked along the street, he happened to see his father, who had been out of town for two weeks. Thinking his father had returned unexpectedly, Mr. F walked faster and called out … but his father disappeared.

Confused and upset, he continued on his way. Later that day, he got a phone call telling him that his father had passed away the previous night.

Now he was really distraught. He called his sister to give her the sad news. He couldn't help it – he had to share his eerie experience.

That's when his sister told him that at 1:45 that afternoon, she too had seen their father, in a different part of town. The brother and sister agreed: their father had loved them so much, he had wanted to appear to them both once more as he was when he was still alive. It was his farewell to his beloved children.

OCTOBER 19
The Murder of Countess Elsa, Dresden, Germany (1756, recurring)

Moritzburg Castle was built as a nobleman's hunting lodge in 1542. It's a tidy little palace with four round towers, and it sits on an artificial island. The whole effect is that of a giant dollhouse.

The woods and lakes that surround the castle have been favorite hunting grounds for the nobility of Saxony for centuries, and it's here, out in the woods, that our ghost story for today begins.

In 1750, the castle was home to Count Ugo von Dentel and his wife Countess Elsa von Karman-Liechtenstein. Their marriage was not a happy one. The countess was unable to give her husband any heirs, so he decided to end the marriage – permanently.

On October 19, 1756, the count invited his wife to go boar hunting with him. When they got to the woods, the count strangled her, and left her body to be savaged by wild boars and hunting dogs. Her mangled corpse was soon discovered and brought back to the castle. The count shed crocodile tears and pretended to be grief-stricken at the accident that had befallen his wife.

The count didn't get to enjoy the single life for long. Soon the apparition of the late countess, her face shredded and dripping blood, began manifesting at his bedside, where she hollowly pleaded for her life. She gave him no rest, appearing nearly every night. And just in case her message was unclear, she always left a trail of blood leading from the bedroom down the hallway, out the door, and out to the spot in the woods where she'd been murdered. The count finally stabbed himself in the heart one night.

The countess got her satisfaction, but her gory apparition still visits the castle. She's been seen many times over the years. Very often, on the morning of October 20, the castle staff find a trail of blood leading out of the bedroom where the count took his life. Clearly, the countess has been there the night before.

OCTOBER 20
Time Slip, Abbeville, LA (1969)

L.C. and Charlie (not his real name) were business associates traveling through Louisiana. October 20, 1969, was a beautiful sunny fall day: clear blue skies, with the temperature at a crisp 60 degrees at 1:30 in the afternoon. L.C. and Charlie had just finished lunch in the small town of Abbeville, and were discussing their work as they tooled down Highway 167, headed north towards Lafayette about fifteen miles away.

There was little traffic on the highway; L.C. and Charlie only saw one car on the road. They were quickly overtaking it, as it was driving very slowly. Their conversation turned from their insurance work to the car ahead of them – it was an older style, but in absolutely mint condition. The men figured the driver must be headed to a car show.

Charlie, who was driving, decided to pass the car, as it was going so slowly. He slowed down too, so they could both get a good look at the pristine antique. L.C. noticed that the large orange license plate had "1940" stamped on it. So it *was* an antique.

As they passed, L.C., who was in the passenger seat, noticed that the driver of the other car was a young woman. She was dressed in 1940s vintage clothing, including a fur coat and a hat with a long, colored feather. A small child stood on the seat next to her, also dressed in a heavy coat and cap.

The woman's windows were rolled up, and L.C. wondered why she wasn't enjoying the crisp fall air. Then his curiosity turned to alarm as he registered the expression on the young woman's face. She was terrified, on the edge of panicked tears. She kept looking around as if she was lost, or in dire need of help.

Charlie slowed the car to a crawl – there was no oncoming traffic – and L.C. shouted to the woman, asking if she needed help. She nodded yes, while giving their car a puzzled look. L.C. waved her over to the side of the road. He had to repeat himself several times, mouthing the words with hand signals, because her window was still rolled up, and it seemed she was having trouble hearing them. They saw her start to pull over, so they finished passing so they could pull over themselves and see if they could help. They rolled to a stop on the shoulder and looked behind them.

The antique car was gone.

Another car pulled onto the shoulder behind them, and a man got out and ran to their car. He frantically demanded to know what had happened to the car he'd been following. All he knew was that an older car had been ahead of him, driving very slowly. A newer car had passed it, then pulled to the shoulder. The older car had started to do the same, momentarily blocking his view of the newer car. Then the older car had suddenly disappeared.

The three men walked around the area for an hour, but no trace of the missing car could be found.

OCTOBER 21
Phone Call From The Dead, Hollywood, CA (1944)

Just past midnight on October 21, 1944, the shrill sound of a ringing telephone dragged actress Ida Lupino from sleep. She was accustomed to late-night phone calls, but as she went to the phone, a strange sensation washed over her.

"It was as if I was floating in a cloud over a big, blue ocean, all shining and vast," she later explained.

When she picked up the phone, she heard her father's voice on the other end. Ida loved her father dearly, but hearing his voice nearly made her faint. That's because Stanley Lupino had been killed in 1942 during a German air raid.

The Nazis were bombing London on a regular basis in 1942. On June 10, Ida was in the middle of shooting on a soundstage in Hollywood when she broke character and shouted, "My father has just been killed in London!" Two weeks later, a letter arrived confirming that the actor had been killed in the Blitz.

Ida later said that her father's voice sounded scratchy and seemed to come from far away, but she was convinced it was him. In his usual cheery voice, the dead actor spoke to his daughter about matters concerning his estate. In particular, he told Ida where to find certain stock certificates and other documents that had been missing since his death.

For the rest of her life, Ida Lupino was convinced that her father had indeed contacted her one last time.

OCTOBER 22
The Sinking of the Regina, Lake Huron (1881)

One stormy November night, the light at the Cove Island lighthouse faltered, then blinked out. The lighthouse stood at the entrance to Georgian Bay from Lake Huron. The beacon had shone from the stone tower since October 1858, warning ships away from the treacherous rocks and tricky shoals. The blackness took over for several heart-stopping moments … then the light beamed from the tower once again. Sailors on the lake breathed a sigh of relief to see the friendly, steady glow.

When the lighthouse keeper was next on the mainland, people asked him why the light had gone out. He brushed the question aside. He'd gotten it going again, hadn't he? The light was safe in his hands. Many years later, though, he admitted the shocking truth: he was not at the lighthouse that stormy night. In fact, he wasn't even on the island. The light had gone out because of his neglect. The beacon, he said, had been relit by the lighthouse ghost, Captain Tripp.

Captain Amos Tripp was the master of the *Regina*, a 75-foot schooner that sailed Lake Huron. On October 22, 1881, *Regina* was crossing the lake with a cargo of salt when she was pummeled by a fierce gale. Leaks flooded the hold, and *Regina* sank lower and lower in the tossing waves.

Tripp thought he could limp the schooner to safety on a sandbar off Cove Island. His crew wasn't about to take the chance of drowning if the captain failed. They cast off in the yawl, leaving Tripp alone on his ship.

Unfortunately, the crew were proved right. The schooner sank just short of the sandbar, and Tripp went down with his ship. His body eventually washed ashore on Cove Island. The old captain was wrapped in a sail and buried behind the dunes.

Captain Tripp's spirit decided to stay at the lighthouse on the island where his body was buried. The unfaithful lighthouse keeper swore it was Tripp's ghost who had relit the beacon that tempestuous night. He said he felt the old captain's energy in subtler ways, too. Wicks were trimmed, brass was polished, and lenses and mirrors were cleaned, as if the captain was just an assistant keeper, albeit an invisible one.

OCTOBER 23
The Surrency Haunting, Surrency, GA (1872)

"Please allow me a small place in your paper to publish a strange freak of nature," Allen Surrency, a sawmill operator, wrote in a letter to the *Savannah Morning News*. This being the 19th century, the newspaper jumped on the story, and published Surrency's letter on October 23, 1872.

The hauntings started in the early 1870s in a small Georgia town, also called Surrency. Surrency (the town) was on the edge of a vast pine wilderness, so Surrency (the man) decided to turn his two-story house into a rest stop for travelers. It seems he had visitors, and not just the human kind.

Glasses and dishes slid off tables and counters and smashed to the floor. Books tumbled from bookshelves. Clocks struck thirteen, or spun backwards. Hot bricks fell out of thin air. Blankets on the beds would roll up and down all night. Witnesses claimed there were at least a dozen poltergeists in the house, and they were all kicking up dickens.

By the turn of the century, the oddities in the house had gotten out of hand. Stories about the haunting ran in newspapers as far away as Russia and Greece. Looky-loos came from all over to see the poltergeists in action, and they were rarely disappointed. The ghosts almost always made their presence known. Plates and cups would dance on the table at mealtimes. A reporter from the *Atlanta Constitution* said that logs rolled out of the fireplace, and that books mysteriously fell off shelves. That was pretty small potatoes compared to the hogs and chickens that appeared in the living room from thin air. The reporter fled the house when that happened.

No one ever figured out for certain who or what plagued the Surrency house. Railroad tracks ran near the front of the house, and rumor had it that a railroad worker was murdered outside the home. It was said his spirit haunted the house in revenge until the house burned to the ground in 1925.

The Surrencys moved across the county when their house burned. The ghosts followed them and continued their torment of the family until Allen Surrency died.

OCTOBER 24
The Battle of Westport, Kansas City, MO (1864)

When John Wornall built his beautiful red-brick home in 1858, he had no idea it would eventually end up on the National Register of Historic Places as one of only four remaining Civil War-era homes in Kansas City.

He also had no idea it would be considered one of the most haunted.

The John Wornall House is one of the oldest homes in Kansas City. It's now a museum decorated as it would have looked around the time of the Civil War. That's because the house is famous for its use as a field hospital during the Battle of Westport.

The battle, sometimes called "the Gettysburg of the West", was fought on October 23, 1864. Union forces soundly beat the Confederates, who were outnumbered. Over 30,000 men fought in the battle, making it one of the largest fought west of the Mississippi River. It was the last major Confederate offensive in the west, and after that, Union forces controlled Missouri. The Union lost 361 men, and 510 Confederates died.

The conflict spilled over into the John Wornall House. Amputations were performed in the sitting room while the battle raged outside. The bedroom where the most grievously wounded soldiers were laid is very active, with witnesses reporting feeling tugging on their pants legs. (This makes sense if the men were laid on the floor to recover – there were only so many beds in the home.) People have reported seeing armed Civil War soldiers patrolling the balconies, and smelling pipe tobacco in "no smoking" areas.

Soldiers are not the only spirits that wander the home. Kandice Walker started as a museum docent in 2006. On her third day on the job, it was her turn to open the museum for the day. When she came up to the door, key in hand, she saw two little girls inside. Thinking the kids had been locked in the house all night, she understandably freaked out. That's when her coworkers relented and told the new kid about the ghosts in the house. The little girls, seen in 1860s dress, are seen in the yard as well as the house. They are believed to be John and Eliza Wornall's daughters, both of whom died of childhood illnesses. (Kandice quickly accepted the idea of ghosts at her new job, and never let it bother her. In fact, she later became the museum's director.)

OCTOBER 25
The Mount Holly Haunting, Mount Holly, NC (1886, recurring)

One of the most terrifying ghosts in North Carolina haunts a house along the bank of the Catawba River. Every year, a mysterious specter shows up to terrify the house's inhabitants. No one knows who the ghost is, or why it haunts this particular house. But everyone knows when it will next appear …

The house was built in the first half of the 19th century. In 1886 it was owned by a couple named George and Mathilda. The haunting began, appropriately enough, on a dark and stormy night.

On the rainy evening of October 25, 1886, George and Mathilda returned home around 11 pm after visiting Mathilda's mother. George dropped Mathilda off at the front porch, and headed for the barn to attend to the horse and buggy. His drive was interrupted by a scream from Mathilda.

George leapt from the carriage and raced back to the house. He found Mathilda at the foot of the stairs in the foyer. She had fainted. George looked up the stairs, and in just a moment, he saw why.

There was a ghostly figure at the top of the stairs. The apparition gave off an unearthly blue glow that filled the entrance hall. It was in the form of a man, with only dark sunken circles where its eyes should have been. Its left arm ended in a stump that dripped dark blue blood in sickening splashes.

George gathered Mathilda in his arms and ran from the house. On the way, the spatter of chilly raindrops on her face revived Mathilda somewhat. George pulled together a makeshift bed of hay bales for her. Going to the barn door, he peered through the rain, and saw a blue light moving through the house. He decided that he and Mathilda should just spend the night in the barn.

George, like many literate people of his day, kept a journal. On October 26, 1886, he ended his daybook entry with the ominous words, "We will possibly never spend another night in our home."

Indeed, the couple spent the next three weeks living with Mathilda's parents. But going back and forth to do farm chores got old fast. On November 16, George confided to his journal, "Tonite I shall risk a night at home. I shall see if the ghost returns." He stayed a couple of nights at the house alone, and absolutely nothing happened. Relieved, he convinced Mathilda to move back home too.

A year passed with no supernatural shenanigans. In his journal for October 25, 1887, George wrote the ordinary observation: "Today is the earliest freeze anyone can recall."

Around 11 pm, George woke from a sound sleep. He looked to the door of the bedroom – blue light seeped under the door. Footsteps clomped down the stairs as the light retreated. George lay in bed, frozen with fear, for over an hour as he listened to the ghost wander the first floor, opening drawers and banging cabinet doors as if looking for something.

The commotion woke Mathilda. At first, befuddled, she thought a burglar had broken in. One look at the expression on George's face told her the truth.

Mathilda's bloodcurdling scream didn't bother the ghost at all.

The next morning, the couple packed their bags. George's journal entry for October 26, 1887, was a terse "Something evil has driven us from our home."

They never returned.

In the mid-1890s, a family named Anson moved to Mount Holly from Tennessee, and bought the house. They lived there for twenty years, and never reported anything supernatural. But there was some mystery surrounding the death of Will Anson, the master of the house. He died of a sudden heart attack at the age of 42. The very next day, his wife, Susannah, packed up their children and all their possessions and moved back to Tennessee. They didn't even return to Mount Holly for Will's funeral.

The date of Will's untimely death? October 25, 1913.

The house stood empty for the next ten years. In 1923, it was bought by Sam and Martha Blake. They remodeled the house, and moved in in early September 1926.

As Sam came upstairs for bed on the night of October 25, 1926, he was thinking how unusually warm the evening had been. At the top of the stairs, though, he walked through a cold spot. Martha had noticed it too.

Around 11 pm, Sam woke to the sound of moaning. Blue light seeped in through the crack under the bedroom door. Sam got out of bed to investigate. There in the hallway was the ghost, glowing blue, its eyeless sockets staring blankly, blue blood dripping from the stump of its left arm.

Sam got his gun from the bedroom closet and started down the hallway. At the top of the stairs, he stepped in something warm and sticky. Looking down at his bare foot, he was horrified to see that he'd stepped in blue blood. He dropped his rifle and ran back to the safety of the bedroom.

The Blakes left for a while after that terrifying night, but much like the original couple, they eventually returned to the home. At the top of the stairs, they found bloodstains on the floor. They tried several times to scrub the stains away, but the spots of blood always came back. Finally, the Blakes bought a rug and put it over the blood spots. To their horror, the spots of blood showed up on the rug. They hired a carpenter to tear up the stained floorboards and replace them with new wood. The bloodstains appeared on the new floorboards too. They are there to this day.

The Blakes spent the next October 25th in the house, and the ghost showed up right on cue. After that, they moved out.

Other families have lived in the house since then. They've made their peace with the blue phantom: every October 25, they just spend the night somewhere else, and leave the ghost to its annual night of rambling around the house.

OCTOBER 26
Animals of Kean Avenue, Chicago suburbs, IL (1927)

East of Route 45, in the south Chicago suburbs, is the intersection of 95th and Kean Avenue. It's tucked away among several forest preserves, a lovely rural area so close to the city. It's next to Hidden Pond Woods, and haunted Archer Woods Cemetery is just down the road. This is yet another hotspot in the incredibly active Archer Avenue Triangle.

The Palos Trail, a bridle path, crosses 95th just about at Kean. Local lore holds that a number of horses and riders have been killed trying to cross 95th Street. Phantoms of both horses and riders began to be seen in the 1970s. Renowned ghost investigator Richard Crowe spoke to a couple, Dennis and Sandy, who said they saw a vision of ghostly riders on a foggy night in 1979. They reported seeing a procession of horses and riders, bathed in an eerie glow, cross the road at Kean Avenue. They noted that the horses' hooves didn't touch the ground.

Horses are not the only ghostly animals to be found near this notorious intersection. Just inside the woods at the entrance to Palos Trail is a small marble headstone, inscribed with the name Felix. Felix was the canine mascot of the local fire station. Felix's spirit sometimes interacts with living horses and riders.

Another dog buried in the area is Nellie, the mascot of the Willow Springs division of the Highway Patrol. The little black-and-tan mongrel was hit by a car in October 1927, leaving behind a litter of pups. Nellie was buried in the woods just north of Archer Woods Cemetery. The area where she was buried has since been paved over by exit ramps for Route 45.

OCTOBER 27
Messengers of Death, County Meath, Ireland (1907)

The family crest of the Prestons of County Meath, Ireland, is a running fox, and a fox also appears on the Preston coat-of-arms. There's a good reason for this: when the head of the house is dying, foxes – not ghost animals, real flesh-and-blood-and-fur foxes – gather around Gormanston Castle. The castle was the seat of the Preston family from the 14th century until it was sold to the Franciscan order of friars in the late 1940s.

When Jenico, the 12th Viscount Gormanston, was dying in 1860, foxes were seen around the mansion. Just before his death, three foxes were playing near the castle. A witness said that foxes came in pairs onto the grounds and sat under the viscount's bedroom window, and yapped and howled all night. The next morning, they wandered through the henhouse, not bothering any of the chickens, just hanging out. After the funeral, they disappeared.

In 1876, Edward, the 13th Viscount, was ill in bed, but expected to recover. The foxes appeared, barking under his window. He died that night.

On October 28, 1907, the 14th Viscount (also named Jenico) died in Dublin. Around 8 pm that night, the coachman and the gardener saw two foxes near the chapel, five or six at the front of the house, and several more yapping in the garden. Two days later, Richard Preston, the viscount's son, was sitting up with his father's body in the castle's chapel. Around 3 am, he heard a shuffling noise on the gravel walk outside. He went to the side door, and opened it to find a full-grown fox sitting on the path. Another fox sat in the shadows nearby, and he could hear several more moving around in the darkness. Curious, he went to the door at the other end of the chapel and opened it. He saw two more foxes sitting there; one was so close he could have reached out and touched it with his foot.

OCTOBER 28
Stuart Pierson, Gambier, OH (1905, recurring)

Kenyon College is known for several hauntings. In addition to the fire on campus (see February 27), the college was the site of a smaller, but no less tragic, incident that created yet another restless spirit.

In 1905, Stuart Lathrop Pierson was one of the new pledges of the DKE fraternity. In fact, he was a legacy: his father was a Kenyon alum and a DKE brother himself. He'd come up from Cincinnati for his son's initiation that night.

Before the initiation, though, Stuart had to endure another fraternity tradition – hazing. A few brothers led him down to a train trestle that crossed over the Kakosing River, and made him lie down on the tracks. They told him to stay in that position until they came back for him. If they returned and found that he wasn't still lying on the tracks, no matter what the excuse, the initiation would be halted and Stuart wouldn't be allowed to join the fraternity.

Stuart was understandably not jazzed about having to lie on the train tracks. It was pitch dark, for one thing. For another, he was in the middle of a trestle high above a river. If a train were to come across, he'd have nowhere to go. But he really wanted to be a DKE. He walked out to the middle of the bridge and lay down. Once they were satisfied that Stuart was in position, the frat brothers left.

What Stuart didn't know was that the brothers had checked the train schedule to make sure no trains were going to cross the bridge that night. They weren't jerks, and they weren't stupid. There were probably a few stifled giggles as the brothers walked away, leaving the terrified Stuart to face his initiation test.

What the *brothers* didn't know was that there was a backup on another set of tracks south of Kenyon College. Since no other trains were scheduled to use the tracks Stuart was lying on, the railroad rerouted one of the trains. When the brothers arrived to collect Stuart after a couple of hours, they came upon the gruesome sight of Stuart's mangled body strewn over several yards of track.

Stuart's ghost began showing up almost immediately after the tragedy. Most of the time, his ghost appears lying down in the middle of the train trestle where he met his grisly end. For years, students would gather at the DKE house and walk down to the train trestle to see if Stuart would make an appearance. The fraternity has a tradition, on the anniversary of the accident, of carrying a coffin to the trestle and reading the coroner's report out loud. The ghost usually shows up, even though the tracks have been converted to a bike path.

Stuart Pierson also haunts the room on the fourth floor of the DKE house where his father waited for him to return from his hazing. John Hepp '04 lived in the room during his junior year. One night, Hepp was drifting off to sleep when he felt an ice-cold touch on the back of his neck. He scrambled out of bed and turned on the light. In the sudden brightness, he noticed a small door next to his closet. The lock was hanging unlatched. Hepp picked up a flashlight and went exploring.

The narrow crawlspace was about ten feet long and two feet wide. It led to a secret room, where Hepp found pledge books, fraternity pins, and other souvenirs from the past. The walls of the tiny room were covered with countless signatures, from brothers leaving their marks for posterity.

One inscription stood out; a set of initials and a date: SLP 1905.

OCTOBER 29
The Clock Collector

Jim Becket loved clocks. Collected them, in fact. His house was filled with old clocks, and he kept a workshop for tinkering. His hobby surrounded him. Sometimes all the ticking and chiming drove Jim's wife, Molly, bonkers, but she put up with it. Jim was retired, and working on clocks kept him busy.

One afternoon, Molly came home from grocery shopping. Bags dangling from her wrists, she struggled with the key. She may have grumbled under her breath a little – why hadn't Jim come to the door to help? She finally got the door open and set the bags down in the hallway.

Something about the sound of the house gave Molly pause. Listening, she finally put her finger on it. It was 4 pm, but none of the myriad clocks in the house were chiming.

Molly instinctively knew something wasn't right. She rushed through the silent house, calling Jim's name. When she got to the back room and saw her husband's body lying on the floor, she realized the awful truth.

Jim had died from a massive heart attack. All of his clocks had stopped exactly at 3 pm – the coroner's estimated time of death.

The clocks never worked properly after Jim's death. But his favorite clock still chimes even today, every year on October 29 … Jim's birthday.

OCTOBER 30
Massacre at Hauns Mill, Cameron, MO (1838)

Jacob Haun moved from Wisconsin to Missouri in 1835, and set up a mill in Caldwell County. Joseph Smith had established the Church of Jesus Christ of Latter Day Saints just a few years earlier, in 1830. By the time Haun's Mill was settled, many Mormon families were moving to that area of Missouri. Tensions began to rise between the Mormons and other settlers in the region.

On October 27, 1838, the governor of Missouri issued an "Extermination Order", telling the Mormons to leave Missouri or be, well, exterminated. The Mormons, obviously, felt they had just as much right as anyone to stay right where they were.

Three days later, there were still around thirty or forty Mormon families at Haun's Mill. That's where 200 militia attacked them on October 30. Most of the women and children escaped to the fields, and the men, mostly unarmed, hid out in the blacksmith's shop. Unfortunately, there were wide spaces between the logs of the building's walls. The militia shot at the workshop, picking off the men and boys inside. Militiaman William Reynolds cornered 10-year-old Sardis Smith behind the bellows and shot him in the head. Mormon Thomas McBride, 78 years old, surrendered to Jacob Rogers and handed him his musket. Rogers accepted the surrender, then shot McBride before hacking at him with a knife.

All in all, seventeen Mormons were killed, and another thirteen were injured. In contrast, only three of the militia were hurt. To add insult to injury, several of the militia members returned the next day, as the women were burying the dead, to ransack the houses and steal whatever loot they could find.

The blacksmith shop is gone now, but next to it was an unfinished well. At least fourteen of the dead were quickly buried in the well as a matter of expediency. Their bodies are still down there.

Paranormal investigators who have visited the site remarked on movement visible in the treeline, and noises that couldn't be explained away as local wildlife. They heard twigs breaking and loud thuds right behind them, but when they spun around, the beam of a flashlight revealed nothing. The investigators also saw flashes of light moving in quick, random directions in the area where the blacksmith's shop once stood.

OCTOBER 31
The Bratty Kid, Manchester, NH (1944, recurring)

"Trick-or-treat!" The chorus of children's voices sings out the refrain every Halloween. A few pieces of candy doled out into pillowcases or plastic pumpkins satisfies the mendicants, until the next time the doorbell rings.

Every Halloween, Frank and Katie Miello hand out candy to every kid who shows up at their home. But every Halloween since they moved into their home in 1969 has meant a knocked-over mailbox, stones thrown at the side of the house, and other minor vandalism.

The first year, Katie was reading in the living room around 11 pm. The trick-or-treaters were long gone, and every one of them had gotten their handful of candy from Katie. Suddenly, three small stones pinged against the window. They didn't break the glass, but Katie was startled. Frank ran outside, but couldn't find the culprit. Then he saw that their mailbox had been knocked over. He was angry enough to call the cops. A young officer checked the yard with a flashlight, but he, too, saw no one. He took the Miellos' report, but warned them it would be next to impossible to catch whoever had vandalized their property.

Around midnight on Halloween 1970, the Miellos heard a loud thump on the side of the house. Frank rushed outside. Again, he saw no one, but a small cinderblock had been thrown against the side of the house, leaving a gash in the siding. Again, the couple called the police.

This time, two officers showed up. One was young, and seemed bored by the whole thing as he jotted his notes. But the second officer was older, a veteran of the force in his early 60s. This cop kept giving the Miellos strange looks as they made their report, almost as if he wanted to say something, but was holding back.

A few days later, Frank and Katie decided to canvas the neighborhood to see if anyone knew of any troublemaking youngsters. Most of their neighbors hadn't lived there very long, and weren't much help. But they told one old woman that their house had been vandalized two Halloweens in a row. She asked which house they lived in. When they told her, she snapped that she didn't want to know anything about that house – then literally slammed the door in their faces.

Another year passed. On Halloween night of 1971, Frank and Katie heard a shower of pebbles hit the side of the house. Frank went outside to find that two garage windows were broken, some shrubs were damaged, and the mailbox was knocked over again.

The next year, in 1972, Frank spent the entire evening of October 31 on patrol, hoping to catch the culprit.

The moon was fairly bright, so Frank didn't use a flashlight. He watched from the shadows of the bushes as kids came to the door and Katie gave them candy. The stream of trick-or-treaters dried up around 10:30, but Frank wanted to stay out until at least 12:30. He was just itching to catch the troublemaker.

Around 11:15, while Frank was patrolling behind the house, he heard rustling coming from the front yard. He rushed to the front of the house. He couldn't see anything … but he heard a child laughing.

Frank went inside for a cup of coffee, then went back outside around midnight. About fifteen minutes later, he heard the kid laughing again – but he still couldn't see anyone. Now feeling a bit unsettled, Frank called out, "Who's there?" There was no answer. Then a rock went whizzing past his head and hit the side of the house.

Frank ran inside and called the police, then went back outside to see if he could catch the vandal. Almost as soon as he stepped back out, another rock hit the side of the house. The mailbox was knocked over yet again. The street was empty, with no sign of kids. Frank heard the laughing again … and this time, it sounded like it was coming from above him. He looked up – and saw a young boy, maybe 12 or 13, sitting on the roof of his house.

"I couldn't believe his nerve," Frank said. "He was just sitting up there on the roof, staring down at me and smiling, like he wasn't afraid of being caught. I figured this must be the kid who'd been throwing rocks, and I yelled for him to come down."

Katie came running, and Frank turned to her for just a moment to tell her the vandal was on the roof. Then he turned back and looked up.

The boy was gone.

Frank tried to explain that the kid had been there, on the roof, he'd been *right there*, but Katie was confused, which only upset her more. The police arrived about ten minutes later. One of them, Frank noticed, was the older officer who'd been out to the house two years before.

"I told them what happened," said Frank. "I said that somehow, even though I had just turned away for a second, the kid had gotten away. I just couldn't explain it. The younger officer smiled and assured me that twelve-year-olds in trouble can be the quickest moving things on earth."

But the older officer pulled Frank aside, away from Katie and the other cop. He said his name was Officer Bernard, and gave Frank his phone number. He said he and Frank needed to talk – but not just then. He asked Frank to call him the next morning.

When the officers left, Katie went upstairs to bed. Too jacked up to sleep, Frank watched TV in the living room for a while. At about 2 am, the doorbell rang. Frank charged out of the house, ready to confront the prankster. He heard a child's soft laughter above him. The kid was back on the roof, smiling down at Frank. Then he vanished again.

At 9 am, Frank called Officer Bernard.

The policeman wouldn't go into details over the phone. He said he'd be at the house within the hour. When he arrived, he didn't waste any time with pleasantries.

"He looked me square in the face and said that the little boy I'd seen on the roof was dead." Frank and Katie sat stunned and silent.

Officer Barnard told the couple that he'd been called out for vandalism reports for years. Then, Frank and Katie learned the tragic story of their house. On Halloween night in 1944, a group of boys were throwing stones at the house. One kid, twelve-year-old Howie Kinder, climbed onto the roof and started pounding on it. The owner, an old man named Wasserman, came out with a shotgun loaded with rock salt and fired. He only meant for the salt to sting, but part of the cartridge hit Howie on the side of the head and killed him. He lay on the roof, dead, until the police arrived.

Wasserman was indicted and jailed. The trouble began the very next year. On Halloween 1945, the new owners reported vandalism. The house changed owners several times, and the reports continued. The ghost boy first appeared on the roof, Barnard said, in 1952. He saw the kid himself in 1963. When he came closer, the boy vanished, leaving behind only the sound of mocking laughter.

Over the next twelve years, Barnard said, three different owners saw Howie on the roof on Halloween night. Katie and Frank have seen him four times. They've come to accept that the ghost isn't angry at them; he's angry at the house, because that's where he died so tragically. They decided that if they ever sell the house, they'll tell prospective buyers to watch out for vandalism on Halloween.

NOVEMBER

NOVEMBER 1
Little Girl Lost, Troy, NY (1971)

Elizabeth, her mother, her husband, and her two children were celebrating her husband's birthday with a trip to McDonald's. She and her mom got the toddlers settled in a booth while her husband went to the counter to order their food.

The kids settled quickly, and Liz had a few moments of quiet. Their half of the restaurant wasn't crowded – their family was the only one there. Liz was roused from her thoughts by the sight of a little girl by the front tables. Four burly workmen sat there, and the little girl stood patiently near them. "Please, may I have something to drink?"

The men ignored her, and the girl turned towards Liz's table. Liz figured the girl was about six or seven, with beautiful long blond hair. She wore a houndstooth coat, of obviously high quality, but the fashion of a previous age. Liz felt sorry for the girl, and wondered how the men could so callously ignore her.

"May I please have something to drink?"

Being a mother, Liz was concerned for the girl's safety. It was only 6 pm, but it was already dark, and the kid was alone. Liz wondered why, and asked the girl where her mommy was.

"She's dead."

Liz asked about a father. "He's dead. They're all dead, you know?"

Liz was shocked, but tried not to show it. She asked the girl where she was from, and how she'd gotten to the McDonald's. The girl said she was from Pleasantdale – a town about four miles north – and that she had walked.

Liz was at a loss for words, and settled for urging the girl to go home. The girl walked towards the front door and turned the corner. At that moment, Liz's husband came around the same corner, carrying their tray of burgers and fries.

How had her husband not collided with the kid? As her husband set their tray on the table, Liz said, "Did you see that little girl by the counter?" She wanted to share the strange conversation with him.

"What little girl?" He hadn't seen her.

Liz jumped up from her chair and ran to the front of the restaurant. No child. She asked the cashier, but he hadn't seen anyone. Now really weirded out, Liz stopped at the workmen's table … and they hadn't seen her either, even though she'd talked to them.

Liz walked slowly back to their table. As she thought about it later, she realized she could only remember details of the little girl above the waist, and that she seemed to glide rather than walk. She also realized that neither her mother nor her two-year-old acknowledged the girl. The girl had been standing only a foot from the toddler's highchair, and Liz's child hadn't once glanced in her direction.

NOVEMBER 2
The Phantom Pig, Berkshire, England (1907)

The Society for Psychical Research wrote up case notes for a strange encounter that happened at Laburnum Villa in 1907. Two young men, Oswald Pittman and Reginald Waud, were painting in the villa's garden. Their friend, Clarissa Miles, was due to join them at 10 am.

Right on time, Oswald saw Clarissa coming up the lane. Trotting along with her like a pet dog was a large white pig. When Oswald mentioned this, Reginald asked him to tell Clarissa to leave the pig outside and close the garden gate securely. Reginald was an avid gardener, and didn't want the pig in his garden tearing up the plants.

But when Clarissa got there, she said she had no idea what they were talking about. She pointed out that if there *had* been a pig following her, surely she would have heard it snuffling and grunting.

Oswald and Clarissa went back out the garden gate and up the lane. They found several children playing, but no pig. And the kids hadn't seen a stray pig either.

NOVEMBER 3
Bruce Castle, North London, England (1680)

The ghost of Lady Coleraine is said to haunt Bruce Castle. Constantia was married to Henry Hare, Lord Coleraine. The marriage wasn't a happy one: Henry had been engaged to Sarah Alston in 1661, but she had married someone else. There is evidence, though, that while he and Sarah were married to other people, they kept up their relationship.

Maybe knowing her husband was in love with someone else wore on Constantia. There were other issues, too. For some reason, Henry kept Constantia locked in the castle's turret. On November 3, 1680, Constantia had had enough. She picked up her baby, forced her way through a window to the balcony, and threw herself over the balustrade.

For many years, her ghost loudly reenacted the fatal fall on the anniversary of her death. Early in the 20th century, a sympathetic priest held a prayer service in the room from which Constantia leapt. The ghost no longer screams, but she sometimes silently goes through the motions of her final jump.

NOVEMBER 4
The Martyred Priest, San Diego, CA (1775)

In the mid-1700s, the Spanish were trying to establish a foothold in the American West. They figured the best way to do this was to start a bunch of missions and convert the natives to Christianity.

The first mission in California was Mission San Diego de Alcala, founded in July 1769 by Fr. Junipero Serra. The mission struggled with Indian revolts in its first few years. The Kumeyaay tribe was not at all happy with the Spanish intruders taking over their land. On November 4, 1775, a band of Indians attacked the compound, setting buildings on fire.

Fr. Luis Jaime tried to soothe the natives and defuse the situation. He walked towards them with his hands outstretched, showing them that he was unarmed. As he came, he said in a warm voice, "Love God, my children." He knew they didn't speak Spanish; he hoped the tone of his voice would convey his message of peace.

It worked – but only for a few moments. The Kumeyaay warriors stood gaping at the priest for a few silent beats. Then they fell on him. Fr. Jaime's body was found near the river the next morning, bristling with arrows. He was buried near the altar of the church he died trying to save.

A woman encountered the priest's restless spirit when she took her son for a visit to the mission so he could write a report for school. The family wasn't Catholic, so the woman was keenly interested in the tour that led through the church. Gazing at the statues and glimmer of candles, the woman noticed a thin man in gray monk's robes standing near the altar. The man was looking at her with a slight, welcoming smile on his face.

The woman smiled back, thinking that here was the perfect person to answer her questions about the paintings and art she saw in the church. As she came nearer, the man spread his arms in welcome.

The visitor noticed small dots of rusty red appearing on the man's robe. At first they were dime-sized, then they spread to the size of a quarter. Unnerved, the woman looked at the priest's face. He still wore that patient, welcoming smile. He didn't seem to be in any pain from the wounds that were bleeding onto his robe.

As the woman watched, the priest began to fade away – first he went transparent, then in a few moments he vanished entirely. A cold shiver ran through her as she realized she'd seen a ghost. Moments later, her son joined her in the chapel. Her encounter with the phantom had taken less than a minute.

NOVEMBER 5
The Black Dog of the Lakes (1875)

Apparently, humans aren't the only creatures that feel compelled to return to claim revenge after a tragic death. A black dog is said to haunt the Great Lakes, a harbinger of doom for ships like *Thomas Home, Mary Jane*, and *Phoebe Catherine*. Whenever the big black dog was seen, disaster was sure to follow.

This specter is described as a huge, shaggy black Newfoundland with eyes of glowing red. It's said to be the ghost of a dog that fell off a ship in the Welland Canal. The dog struggled and sank under the water as the men on board pointed and laughed. A little later, the boat got stuck in the lock. After working the boat loose, the crew discovered that the dog's water-soaked body had gotten jammed between the side of the boat and the wall of the canal.

The dog's revenge was just beginning. The boat was later lost in a storm, with only one survivor – the one guy that had been kind to the dog when it was alive. The man later said that in the shrieking winds that had sunk the boat, he'd heard the mournful howls of a big dog.

In November 1875, the schooner *T.G. Jenkins* was traveling on Lake Erie, loaded with grain going from Chicago to Ontario. The night was pleasant with a light breeze. Suddenly the helmsman started yelling that he'd seen "the Dog". He explained to his groggy shipmates that the dog had climbed up the side of the boat from the lake's surface, trotted across the deck, then hopped over the rail and continued its stroll across the lake.

Captain John Brown didn't believe that for a moment. Searching the helmsman, he found a bottle of booze in his pocket. He threw the guy in the brig, and at Port Colborne, he kicked him off the boat altogether.

As the boat made its way down the Welland Canal, the helmsman followed it on shore, pleading with his mates to leave the cursed ship. The crew kept driving him away, but he kept yelling his warning.

By the time the schooner reached Port Dalhousie, the crew had had time to think about the helmsman's warning. Men began to mutter about leaving the ship after all. To keep his crew, Captain Brown didn't hang around in port, but cast off as soon as he could. Somewhere between Port Dalhousie and Oswego, New York, the *Jenkins* went down. All hands were lost, and no wreckage was ever found.

The *Jenkins* had disappeared, but the black dog had not. The night the schooner went missing, a farmer at Sheldon's Point, west of Oswego, saw a strange black dog haul itself ashore. The dog's fur was soaked and stuck to its body, and it dragged its back legs as it walked, as though it was paralyzed. The farmer said the dog had sort of a satisfied expression on its face. He watched the dog until it disappeared.

NOVEMBER 6
"Goodbye, Sissy!", Mussoorie, India (1868)

Colonel V's wife and daughter were in their bedroom in Mussorie, India. The daughter was brushing her hair in front of the mirror when she exclaimed that she could see Colonel B, a friend of the family who lived in Meerut, about 80 miles away. The girl claimed that the colonel said, "Goodbye, Sissy – goodbye!", then vanished.

Her mother, unsure of how to interpret this announcement, searched the entire house and the garden, but the colonel was nowhere to be found. The girl repeated her story to her father, and described the clothes Colonel B was wearing.

Two days later, Colonel V read in the paper that his friend had shot himself on the day his daughter reported seeing him. The East India Company reported the date of death as November 6, 1868.

NOVEMBER 7
The Helpful Monks, Glastonbury, England (1907)

Glastonbury Abbey holds a special place in English history. It's said to be the burial place of King Arthur and Queen Guinevere, and legend has it that the Holy Grail ended up here. With such a mystical background, the abbey is the setting for many ghost stories. They say Arthur rides through the courtyard every Christmas Eve, which is a lovely thought. But there are ghosts here that have their origin in history, not just in fanciful folklore.

Early in the 20th century, two archaeologists, Frederick Bligh Bond and J. Allan Bartlett, were put in charge of excavations at the abbey. But these guys were interested in more than just what they could see and measure. They both believed firmly in ghosts, and they had the bright idea to invite the spirits of the abbey to help with the dig – my kind of archaeologists!

They experimented with automatic writing. One of the men would hold a pen in his hand, and they would just sit there shooting the breeze. Sometimes, the man holding the pencil would find his hand starting to write on its own.

The first message came through on the night of November 7, 1907. It was a rough drawing of the floor plan of Glastonbury Abbey, with a signature – "Gulielmus Monachus", or William the Monk. He wasn't the only one who was eager to chime in; messages came from other monks as well. They all said they'd lived at Glastonbury during the 13th century. The first messages were written in medieval Latin, but the monks soon switched to an archaic form of English. (They couldn't always make their messages understood by the modern archaeologists.)

The ghostly monks gave the scientists information about the original construction of the abbey, telling them where to excavate and what they would find. The monks seemed just as excited about the dig as the archaeologists were.

"When you dig excavate the pillars of the crypt six feet below the grass ... they will give you a clue ... You will soon learn as you proceed ... We have much to do this spring."

The archaeologists used this technique from 1907 to 1922, with stunning success. Everything the old monks told them about the abbey was correct.

The ghostly monks seemed to relish this contact with the world of the living. They eventually got quite chatty with the scientists. One monk, named Johannes, told the men what he remembered about abbey life in the 13th century.

"I remember using the stairs often for my fitness. But it availed me not, though my father prior recommended it often. Alas! I waxed more fat." You can almost hear the rotund monk's sigh of resignation.

Another memory was just as human. "I loved the rain on our hundred roofs and myriad voice that came from the waterspouts, when the gargoyles shouted each to each. The cloisters whispered comfort and refreshment as we lay under the dormer roof in parched and sultry nights."

NOVEMBER 8
Arlington Mansion, Arlington, VA (1980)

The mansion at Arlington, within view of Washington DC, was built in 1802 by George Washington's adopted grandson, George Washington Parke Custis. Custis intended the grand mansion as a memorial to the nation's first president. It is one of the ironies of the Civil War that it was once the home of Robert E. Lee. Custis's only child, Mary, married Lee in 1831, and the couple lived happily on the estate – at least for a while.

In 1846, Lee was called to serve in the Mexican War, and in 1852 he left Arlington again, to become superintendent of West Point. He came home after that, but he'd been enjoying life at the mansion only a few years when the Civil War called him away yet again. Union troops soon occupied Arlington, which was confiscated to punish the Rebel general and his family. Federal authorities started burying fallen Union soldiers on the estate – a temporary arrangement that later became permanent. We know it today as Arlington Cemetery.

With such a history, it's no wonder the whole area is haunted. There are Civil War soldiers aplenty, but spirits from other eras hang out there too. Native American ghosts are sometimes seen swimming in the Potomac.

Ghosts also inhabit the historic mansion. Three sisters visited Arlington on Veterans Day, 1980. Katy and Maryanne were in town visiting their married older sister, Joan. By the time their sightseeing brought them to Arlington, the day had turned wet and chilly. The sisters decided to tour the mansion instead of walking around the cemetery.

The mansion was open to visitors, but no guide came to greet them at the door, and they didn't see anyone else waiting for a tour. They decided to wander through the vast house on their own. They passed room after dim room, many of them roped off to discourage tour guests from entering.

The three sisters wandered down the main hallway until they came to a room that was closed off by a metal gate rather than a velvet rope. This was yet another grand room, with a fireplace over which hung the portrait of a young woman. There they saw another person at last.

The woman was wearing a period dress and a white bonnet. She was standing with her back to the door, lighting candles on the mantel. The sisters called to her, but she ignored them and continued fussing with the tapers. The sisters gave up trying to get a response from the oblivious woman, and continued down the hallway. They turned a corner and found another doorway, again with a metal gate, that led into the same room.

But when they looked in, the woman had disappeared.

As they gazed around the room in disbelief, the sisters realized that the two barred doorways were the only ways in or out of the room. Joan turned to her younger sisters and suggested they cut their impromptu tour short. The others agreed, and all three made a mad dash for the front door.

NOVEMBER 9
Where'd He Go?, Quincy, IL (1878)

On the evening of November 9, 1878, Charles Ashmore took a drinking bucket to the spring near his family's cabin to fill it with fresh water.

He was never seen again.

When the 16-year-old didn't return from his errand, his father and older sister took a lantern and went searching for him. A light snow was falling, so Charles' tracks were plainly visible on the path from the house to the spring. Father and daughter followed the footprints until ... they just stopped, with no sign of sliding or jumping, or of any struggle. It was as if, between one step and the next, Charles had ceased to exist.

His family searched for him, but he was nowhere to be found. The ice on the creek was solid, so he hadn't fallen in. And there was still the puzzle of the footprints that simply ... stopped. Four days after Charles disappeared, his mother said she could hear his voice coming from the air, out where he'd vanished. She couldn't tell what he was saying, but she – and others – heard his voice clearly.

They just couldn't see him.

Charles Ashmore's voice was heard for the next several months, but it grew fainter as time went on. By midsummer, his voice, too, had vanished.

NOVEMBER 10
The Edmund Fitzgerald, *Lake Superior (1975)*

When the *Edmund Fitzgerald* was launched on June 7, 1958, it seemed to be plagued with bad luck right from the jump. Mrs. Edmund Fitzgerald, wife of the ship's namesake, was given the honor of smashing the traditional bottle of bubbly to christen the ship. It took her three tries to break the champagne bottle – if the bottle doesn't break on the first strike, it's obviously bad juju.

The boat launched cattywampus, sliding awkwardly into the water, sending waves crashing up to wet onlookers and damaging itself. It damaged the audience too – the water was so cold that one guy who got splashed suffered a heart attack and died from the shock.

When launched, the freighter was the largest ship on the Great Lakes. And when she foundered in a storm on November 10, 1975, with the loss of the entire crew, she was the largest ship to have sunk there.

For seventeen years, the *Fitz* carried iron ore from mines near Duluth, Minnesota, to iron works in Great Lakes ports such as Detroit and Toledo. She set records six times for hauling ore, even breaking her own previous best. The *Fitz* was beloved by boat enthusiasts for her size, her record-breaking performance, and the geniality of her captains. One of them, Peter Pulcer, was fondly known as the "deejay captain"; he was known for broadcasting music day or night over the ship's intercom while navigating the St. Clair and Detroit rivers.

On the afternoon of November 9, 1975, the *Edmund Fitzgerald* left Superior, Wisconsin, loaded with ore from Duluth, headed for Detroit. She joined another freighter, *Arthur M. Anderson*. The next day, the two ships were caught in a violent storm on Lake Superior. Waves up to 35 feet high smashed into the freighters, lashed by winds of hurricane strength.

The *Fitz* radioed to *Anderson* that she was in trouble – Captain Ernest McSorley reported to *Anderson's* captain that it was "one of the worst seas I've ever been in." But *Edmund Fitzgerald* never broadcast any distress signals; McSorley's last message to *Anderson* was a simple, grim "We are holding our own." That message proved false. *Edmund Fitzgerald* sank in 530 feet of water, taking all 29 crew members down with her. No bodies were ever recovered.

The loss of the beloved *Edmund Fitzgerald* has become one of the most famous disasters in Great Lakes history ... and one of the most mysterious.

Remote vehicles have been sent down on several occasions to explore the wreck. Jacques Cousteau's research team went down themselves in 1980 – and came right back up again. They reported seeing lights in the freighter's pilothouse. Common sense said they were seeing the reflection of their own lights in the glass, but in 530 feet of dark water, it freaked them out so badly they cut the dive short.

A team went back in 1989. This time they sent a remote vehicle down, only to have it suffer a catastrophic power failure when it reached *Fitz's* stern. The team hauled it back up, and technicians checked it thoroughly. They found nothing wrong. They sent the fully-functioning ROV down a second time. As it approached the stern of the sunken ship, it conked out again. Again, no reason for the failure could be found.

In 1995, the Canadian Navy sub tender *Cormorant* was sent to the wreck site to help retrieve the *Fitzgerald's* bell. Just as they motored into place above the wreck, *Cormorant's* bell fell off its mount, crashing to the deck. Captain John Creber said, "It's never fallen before and we've been through 30-foot seas with it!" Was some energy reaching out from *Fitzgerald* to communicate with the men on *Cormorant*?

NOVEMBER 11
The Unknown Warrior, London, England (1920)

Westminster Abbey is the final resting place of kings, queens, writers, musicians, generals, doctors, and scientists. Elizabeth I, Charles Darwin, Geoffrey Chaucer, Rudyard Kipling, Laurence Olivier, and Stephen Hawking are only a few of the illustrious folks whose bodies (or cremated remains) are buried here. As is the custom in European churches, some of the graves are in the floor, and people walk over them every day. But there is one grave that never feels the mundane pressure of tourists' feet. It's forbidden to walk on the Tomb of the Unknown Warrior.

In 1916, a clergyman serving at the Western Front saw an anonymous war grave in France, and it gave him an idea. The Reverend David Railton was in Armentieres when he saw a grave in a back garden. A rough cross stood at the head of the grave. On it was penciled "An Unknown British Soldier." Railton was inspired – what if the people of Britain could have a place to go to honor the unknown war dead? A million British died in World War I, and many bodies were still unidentified. What if there was a way the nation could honor those who'd made the ultimate sacrifice for king and country?

In August 1920, Railton wrote to the Dean of Westminster to suggest the Tomb of the Unknown Warrior. But how to choose one corpse to represent thousands of unnamed dead?

The bodies of British servicemen exhumed from four battlegrounds – the Aisne, the Somme, Arras, and Ypres – were brought to a chapel for review by Brigadier General L.T. Wyatt, the officer in charge of troops in France and Flanders. The bodies were laid on stretchers and covered with Union Jacks. None had been identified.

"The point was that it literally could have been anybody," says Terry Charman, a historian at the Imperial War Museum. "It could have been an earl or a duke's son, or a labourer from South Africa … it could have been someone from any rank."

General Wyatt selected one body – he may have been blindfolded when he made his choice – and the corpse was placed in a plain coffin, which was sealed. The other bodies were reburied.

The next day, the dead soldier began the long journey home. The body was sent to London, and on the morning of November 11, 1920, two years to the day after the war had ended, the Unknown Warrior was taken in a procession through the streets to the Cenotaph. King George V dedicated the new war memorial, with the Unknown Warrior in attendance.

At 11 am – the "eleventh hour" – there was a two-minute silence. Then the body was taken to Westminster Abbey and buried. The grave was filled with soil from the main French battlefields, and the stone covering the grave was black marble from Belgium. An estimated

1,250,000 people visited the Abbey to see the grave just in the first week.

From time to time, when the tourists and other visitors have gone, and Westminster Abbey settles into the stillness of ages gone by, a ghostly soldier materializes next to the tomb. No one knows who he is – that's the point – but he stands in respectful silence, his head bowed, gazing thoughtfully at the grave where his earthly remains lie, unknown but venerated nonetheless.

NOVEMBER 12
The Faithful Rajah, New York State (1930)

Ruth Rockwell was a moody, troubled 18 year old, filled with teenage angst and obsessed with death. She'd been staying for a few months at her brother Donald's place, a small farm in New York's Westchester County.

On November 11, 1930, Ruth told her sister-in-law she was going out, and might not be back that afternoon. Mrs. Rockwell nodded absently. It would be good for Ruth to get out of the house.

Around 3 pm, Mrs. Rockwell was sitting in the living room when the family dog, a Great Dane named Rajah, started acting strangely. He ran upstairs, then came back down with a pillow in his mouth. Mrs. Rockwell gave the dog a pat, thinking he'd brought it for her. But Rajah raced back upstairs, coming back down with Ruth's coat in his massive jaws. He laid the coat on top of the pillow.

Now Mrs. Rockwell was really confused, but Rajah wasn't finished yet. He ran back upstairs once more, and returned with one of Ruth's hats. He lay down, put his head on the pile of pillow, coat, and hat, and heaved one of those deep, heartfelt sighs that dogs pull off so well.

Half an hour later, the Rockwells got a call from the police: Ruth was dead. She'd chosen a novel but effective way of committing suicide – she'd gone up as a passenger on a small private plane that took people sightseeing over Long Island. The pilot had felt the plane sway a bit, and when he looked back, Ruth was gone. She had jumped.

When the Rockwells got home that night from their terrible errand, Mrs. Rockwell told Donald about Rajah's weird behavior that afternoon. He asked what time this had happened, and she said it had been around 3 pm, right around the time Ruth had jumped from the plane.

Just then – it was around 9 pm – Rajah, who had been lying next to their bed, jumped up, ran to the window, and started barking ferociously. He came back to Mrs. Rockwell for a moment, then ran back to the window, snarling and growling at something only he could see. Donald tried to calm the dog, but Rajah didn't settle for a long time afterward.

Later, when going through Ruth's room, the Rockwells discovered a suicide note. It read, "If there is a spirit world, I will attempt to communicate with someone in the family at nine o'clock." Was Rajah the "someone" who picked up on Ruth's wandering spirit?

NOVEMBER 13
College Ghost, Northampton, MA (1925)

Smith College, one of the Seven Sisters, has its fair share of ghosts. There's Francine, of Northrop House, who disappeared after having her heart broken, but who still comes back to sit in her old rocking chair. There's the trysting couple in Sessions House, British officer "Gentleman Johnnie" Burgoyne and his secret ladylove, Lucy Hunt. And Park House has the ghost of Jeanne Robeson.

Jeanne was a senior at Smith when she died. Her death on November 13, 1925 was a series of missteps that added up to tragedy. She was in the kitchenette at the house ironing her laundry, and had closed the door so as not to bother her housemates who were sleeping in rooms just off the hallway from the kitchen. She turned on the gas stove, but was interrupted before she could light it. Maybe she tripped, and, falling, hit her head and knocked herself cold. No one knows. But as she lay on the floor, the gas was still seeping into the air of the kitchen. Jeanne died of asphyxiation sometime during the night.

Jeanne has chosen to spend eternity watching over the residents of Park House. Many girls are comforted by her strong presence, and say she has helped them in countless ways. Jeanne has only one fault, which is that she either doesn't understand or doesn't trust modern technology. Cellphones fritz out when Jeanne is around. MP3 players refuse to work. And students have found their Kindles or tablets covered with random papers or tipped into the garbage can.

NOVEMBER 14
The Ghost of Roy Simms, College Station, TX (1959)

Texas A&M is another university that several spirits call home. The Animal Industries Building is the stomping grounds of the ghost of Roy Simms. Built between 1929 and 1931, it housed the animal science department, and a meat laboratory was located in the basement. Simms was once the laboratory foreman. On November 14, 1959, he was alone in the building. He was slicing a slab of bacon when his knife slipped and severed his femoral artery. He dragged himself into the freight elevator, trying to get upstairs to get help, but he bled to death before he could work the controls.

Simms's ghost is a rowdy spirit. No one's ever seen him, but he has other ways to show his presence. He walks the halls at night with a heavy tread, screaming and slamming doors. At one point, Simms was creating havoc in the meat lab at night, moving furniture, opening containers, and messing with equipment. The custodian at the time was Henry Turner. Turner figured that Simms was causing trouble because he couldn't rest. He had the bright idea to leave the elevator in the basement all night with the door open, so Simms would have a place to sleep. It worked for a while, but now Roy Simms is as active as ever.

NOVEMBER 15
The Nighttime Visit of Captain Wheatcroft, Cambridge, England (1857)

Captain German Wheatcroft left England in September 1857 to join his regiment in India. He left his wife behind in Cambridge.

On the night of November 14, Mrs. Wheatcroft tossed in the grip of a terrible nightmare. She saw her husband, looking anxious and ill. She gasped herself awake, her heart pounding. Thank heaven it was only a dream.

But in the moonlight that streamed through the window, she still saw her husband. The captain stood by her bedside in his uniform. He had "that look" on his face, the look he got when he was upset. His hands were pressed to his chest, fingers splayed, and she could see the fabric of his uniform between his fingers. He opened his mouth and seemed to tell her something urgent, but she couldn't hear his voice. After a minute or so, he faded away.

Mrs. Wheatcroft's first thought was to make sure she was actually awake. Instead of the customary pinch, she lifted the sheet and rubbed her eyes. The touch was real. Her young nephew was in the bed with her, so she leaned over and listened to the sleeping toddler's breathing. The child's quiet breaths calmed her a bit ... but she found it impossible to get back to sleep after seeing such an unsettling, vivid vision of her husband.

The next morning, she shared the disturbing scene with her mother. She'd seen no blood in the vision, but even so, she felt that Captain Wheatcroft had been killed or severely wounded. What other reason could there be for his phantom appearance at her bedside? She was so convinced of the truth of her experience that she refused all social invitations for the next few weeks. She told her friends that even if she wasn't yet a widow, she didn't feel right enjoying a social engagement with such uncertainty weighing on her heart. She resolved not to attend any social functions until she'd read a letter from her husband – one dated after November 14.

In December 1857, Mrs. Wheatcroft finally got the news she'd been expecting. The telegram said that Captain Wheatcroft had been killed in action at Lucknow, India. But the telegram gave the date of his death as November 15. Mrs. Wheatcroft was sure this was wrong – she even told the captain's lawyer this when she met with him to settle the estate. Even the death certificate from the War Office, dated November 15, 1857, failed to shake her conviction. After all, the ghost of her husband had appeared to her on November 14.

Trying to put the widow's mind at ease, the lawyer, Mr. Wilkinson, contacted the army office. He was told that the commander-in-chief had in fact sent two separate dispatches. Just as in the telegram, both dispatches gave the date of Captain Wheatcroft's death as November 15.

In March 1858, a letter was delivered to the captain's family. It had been written near Lucknow in mid-December 1857. The writer was an officer who'd served with Wheatcroft. He shared the sad news that Wheatcroft had been killed while leading the squadron – on the afternoon of November 14.

The officer said he'd been riding near Wheatcroft when he'd seen the captain go down, hit in the chest by a shell fragment. The captain had been buried at Dikooska, and his fellow soldiers had put a wooden cross at the head of his grave. On the cross were carved the captain's initials and the date of his death – "GW, 14th November, 1857."

Mrs. Wheatcroft wept at the news, but she was relieved that her mind hadn't been playing tricks on her. She took the letter to the War Office, and the authorities corrected the date of the captain's death in the official records.

NOVEMBER 16
Ghosts of the Commons, Boston, MA (1688)

Boston's Central Burying Ground runs along the south side of Boston Common, along Boylston Street. As you'd expect from such an ancient cemetery, many of the people buried here have been lost to time. But we do know that many of the inhabitants here fought in the Revolutionary War – on both sides. Patriots who fought at the Battle of Bunker Hill rest here, as do British soldiers who died during the Siege of Boston. Gilbert Stuart, who painted the famous portrait of George Washington, is buried here too.

Boston Common, the beautiful 50-acre park in the heart of the city, was founded in 1634, making it the oldest city park in the United States. Historic-minded visitors might wander through the Central Burying Ground during their visit to Boston Common ... but what they may not realize is that the Common is actually a big anonymous cemetery.

The Puritans weren't shy about offing people who didn't fit the mold. Untold numbers of undesirables were executed on the Common, and buried right there. Included in this rogues' gallery were pirates, murderers, Indians, Quakers, suspected witches, and thieves – including the dastardly Rachell Whall, who in the late 1700s stole a bonnet worth 75 cents.

One of the "witches" executed on the Common was Ann Glover, an Irish woman who spoke fluent Gaelic but very little English. This got her in trouble during her trial, when she was required to recite the Lord's Prayer – in English – to prove she wasn't a witch. Goody Glover, a widow, had been hauled into court for various crimes, namely being self-sufficient and not afraid to speak her own mind. One day, her daughter picked a fight with a neighbor's daughter, and soon after, the neighbor's children were afflicted with "horrible fits." This was enough to get Goody Glover accused of witchcraft, then hanged on November 16, 1688.

In 1988, the Boston City Council tried to make amends for the failings of history by proclaiming November 16 as Goody Glover Day. Glover is the only witchcraft hysteria victim to receive such an honor.

Goody Glover's spirit, along with other innumerable lost souls, still wanders Boston Common. The park seems idyllic, but if you look closely, you'll notice that few flowers are planted here. Other parks in Boston are riots of color, but here, in this place of unjust killings and needless death, the festive air just doesn't seem to last. Colorful flowers simply don't flourish here.

NOVEMBER 17
The Night the Ghost Got In, Columbus, OH (1915)

"The ghost that got into our house on the night of November 17, 1915, raised such a hullabaloo of misunderstandings that I am sorry I didn't just let it keep on walking, and go to bed."

James Thurber is generally considered one of America's greatest humor writers. And one of his best stories, published in the collection *My Life and Hard Times*, tells the story of a ghostly visit.

The story begins as Thurber, narrating the story as a teen, has just gotten out of the bathtub. From downstairs, he hears unfamiliar footsteps walking around the dining room table. At first he thinks it's his father or his brother Roy. Then he suspects it's a burglar.

Going on this assumption, he wakes up his other brother, Herman. James and Herman go to the back stairs to listen to the mysterious footsteps, but they've stopped. There's no sound from downstairs. When James insists that *something* is down there, the footsteps immediately thunder up the back stairs towards the boys – but they see nothing. James slams the door to keep the ghost at bay. After an agonizingly long moment, he opens it to find ... nothing. The family never heard the ghost again.

But the slamming of doors has roused the household. Thurber's mother buys his burglar theory, and decides to call the police. The phone, though, is downstairs ... where the ghost-slash-burglar is. So Mrs. Thurber hauls up a window and chucks a shoe through the neighbor's bedroom window, and makes Mr. Bodwell call the cops. (She has so much fun throwing the shoe, James has to talk her out of throwing a second one.)

The police show up en masse, along with a few reporters. The police toss the place, but find neither burglar nor ghost. They do, however, find Grandfather in his attic bedroom. Grandfather, under the delusion that the police are deserters from General Meade's army hiding from Stonewall Jackson in his attic, grabs one of the cops' guns and shoots him.

The police get Grandfather barricaded back in his bedroom, and poke around the house some more, hoping to find *someone* to arrest. One of the reporters comes up to James, hoping for a juicy story. "Just what the hell is the real lowdown here, Bud?" he asks.

Thurber decides to tell the truth, and admits that he'd heard a ghost.

"He gazed at me a long time as if I were a slot machine into which he had, without results, dropped a nickel," Thurber writes. The reporter wanders away, disappointed, and the cops soon follow.

The next morning, Grandfather, no worse for wear, comes down for breakfast. The family assumes the old man has forgotten all about the mayhem of the previous night, but over his third cup of coffee, he glares at James and Herman. "What was the idee of all them cops tarryhootin' round the house last night?" he demands.

The boys just shrug. How to answer?

"He had us there," admits Thurber.

NOVEMBER 18
The Jonestown Massacre, Jonestown, Guyana (1978)

Jim Jones was a cult leader who held a deadly sway over his followers. He started the Peoples Temple in Indiana in the 1950s, which grew in popularity and notoriety. He moved the church to California in 1965, where the strangeness continued. In the 1970s, Jones moved his congregation again, from San Francisco to a commune called Jonestown, in the jungles of Guyana. On November 18, 1978, amid an investigation of the cult, Jones arranged a mass murder-suicide of himself and 918 commune members, 304 of them children. Many cult members died from drinking FlavorAid that had been laced with cyanide.

After the suicides, the bodies were flown back to the United States in a huge C-5 Air Force cargo plane. After unloading the bodies, the plane's crew reported loud unexplained banging sounds in the hold, mysterious whispers, and an unsettling laugh that came out of nowhere. The plane's next trip was to Aljubail Airport in Saudi Arabia. By the time the plane landed, the crew was so rattled they refused to stay in the cargo hold.

A contingent of Marines was stationed at the airport, and they decided to do some ghostbusting. They ordered the Air Force personnel out of the plane and shut themselves inside the cargo hold. Soon the plane was bombarded by a deafening banging noise, like a sledgehammer hitting an empty metal barrel. The Marines cleared out quickly and tore the plane apart, but nothing was found to explain the cacophony. Soon afterward, apparitions started to manifest in the hold. The plane was placed under guard for the rest of its stay at the airport. After it returned to the US, there were no reports of further haunting.

NOVEMBER 19
The Slawensik Poltergeist, Silesia, Poland (1806)

In 1806, the resplendently-named Prince Friederich Hohenlohe-Ingelfingen was captured by Napoleon and taken to France as a prisoner of war. The prince asked his friend August Hahn to oversee his castle at Slawensik until Napoleon decided to release him.

Hahn wouldn't be alone in the drafty old castle. His personal servant, Johannes, would accompany him. In addition, two coachmen lived at the castle, along with a caretaker and her son. Hahn wanted someone other than servants to talk to during his stay, so he asked his friend Karl Kern to come with him. They arrived at the castle on November 19, 1806.

On the third night after their arrival, Hahn and Kern were sitting in the first-floor room they'd staked out for their stay, when a shower of limestone chunks and other debris tumbled down on them. Thinking that the medieval structure was falling down around their ears, the men jumped up, cussing – but there were no cracks in the walls or ceilings. The next night the men were actually pelted with chunks of stone, again from thin air.

The poltergeist activity continued, and got weirder. Once, after Hahn had heated some water and poured it into a basin, preparing to shave, the water vanished from the bowl before he could wet his razor.

A local bookseller visited the castle and had his hat stolen by the entity. At the end of his visit, he just couldn't find his hat. The servants searched the place – no hat. Just then, the hat appeared, floating teasingly in the air a few inches from the bookseller's face. The man snatched for his hat, and it jerked away from his fingers. He chased the hat for several minutes before it dropped at his feet.

By this time, Hahn was exhausted from several months of sleep deprivation. One evening, he announced to the ghost that he didn't want a single thing thrown at him that night. He climbed into bed and waited, nerves on edge. Nothing happened. Hahn heaved a sigh of relief, then tensed … nothing happened. Hahn finally drifted off into a deep, restful sleep – and a huge splat of water drenched his face.

The weirdest thing happened one evening when Kern and Hahn's servant Johannes were alone in the castle. They witnessed a jug of beer rise slowly from the table, and pour itself into a mug. Then the mug lifted and tilted, as if someone invisible was drinking from it. As unsettling as this was, the men were even more freaked out when they went to where the mug had just been emptied – and found not a drop of beer on the floor.

Hahn and Kern stayed at the castle another six months, until the prince was released from imprisonment in France. Hahn wrote the last entry in his journal on November 19, two years to the day they had arrived at the strange castle.

NOVEMBER 20
First Unitarian Church, Alton, IL (1934)

The hilly riverside town of Alton is simply stuffed with ghosts and other mysteries. One of these is the haunted First Unitarian Church.

In the 1850s, St. Matthew's Catholic Church was destroyed by fire. Rather than rebuild on the site, the Catholics decided to build a new church elsewhere. In 1854, they sold the land, and the rubble, to the Unitarians, who used the foundation and the remaining stone to build their own church.

In 1928, Philip Mercer became pastor of the First Unitarian Church. He was an Englishman who emigrated to America in 1886, when he was 18 years old. He worked for a while in St. Louis, on the railroad, before becoming a minister ... and beyond that, people knew very little about him. Mercer was friendly and outgoing, and enjoyed social outings connected with the church, which are good qualities in a minister. Mercer was a great conversationalist – but he never spoke of his family or his personal life. He was well-liked, and well-respected; people just didn't know much about him.

In 1934, something in Mercer's life ... changed. He'd gone on vacation – normally a rejuvenating experience – but had come back very stressed. He began to complain of weakness and various health problems, and dropped weight at an alarming rate. His doctor couldn't find anything wrong with him, and Mercer went into a moody funk.

One Sunday in November 1934, Mercer was acting very strangely as he delivered his sermon. He was sweating profusely, and he seemed to race through the service, as though eager to get it over with.

The next day, a woman who lived next door to the church saw Mercer leaving the church around 1 pm. By that evening, he hadn't returned. It wasn't unusual for Mercer to spend the night in St. Louis, but he hadn't mentioned any plans to see a play or concert that night. James McKinney, Mercer's friend, was concerned.

On Tuesday morning, McKinney was worried enough to call the church repeatedly. When no one answered, he went over in person. McKinney entered the church and found Mercer's body hanging by a cord in a doorway. A kicked-over chair lay on the floor beneath him.

The coroner ruled Mercer's death, committed Monday, November 20, a suicide. His fiancee, Dorothy Cole of Minneapolis, said that Mercer had slipped into depression, and that she was unable to help him. But he left no note, and to this day, his death remains a mystery.

Luke Naliborski, a guide with Troy Taylor's Alton Hauntings Tours, is very familiar with the First Unitarian Church, and has led many groups through the building. He's had the odd experience of hearing notes play on a piano when no one was near it. Other manifestations include footsteps, cold spots, and a male presence who gives people an unwelcome feeling, as though they're trespassing on his space. People have also seen an apparition of a man wearing a white shirt and black pants. The doors of the church mysteriously lock and unlock on their own. Some doors slam themselves open, as if blown by a violent wind.

NOVEMBER 21
Daddy and Daughter, Jackson, MI (1883, recurring)

It's always nice to have family close enough for a visit. Every year, a father and his daughter reunite to catch up on things. People in the area say they've been having these tender family meetings for many years. There are a couple of things, though, that make these reunions unique. One is that they always take place in a small rural cemetery, but neither of them have far to travel – the daughter is less than five miles away.

The other is that both father and daughter have been dead for over a century.

Two spirits haunt the Crouch-Reynolds Cemetery in rural Jackson, Michigan. Jacob Crouch is buried in an unmarked grave near the main gate under a spirea bush. His daughter Eunice White is buried in nearby St. John Catholic Cemetery. On November 21 every year, Eunice's spirit rises from her grave and travels down the road to Jacob's resting place. Or perhaps the white mist that appears over Jacob's grave is Jacob himself, preparing to go visit Eunice. No one really knows.

Why does the spirit of Jacob Crouch (or Eunice White) hover over Jacob's grave every November 21? Because that's the day they were both murdered.

Jacob Crouch was, at 74, one of the richest farmers in Michigan. Four years before his death, he'd bought a 15,000-acre ranch in Texas that was said to be worth over $1 million. He had other ranches in Texas, all of which earned him hefty profits. Sometime during the night of November 21, 1883, someone broke into the Crouch farmhouse and murdered four people as they slept. It was believed that Jacob had just gotten a payout of ranch profits, so whoever committed the murders was after Crouch's money.

Shot to death were Jacob, his very pregnant daughter Eunice, her husband Henry White, and Moses Polley, a cattleman from Pennsylvania who was in town to do business with Jacob. One of the more workable theories about the unsolved murders is that one his way to the Crouch farm on the train, Polley bragged about his wealth. Some shady characters may have followed him to the farm, and robbery turned to murder.

Many locals say that the white mist can be seen over Jacob's grave any time of year. But legend holds that Eunice and Jacob reunite at the secluded cemetery on November 21.

NOVEMBER 22
An Omen of Death, Boston, MA (1963)

In the 1960s, a successful Boston businessman shared a strange story. Though he wished to remain anonymous, his tale was unforgettable.

The man was Irish, and his story concerned the *bean sidhe* – pronounced banshee, the "fairy woman" whose terrifying wail portends the death of a family member. This man's Irish Catholic ancestors had come to Boston to escape the potato famine. His great-great-grandfather had opened a small grocery store, and done well for himself. That first store was the precursor to a chain of supermarkets. The storyteller was a respected businessman.

When he heard the *bean sidhe* the first time, he was ten years old. He woke on a sunny spring day to the sound of birds chirping outside his window. He smiled sleepily, maybe thinking of a baseball game later that day. But another sound drove the cobwebs of sleep from his mind – a low, keening wail that soon drowned out the birdsong, like a rising wind. He looked out his window, but not a breeze rustled the bushes. And now the howl of the wind became the sobbing of a heartbroken woman – but there was no woman outside his window either.

Confused, the boy hurried downstairs, and found his father with his head in his hands, weeping. The boy's mother explained that they'd just learned that the boy's grandfather had died.

The family hadn't told the boy about the lore of the *bean sidhe*; it was Old-World stuff that had no place in their modern lives. But a few years later, the boy heard the folktale, and it got him thinking. Had he heard the *bean sidhe* the morning of his grandfather's death?

The *bean sidhe* returned in 1946. The boy was a young man now, serving in the Air Force. He was stationed in Asia, but the *bean sidhe* found him anyway with her heartbreaking news. The man was pulled from sleep again, the cry of the *bean sidhe* jolting him awake, "rising and falling like an air raid siren," as he described it. The howl faded, and the man was overcome with a feeling of deep sadness. It came as little surprise to him hours later when news reached him of the death of his father.

Twelve years passed. The man was in Toronto on business. Again, the *bean sidhe* cried in the morning, but this time, the man was awake. He was reading a newspaper in bed when he heard a woman's moans from the window. The moans escalated into shrieks of lamentation. The man covered his ears against the pitiful cries. Was the *bean sidhe* warning him about his wife? His young son?

As soon as the wailing died down, the man leapt out of bed and lunged for the phone. Several calls later, he'd been reassured that all was well at home. Still, he puzzled over the warning. When he came down in the elevator and heard the day's news from the desk attendant, he knew who the *bean sidhe* had cried for.

The date was November 22, 1963. His boyhood friend, another Irish-Catholic kid from Boston, John F. Kennedy, had just been shot by an assassin.

NOVEMBER 23
The Haunting of Haw Branch Plantation, Amelia, VA (1965, recurring)

Haw Branch Plantation was once one of the largest in the South, encompassing 15,000 acres of rich Virginia land. The mansion was built in 1745, but after the Civil War, it fell into disrepair as the plantation fell on hard times.

Today, it is a private home. It was purchased in 1964 by the McConnaughey family, whose ancestors had lived in the house fifty years earlier.

And it is one of the most haunted locations in America.

On November 23, 1965, the family was awakened by bloodcurdling screams coming from the attic. They raced upstairs, but found nothing. Every six months, on May 23 and November 23, the horrifying sounds came again. In 1967, a ghost showed up in the house – an apparition of a slim girl dressed in white. The ghost was eventually identified as the family's great-grandmother, Harriet Mason.

By 1969, the family had restored the mansion, and a cousin gave the family an old portrait of a distant relative, Florence Wright. The charcoal portrait was done in shades of gray, and the family decided it would look good over the fireplace in the library. Soon after the portrait was hung, one of the family members saw the Lady in White materialize directly in front of the portrait, as if she had stopped in to admire it. Not long after that, colors gradually began to brighten the gray shades of the charcoal portrait. As it turned out, the portrait had originally been done in pastels, and the colors had faded in storage. When the picture was displayed in a place of honor, Florence's spirit showed her approval by colorizing the picture, bringing it back to its original appearance.

Spirits like to be appreciated, too.

NOVEMBER 24
The Death of Lord Lyttleton, England (1779)

Thomas, Lord Lyttleton, was the kind of rakehell that Regency romances are written about, but he didn't have a heroine to redeem him and give him a Happy Ever After. He did marry, then promptly deserted his wife and started dating a barmaid, whom he whisked off to Paris. Lyttleton was 35 in 1779 when scandal connected him to the Amphlett sisters – yeah, all three of them.

In November, he had returned to his home in London when he began to suffer from fits. One night, he had a horrifying vision, one that seemed to portend the future.

He woke to the noise of a bird fluttering at the window. Then the room filled with light, and instead of a bird at the window, he saw a woman dressed in white. It was the spirit of Mrs. Amphlett, the mother of the three girls, who had recently died.

"I have come to warn you of your death," the ghost said. She pointed to the clock on the mantel, whose hands stood at midnight. She told Lyttleton that in three days, exactly at midnight, he would die. Then she vanished, and the room was dark once more.

Lyttleton was understandably upset at this dire news. He called his manservant into the room and told him what the ghost had said. He told other people, too, over the next couple of days.

By the third day, Saturday, November 27, Lyttleton was trying to joke about his fate. Over breakfast, he told his guests (which included two of the Amphlett sisters) that he felt fine. Later that day, he was walking past a graveyard with his cousin, and commented on how many of the people buried there were 35 years old – his own age. But, he told his cousin, he planned to live to a ripe old age.

In the afternoon, Lyttleton and his guests traveled to Lyttleton's country house. Soon after they arrived, he had another fit, but he was well enough to join his guests for supper at 5 o'clock.

No one had told Lyttleton, but as a precaution, everyone had set their watches – and his – ahead half an hour, and the servants had also set the house clocks ahead. Around 11 pm, everyone headed for bed.

Now that he was undressed and ready for bed, Lyttleton started to get nervous. He kept looking at his watch, and his valet's watch, holding them to his ear to make sure they were both ticking. The watches soon read 12:15, and Lyttleton began to relax.

When the watches read close to 12:30 – when it was actually nearly midnight – Lyttleton decided to take his medicine and try to sleep. The valet brought the medicine and began to stir it with a toothpick. Lyttleton scolded him, and sent him to get a teaspoon.

The servant returned a few minutes later with the teaspoon, and found Lyttleton in the throes of another fit. Because his head was propped up on pillows, his chin was resting on his neck as he seized, and his airway was cut off. The valet ran for help, but when he returned, Lyttleton was dead.

There's another weird angle to this story. One of the friends of Lyttleton's who was at the country house that afternoon was Miles Andrews. Andrews was a partner in the Dartford powder-mills about thirty miles away, and had to attend to some business at the mills, so he hadn't stayed at the house with the others. Andrews had heard about the ghostly warning, but before he left, he reassured himself that Lyttleton was in good spirits. He, like Lyttleton, didn't believe in the death portent, so he didn't even remember when that night the event was supposed to occur. He stayed the night at the house of his business partner. Around midnight, the curtains at the foot of his bed were yanked open, and there stood Lyttleton in his nightclothes.

Andrews was stunned to see his good friend standing there in dishabille in the middle of the night. As soon as he could speak, he started grumbling at Lyttleton for coming to see him with no warning. Still grousing, Andrews turned over in bed and rang the bell for his valet.

When he turned back, Lyttleton was gone. Thinking his friend had simply left the room, when the valet came in, Andrews asked, "Where is Lord Lyttleton?" The servant said he hadn't seen Lyttleton since they'd left the country house earlier that day.

Andrews started yelling at the valet, telling him that Lyttleton had just been at the bedside. The servant insisted that was impossible.

Now Andrews was really enraged. Thinking Lyttleton was pranking him, he had his servants search the entire house, but his friend was nowhere to be found.

Andrews fumed about Lyttleton's epic prank … until at 4 o'clock, a message arrived informing him of Lyttleton's death. Realizing that the figure he'd seen was a ghost, Andrews fainted dead away.

NOVEMBER 25
The Monks of St. James-Sag, Lemont, IL (1977)

Every paranormal researcher has an origin story. My introduction to the world of the supernatural came when I was a kid. My father loves to read as much as I do, and he is an amazing storyteller. He'd regale us kids with stories at the dinner table. There I'd be, listening to him wide-eyed, my pork chops and green beans forgotten on my plate, as he'd spin tales of Resurrection Mary, the screaming mummy at the Field Museum (still one of my personal all-time faves), and the ghostly monks of St. James-Sag. At the time, I honestly thought he was making up stories for my personal entertainment (and to scare the paste out of me). Imagine my thrill when I grew up and realized that all the stories my dad told me, every single one of them ... were *true*.

(At my sister's wedding in October 2000, I finally asked my dad where he'd heard all the stories he'd shared with me, stories that led me to be a writer of true ghost tales. He said he couldn't remember – he just read an awful lot of books. Which, honestly, is how I get most of my stories too. So now you know where I get it.)

One of my father's stories was about the ghost monks of St. James-Sag Church. Hearing his tales, I always pictured the church as this dark, brooding Gothic monstrosity, but that couldn't be further from the truth. The church is a trim white confection fronted by the bell tower. Built in 1856, it's the second oldest Catholic church in northern Illinois. The grounds around the tidy church are the resting place of thousands – before it became the church's cemetery, that high ground was also used by the local natives as a burying ground. Fr. Jacques Marquette offered the first Mass there in 1673. The French set up a signal post in the late 1600s. The site then became a mission, then the church.

The first ghost story involving the church dates back to September 30, 1897, and was reported in the *Chicago Tribune*. Two musicians, William Looney and John Kelly, had given a performance at the church hall that lasted until 1 am. Rather than go back to Chicago that night, they decided to sleep in the hall.

One of the musicians woke up later to the sound of horses' hooves on the gravel road. Looking out the window, he saw a carriage. It stopped, and a girl in a white robe appeared from nowhere. She got into the carriage, and as it began to move again, horses, carriage, passengers and all simply vanished. It's said that the spectral woman and the disappearing carriage date back to the early 1880s. A young housekeeper at the rectory and an assistant to the priest fell in love and planned to elope. As the girl climbed into the wagon, the horses bolted and the wagon overturned, killing them both. The young lovers were buried together in an unmarked grave in the cemetery, and periodically reenact their doomed elopement attempt.

But that's not the story my dad shared with nine-year-old me. He told me the story of the phantom monks. According to urban legend, if trespassers are caught on the grounds at night, a group of monks force them to kneel on ball bearings all night in prayer. The snag in this story is that there were never any monks at St. James-Sag.

And yet ... and yet ... there is the two-page report filed by Herb Roberts, a Cook County police officer, the Friday before Thanksgiving, 1977. He was on patrol that night, and drove past the cemetery around 2:30 am. His glance through the locked gates showed him a line of eight or nine hooded figures dressed in monks' habits and cowls walking slowly up the hill to the church.

Roberts yelled at the figures to stop, but they kept walking. He radioed for backup, then grabbed his shotgun and went to deal with the intruders himself. He stumbled over gravestones in the dark, and nearly lost his footing several times on the uneven ground. Meanwhile, the dark, hooded figures simply glided up the hill without a sound. Their footsteps made no noise in the fallen leaves that blanketed the ground.

When Roberts arrived at the top of the hill, he could find no sign of the intruders. His backup brought the K9 unit, and the highly trained dogs couldn't catch any scent of the trespassers. Roberts and his colleagues came to the conclusion that what he'd seen was indeed a ghostly gathering of phantom monks.

NOVEMBER 26
The Sinking of the Jane Miller, Ontario, Canada (1881)

White Cloud Island, deer season, 1906. The campfire crackled as the hunters huddled around it. "The worst day hunting's better than the best day working," someone joked, getting a chorus of chuckles. Someone else went back for the last of the stew. As he dropped the spoon back into the empty pot, he hesitated. Then he shook his head. Probably just the wind in the trees.

But another hunter spoke up. "You hear that?"

They all stood up, looking out over the dark waters of Georgian Bay. The wind whipped the black lake into choppy waves. One of the men shivered.

"Thought I heard –"

The faint cry came again. "Help me!" And even more chilling, "God save us!"

"Sounds like a boat's in trouble," someone muttered. "But what can we do? We've only got the skiff. We wouldn't last long enough out there to rescue anyone."

"I can't tell where the yellin's coming from," someone else said. "Seems like it's all around us – but how is that possible?"

The next day, the hunters searched the beach, and gazed out towards the lake. They all remembered the plaintive shrieks of the night before. But they found nothing to explain the desperate cries. When they got back to town, they shared their strange experience.

That's when they heard of the tragedy of a quarter-century before – the unexplained sinking of the *Jane Miller*.

The *Miller* was a small steamer that worked Georgian Bay near Ontario. She wasn't a graceful craft, but she did her job well.

Her last trip started on the morning of November 25, 1881. She loaded up with freight and passengers at Meaford, then headed west. She battled a strong southwest gale, but made it safely to Colpoys Bay, where she took on a load of wood. At 8:30 pm, she headed west again, making for Wiarton. She chugged into the darkness … and was never seen again. Still fighting the southwest wind, *Miller* never reached Wiarton, only twelve miles away. What little wreckage there was – a smashed lifeboat, a few oars, the crew's uniform caps – was found washed up on White Cloud Island. The 28 people on board were lost.

NOVEMBER 27
The Wedding, Devon, England (1667)

Weddings are joyous occasions, and the wedding of Dorothy Ford and William Streat was no exception. There'd been some doubt that the wedding would actually take place. The groom, rector of the parish in South Pool, was 66 years old – a bit long in the tooth for marriage. And the wedding had been postponed.

But now here was Dorothy, standing next to William in his own church, as a visiting priest recited the marriage rites. The church was packed; everyone there knew of the couple's love for each other, and they wouldn't have missed this wedding for anything.

Especially since William Streat had died a year and a half before.

He'd been killed in a riding accident. His bride-to-be, Dorothy, was distraught, and William was greatly missed by his parishioners. After his funeral, many people in town began to dream about William. In these dreams, he would tell the dreamer that his soul was restless and tormented, unable to find peace.

Only his wedding, he told them all, would bring him solace.

After months of this shared nightmare, the villagers decided to honor their late rector's wished. They decorated the church for a wedding, William's coffin was exhumed, and Dorothy, the radiant bride, stood beside it while the priest performed the ceremony. After that, William was reburied, and the dreams stopped.

NOVEMBER 28
The Cocoanut Grove Fire, Boston, MA (1942)

The Cocoanut Grove supper club was built in 1927, and was enormously popular during Prohibition. It slumped a bit in the 1930s, but by the early years of World War II, it had become Boston's most popular hangout.

The restaurant was a single-story building with a basement. The kitchen, freezers, and storage areas were in the basement, as well as a bar called the Melody Lounge. On the first floor was a large dining room and a ballroom, along with several other bar areas.

Around 10:15 pm on the night of November 28, 1942, a bartender asked a busboy to fix a lightbulb at the top of an artificial palm tree in the Melody Lounge. (Popular theory has it that the bulb had been unscrewed by a patron in search of a dark corner for more privacy with his date.) The busboy lit a match to locate the socket in the dim light.

Moments later, the palm tree burst into flames. Quick-thinking bartenders tried to put the fire out with seltzer bottles, but the fire spread rapidly. The flames devoured furniture and decorations, and panicked patrons rushed for the four-foot-wide set of stairs that led from the Melody Lounge to the foyer on the first floor. The fire spread incredibly quickly; some people were burned alive, their hands still clutching their drinks.

A few people made it out through the front door, but the revolving door soon became jammed with bodies, crushed by the weight of the panicked crowd behind them. A fireball then exploded into the dining room, where patrons were crowded together waiting for the 10 pm show to begin. It was later estimated that the club was packed with over 1000 patrons – roughly double its legal capacity. Panic reigned as flames and toxic gases filled the building.

In a strange coincidence, the Boston Fire Department received a call at 10:15 pm from an alarm box three blocks away from the Cocoanut Grove. Responding firefighters found a car fire on Stuart Street. They dealt with it quickly – then one of the firemen noticed smoke coming from the supper club. The firefighters arrived at the Cocoanut Grove moments later, to find the building fully involved.

Firefighters extinguished the fire in minutes, but the damage had already been done. Getting into the building to rescue people was almost as hard as getting out. Bodies, both living and dead, were piled shoulder-high at the exits. Some patrons hid from the fire in the refrigerators and meat lockers in the basement. Some protected their lungs against the smoke by soaking handkerchiefs in urine (presumably their own). Some emerged with backs bloody from where people had clawed them like wild animals in their frenzy to escape the flames.

The bodies were sent to a temporary morgue in a nearby garage. Some victims thought to be dead were found to be alive, and were moved to the hospital. Happily, they survived. Morgue staff worked to identify the deceased. Identifying female victims was difficult, because personal identification was usually carried in purses, which of course were left behind in the confusion and panic.

The Cocoanut Grove fire injured 166 people and claimed 492 lives. It was the deadliest club fire in American history – but there was a bright spot. The injured were taken to local hospitals, where they received newly developed methods of care. The first recorded use of penicillin to fight infection in burn victims was in response to this fire. As a result of the tragedy, Boston hospitals made advances in burn treatment in fluid retention, prevention of infection, treating respiratory trauma, and in skin surface treatment. Building codes were also revised.

One of the buildings used as a temporary morgue was the Jacques Cabaret, now a drag lounge. A bartender was cleaning up late one night and saw several bodies lying on the floor of the bar area, which was in darkness. The bodies looked like they'd been lined up in rows. When the bartender turned on the light to get a better look, the bodies disappeared.

Wendy Reardon is a dance instructor. She owns Gypsy Rose Dancing Studio on Boylston Street. After taping a demo video of herself pole dancing, she noticed that the video had multiple moving orbs and streaks of light. Even stranger, the anomalies were moving in sync with her, as if they too were dancing. These anomalies show up in Wendy's videos so often that she has named some of them. "Bullet" moves with incredible speed, and "Blinky" flickers in and out like a firefly.

The spirits of Cocoanut Grove are still dancing the night away.

NOVEMBER 29
The Gray Wolf, Sand Creek, CO (1864)

By late 1864, with the Civil War raging, mistrust between white settlers and Native Americans in the western territories was also boiling over into violence. Some chiefs sought peace for their tribes, and were promised the protection of nearby US Army forts.

One of these leaders was Black Kettle, a Cheyenne chief. About 800 of his people lived in Sand Creek, a village in southeast Colorado. On November 28, 1864, Black Kettle was assured by the authorities at Fort Lyon that as long as he flew a white flag and the United States flag over his camp, his people would be safe. The two flags would be a symbol, the authorities said, that the Cheyenne were friendly. Besides, that territory had been promised to the Cheyenne by an 1851 treaty.

The very next day, that promise blew up in Black Kettle's face.

On the morning of November 29, a force of about 675 US soldiers, members of the Colorado Volunteer Infantry led by Major John Chivington, surrounded the village. Disregarding the flags, the soldiers opened fire on the village, slaughtering men, women, and children alike. Women and children fled to the creek bed, frantically scrabbling holes in the sandy ridges for cover. It did them no good; the soldiers chased them down and bayoneted them.

(There was one company of soldiers that refused to fire on the Indians. It was led by Captain Silas Soule, who later testified against Chivington in the army's investigation in January, 1865. On April 23, 1865, just after he married Hersa Coberly, Soule was assassinated on a street in Denver for testifying against Chivington. Soule is still revered today by the Cheyenne for disobeying orders and refusing to attack the village. And, I'm proud to say, I'm related to him. We're both descended from George Soule, who came over on the Mayflower.)

In all, about 140 women and children and 60 men were slaughtered and horribly mutilated at the Sand Creek Massacre. Here's where the supernatural steps in to lend a hand … or a paw. The phantom of a gray wolf appeared to the surviving women and children and led them to safety. The mysterious animal escorted them all the way to another Cheyenne camp near the forks of the Smoky Hill and Republican rivers.

NOVEMBER 30
The Wreck of the Isidore, York, ME (1842)

The lighthouse at Cape Neddick, near York, Maine, sits on a barren chunk of rock known to locals as "The Nubble". Millenia of pounding waves have sculpted the red stone here into fantastical shapes, with names like the Devil's Oven and Washington's Rock (supposedly a likeness of our first president, but most agree that seeing it takes some imagination and a lot of squinting.)

There are other faces in the stone here too, and thereby hangs our tale for today.

Two days before the *Isidore* was to set sail in November 1842, a sailor named Thomas King woke in panic from a horrifying nightmare. He'd dreamed of a wrecked ship, and drowned sailors floating limply on the waves. King's dream had one weirdly specific detail: the sinking ship dissolved into fog and was blown away by the wind, and the faces of the sailors turned to stone and were washed up on a barren island.

King told Captain Leander Foss about his dream, and asked to be released from his contract. Predictably, Foss laughed at him and told King he'd better be ready to sail in two days.

The next night, another member of *Isidore's* crew had a disturbing dream. The details of this nightmare were even more specific than King's dream: the sailor saw seven coffins, and saw himself in one of them. Foss heard about this dream too, but he wasn't about to let superstition disrupt his schedule.

The *Isidore* left Kennebunkport early on November 30. Snow began to fall from a leaden sky, and a bitter north wind followed *Isidore* out to sea. Thomas King watched the ship fade into the gray distance – from the Maine shore. He had hidden in the woods until he was sure the ship was under way.

DAYS *of the* DEAD

The next day, King was glad he'd trusted his gut. Word came that pieces of the *Isidore* were scattered all along the shore near Cape Neddick. There were no survivors, and only seven bodies washed ashore – one of them being the sailor who'd dreamed about the seven coffins. Captain Foss's body was never found.

Locals have reported seeing the ghostly gray form of the *Isidore* off Cape Neddick, floating on a bank of fog rather than riding the waves. But the most tangible evidence of the sinking of the doomed ship may be those tortured faces in the rocks on The Nubble. Maybe that's not Washington after all …

DECEMBER

DECEMBER 1
Left Behind, Athens, OH (1978)

The Athens Lunatic Asylum opened on January 8, 1874, specializing in the treatment of criminally insane patients. In its early years, "The Ridges" was a peaceful place, a stately red-brick building with white trim, a safe place where minds could heal. But as with many other institutions, overcrowding over the years led to a decline in patient care.

On December 1, 1978, a patient named Margaret Schilling wandered away from her caretakers, unnoticed. Attendants searched for her ... but they didn't look everywhere. On January 12, a maintenance worker discovered her body in a locked, long-abandoned ward that once housed patients with infectious diseases. Margaret had died of heart failure. Before she passed, she took off all her clothes, folded them neatly in a pile next to her, and lay down to die. Sunlight shone on her corpse through a nearby window. The fluids from her decomposing body left a permanent stain on the concrete.

The asylum donated all its land and buildings to Ohio University in 1988, and closed in 1993. But the eerie stain where Margaret lay is still there – and so, it seems, is she. People have reported seeing Margaret's gaunt figure staring out of the window of the room where she died, or wandering the building – now the Kennedy Museum of Art – at night. Other hauntings in the building include full-bodied apparitions in empty rooms, and the sounds of squeaking gurneys and disembodied voices.

DECEMBER 2
Ambrose Small, Theater Lover, Ontario, Canada (1919)

Theater people tend to be passionate about their craft. This holds true not only for actors, but those behind the scenes as well.

Ambrose Small can safely be said to be a fan of the theater – he owned ninety of them. He opened the resplendent Grand Theatre in London, Ontario in 1901, adding it to his collection. He owned venues in seven cities around Ontario, but the Grand was his favorite. Small built it to replace an 1881 opera house that had been ravaged by fire on February 23, 1900. The new theater opened on September 9, 1901, with seating for 839 patrons. It was one of the shining jewels on the vaudeville and live theater circuits. In 1924, it was sold to a film syndicate, and was converted into a movie house six years later.

However, Small was not around to see this change. On December 2, 1919, he mysteriously disappeared while on a trip to Toronto. At first, no one realized this was the last know sighting of the theater magnate. He was in the habit of traveling without telling anyone where he was going. (This is because when he was gone, he was usually up to no good – he'd regularly take off to carouse and see loose women.) But when weeks went by, and no one heard from him, people began to get concerned. He was reported missing in early 1920, but his date of death is generally regarded as December 2. The day before, he had sold all his theater holdings for a profit of $1.7 million. On December 2, he deposited the check, and had brunch with his wife downtown.

Then he simply disappeared. He didn't take any of that money with him, and his wife

Teresa never got a ransom note. He was just … gone.

But he returned in spirit to his favorite theater. Small is a trickster spirit, more playful than annoying or scary. He enjoys ogling women, who feel the lascivious stare of an unseen admirer. (This fits perfectly with his behavior in life.) Every once in a while, Small will materialize fully in dressing rooms or on catwalks.

Small still watches over his theater. In the 1970s, Small's spirit saved an irreplaceable part of the building from inadvertent destruction. During renovations, a backhoe was tearing down part of the west wall when it suddenly stalled for no reason. Then, someone realized the backhoe was dangerously close to an arch featuring a hand-painted mural. Technicians who were summoned to the scene determined that if the backhoe had removed just one more brick, the arch would have toppled, destroying the historic mural. The wall was immediately reinforced, and the last supporting brick was given a place of honor in a display case.

DECEMBER 3
The Equator, Everett, WA (1894)

Ships carry the romance of the sea, inspiring tales of adventure. Some of these stories make it into print, becoming beloved works of literature. Others just live in the hearts of those who experienced life aboard ship.

The *Equator*, a two-masted schooner, was built int the late 1880s to sail as a trading vessel in the warm, welcoming waters of the South Pacific. After its service it was moored in Everett Harbor in Everett, Washington. The ship was known for the strange paranormal activity that stalked her decks – phantom figures, mysterious floating lights, and workmen's tools disappearing.

In response to all this activity, the ship's caretakers invited some psychics aboard for a séance. During the séance, two glowing lights hovered near the stern, dipping down as if to greet the psychics. As a result of this spirit communication, the mediums were able to discern the identities of both ghosts.

The glowing lights were the manifestations of Robert Louis Stevenson and King Kalakaua, the last king of Hawaii. Why would these two historical figures be hanging out together on the freighter?

Simple – the two men knew each other. And the ship held happy memories for them both.

Beloved adventure author Robert Louis Stevenson was not a well man. Living in England during the Industrial Revolution led to his contracting tuberculosis, in addition to other health problems. He went to Hawaii to get away from the choking smog of his native country. While there, he was a frequent guest of King Kalakaua. The king was famous for his hospitality, and he was delighted to host the renowned author.

Unfortunately, Hawaii's heat and humidity didn't agree with Stevenson. He booked passage on the *Equator* for himself and his family, hoping that the sea air of the South Pacific would ease his lung troubles. King Kalakaua was sorry to see his friend go. The royal family hosted a farewell luncheon on board the ship for the departing Stevensons.

The Stevensons lived aboard for six months as *Equator* made her way through her ports of call. In Samoa, Stevenson bought a large estate, and the family settled there. And it was there that Stevenson died on December 3, 1894. His ghost still resides there – his mother saw his ghost on her own deathbed in 1897.

Stevenson was a Scot, and most likely believed in ghosts as part of his heritage. And spirits abound in Hawaiian folklore; King Kalakaua would certainly have believed in an afterlife of contented haunting. The ship on which they shared a last meal and a bittersweet parting is now the place where they can enjoy each other's company as much as they like.

DECEMBER 4
Ghosts of the Watertown (1924)

Today we have another ship story, but this time, it's not the ship that's haunted. It's the water around the ship.

In 1924, the oil tanker *Watertown* sailed from California en route to New Orleans and New York via the Panama Canal. All was smooth sailing until the day two crew members, Michael Meehan and James Courtney, went belowdecks to the ship's hold to clean out a cargo tank. They were both overcome by fumes and died.

On December 4, Captain Keith Tracy had the men buried at sea. But the dead men returned. The next day, sailors saw the eerie apparition of Courtney's and Meehan's faces floating in the waves off the port side of the ship, at the same spot the men's bodies had been lowered overboard. The phantom faces bobbed in the water for about ten seconds before dissolving into the spray. Even creepier, the faces kept appearing.

When *Watertown* docked in New Orleans, Captain Tracy told the ship's owners about the ghostly faces. They suggested he try to take a picture. When the ship continued on its way, the faces reappeared, still keeping pace with the ship. Tracy snapped six photographs of the creepy faces, then locked the camera and film in the ship's safe.

Watertown reached New York safely, and Tracy handed the film over to the company's offices, who had it processed. Five of the six pictures showed nothing at all, just the chop of the waves. But the sixth picture is one of the most famous ghost photographs in the world.

Unfortunately, in April 2010, paranormal researcher Blake Smith cast doubts on the photo's authenticity. Using measurements from *Watertown's* sister ship, *Baldhill*, Smith recreated the famous photograph. He found that the faces would have been 7.5 meters tall, which seemed weird to him. Of course, Captain Tracy wouldn't have had the technology onboard to futz with the picture. But spirit photography, and fraud, had been around for decades at that time. On the other hand, the negative of the original photo had been investigated by the Burns Detective Agency, which found no evidence of tampering. And the ship's company never tried to profit from the picture.

So is the *Watertown* ghost picture actual proof of the paranormal? I'll let you decide.

DECEMBER 5
The Ghost of Clet Hall, Niagara, NY (1864)

The Seminary of Our Lady of Angels was founded in 1856 and built on the northernmost edge of Niagara Falls. Now known as Niagara University, it's home to the ghost of Thomas Hopkins.

At 2:30 pm on December 5, 1864, a fast-moving fire swept through the Seminary, the first building to be constructed on campus. The fire began where a stove pipe met the dry wood of the ceiling. The building was destroyed, with only one casualty. A student from Brooklyn, Thomas Hopkins, bravely but foolishly rushed into the building to make sure everyone had escaped. They had – but he didn't.

The Seminary was rebuilt as Clet Hall, and campus legend holds that Hopkins is still there, watching over his fellow students. He may be a guardian, but he's also a trickster who isn't above pranking the hall's residents. Doors will swing open on their own, sometimes accompanied by mocking laughter. Faucets turn on in the empty building over summer break. Footsteps and clanking noises echo in the hallways. According to lore, Hopkins "lives" in the attic, but that's just his home base. There are some nights that people experience poltergeist activity all over the building.

DECEMBER 6
Ghost of the Royal Hotel, Cumbria, England (1820)

Another ghost that rose from the ashes of a fire haunts the Royal Hotel in Kirkby Lonsdale, a town in the north of England. It was once known as the Rose and Crown Inn, and 200 years ago, it was the scene of a horrible tragedy.

On December 6, 1820, the Rose and Crown Inn went up in flames. A glowing ember popped out of a fireplace and landed in the dry straw of a nearby broom. The town had no fire service at the time, so there was little help fighting the inferno. Mrs. Roper, the landlady, was able to save her two children, and ran through the burning inn trying to wake all the servants she could. One maid also escaped, but five women who were asleep in the attic succumbed to the flames. Agnes Nicholson (17), Hannah Armstrong (18), Bella Cornthwaite (20), and Agnes Waller (25) all worked as maids at the inn. Their friend Alice Clark (31) used to work there, and had come back for a visit.

One of these young ladies – it's impossible to know which one – now haunts the rebuilt Rose and Crown, now known as the Royal Hotel. She manifests as the misty apparition of a petite woman with short blond hair. She wears a traditional maid's uniform. She doesn't seem to like the upper floors of the hotel, perhaps reminded of the attic where she perished. She sometimes appears in the lobby and in the women's restroom, but her favorite spots seem to be Rooms 20, 21, and the landing between the two rooms.

The town of Kirkby Lonsdale has not forgotten the tragedy. Soon after the fire, townspeople raised funds to erect a monument to the five lost women in the churchyard of St. Mary's Church. Those same generous folks donated money to help Mrs. Roper get back on her feet with another inn. The town's first fire station was built as a result of the fire, so the girls didn't die in vain.

On December 6, 2020, the 200th anniversary of the fire, the town held a memorial service for the lost. Girls from the primary school, dressed in period costumes, sang a Christmas carol. And mourners laid five white roses, their stems tied with pale pink ribbons, at the base of the monument in remembrance.

DECEMBER 7
The Sinking of the Westmoreland, Lake Michigan (1854)

The Great Lakes are the source of many a ghostly tale. One of the ships lost to the frigid waters of Lake Michigan was *Westmoreland*, in 1854.

The ship battled blizzard conditions for eighteen hours before finally succumbing at 10 am on December 7. Rising water extinguished the boiler, leaving the steamer without power. Ice built up and capsized the top-heavy ship, taking seventeen men – half the crew – under the icy waves.

The wreck of *Westmoreland* was lost for 155 years – but divers had been searching for her all that time. When she went down, she was rumored to be carrying 280 barrels of whiskey in her hold, and $100,000 in gold coins in her safe.

On July 7, 2010, Diver Ross Richardson discovered *Westmoreland*. She was sitting upright and relatively undamaged on the lakebed, 200 feet below the surface. She's one of the best-preserved shipwrecks from the 1850s.

That preservation has led to a very strange tale. The story goes that a diver went down to the wreck and made his way inside, eventually reaching one of the cabins. There he found half a dozen men seated around a table playing cards. A stack of coins was in the middle of the table, and several of the men clutched cards in their skeletal hands.

The diver did not stick around to see who had the winning hand.

DECEMBER 8
Forbidden Love, San Juan Capistrano, CA (1812)

Ah, young love. How often it can go awry ... Magdalena was a beautiful girl of fifteen or sixteen years. A parishioner of San Juan Capistrano, she fell in love with a young man named Teofilo. He was a talented artist who painted the wall frescoes, decorating the newly completed Great Stone Church at the mission.

Magdalena's father forbade her to see Teofilo, as he was not of the same social standing. But love finds a way, and the girl regularly slipped out to see her beloved. One day, though, her father caught the young couple together.

Magdalena's father made her confess to the priest at the mission. As part of her punishment, she was required to walk to the front of the congregation holding a lit candle of penitence, so everyone would know her shame. The day set for her public penance was

December 8, 1812 … but God had other plans that day.

That was the day a 6.9 magnitude earthquake struck southern California. Magdalena came to the Great Stone Church for early morning Mass. Chastened by the friars, Magdalena dutifully held her lit candle as she walked up the aisle. She lost her footing as the earth shook underneath her, but still she kept the candle in her trembling hands. The bell tower swayed for a heart-stopping moment, then crashed onto the church. In a few horrible seconds, forty people were buried alive. It took months to clear away the rubble and find the bodies. Among the dead was Magdalena, still clutching a candle in her cold hand.

According to local lore, Magdalena can be seen looking out a window in the Great Stone Church, on nights when a half-moon lights the sky.

DECEMBER 9
The Hole That Wouldn't Stay Filled, Newton, AL (1864)

By the last months of 1864, the end of the Confederacy was in sight. The South was desperate for fighting men, and gangs calling themselves "Home Guards" patrolled the area, looking for deserters and slackers to punish.

Bill Sketoe had a sick wife at home. He'd gone out to get medicine for her, and was hurrying back with it when he ran into Captain Joseph R. Breare's company near the Choctawhatchee River near Newton, Alabama. This was not a unit of the Home Guard, but rather a Confederate unit assigned to enforce military service.

The men accused Sketoe of being a deserter. Actually, Sketoe was a Methodist minister, which exempted him from military service. He protested his innocence, explaining about his sick wife, but the men wouldn't listen. They threw a rope over the limb of an oak on the riverbank and prepared to hang Sketoe for desertion. It's said his last words were a prayer for God to forgive his killers.

Bill Sketoe did not die easily. He was a tall man, and when he was hanged, his feet still touched the ground. This wasn't an efficient way to hang a man, obviously, so one of the vigilantes used his crutch to dig the soil out from under Sketoe's feet. That got the job done.

After Sketoe's death, his family had him buried in nearby Mount Carmel Cemetery. But the hole dug by his hanging remained on the riverbank, a mute testimony to the unnecessary killing. It soon became known as "the hole that wouldn't stay filled," because no matter how much debris and riverbank duff found its way into the hole during the day, overnight it would mysteriously be swept clean. Highway workers once filled the eight-inch-deep hole with dirt and pitched their tent directly over it, and slept there all night. In the morning, they discovered that the haunted hole was once again completely empty.   Legend had it that the ghost of Bill Sketoe still swung from the hanging tree, and his dragging feet cleaned the hole every night.

DECEMBER 10
The Black Cat, Shepherdstown, WV (1910)

On the campus of Shepherd College stands a building called Yellow House. The place has a long, interesting history: the original structure was a one-and-a-half-story, 360-square-foot log cabin built sometime between 1772 and 1793. Some historians believe it was the first home built in Shepherdstown. In 1926, it was purchased by Shepherd College, and has served as a sorority house, a daycare center, and simply as storage. But at the time of our story, it was still a private home.

In the early 20th century, this was the home of a cobbler named George Yonts. Yonts was said to be somewhat of a strange character, but well-liked in the community. He lived alone, and rumor had it that he had a fortune hidden somewhere on his property.

This is probably why Yonts was found murdered outside his cabin on the morning of December 10, 1910. His killer was never found. After Yonts was buried, treasure hunters swarmed the place, but no one ever discovered his rumored stash.

The first person to live in the cabin after Yonts' death was Net Entler. She moved into the cabin and decided to keep the furnishings Yonts had left behind. She also adopted the cobbler's black cat.

On the first anniversary of the murder, the cat acted weird all day, pacing the cabin restlessly, pausing once in a while to stare at the attic door. By the time evening came, the cat was scratching insistently at the door. Finally, Miss Entler opened the door, and the cat darted up the stairs. Immediately all hell broke loose: there were sounds of a titanic brawl coming from the attic. Miss Entler slammed the door in horror. The ruckus continued for about an hour. Then, all fell quiet. The cat came downstairs and mewed to be let out. It looked exhausted.

This phantom battle royale happened every year on the anniversary of Yonts' death. No one ever discovered who or what the cat was brawling with. Even after the cat died, the sounds of fighting in the attic manifesting once a year. The annual dustup continued until Shepherd College bought the property in 1926.

DECEMBER 11
Shadow of a Doubt, Rutherfordton, NC (1880)

Dan Keith was a mountain of a man. Six feet four inches, 230 pounds, he was not someone you'd want to cross. He had an outsized personality to match. Born in 1848 in Kentucky to Clayborn and Permillia Keith, he was the youngest of eight children. Clayborn died young, worn out by a lifetime of working poor ground. Dan, a rebellious kid, ran away from home to join the Confederate army. (Which he deserted.) After that, he moved to Indiana and became a petty thief. Then he came back to Kentucky and rejoined the army. (And deserted again.)

Over the next fifteen years, Dan lied, swindled, stole, and cheated as he wandered around the South. Meanwhile, he married three wives. (He deserted them too.)

In 1878, Dan settled in North Carolina with his fourth wife. He was thirty years old, she was fifteen. His swindles had gotten elaborate over the years. The area of North Carolina where he now lived was known for gold deposits. He took a 68-pound stone and rubbed it with brass until it took on a shine, then told people he'd found a gold mine. Several suckers fell for it. When his fraud was revealed, his enemies vowed revenge.

On January 28, 1880, the community was rocked by a gruesome crime. Alice Ellis, a Black girl, was found brutally raped and murdered. The eight-year-old was discovered in a wooded area of Rutherford County. Her head had been smashed to a bloody pulp with a large rock.

As Dan Keith was a big guy, suspicion naturally fell on him. Sheriff Noah E. Walker came to Dan's home to question him. Dan denied any knowledge of the killing, but when Walker searched the cabin, he found a bloodstained shirt. Dan protested that he'd gotten the shirt bloody while skinning rabbits, and even pointed out the carcasses of the skinned game. But Walker figured he had his man, and took Dan into custody. Dan went quietly. He was confident his innocence would be proven in court.

However, that's not what happened. By the time the trial was held, Dan had already been convicted in the court of popular opinion. The evidence presented at the trial was completely circumstantial. Not one of the fifteen "witnesses" called had actually witnessed the murder. The jury deliberated only half an hour before finding Dan Keith guilty.

The judge allowed Dan to make a statement before passing sentence. Dan showed no remorse at all – he was innocent, and he knew it. "Those who say I kilt anybody are liars," he thundered. "And each of you will be haunted every day for the rest of your life. Then the devil will have ye."

Dan was hanged on December 11, 1880, at Gallows Field in Rutherfordton. A few days after the hanging, people began to notice something weird abut the jail where Dan had been held. There was a shadow on the south wall that looked like a hanged man – a *big* hanged man.

Sheriff Walker ignored the shadow for a while. Then he ordered the wall cleaned. Workers scrubbed at the wall until the paint wore away to the wood beneath, but the shadow was still there. Walker had the wall repainted, but the shadow remained. Even creepier, the shadow was visible even in the dark of night.

When another site was chosen as the county jail, the building was converted into a private home. The new owner was disgusted by the looky-loos who still came to gawk at the shadow, so he planted ivy to grow over the wall and hide it. In 1949, the home became an office building. After a few more coats of paint, the shadow was finally eradicated.

But Dan Keith wasn't finished with his vengeful haunting. In 1971, the old jail was torn down, and a Burger House restaurant was built on the site. It failed within two years. Several other franchises followed, and they all went bust.

In one of those restaurants, Dan seems to have reappeared. Wait staff were deeply freaked to see an eerie shadow on the wall when they took the garbage out late at night. The manager would lock the building at the end of the evening – and come in the next morning to find a corner table set for one.

DAYS *of the* DEAD

DECEMBER 12
A Trooper to the End, Anniston, AL (1989, recurring)

When faced with a terminal diagnosis, people can have differing reactions. Captain E.C. Dothard was 58 years old when he was admitted to Stringfellow Memorial Hospital in December 1989 following a cancer diagnosis. Dothard was no stranger to hardship and stress. The state trooper was wounded in the May 1972 assassination attempt that left Governor George Wallace paralyzed. Dothard suffered a gunshot wound to the stomach. It was a graze, but still, it dropped him to the ground. Another trooped described Dothard "still barking out orders while on the ground after being shot."

Captain Dothard was a tough old guy, but he decided he couldn't face a long, slow, painful death by cancer. He wanted to depart this life on his own terms. He had brought his gun to the hospital, and after getting the news, Dothard shot himself in the head.

It wasn't a neat job, either. The gunshot obliterated part of Dothard's face. This violent, traumatic suicide has resulted in a unique haunting.

Dothard's headless ghost is sometimes seen in the hallways at Stringfellow Memorial. An even more unforgettable apparition is the lone eyeball that is seen rolling across the floor and out the door of the room where Dothard took his own life. The eyeball always appears in December, and sightings cease by the 25th. Some people suspect that Dothard just wants to hang around for another Christmas.

DECEMBER 13
Ghost Cat, Columbia, SC (late 1960s)

Patterson Hall, on the Columbia campus of the University of South Carolina, is haunted by the ghost of a kitten that only shows up on the ninth floor, and only in December. The phantom kitten crawls into the beds of sleeping students and goes through the motions of finding food, first gently kneading the sleeper's neck with its wee front paws, then biting just a little. If the student wakes up, she might catch a glimpse of the kitty.

The origin story of this tiny ghost is deeply tragic. In the late 1960s, a student named Linda Mossey enrolled at the university. She was the oldest daughter of a Free Will Baptist minister … and she was pregnant. She managed to hide her condition from her family until she went off to college, then from her professors and classmates. Linda kept to herself, spending most of her time in the library. Even her roommate rarely saw her.

In early December, Linda huddled alone in a shower stall, her body wracked with the pain of birth. Her baby, born prematurely, didn't survive.

Linda healed physically, but emotionally, she was gutted by guilt and the loss of her child. She withdrew even further, and stopped going to classes. She wandered the campus, avoiding other students entirely.

It was on one of these lonely walks that Linda found a tiny kitten abandoned near the dumpsters behind Patterson Hall. The stray was only a week or two old. Linda scooped up the miniscule ball of fluff and snuck back to her room.

She poured all her mothering instinct into the wee kitten, feeding it, cuddling it, singing lullabies. When she went out, she tucked the kitty into her winter coat, protecting it from the bitter weather.

Christmas drew near, and Linda realized with dull despair that she would soon have to go home for winter break. Unable to face what she had done, she committed suicide. But before she took that final step, she strangled her beloved kitten, so it wouldn't be left alone by her death.

The little ghost kitten of Patterson Hall still looks for food and human comfort. That's all it knew in its short life. It returns every December in search of imaginary milk … and phantom cuddles.

DECEMBER 14
Old Main, Fredonia, NY (1900)

Another college theater that has a ghostly presence is Old Main at the state university in Fredonia, New York. The university began as a "normal school" – that is, a school for training teachers.

When the building was Old Main Dormitory, it was fitted with iron grilles on the windows to keep out prowlers. Those iron bars may have given the female students a sense of security, but they spelled disaster on December 14, 1900, when fire broke out in the dorm. Six students and a custodian were trapped inside, unable to get to the fire escapes or break a window to escape the inferno. The seven were burned beyond recognition – May Williams' body was only identified by her ring – and buried in a common grave in Forest Park Cemetery.

The dormitory was demolished by the flames, but a new structure was built on the foundation. It later housed the theater. In December 1974, on the anniversary of the tragedy, sixteen students decided to do an investigation of the building. The activity that night was subtle, but undeniable. The group experienced inexplicable cold spots, as well as indistinct voices. The creepiest-but-coolest experience was that the group heard a girl singing somewhere in the building. Recorders out, the investigators combed the place, but never found the source of the hauntingly lovely voice.

DECEMBER 15
The Birth of Nero, Rome, Italy (37 AD)

Nero is one of the Roman emperors that even people who aren't Classics nerds recognize. He's best known for denying he set the fire that burned for six days in 64 AD and destroyed two-thirds of Rome. (He blamed the Christians.) Four years later, while facing his execution, Nero committed suicide.

He wasn't buried in Augustus' mausoleum, the resting place of other members of the Julio-Claudian dynasty. Instead, he was buried in the family tomb of his ancestors, the Ahenobarbi, on the Pincian Hill. Legend has it that a massive walnut tree grew near his grave, and flocks of ravens came to roost in it.

Superstitious Romans claimed that Nero's soul was trapped on earth, pinned by the tree and guarded by the spooky ravens. They also claimed that Nero's evil soul had attracted a bunch of demons who infested the area. Apparently, Nero was still partying in the afterlife – only now his dinner companions were demons. Over the centuries, people living in the area reported feelings of terror, mysterious injuries, possessions, and inexplicable killings. In 1099, the Christian population asked the Pope to do something about the creepy tree, the demons, and Nero's ghost.

Pope Pascal II retreated for three days of fasting and prayer. It's said he was visited by the Virgin Mary, who told him how to settle the situation. The Pope ordered the tree cut down, and Nero's tomb destroyed. The human remains found in the tomb were burned and thrown into the Tiber River. To consecrate the ground, a church was built on the site and dedicated to Mary. In 1472, Pope Sixtus V rebuilt the church and named it Santa Maria del Popolo (from the Latin *populus*, people, because it was the people who had demanded the demons be removed).

It's said Nero's ghost still wanders the Piazza del Popolo at night, scaring unwary tourists. The emperor had his own run-ins with ghosts during his life. He tried really hard to kill his mother, Agrippina. He tried drowning her in a collapsible boat, but she swam to safety. He had her bedroom ceiling rigged to collapse on top of her, but that failed to kill her. Finally, he stopped messing around and had one of his guards just stab her. After Agrippina's death, her ghost came back to haunt him. Nero tried to conjure her spirit with the help of necromancers and magicians, to beg her to leave him alone, but no – she haunted him for the rest of his life. (Serves him right.)

DECEMBER 16
One For The Gipper, South Bend, IN (1920)

The University of Notre Dame is renowned for its football team, the Fighting Irish. This is mostly down to one iconic player, George Gipp, who was a student and star player at the university. Playing under the famous coach Knute Rockne, Gipp was recognized as a football phenomenon, leading his team to twenty consecutive victories and two championships.

In addition to a promising career on the gridiron, Gipp also had a vibrant social life. He was infamous for wandering in well after the 11 pm curfew. Eventually, Brother Maurilius, the stern monk who supervised Washington Hall dorm, threatened disciplinary action. This would have jeopardized Gipp's position on the team, so he took the warning seriously ... for a while.

In mid-November, though, Gipp found himself caught out after curfew again. He snuck to the back door of Washington Hall, but found it locked. He had little choice – he curled up on the steps and slept outside.

This did not do him any favors. Gipp woke with a scratchy throat. He played anyway, leading the team to victory over Northwestern University. But on November 23, he was admitted to St. Joseph's Hospital with pneumonia. His condition deteriorated over the next couple of weeks, and on December 12, he spoke his immortal request to Coach Rockne: "Tell them to go in there with all they've got and win one for the Gipper." Two days later, Gipp drifted into a coma, and died December 14, 1920.

He soon returned to Washington Hall as its resident spook. Students returning from Christmas break in early 1921 heard weird moaning sounds coming from the band room. Instruments played themselves, adding to the eerie cacophony. The ghostly shenanigans came to the attention of none other than Brother Maurilius. The dorm supervisor was skeptical … until the night he was woken by an almighty crashy explosion noise in the hallway. Running out to see what had happened, he heard the mournful blat of a tuba drifting from the band room. He raced to the room, intending to unmask the hoaxer, but the room was empty.

Students no longer live in Washington Hall; it's now a theater. The ghost of the Gipper is still there, slamming doors and turning lights on and off. One student, on a ladder setting lights for a production, had just screwed in a lightbulb. He watched the bulb unscrew itself and drop to the floor, shattering under his ladder.

But the ghost isn't always destructive – he can be helpful. In the late 1970s, a group of students decided to hide out after play practice and do some investigating. Lori Wright was one of them. She says that one student hid on the catwalk while the director locked up the building. Then the stowaway snuck down and let the other students in. They all sat on the stage, lit candle, and got out a Ouija board.

"We asked if there was anyone in the hall that wanted to speak to us, and the planchette immediately slid to the letters 'S' and 'G' and then slid over to the part of the board that reads 'Goodbye'." Confused, the students repeated their question – and again, they got the message "SG – Goodbye." This really creeped them out, so they decided to leave. They packed up and let themselves out the side door.

As soon as they were out, they looked back – and saw a light bobbing inside the theater. The light passed the window, then reappeared in the stairwell, headed for the side door they'd just come through. With a start, the students recognized the beam of a flashlight. They dove into the bushes as the door opened – and a security guard stepped out.

" 'SG'. Security guard. I think whatever was there was trying to keep us from getting in trouble," Lori says.

DECEMBER 17
Jimmy Garlick, London, England (1765)

Old churches can hide many intriguing artifacts … especially a church like St. James Garlickhythe in London, built in the twelfth century, destroyed in the Great Fire in 1666, and rebuilt by legendary architect Christopher Wren. In 1855, workmen were clearing out a storeroom when they found a dessicated corpse. He became sort of a mascot for the church; he was displayed in a glass case in the church, and parishioners nicknamed him "Jimmy Garlick". Prankster choirboys would regularly take Jimmy out of his case on Sunday mornings and prop him up in a pew.

During the Blitz, a German bomb came perilously close to the exquisite church, shattering the display case and sending splinters of glass all over the corpse. Since then, the ghost of Jimmy Garlick has been free to haunt the church. Later in the war, a guard saw a dark figure walking in the aisle during an air raid. He shouted for the person to take cover, but the figure vanished.

Jimmy's corpse survived the war, and is now kept in a room in the church's tower. There are no plans to put him back on display. Researchers have concluded that the mummy is the body of sixteen-year-old Seagrave Chamberlain, who died from a fever on December 17, 1765. His tombstone can be seen in the wall of the church.

An American tourist had a deeply unsettling experience in the 1970s. She was visiting the church with her two sons, and the older son went off exploring. He climbed the stairs to the balcony – and came face-to-face with a skeletal apparition. The silent phantom stared at the terrified boy, white eyes bulging from bony sockets. The boy shrieked for his mother, but by the time she ran to him, the specter had melted away.

DECEMBER 18
Donner Dinner Party, Truckee, CA (1846)

One of the most memorable tales of the Old West is the story of the Donner Party. Even if you have zero interest in history, the mention of this ill-fated expedition is likely to send chills down your spine. And the sad thing is, it should never have happened. Those folks would probably have simply made their trek, settled in California, and disappeared into history except for the incredible run of bad luck and stupid decisions that left them stranded in the Sierra Nevada mountains.

Westward migration in the mid-19th century had to follow a tight schedule. Leave too early, and there wouldn't be enough grass along the way to feed your pack animals. Leave too late, and you risked getting stuck in a mountain pass over the winter. The ideal time to leave Independence, Missouri, was mid- to late-April, but the Donner Party poked around until May 12.

Then, when they got to Wyoming, the leaders of the party, George Donner and James Reed, decided to take a nifty shortcut they'd heard about, called the "Hastings Cutoff". Most pioneers heading to California went north through Idaho, then south through Nevada. A shady guidebook author, Lansford Hastings, touted a shortcut through the Wasatch Mountains. There was a serious problem, though, with this route: no one had ever actually taken wagons through this shortcut … not even Hastings himself. (In an exquisite irony, on the same day the Donner-Reed party left Springfield, Illinois, heading west, Hastings left California heading east – to see what the shortcut he'd written about was really like.)

Nevertheless, the twenty wagons of the Donner-Reed party decided to break off from the rest of the group and take Hastings' spurious shortcut. This was a colossal mistake. The travelers had to break their own trail, wasting precious time cutting down trees to let the wagons through. The "shortcut" added nearly a month to their journey.

The final misfortune came in early November 1846. The group had only 100 miles to go when they reached the Sierra Nevada mountains. But as they slept one night, fat snowflakes began to drift down. Overnight, a blizzard dumped several feet of snow. Mountain passes that were clear just the day before were now impassable, choked with ice and snow. The settlers had to back up, making camp at Truckee Lake.

Weeks passed. Then months. People lost weight, growing gaunt and hollow-eyed. Food ran low … then ran out. One survivor put the dilemma in stark terms.

"What would you do if you were a mother watching your children starve or freeze to death? You've already eaten the horses and oxen, and boiled their hides into a horrible gelatinous concoction; you've eaten field mice and finally cut the throats of your beloved family dogs and eaten them, paws and all. But you know that there's protein that will keep you alive in those snow banks."

As delicately as she could, she was referring to one of the most powerful human taboos: cannibalism. In the extremity of their starvation, some of the group ate the bodies of the dead. About half of the Donner Party survived their ordeal. About half of those survivors resorted to eating human flesh.

The last members of the Donner Party eventually made it to California, but their arrival had come at a terrible cost. The Donner Party will forever be synonymous with bitter cold, bleak starvation, and the most horrible choice.

Donner Pass is still haunted by the ill-fated group. Visitors to the memorial site capture ghostly images in photographs, many of them children; most of the group were under eighteen years old, and the vast majority of the survivors were children. Invisible hands tug at tourists' clothes, and a feeling of desperate gloom hangs over the site.

The ghost of Tamsen, George Donner's wife, manifests as a yellowish glowing figure. George, Tamsen, and their children were found by rescuers. George had injured his hand at the beginning of the ordeal, and by the time help arrived, it had turned gangrenous. Tamsen sent her children with the rescue party, but refused to leave George. George died of his septic injury, and by staying with him, Tamsen sealed her own fate as well. Her body was never found.

DECEMBER 19
Death of Emily Bronte, Haworth, England (1848, recurring)

One of the giants of English literature is Emily Bronte, despite the fact that she died at the age of thirty, having published only one novel.

Emily was a shy child who grew into an introverted woman. People found her standoffish, but that masked a personality that was painfully ill at ease with strangers. Emily was homeschooled all her life; at 17, she tried formal schooling but had a nervous breakdown. She was happiest when she was out on the moors, the wild, lonely places that played such a large part in her novel.

She published *Wuthering Heights* in 1847, and likely would have gone on to write more classics of Western literature. But in addition to being fabulous writers, the Brontes had something else in common: they were prone to tuberculosis. Emily's brother Branwell died in September 1848, and she caught a chill at his funeral. A few weeks later she was suffering with a fever. She developed the dry, wracking cough of consumption. Her downward spiral was hastened by her refusal to take any medication or undergo any treatment.

Emily died at 2 pm on December 19, 1848, on the sofa in the sitting-room of Haworth Rectory. She still haunts her former home. Beginning on December 19, and through Christmas, she can be seen wandering the grounds of the rectory. She vanishes if approached, just as shy in death as she was in life.

She makes appearances in town as well. Weavers Restaurant in Haworth is packed on December 19 with patrons hoping to catch a glimpse of the Gray Lady. This ghost only appears on the anniversary of Emily's death. She's described as a slender young woman wearing a bonnet, shawl, and long skirt. She wanders through the restaurant, disappearing into one of the walls at the end of her annual visit.

Every so often, Emily's ghost wanders farther afield; maybe in death, she's getting more adventurous. In May 2000, an employee of the British Library took a cab across London to an exhibition. He carried with him the original manuscript of *Wuthering Heights*. When he got to the venue, the cabbie asked him where his lady companion had gone.

The librarian was flummoxed. He was alone in the cab's back seat. But the driver insisted he'd seen a pale young woman dressed in black sitting next to the librarian.

After all, he'd been carrying her manuscript.

DECEMBER 20
The Dancing Ghost, Orensburg, Russia (1870)

The country estate of a wealthy landowner named Shchapoff was the site of an intriguing poltergeist case in 1870. On the night of November 14, Helena Shchapoff, his 20-year-old wife, had been visiting with the miller's wife. The two women had been chatting in the manor's living room when a servant came in to tell Helena that her baby daughter was being fussy, and refused to settle down to sleep. Helena asked Maria, the cook, if she would entertain the infant. Helena knew that Maria had a magic touch with the baby: whenever the cook danced a little three-step jig, it put the baby in a good mood, and she'd settle down and stop fussing. Sure enough, Helena heard the tapping of Maria's feet as she danced. Soon, Maria came in to report that the baby had dropped off to sleep. Helena thanked her, and dismissed her for the evening.

Helena and the miller's wife continued their conversation, but the guest broke off her gossip to scream – she'd seen a frightful face peering in the window, she said. Helena got up to investigate, but suddenly a cacophony erupted above their heads. Someone was making a hell of a racket in the attic. In a few moments, the rapping slowed, becoming recognizable as Maria's jigging.

Helena was perplexed. Why was Maria still dancing? The baby was asleep; she'd said so. The two women went to the cook's room … where they saw Maria fast asleep.

Now wondering just who was in the attic, Helena and her guest took a lantern and went up to investigate. They still heard the rapid patter of dancing shoes, but there was no one in the attic. The women fled down the stairs as the rapping surrounded them down the stairwell.

At 10 pm the next night, the dancing footsteps began again. Helena had her servants search the house, but the invisible dancer remained elusive.

When Mr. Shchapoff returned from his business trip the afternoon of November 16, he scoffed at Helena's story. He was a no-nonsense kind of guy, and dancing ghosts just didn't fit into his worldview. Even when his mother and mother-in-law backed up Helena's account, he refused to believe it.

Then, that night after everyone else had gone to bed, Shchapoff was in his study reading.

Around 10 o'clock, he noticed a scratching noise above him. Thinking that a pigeon had gotten into the attic, he listened more closely. He soon realized the sounds weren't the random skritches of a bird's claws; they were the lively pattern of a three-step.

Shchapoff thought Helena was pranking him. He crept upstairs to their bedroom, intending to catch her at it. Once he was sure the sounds were coming from their room, he threw open the door, ready to lecture her.

The sounds stopped immediately. Helena lay in bed, sound asleep. Baffled, Shchapoff started to close the door, when the rapping started up again. One particularly loud thump woke Helena. She sat straight up, saw her husband, and asked, "Did you hear that?"

"I didn't hear a thing," Shchapoff fibbed, not wanting to scare her. Just then, two explosive bangs rocked the house. Shchapoff grabbed a pistol, whistled up his dogs, rousted the servants, and went to put a stop to the nonsense.

He didn't find the prankster. Those searching inside the house said that the noises were outside. But the people outside swore that the ruckus was coming from inside. Shchapoff finally gave up for the night.

The next night, rapping and dancing filled the attic again as Shchapoff and his neighbors listened – he'd invited even more backup. The night's performance ended with a violent finale: a heavy wooden door was struck by an invisible force that tore it off its hinges.

After that, the footsteps stopped ... for a while.

On December 20, the Shchapoffs were entertaining guests. They told the tale of their mysterious rapping visitor, and the guests were skeptical. Instead of letting it go, Shchapoff was irritated that his friends doubted his story. He called Maria into the parlor and insisted she dance, saying loudly that the ghost just needed a little coaxing to come back.

Shchapoff got his wish, all right. Maria danced her little jig, and the attic erupted with a flurry of rapping as the poltergeist mimicked her steps precisely. Guests ran up to the attic to see if Shchapoff had planted another servant up there to trick them, but found no one. On New Year's Eve, Shchapoff again made Maria perform for his guests, with the same result.

Then, the activity turned violent. Balls of fire circled the house and threw themselves against the windows. Dresses hanging in closets burst into flames. Once, a mattress started burning while a guest was in the bed.

The climax came when Helena, the local miller, and another guest were talking in the house. A crackling noise erupted beneath the floor, and the room was filled with an eerie wail. A bluish spark jumped at Helena, and her dress instantly burst into flames. She screamed and fainted. The guest lunged at her and beat out the flames with his hands. He was severely burned – but Helena didn't get so much as a sunburn, even though her dress was nearly consumed by the flames.

The Shchapoffs left their country estate soon afterwards. They moved to their townhouse, and fortunately, left the terrifying phenomena behind.

DECEMBER 21
More Stevenson, Monterey, CA (1879)

Before Robert Louis Stevenson fetched up in Hawaii as King Kalakaua's guest, he spent some time in California. He'd come to the western United States from England in August 1879, following an alluring woman named Fanny Osbourne. He'd met Fanny in September 1876, and had been quite taken with the talented young woman, herself a noted writer of short stories for magazines. In May 1880, they would marry, but that was in the future. Fanny moved to the States, and Stevenson knew he had to follow her. He landed in New York City and traveled by train to California. By the time he arrived in Monterey, his health, always precarious, was utterly broken, and he had to take some time to recover.

Stevenson took a room at the French Hotel, which was owned by Manuela Girardin. During Stevenson's stay, the hotel was visited by tragedy.

Manuela lost her husband, Juan, in the summer of 1879 to the typhoid epidemic that was raging at the time. Then in early December, her two grandchildren fell ill with typhoid too. Manuela cared devotedly for her young patients, nursing them through their illness night and day. This attention was her undoing, though. She contracted typhoid herself, and died on December 21.

Manuela Girardin has stayed in the house where she nursed her grandchildren back to health at the cost of her own life. It's now a museum. The haunting is concentrated during the first three weeks of December, when people will smell the sharp tang of carbolic acid, a sickroom disinfectant of old. Or they'll see a rocking chair in the nursery start rocking on its own – maybe with Manuela, invisible, cuddling a feverish child. Every year, a guest at the museum will see an extra costumed interpreter. They'll comment on her authentic outfit – while pointing at a blank wall.

DECEMBER 22
The Manhattan Well Murder, New York City (1799)

Gulielma Sands, known as Elma, lived in a boarding house in New York City. In December 1799, she was in a relationship with another tenant, a carpenter named Levi Weeks. The couple made plans to elope on December 22.

Around 8 pm that evening, Elma's cousin, Catherine Ring, heard the front door open and close. She assumed it was Elma sneaking out to meet Levi. But Levi showed up at 10 pm demanding to know where Elma was. This unexpected development led to a search of the neighborhood.

Witnesses saw Elma in Lispenard's Meadow, a nearby lover's lane of sorts, walking with two unidentified men. Lispenard's Meadow was also the site of the Manhattan Well. On January 2, Elma's body was pulled from the well. She'd been dumped there, her neck broken.

Levi Weeks was accused of Elma's murder. For his trial, his wealthy oldest brother Ezra hired the best lawyers in town: Alexander Hamilton and Aaron Burr. The two-day trial was the first recorded murder trial in American history.

The case was expected to be a slam-dunk for the prosecution. Levi Weeks was in a relationship with Elma, and he was the last person to actually be seen with her. There were rumors (untrue) that Elma was pregnant, which seemed to give Levi motive for her murder.

But Hamilton and Burr knew their business. They cast serious reasonable doubt on the case, painting Elma as a loose woman, addicted to laudanum. Any guy could have killed her, they said. After only five minutes of deliberation, the jury found Levi Weeks not guilty.

Not that it did him any good. Weeks was so hated after the trial, he had to leave town. And Catherine Ring, Elma's cousin, had a few tart words for Alexander Hamilton.

"If thee dies a natural death, I shall think there is no justice in heaven!"

Catherine's curse backsplashed on pretty much everyone involved in the trial. Hamilton was killed in 1804, in a duel with his former partner, Aaron Burr. The judge in the trial simply disappeared after leaving his hotel one night. And Burr was loathed for killing Hamilton, tried for treason in 1807, lost his beloved daughter Theodosia to shipwreck in 1812, and died broke in 1836, the same day his divorce was finalized.

In 1817, houses were built in Lispenard's Meadow. The Manhattan Well ended up hidden in the basement of a four-story building at 129 Spring Street. The upper-middle-class home eventually became commercial property. In 1954, the building was purchased by the DaGrossa family, who opened a restaurant. In 1980, Manhattan Bistro had grown so much that they needed more storage. They excavated the cellar, and exposed the well that had been buried for nearly 200 years.

Since then, the spirit of Elma Sands has made her presence known. Witnesses have heard her screaming for her life, and have seen the apparition of a young woman, soaking wet, dressed in 18th-century clothing.

Restaurant manager Thomas King had many paranormal experiences during his time at the Bistro. One evening, he went down to the basement to get a bottle of wine from the large cage where the liquor was stored. He unlocked the gate, leaving the key in the lock, and went to the back wall for the bottle. When he turned around, he found the gate locked behind him, trapping him in the cage. The keys had been removed from the lock and placed on a box just out of reach. King was down there for an hour before other employees realized he was missing and came downstairs to rescue him.

Manhattan Bistro went out of business in 2013. In 2014, the building was gutted, renovated, and became an upscale clothing boutique. The well was preserved, and is now in the corner of the men's department.

DECEMBER 23
The Hitchhiking Ghost, Franklin, TN (1864)

Advances in military technology during the Civil War led, naturally, to advances in medicine and surgery. Military units couldn't travel with entire hospitals, so surgeons went to the battlefields, and set up field hospitals for the care of the wounded. The surgeons did the best they could for the men under their care, and these makeshift camps were better than nothing.

Deering J. Roberts, a Confederate surgeon, was charged with setting up a temporary hospital after the Battle of Franklin on November 30, 1864. When he arrived with his hospital steward, he went to work finding suitable buildings to set up as hospitals. One such building was an old wagon shop, two stories high, with plenty of windows for good lighting. Roberts set his team to preparing this building and two others to house wounded soldiers.

The Battle of Franklin turned out to be one of the bloodiest engagements of the war. It lasted only five hours, but the Confederate assault was bigger than Pickett's Charge at Gettysburg. The Confederates lost 1,750 men that day, and 3,800 were wounded.

Roberts was a talented, caring surgeon who did his best for the men entrusted to him. His policy was not to amputate a limb without the patient's consent.

One soldier, wounded in the battle, adamantly refused amputation, even though the bones of his arm had been shattered by a Minie ball, and the wound was already badly infected. Roberts took pity on the terrified soldier, and accepted his decision not to amputate, although privately he described wounds left by Minie balls as "both remarkable and frightening." Roberts later wrote in his journal that the soldier suffered not only from his grievously wounded arm, but also "nostalgia and despondency." The man had but one wish: to walk home in time for Christmas.

Unfortunately, the soldier didn't achieve his goal. He died at the hospital December 23, 1864.

Apparently, though, he hasn't given up on getting home for Christmas. Travelers on the highway outside of Franklin have reported appearances of the hitchhiking ghost of a Confederate soldier. Maybe one of these years he'll make it home.

DECEMBER 24
The Ghost and Mary Pepper, Liverpool, England (1887)

Every so often, we hear of ghosts helping the living. It's rarer still when a living person has the chance to help a ghost.

Mary Pepper was an orphan living in Liverpool in the 1880s. At seven years old, she was on her own, living in the cellar of an abandoned building. Like many other street waifs of the Victorian era, Mary scavenged the streets for anything of value – lumps of coal that had fallen from carts, coins dropped from the pockets or purses of those more fortunate. She would beg for day-old bread from the Dow Street bakery. Sometimes she would hang around the door of the candy shop, hoping for a few hard candies or bits of toffee from Mr. Mallard, the owner. That was a real treat.

Even in her poverty, Mary found beauty on the rough streets. On Christmas Eve, 1887, she was following a robin as it hopped down Crosshall Street. The bird's red breast was a cheerful spot of color against the snow. Mary's reverie was interrupted by the sudden appearance of a ghost.

Mary knew the man was a spirit. For one thing, she'd seen ghosts all her life. For another, this man was completely devoid of color – he was stark white, from the top hat perched on his white hair to the tips of his polished boots. And for a third, she recognized him. It was Henry Silver, who had died in the 1860s.

The ghost stared at her with shocking-pink eyes, the only part of him with any color at all. It reached out for her with bony pale hands, groaning as if in distress. It staggered through the snow, leaving no footprints. Mary just sighed. He'd scared the robin away.

"Aren't you afraid of me?" the ghost demanded.

"No. You're nothing – just a sad ghost," Mary replied calmly.

"I'm not nothing!" Silver retorted. "I'm an evil spirit!"

Mary just wandered away, unimpressed. Perhaps she could spot the robin once more.

Silver followed Mary down Crosshall Street. Trying to scare her, he swooped through her several times. He followed her home to the dank cellar where she lived, and squeezed through a hole in the wall. Finally, seeing that Mary could not be spooked, he told his story.

During his life, Henry Silver had a curious, unpleasant hobby. He would plant fake love letters that led to quarrels between couples, often making them break up as a result. One of these pranks backfired terribly when a young woman, thinking she'd been deceived by her lover, threw herself into the Mersey River and drowned. She happened to be a Gypsy, and here's when Silver's penchant for mischief caught up with him. A relative of the girl came to see him and placed a Gypsy curse on him. Because of his cold-hearted tricks, the old woman cursed him to be cold forever. Despite his doctor's best efforts, Silver soon died of hypothermia … in summer.

Silver cried out to Mary that he longed to feel warmth once more – the cozy fireside, the glow of love – as he wept for his loss. Mary snapped, "Then go into St. John's Church and ask for forgiveness."

"I can't – I'm too proud!" Silver argued. Mary finally talked him into it, and led him to the church herself. Silver squared his shoulders, and walked into the church.

He was in there for quite some time. Mary waited for him patiently outside. She felt a bit responsible for the poor sad ghost. When he came out, Silver was a changed man … literally. His color had returned; now he sported a black top hat and a brown suit, and his cheeks were a healthy, rosy pink. He gave Mary a hug, and said, "Thank you, little one." Then he disappeared.

The ghost's gratitude wasn't just lip service. Several years later, when she was fifteen, Mary was adopted, and later emigrated to America. There, she married a rich oil tycoon and, presumably, lived happily ever after.

DECEMBER 25
The Headless Horseman, County Limerick, Ireland (1700s, recurring)

Castle Sheela in Ireland is haunted by a really spectacular ghost, one without a head. What's more, he makes an annual appearance in grand style – throwing the castle door open every Christmas Day and riding his horse up the stairs.

The story begins in 1739, when Galty Mallory, heir to Castle Sheela, visited Hungary on his Grand Tour of Europe. He fell in love with Countess Hoja in Budapest, and married her. After a year of travel, the couple returned to Ireland and settled in the ancestral castle. In 1740, their first son, Ormond, was born, the oldest of five children.

Ormond grew up to be a selfish, unpleasant lout who only cared about his own pleasure. When he was eighteen, Galty died, and Ormond inherited the castle and the family fortune. He lived the life of a womanizing jerk, chasing all the tail he could find. He had a knack for seducing women who were already married. His mother was so disgusted by his behavior that she took her two daughters and her son Dominic and moved back to Hungary. (Another son had died in childhood.) She had some parting words of warning for her son: "Beware of the village men. They'll surely take their revenge."

Ormond took up with Moira Carmichael, completely ignoring the fact that she already had a husband. John Carmichael mysteriously died soon after, and Moira moved into the castle. She and Ormond allowed the castle to fall into ruin – furniture broken in the couple's drunken fights, wall hangings dusty and faded, dishes and goblets carelessly chipped. No self-respecting servant would work there, so the castle declined further as the years wore on.

The one creature on earth that Ormond really cared for was his horse. He'd named it Follow, because ever since it was a colt, it would follow Ormond anywhere – even up the stairs to its master's bedroom. Ormond had a ramp installed next to the staircase, a gentle lift with four shallow rises, to make Follow's daily trek easier.

Ormond and Moira argued more and more often, because even though he had her at home, he was still tomcatting around. Ormond started seeing a Mrs. Fermoy. One day while the couple was strolling in the local lover's lane, Jason Fermoy – her husband – jumped Ormond and beat him so badly that Ormond's shoulder was broken. He spent several months convalescing (during which Follow came up to see him every day).

While Ormond was laid up, his mother came for a visit. Since she planned to be there over the Christmas season, she asked him to do two things for her. She wanted him to have his portrait painted, to hang in the castle's gallery with his ancestors. And she wanted to bring the family together for a Christmas feast. Ormond agreed to both.

There was a hunt also planned for Christmas Day. Ormond was well enough to attend, but he showed up late. Others who were there said he looked like he'd been in a fight – he was bruised, and there was a jagged cut near his mouth. He seemed on edge, constantly looking around as if fearing another attack.

The hunt was over by 4 pm, and Christmas dinner at Castle Sheela was supposed to start at 6 pm. Ormond was expected home soon after 4, but by 6, there was still no sign of him. Dominic, his brother, took some servants out to look for him, but they soon returned, half frozen.

At 8 pm, there was a noise at the door … a noise everyone recognized. It was Follow, coming up the front steps to be let in. Dominic rose to open the door – and sank to his knees in horror.

Follow was covered in lather, badly winded. His sorrel hide was mottled with dried blood. He staggered into the great hall, with his master on his back … most of him, anyway. A body, dressed in the clothes Ormond had worn to the hunt, was tied in place on Follow's back … only a body. No head. The neck ended in a bloody stump.

As everyone watched aghast, Follow carried his gruesome burden slowly up the ramp. When he got to Ormond's room, he fell to his knees, then collapsed onto the floor, stone dead.

Ormond's head was never found, and his murder was never solved. He was buried in the family cemetery. For many years, one person frequently visited his grave – a heavily-veiled Mrs. Fermoy.

Dominic inherited Castle Sheela on Ormond's death. The first thing he did was to order the ramp torn out. This doesn't stop Follow's ghost from coming up. The castle's inhabitants have seen the phantom horse and headless rider making their way up the stairs many times. Other times, only the somber sound of slow hoofclops is heard.

In addition to his visits throughout the year, Ormond manifests every year on Christmas Day, and he does it in two distinct ways. His portrait changes: on that day, his face vanishes, replaced by a dark smudge. The next day, Ormond once again regards the hall with his thin smile and cold eyes.

And every year on Christmas night, the front door of Castle Sheela bangs open, and a spectral horse shuffles in, bearing a headless body. The horse makes its exhausted way up an invisible ramp, step by painful step, once more making its desolate journey.

DECEMBER 26
The Chicken Ghost, London, England (1943)

One evening in December 1943, a British airman stationed in London was out for a stroll. He was crossing Pond Square when he heard the anachronistic rumble of carriage wheels on cobblestones. Then he heard a sound that was even more out of place: the squawk of a chicken.

The airman looked around. He didn't see a carriage, but he did see a chicken running around in confused circles. He was surprised to see a chicken in the middle of wartime London. What was even stranger was that the chicken had no feathers. The airman took a couple of steps, hoping to help the poor shivering thing. Before he got too close, though, the chicken ran through a brick wall and disappeared!

The chicken ghost has been seen in Highgate for over 300 years. The poor thing has every reason to haunt the square. That unfortunate bird was the world's first frozen chicken – the ancestor to every bucket of KFC.

Legend has it that in March 1626, Sir Francis Bacon, the eminent scientist, was riding in a carriage with his friend Dr. Witherborne. Looking out the carriage window, Bacon noticed that the wheels were packed with chunks of snow, and that the grass revealed by the passing of the wheels looked fresh and green, even at the end of winter. He wondered aloud if snow could be used for food preservation.

Witherborne pooh-poohed the theory, but Bacon ordered the carriage to stop. He trotted to the nearest house and bought one of the household's chickens. He wrung its neck, plucked it, gutted it, and stuffed the carcass with snow. Then he packed more snow around the prepared bird. Weeks later, the chicken's meat was still good.

Bacon wasn't around to enjoy his triumph, though. As a result of his impetuous adventure in the snow, he developed pneumonia. By April 9, he was dead.

The chicken had its revenge.

DECEMBER 27
Albert Balch, Steilacoom, WA (1862)

Lunacy, an old-fashioned description of mental illness, was so named because people thought the moon could cause lapses in reason. This is no longer a viable diagnosis in modern times. But storekeeper Albert Balch really did seem to suffer with the phases of the moon.

Whenever there was a new moon, Albert seemed to lose focus. He would wander the streets at night, gazing up at the sky. He was often dazed, but not violent. His family sent him to an asylum in San Francisco for treatment, which seemed to help.

Soon after his return home, though, he seemed to relapse. In 1859 the owner of the store where Albert worked sent him to San Francisco to buy merchandise. In the grip of one of his spells, Albert went missing. His brother eventually found him wandering the streets with $2,500 in gold coins in a suitcase.

His dementia grew worse, and soon paranoia sunk its claws into his mind too. Albert became convinced he had enemies who were trying to kill him. On December 27, 1862, the new moon drew him outside once more. He ran out dressed only in his nightshirt. He was later found dead. The coroner's inquest determined that Albert had either fallen and died as a result of the fall, or had run from imaginary pursuers until he collapsed from exhaustion and died of exposure.

Albert Balch's ghost still roams the trail to Fort Nisqually, where his body was found. Perhaps he has finally found peace in his perpetual moonlit travels.

DECEMBER 28
Tay Bridge, Scotland (1879)

The weather on the night of December 28, 1879, was foul in Scotland. Freezing winds howled across the crags, and the powerful locomotive NBR (Northern British Railway) 224 battled the elements as it steamed along the cold, dark, rain-lashed tracks towards Dundee.

The train approached Tay Bridge at speed. As it reached the middle, the center span shuddered and groaned with the twin stresses of the train above it and the violent winds all around it.

The bridge suddenly collapsed, sending NBR 224 and all its cars into freezing water. Everyone on the train died that night, including the son of the bridge's designer, Sir Thomas Bouch. Some bodies were never recovered.

The locomotive itself was raised, salvaged, and put back into service. The bridge, too, was rebuilt, incorporating some of the original beams. In an ironic twist, the reconditioned locomotive was named "The Diver". Many engineers were too spooked to drive it, especially over Tay Bridge. Despite its dire reputation, The Diver remained in service until 1919.

Witnesses say that if you stand on shore near Tay Bridge at 7:15 pm on the anniversary of the crash, you can see the phantom lights of a spectral locomotive, and hear screams and the desperate shriek of brakes as the tragedy repeats itself.

The podcast Ron's Amazing Stories featured a story sent in by Alexander Short of Manchester, England, in Episode 436. Ron graciously allowed me to share Alexander's story.

In Alexander's journal entry from December 28, 2005, he wrote that something terrible had happened to him that evening. He's an actor, and had been touring in Edinburgh. He'd boarded a train that evening that would take him to Dundee. He'd brought a book with him for the trip, but the motion of the train soon lulled him to sleep.

When he woke about an hour later, the first thing he noticed was that the car was redolent with an awful stench. He looked around, and everything felt different ... wrong, as if the world was just about to get a dose of really bad news. He also noticed that the car was much dimmer. The reason? The electric lights had been replaced – by candlelight.

Now starting to panic, Alexander looked around for any sign of life. He was alone in the car, but he saw a man coming towards him from the adjacent car. Alexander's relief turned to dread when he realized that even though the man was less than six feet away, Alexander couldn't see his face clearly. Alexander's nerve broke, and he yelled at the man, demanding to know what was going on.

The man, whose face resolved into detail, sighed, and pointed behind Alexander. He turned, and saw the car filled with passengers once more ... passengers dressed in the clothing of a bygone era. The man introduced himself as Mr. Bouch, and asked Alexander to return to his seat. He did so, still hoping he was in the grip of an extraordinarily detailed dream. But the crack of thunder from the storm raging outside as the train raced along was all too real. He even watched lightning strike, splitting trees along the track.

Alexander watched in horror as the faces of his fellow passengers began to fade. The rancid stench of death still surrounded him. He looked out the window and saw that the train was rapidly approaching a bridge. The train rocked back and forth more violently, and Alexander was convinced he was going to die. The car leapt into the air – then began to fall.

Alexander wrote that he could remember the splash as the train hit the water, the chill as the car started to fill. He was surrounded by chaos – people grabbed at luggage, screamed in panic, tried to force windows open. A thump shuddered through the car as the train smashed into the riverbed. The screams turned to gurgled cries, and darkness overtook everything as the candles drowned. Bodies floated around him in the inky, freezing water. Alexander let go of his last breath and surrendered to the blackness.

Then he snapped back to consciousness. He found himself back in his regular seat on the modern train. When he got off at Dundee, he noticed a small historical marker. It commemorated the collapse of Tay Bridge during the worst storm in thirty years ... the collapse that sent NBR 224 plummeting to the bottom of the river.

Alexander wrote that he hasn't ridden a train since.

DECEMBER 29
Death At Wounded Knee, South Dakota (1890)

In 1889, a Paiute prophet named Wovoka had a vision. He discerned that Natives would rise again, that buffalo would return to the Plains, and peace would return to the land. He encouraged his followers to pray for this peace through movement: the Ghost Dance, in which people would dance themselves into a trance meditation. Several tribes took up the Ghost Dance philosophy, which was Wovoka's aim. He wanted to bring tribes together in unity.

Whites saw the movement, and the resulting tribal cooperation, as a threat, so they moved to squash it. On December 28, 1890, the Seventh Cavalry attacked 300 Hunkpapa Sioux at Wounded Knee. According to some accounts, the soldiers ordered the Indians to lay down their rifles. One man, who may have been deaf, ignored the command. Chaos ensued. Four Hotchkiss guns, each firing fifty explosive shells per minutes, tore into the crowd, killing men, women, and children indiscriminately. Many victims were mutilated while still alive, and left to die in the freezing weather. The dead were eventually collected and thrown into a mass grave.

The massacre led to deep, lasting haunting. On Pine Ridge Reservation, ghost children are seen running and screaming as they relive the atrocity. The ghost of a young woman beheaded by a soldier's saber is seen walking with her small daughter – the two are looking for the mother's head.

DECEMBER 30
Music In The Night, Murfreesboro, TN (1862)

The Battle of Stones River (December 31, 1862-January 2, 1863) was one of the major battles of the war, with the highest percentages of casualties on both sides. Nearly one in three soldiers on the field was killed, captured, or injured. Union troops successfully fought back several Confederate advances, gaining much-needed confidence after their loss at the Battle of Fredericksburg.

Witnesses report the sounds of an army on the move. They also tell of hearing period music in the air.

On the evening of December 30, both armies were preparing for the coming morning's battle. The Union band played the tune "Yankee Doodle", followed by "Hail Columbia". The Confederate musicians cheekily responded with "Dixie". Soon after this musical conversation, the Northerners went into the song "Home Sweet Home". After a moment, the Southern troops joined in. The cold air was filled with the sound of men's voices raised in song, sworn enemies singing the same bittersweet tune, finding harmony for a few moments before the appalling bloodshed to come.

DECEMBER 31
Remembrance At The Cemetery, Amana Colonies, IA (1854, recurring)

Seven villages in the Iowa River Valley make up the Amana Colonies. The seven villages are Main Amana, East Amana, High Amana, Middle Amana, South Amana, West Amana, and Homestead (because they ran out of Amanas). The peaceful communities are a tourist destination for all the right reasons. This is a place where community is cherished and hospitality is a way of life. Historic homes line the quiet streets, and the people who live here share their sense of the past. If Colonial Williamsburg was a modern working town, rather than a historic recreation, it would be the Amana Colonies.

The cemeteries in the Amana Colonies were all laid out at the same time as the towns themselves. In the Amana faith, everyone is equal – no one is more important than anyone else. So the gravestones all look alike: made of cement, with the deceased's name, date of death, and age. There are no family plots, as everyone is considered family. The burials are arranged facing east, the direction of the Resurrection. The cemeteries are planted with a border of pines. The evergreen trees keep their leaves all winter ... and these trees are what give us our final ghost story. The ghosts of children buried here are said to rise up on Christmas to claim pine boughs left on their graves by living children.

And here's one more for the road: the Granny Sprague Cemetery in Homestead holds only one grave. It's the resting place of Mary Wright, who died of an infection in 1854 at the age of six. Mary manifests as a blue glow above her grave. She appears during the final moment of every year.

Happy New Year!

BIBLIOGRAPHY

As you can well imagine, collecting three hundred and sixty-six stories took some doing. Here are some of the resources that helped out with that.

Baltrusis, Sam. *Ghosts of Boston: Haunts of the Hub.* Charleston, SC: Haunted America (A Division of The History Press), 2012.
Belanger, Jeff. *Weird Massachusetts: Your Travel Guide to Massachusetts's Local Legends and Best Kept Secrets.* New York, NY: Sterling Publishing Company, 2008.
Christensen, Jo-Anne. *Victorian Ghost Stories.* Ghost House Books, 2004.
Cline, Bruce L. and Lisa Cline. *History, Mystery, and Hauntings of Southern Illinois.* Illinois History.com, 2014.
Colby, C.B. *Strangely Enough.* New York, NY: Sterling Publishing Company, 1959.
Coleman, Christopher K. *Ghosts and Haunts of the Civil War: Authentic Accounts of the Strange and Unexplained.* New York, NY: Barnes and Noble Books, 1999.
Crain, Mary Beth. *Haunted Pet Stories: Tales of Ghostly Cats, Spooky Dogs, and Demonic Bunnies.* Guilford, CT: Globe Pequot Press, 2011.
Dwyer, Jeff. *Ghost Hunter's Guide to California's Gold Rush Country.* Pelican Publishing, 2009.
Edwards, Peter. *Night Justice: The True Story of the Black Donnellys.* Toronto, Canada: Kay Porter Books Ltd., 2004.
Hansen-Steiger, Sherry. *Hollywood and the Supernatural.* New York, NY: St. Martin's Press, 1990.
Lewis, Chad. *The Most Gruesome Hauntings of the Midwest.* On The Road Publications, 2012.
Ludlam, Harry. *The Restless Ghosts of Ladye Place, and Other True Hauntings.* Taplinger Publishing Company, 1968.
Markus, Scott. *Voices From the Chicago Grave.* Michigan: Thunder Bay Press, 2008.
Martin, Joel and William J. Birnes. *The Haunting of the Presidents: A Paranormal History of the United States Presidency.* New York, NY: Signet, 2003.
Mayo, Matthew P. *Haunted Old West: Phantom Cowboys, Spirit-Filled Saloons, Mystical Mine Camps, and Spectral Indians.* Guilford, CT: Globe Pequot Press, 2012.
Miller, Orlo. *The Donnellys Must Die.* Toronto, Canada: Macmillan of Canada, 1962.
Morris, Jeff and Vince Sheilds. *Chicago Haunted Handbook: 99 Ghostly Places You Can Visit In and Around the Windy City.* Covington, KY: Clerisy Press, 2013.
Musick, Ruth. *The Telltale Lilac Bush and Other West Virginia Ghost Tales.* The University Press of Kentucky, 1965.
Naliborski, Luke. *Creepy With a Chance of Ghosts.* Jacksonville, IL: American Hauntings Ink, 2017.
Newman, Rich. *Ghosts of the Civil War.* Woodbury, MN: Llewellyn, 2017.
Norman, Michael. *The Nearly Departed: Minnesota Ghost Stories and Legends.* St. Paul, MN:

Minnesota Historical Society Press, 2009.

Norman, Michael and Beth Scott. *Historic Haunted America*. New York, NY: Tom Doherty Associates, 1995.

Ogden, Tom. *Haunted Colleges and Universities: Creepy Campuses, Scary Scholars, and Deadly Dorms*. Guilford, CT: Globe Pequot Press, 2014.

_____. *Haunted Hollywood*. Guilford, CT: Globe Pequot Press, 2009.

_____. *Haunted Theaters: Playhouse Phantoms, Opera House Horrors, and Backstage Banshees*. Guilford, CT: Globe Pequot Press, 2009.

Pitkin, David J. *Ghosts of the Northeast*. Salem, NY: Aurora Publications, 2002.

Price, Harry. *Poltergeist Over England: Three Centuries of Mischievous Ghosts*. London: Country Life Ltd., 1945.

Robinson, Charles Turek. *The New England Ghost Files*. North Attleborough, MA: Covered Bridge Press, 1994.

Rule, Leslie. *Ghost in the Mirror: Real Cases of Spirit Encounters*. Andrews McMeel Publishing, 2008.

Russell, Randy and Janet Barnett. *Ghost Dogs of the South*. Winston-Salem, NC: John F. Blair, Publisher, 2001.

Scott, Beth and Michael Norman. *Haunted Heartland*. New York, NY: Warner Books Inc., 1985.

Shatkins, Candice. *Haunted Kenosha: Ghosts, Legends and Bizarre Tales*. Charleston, SC: Haunted America, 2009.

Shuker, Karl P. N. *The Unexplained: An Illustrated Guide to the World's Natural and Paranormal Mysteries*. North Dighton, MA: J.G. Press, 1996.

Shults, Sylvia. *Spirits of Christmas: The Dark Side of the Holidays*. Jacksonville, IL: American Hauntings Ink, 2017.

Slocum, Joshua. *Sailing Alone Around the World: A Voyage Beyond Imagination*. Dover Publications, 1956.

Smith, Barbara. *Haunted Hearts: True Ghostly Love Stories*. Auburn, WA: Ghost House Books, 2005.

Smitten, Susan. *Ghost Stories of New York State*. Auburn, WA: Lone Pine Publishing, 2004.

Steiger, Brad. *Real Ghosts, Restless Spirits, and Haunted Places*. Canton, MI: Visible Ink Press, 2003.

Stonehouse, Frederick. *Haunted Lakes: Great Lakes Ghost Stories, Superstitions and Sea Serpents*. Duluth, MN: Lake Superior Port Cities Inc., 1997.

_____. *Haunted Lakes II: More Great Lakes Ghost Stories*. Duluth, MN: Lake Superior Port Cities Inc., 2006.

Taylor, Troy. *The Big Book of Illinois Ghost Stories*. Mechanicsburg, PA: Stackpole Books, 2009.

_____. *The Big Book of Missouri Ghost Stories*. Mechanicsburg, PA: Stackpole Books, 2013.

Taylor, Troy and Rene Cruse. *And Hell Followed With It: History and Hauntings of American Disasters*. Jacksonville, IL: Whitechapel Press, 2011.

Thurber, James. *My Life and Hard Times*. Harper Perennial Modern Classics, 1999.

Ward, Frank and Troy Taylor. *Close Behind Thee: American Ghost Stories*. Jacksonville, IL: Whitechapel Press, 1998.

ABOUT THE AUTHOR

Sylvia Shults is the author of several books of paranormal nonfiction, including 44 Years in Darkness, Fractured Spirits: Hauntings at the Peoria State Hospital, and Ghosts of the Illinois River. She sits in dark, spooky, haunted places so you don't have to. She has spent the last nineteen years working at a public library, slowly smuggling out enough words in her pockets week after week to build a book of her own. She lives a short, ten-minute motorcycle ride away from the haunted asylum that features in so many of her books. She considers it the highest privilege to share the incredible, compassionate history of the Peoria State Hospital.

After battling an intense, lifelong fear of the dark, Sylvia decided to become a ghost hunter. (What WAS she thinking?) As a paranormal investigator, she has made many media appearances, including a tiny part in the Ghost Hunters episode "Prescription for Fear", about the Peoria State Hospital.

Sylvia loves hearing from her readers, especially when they have spooky stories of their own to share with her. She can be found at www.sylviashults.com, and on Facebook at the pages for Fractured Spirits and Ghosts of the Illinois River.